T4-AFX-986

821.76
 Byr
 Gre
    Grebanier.
    The uninhibited Byron.

            The Library
    Nazareth College of Rochester, N. Y.

THE UNINHIBITED
BYRON

OTHER BOOKS BY BERNARD GREBANIER

The Great Shakespeare Forgery
The Truth About Shylock
The Heart of Hamlet
Thornton Wilder
Playwriting
Racine's Phaedre, *an English Acting Version in Verse*
Molière's The Misanthrope, *an English Acting Version*

POETRY

The Other Love
Mirrors of the Fire
Fauns, Satyrs, and a Few Sages

THE
UNINHIBITED
BYRON

An Account of His Sexual Confusion

BERNARD GREBANIER

CROWN PUBLISHERS, INC.

NEW YORK

WITHDRAWN
NAZARETH COLLEGE LIBRARY

ACKNOWLEDGMENTS

Grateful acknowledgment is made to the following for permission to quote copyright material:
The Henry W. and Albert A. Berg Collection of the New York Public Library, Astor, Lennox and Tilden Foundations, for unpublished portions of Hobhouse's diary and a poem in the handwriting of the Lady Caroline Lamb; The Pierpont Morgan Library for the Elizabeth Medora Leigh manuscript autobiography and the last letter she wrote to her mother; John Murray for quotations from Leslie Marchand's *Byron, Lord Byron's Correspondence,* D. L. Moore's *The Late Lord Byron,* and Paston and Quennell's *To Lord Byron,* and to Alfred A. Knopf, Inc., for the Marchand material; Chatto and Windus, Ltd., for extracts from R. M. Lovelace's *Astarte;* Constable Publishers for extracts from E. C. Mayne's *Lady Byron;* MacDonald, London Ltd. and Harcourt, Brace and World Inc., for extracts from M. Elwin's *Lord Byron's Wife;* G. Richards for quotations from J. C. Fox's *The Byron Mystery;* Elizabeth Jenkins for quotations from her *Lady Caroline Lamb;* and to L. B. Lippincott for the D. L. Moore material.

© 1970 by Bernard Grebanier
Library of Congress Catalog Card Number: 70–127498

All rights reserved. No part of this book may be reproduced or utilized in any form or by any means, electronic or mechanical, including photocopying, recording, or by any information storage and retrieval system, without permission in writing from the Publisher. Inquiries should be addressed to Crown Publishers, Inc., 419 Park Avenue South, New York, N.Y. 10016.

Printed in the United States of America
Published simultaneously in Canada by General Publishing Company Limited

821.76
Byr
Gore

For Philip Winsor
With respect, love, and gratitude

CONTENTS

LIST OF ILLUSTRATIONS

PREFACE

IT WAS PROBABLY THROUGH SOME SUBTLE ASSOCIATION OF IDEAS THAT I first decided to do a book on Byron. Nearly a decade ago, when I made my first extended stay at Venice, I noticed that although the palaces and houses on the Grand Canal and interior streets are bristling with commemorative plaques, there is one remarkable omission. It is not astonishing that there should be stones to mark the birthplaces or residences of Petrarch, Titian, Tintoretto, Veronese, Goldoni, Cimarosa, and others dear—one hopes—to Venetians. Nor have celebrated foreigners been overlooked: Wagner, for instance, at the Palazzo Vendramin and Browning at the Rezzonico. There are, besides, quite as many memorials to potentates and politicos who now are nobodies. But in Venice itself there is nothing to signalize the fact that Byron spent some of his most important years in this city, even though he was surely the most influential and talked-about poet of his century, and the fascination of his life, whatever the future of his poetry, renders it unlikely that he will ever be a nobody.

Byron had lived—quite conspicuously—in Venice; I was there, too, and I was spurred to find out all I could about his life in La Serenissima. I had not made many tentative investigations before new perspectives on his biography opened before me. By the time I returned to Venice the following year, I had determined to make him the subject of my next book, though Venice was to decide for me that I should have somewhat to postpone that intention. I have been back every year since then, often for the better part of the year.

As my material on Byron began to take shape, my original idea was to write a biography that would begin with the breakup of his marriage and his self-imposed exile from England, bring him to Venice, and end with his leaving for Ravenna to commence his dreary quasi marriage with Teresa Guiccioli. I did not then, and I do not now, see the value of writing just another book on Byron or on Byron and His Times; we have enough of them. No one is justified in writing any biography unless he has either new information on his subject or a fresh view of it, and I felt I had both. But the more I considered Byron, the more I read his remarkable letters, the more I looked into the lives of those connected with him, the more convinced I

9

became that, despite the numerous and, in several instances, important works on him, there were serious gaps and in some portions a scanting or hurrying over in what has been presented of his life.

I soon found myself in the dilemma of the author of *Tristram Shandy:* the futher I went into Byron's past the further I found I had still to go. I eventually saw that if I persisted in including the Venetian years what I had to say could not be managed within the confines of a single volume, and that I actually had two different themes, each requiring totally different treatment. One, terminating with the dissolution of his marriage, was his sexual confusion, which began in his childhood and worked havoc on himself and almost everyone connected with him, and which made the success of his marriage wholly improbable. That is the theme of the present book, and should not and does not bring him as far as Venice, for by that time the damage had been done. The other theme, which had been the first in my thought, will require a quite different sort of book, if and when I write it, a book which must not be entirely a biographical study of Byron.

Relative to those years of his life spanned in this book there are a number of matters, I believe, here presented either for the first time in a biography of Byron, or else given the attention they merit. No one seems to have seen how cardinal an influence in his life was his traumatic experience with the nurse May Gray. Concerning the most hectic affair of his life, that with Lady Caroline Lamb, there have been curious lapses in the biographies of Byron: though mention has been made that she wrote one novel about their relationship and another in which he figures as the hero, nothing has been told us about the books, and I therefore made it my business to read them—and found them full of interest for their portraits of him and herself; no biography of Byron has had anything to say about the novels by others in which he and she are portrayed as characters, and I have read those; none has much to say about her life after Byron's final break with her. Despite the overwhelming evidence, biographers have avoided the conclusion that beyond doubt his relationship with his sister was physically an incestuous one. The child of that incest, Medora Leigh, is more often than not dismissed in a line—here I was fortunate not only in tracking down the manuscript of her autobiography but also in discovering a most moving letter, apparently the last she wrote to her mother, and never before published. No one has been willing to gauge the meaning of the poems he wrote as a schoolboy or to follow the career of his friend Bankes. I see Lady Melbourne quite differently from other biographers. Byron was an extremely voluminous correspondent and some of his best letters—and there are no better letters in English than his best—have not been quoted in the biographies. Long as it is, Professor Marchand's three-volume work, magnificent and invaluable to all later biographers, had no room for many of these and other particulars of interest to me, partly because he covers Byron's entire life, partly because of documents published after his book, and even more because he is so largely concerned, as I am not, with Byron's career as a poet. I am interested here in Byron's poems only insofar as they reveal his emotional life. G. Wilson Knight's rehabilitation of the anonymously issued *Don Leon* poems, some of the most brilliant bawdry in our language—many passages from which I quote for the first time—has been of exceeding importance as pointing to the truth behind Lady Byron's separation from her husband; but I thoroughly disagree with him on Byron's relation to his sister and cannot accept his interpretation of Byron's attraction to boys. Again, having been granted access to the Lovelace Papers, Malcolm Elwin has been able to publish extremely significant letters and memoranda of and to Lady Byron, but his emphasis is, as it should be, on her; the involutions of the separation which this new material affords, when it is coupled with what the *Don Leon* poems tell us, have for me the fascination of a Henry James novel. Naturally, what I have just said is not in criticism of my predecessors: in dealing with such a life as Byron's no one can include everything—a reason for my limiting my subject—and I do not forget that every writer has been entitled to his own views.

Having thus stated the most significant contributions in recent decades to Byron's biography, I cannot omit Doris Langley Moore's remarkable and fascinating *The Late Lord Byron*.

Bernard Grebanier

Portrait of Byron when he was thirty,
sculptor the celebrated Albert Thorwaldsen.
Byron sat for the bust.

BEFORE CARO

1.

"IF THERE IS ONE HUMAN BEING whom I utterly *detest* and *abhor*, it is she," wrote Byron of Lady Caroline Lamb, a creature, he added, lost to shame and feeling and without "one estimable or redeemable quality"; she had been "an adder" in his path, and he would much rather "be with the dead in purgatory, than with her." It was in June 1814 that he was thus shuddering with aversion for the hazel-eyed, golden-curled "Caro" of the lovely voice and fetching manner whom some of her friends had variously nicknamed the Fairy Queen, the Sprite, Ariel, and the Squirrel.

Scarcely two years earlier, when he was twenty-four, they had come to know each other. Returned from his travels in lands then exotic, Byron had become overnight the rage of Caro's London circle with the opening cantos of his *Childe Harold*. A work of which its author felt none too sure, it was crammed with the oratorical flourishes perfectly timed for the era, and had as hero, excitingly, Byron himself, and at the same time the sort of hero who was very much à la mode. And what wonderfully strange places Byron had seen—Albania, Greece, and Turkey!

Not to speak of the marvelous attractiveness of the poet himself. "So beautiful a countenance I scarcely ever saw," affirmed an observer, who also felt that the poet's eyes (light gray or grayish brown) were like "the open portals of the sun." The auburn locks fell engagingly over his brow in careless ringlets. (Scrope Davies discovered their secret when he came into Byron's bedroom to find his friend in bed with his hair done up in curlers.

With his amusing stammer he confessed having been deceived, like everyone else, into believing the hair curled naturally. "Yes, naturally, *every night*," Byron retorted, "but don't let the cat out of the bag.") Noting the signs on the face of "keen and rapid genius," the "pale intelligence, its profligacy and its bitternesss—its original symmetry distorted by the passions, his laugh of mingled merriment and scorn," the famous painter Sir Thomas Lawrence was equally arrested by the well-formed mouth "wide and contemptuous even in its smile, falling singularly at the corners," its expression "vindictive and disdainful."

It was a decade later that Lawrence thus depicted him, but in 1812 this was already Childe Harold—that is, more important to the ladies, Byron himself. It was perhaps a tiny shock for them that the poet was rather under average height. But he had one feature of which Byron's hero was deprived, the limp owing to his clubfoot on the right leg, which, however embittering to himself, only caused the female heart to skip a beat with compassion.

Lady Caroline, having read the poem everyone was talking about, wrote anonymously to its author to tell him that she and everybody she knew thought it beautiful. He ought to be and must be happy, she said; he must cease regretting the past and expending his talents in gloom. She was not worth his notice, she added. He was unacquainted with her and was not to trouble finding out her identity, but rather burn the note—a thing Byron never did with his correspondence. Then came a truly feminine touch: of course, if he wished to, he could easily enough discover who she was, though that would be a disappointment to her. (Her greatest wish, actually, was one day to get to know him.)

This message was followed by another, opening with flattering and misspelled tributes to his "superior mind." He was not to think she was in love with him, for she was already in love with one she would not name. Byron could not rest until he knew the identity of this female worshiper.

Her two missives were penned during the second week of March 1812, and she saw him for the first time later that month, with the moths of the London world of fashion fluttering about him asking to be singed. When Byron asked to be introduced to her, probably having learned that she was the author of the letters, she turned on her heel away from him, a choice piece of coquetry. At home she noted in her diary that he was "mad, bad, and dangerous to know." Doubtless as one of his admiring readers she must have been prepared to find him so, but, then, Caro was quite capable of posturing before herself in her own diary. Not many women can defend themselves against the challenge presented by such a man. Certainly Lady Caroline was not one.

Those to whom she was the Fairy Queen did not know her thoroughly.

It is true that when at the age of nineteen she married the sophisticated William Lamb and the alliance was held a love match, she had friends who could not bear to think of the delicate Ariel as a wife who might soon be a mother; but some took comfort in observing that matrimony had left their Caro still "the same wild, delicate, odd, delightful person," unlike anyone else under the sun. Caro was not, however, pure spirit. Before meeting and snubbing Byron she had already had her fling at adultery. Ariel was also known to others, who saw another side of her, as the Little Savage and the Bat.

Byron, used to having women throw themselves at him, was, of course, brought to attention by her affront. He had heard of her unconventional personality and been curious about her. Besides, for all his republicanism and love of liberty, he was a snob about rank, and he was not the less interested in her for being the daughter of the Earl of Bessborough, the niece of the Duchess of Devonshire, and the daughter-in-law of Lord and Lady Melbourne. He contrived to be presented to her himself, and came to Melbourne House the next day to visit her.

The poets Samuel Rogers and Thomas Moore were there, and Lady Caroline had just come in from riding, and was sticky and overheated. When she heard that Byron was on his way upstairs, she dashed out of the room. Rogers congratulated him: "Lady Caroline has been sitting here in all her dirt with us, but when you were announced, she flew to beautify herself."

The entry which Caro was soon making in her diary was quite different from her recent one: "That beautiful pale face is my fate." She could little have guessed how prophetic were those words.

She never was to forget that three days after his first visit Byron brought her "a Rose and Carnation . . . with a sort of half sarcastic smile,— saying, 'Your Ladyship I am told likes all that is new and rare for a moment.'" On March 27, Good Friday, she wrote him a letter of studied coquetry: "The Rose Lord Byron gave Lady Caroline Lamb died in despight of every effort made to save it; probably from regret at its fallen Fortunes"; she further identified herself with the sunflower, because "however deficient its beauty and even use, it has a noble and aspiring mind, and, having *once* beheld in its full lustre the bright and unclouded sun that for one moment condescended to shine upon it, never while it exists could it think any lower object worthy of its worship"; after this elaborate adulation, she acknowledged having many faults, but assured him "there is not one, however, . . . that shall not be instantly got rid of, if Lord Byron thinks it worth while to name them." Caro copied out in her own hand—spelling was not her forte—his first message to her. She had given him a gold chain to wear about his neck, and he had sent her these lines:

> Yet feign [*sic*] would I resist the spell,
> That would my captive heart retain.
> For tell me dearest is this well
> Ah Caro! do I need the Chain? . . .

The gold chain was but a beginning. They began to exchange letters. She had, in truth, many faults, but she had also the unusual trait of great generosity. She soon was besieging him with pleas to let her know if he were out of funds; if so, all her jewels were at his disposal. But their physical intimacies were punctured by fierce quarrels. Often Rogers, who lived near Byron, found her "walking in the garden, and waiting for me, to beg that I reconcile them." Her passion rapidly approached insanity. "When not invited to a party where he was to be, she would wait for him in the street till it was over." Her aunt, the Duchess of Devonshire, wrote on May 4 that her niece "as usual, is doing all sorts of imprudent things for him and with him"; and within a week observed, "The ladies, I hear, spoil him, and the gentlemen are jealous of him. He is going back to Naxos, and then husbands may sleep in peace. I should not be surprised if Caro . . . were to go with him, she is so wild and imprudent."

The Duchess also described the buzzing, curiosity, and enthusiasm in her circle over *Childe Harold* and its author. The book was "on every table, and himself courted, visited, flattered, and praised whenever he appears. He has a pale, sickly, but handsome countenance, a bad figure, animated and amusing conversation, and, in short, he is really the only topic of conversation—the men jealous of him, the women of each other."

He had been compared by Caro to the sun, and like the sun he shone on many. He was already incapable of devoting himself to one woman, and during the time of his wild passion for her, he was distributing his affections elsewhere, too. But for three months he was fascinated by this chameleon, though there were ominous signs in the brutality with which he mixed words of endearment: "Every word you utter, every line you write, proves you to be either *sincere* or a *fool.* Now as I know you are not the one, I must believe you the other. I never knew a woman with greater or more pleasing talents . . . But these are unfortunately coupled with a total want of common conduct . . . Then your heart, my poor Caro (what a little volcano!), that pours *lava* through your veins; and yet I cannot wish it a bit colder . . . I have always thought you the cleverest, most agreeable, absurd, amiable, perplexing, dangerous, fascinating little being that lives now . . . This nonsense is the first and last compliment (if it be such) I ever paid you. You have often reproached me as wanting in that respect; but others will make up the deficiency."

The compliment was ambiguous enough, yet she loved him with utter abandon, utter indifference to what people thought or said. But even if she had been a woman of discretion, it was already too late.

2.

FOR BY HERITAGE, BIRTH, AND CHILDHOOD EXPERIENCE BYRON WAS destined to erotic confusion.

His ancestry on both paternal and maternal sides was not such as to endow him with the temperament for a tranquil life. The Byrons were "bad"; the Scottish Gordons, his mother's family, were, if anything, worse. The latter were notorious for centuries for their savagery and violence.

When Henry VIII seized upon the properties of the former monasteries, he sold Newstead Abbey, situated in Sherwood Forest in Nottingham, to John Byron, who was knighted by Queen Elizabeth in 1579, and presently much talked of for his luxurious style of living. A later Byron of the same name was with the banished Charles II in France; his wife Eleanor is mentioned by Pepys on April 26, 1667, as being the king's seventeenth mistress while in exile. Of the three wives of the fourth Lord Byron the last was our poet's great-grandmother. Their son William became the fifth Lord Byron. His brother, an admiral, was the poet's grandfather. Lord William succeeded to the title at fourteen and was still young when known in London to be a roué; among his escapades was an attempt to abduct the actress Miss Bellamy. In the country he had the reputation of an eccentric and a wild spendthrift. He built on his grounds a small castle, where as an older man he lived as a recluse, and was the subject of much local gossip as a "Wicked Lord" who entertained depraved cronies at parties too lascivious to describe. Having been for a while in the Navy, he erected two forts on the shore of one of his lakes and there superintended, somewhat in the manner of Uncle Toby with his soldiers, naval engagements in miniature. These extravagances were so costly that he cut down most of the magnificent oaks of his park to sell as lumber.

But his most notorious exploit was connected with William Chaworth of Annesley Hall, relative and neighbor, ancestor of the Mary Chaworth who was to figure importantly in our poet's biography. In January of 1765 both men were dining with others at a tavern in Pall Mall. Lord William, forty-three at the time, during a discussion with Chaworth on the science of preserving venison, had angry words with him. They demanded a vacant spot at the tavern, and in a dark room lit only by a candle began to duel.

Chaworth blundered and Lord Byron ran him through. Chaworth died the next day; while still conscious he refused to accuse his slayer of unfairness and lamented only his folly in fighting in so obscure a room. Tried before his peers, Byron was found guilty of manslaughter.

Many tales were circulated about Lord William. At this date it is impossible to disentangle fact from legend, but the stories at least illustrate the character he bore in the world and also explain why his wife should have found it intolerable to live with him and eventually have left him. He is said, for instance, to have thrown her into a small lake, and also to have, on trifling provocation, shot his coachman to death, then to have hurled the body into the coach where his wife was seated, and, mounting the coach, driven away himself.

Lord William had an only son, who disappointed him by running off, just before his marriage to an heiress was to take place, with his cousin, the daughter of our poet's grandfather, and a girl without any fortune. Lord William, as a result, became more and more bitterly eccentric and never went anywhere without pistols. He not only stripped his forest further, but is reputed to have slaughtered twenty-seven hundred deer in his park to sell in neighboring markets. As an old man he cut off all connections with society and amused himself with crickets he had trained to crawl all over him.

Lord William's grandson died in 1794; thus, our poet when little more than six, became next in line for the Byron title and holdings.

Lord William's brother John, the poet's grandfather, quit school when very young, because, it is said, of his erotic bouts there, and joined the Navy. His ship, the *Wager,* foundered near the Strait of Magellan, when he was but eighteen; he later told how, when famine became unendurable, he had dined on the skin and leg of a dog he had been fond of. (Byron was inspired in the second canto of *Don Juan* to recreate the episode of the shipwreck.) Back in England, after earning some notoriety as a philanderer, John Byron in August 1748 married his cousin from Cornwall, Sophia Trevanion. (We shall meet with another Trevanion later in our story.) Of her nine children, the eldest son was John Byron, the poet's father. Her husband, Vice-Admiral John Byron, after sailing through an almost incredible number of storms at sea—he earned the nickname of "Foulweather Jack"—retired to the country, where he was as celebrated for his hospitality as notorious for his infidelities. One of many of these was with a good-looking servant who, found in his bed, was dismissed from service; Foulweather Jack established her as his mistress in London, and when his wife traced his steps to her living quarters, moved her to other lodgings.

He could never, however, have competed in dissoluteness with his son, the poet's father, "Mad Jack Byron." In fact, because of Mad Jack's talent for running through money with extraordinary speed, Foulweather Jack was

impelled to disinherit him. Schooled at Westminster, then at a French
military academy, after which he became a Guardsman, Captain Mad Jack,
very handsome, heartless, and unprincipled, had no scruples in extracting
money from the women he slept with.

In the summer of 1778, when he was twenty-two, he met the beautiful
Lady Carmarthen in London during her husband's absence. Her attractions
included a sizable fortune. Soon their intimacies caused scandal of sufficient
volume to reach the ears of Lord Carmarthen in Yorkshire. He hurried
home, locked his doors against his wife, vowed never to admit her again,
and started divorce proceedings. Lady Carmarthen, not at all discomfited,
declared herself happy to be rid of him and sent for her clothes and jewels.
She and her lover at once began living together in various of her properties.
The next year Lord Carmarthen procured from Parliament a bill of divorce-
ment from her; shortly after, on June 9, 1779, Captain Byron married her.
A month later she gave birth to a daughter. He wasted no time in spending
her fortune, and to escape creditors the pair went to France. She died in
January of 1784 at the birth of Augusta, the only one to survive of their
three children.

The next spring Captain Jack, leaving the infant Augusta behind, set
out again for England to find another heiress. Avoiding the creditors of
London, he made for Bath, the watering place where heiresses might be
found in quantity. There handsome Mad Jack quickly captivated Catherine
Gordon of Gight, a rich, plain, and gauche girl of twenty.

She had been sent that same year to Bath, it is said, to escape the
adventurers of her native Scotland; destiny decreed that she should make
herself miserable by marrying an English one instead. Indeed, there appears
to have been an ironic fatality about the match. Sir Walter Scott remembered seeing her in Edinburgh before she had ever known of Captain Jack's
existence, at a performance of Southerne's *The Fatal Marriage,* a play of
which the hero's name was Biron; Mrs. Siddons had been featured in the
drama and had succeeded so much in affecting the ladies of the audience
that they were "often led out in a fit of hysterics"; Catherine Gordon, already
a girl of uncontrolled emotion, made something of a spectacle of herself
even in that gathering by falling "into violent fits" and being "carried out
of the theatre, screaming loudly" the words of Mrs. Siddons in the character
of Isabella, 'O my Biron! my Biron!' "

It has been noted that she came of a stock whose barbaric acts, violence, and lawlessness make the sins of the Byrons seem tepid. When, for
example, the messenger of the Privy Council was sent to William Gordon
in 1601 on the complaint of the Mowats for his banditries, the emissary
missed being slain only because Gordon was held back from shooting him;
he nevertheless was thrust into the hall, his official papers seized and thrown

into some broth, and he was compelled, a dagger the while at his heart, to swallow them. For the rest of that century the depredations of the Gordons continued unabated. When a Davison married a Gordon in 1701 he paid her family £40,000, a sum which proved inadequate to liquidate their debts. A later laird, after siring fourteen children, was found dead in a river in January of 1760, apparently a suicide.

His eldest son, who died in 1779, was the father of Catherine Gordon. She was raised by her grandmother, an old lady whose narrow Calvinism was on a par with her general ignorance and who, depriving the girl of the education to which her rank entitled her, did her best to create her in her own image. Catherine was taught to believe in ghosts and fortune-tellers, and to entertain all sorts of superstitions. She never mastered either grammar or spelling.

It was not long after his arrival at Bath that Mad Jack married his unhandsome heiress—on May 13, 1785. It was not long, either, before he was spending her money freely. For nearly a year they lived at the family seat, Gight, a castle fairly in ruins. Within that year he had not only run through her money but the £8,000 for which the estate had been mortgaged because of his expenditures. By August of 1786 they were living in a house in Hampshire and Gight was sold. Too late she realized her error in never having thought of insisting on a settlement for herself before her marriage; she wrote to her relative, Miss Urquhart, asking her to deal for her with the commissioners, in a strain which is pathetically eloquent of her inability to trust herself to withstand the blandishments of the husband to whom she was so passionately attached: "The best that I could wish or expect would be 10,000£, and, I would have that settled in such a manner that it would be out of Mr. Byron's power to spend, and out of my power to give up to him . . ." She was equally anxious that he never know "that I wrote or spoke to anybody on the subject, because if he did he would never forgive me."

In 1787 the Byrons were on the Isle of Wight. Having promised to pay some of his debts with £700 of his wife's money which came into his hands, he preferred to go off to Paris to spend it, and managed to dissipate all of it in a few months. When his wife, already big with child, followed him, he was down to his last shilling. Little Augusta, four years of age, was seriously ill, and Mrs. Byron undertook the care of her and brought her back to health. During Catherine Byron's brief stay in Paris the debts of her husband began to soar again. Unlike him, who was fluent in French, she knew not a word of the language; not surprisingly the poor woman wished to bear her child in surroundings not so utterly foreign to her. As her time neared, she therefore came back to England, unaccompanied by Captain Jack, but bringing with her Augusta, whom she delivered to Lady Holderness, Lady Carmathen's mother, and the child's grandmother. She herself rented a furnished room in London between Oxford Street and Cavendish Square on Holles Street—the house no longer exists—and awaited the day of her accouchement. Mad Jack did turn up in England in January of 1788 but because of his creditors had to avoid the city, except on Sundays. We do not know whether he was present when his son was born on Tuesday, January 22. The child was christened at Marylebone church with the name of Mrs. Byron's father, George Gordon. He was born with a clubbed right foot. A surgeon was called in and prescribed a shoe that might enable the youngster, when of age, to walk with less pain, but did not raise any hopes that the condition might ever be corrected.

Captain Jack's talent for incurring further debts had not diminished, and his wife was again appealing, this time to her trustees, to stand between herself and her inability to deny his heartless and unending demands for money: they were to ignore, she begged, any requests coming from her through her husband for more cash.

After many changes of residence to escape the bailiffs, she went with her son to Aberdeen to live within her now severely limited resources. First Captain Jack took a house at Folkstone, then joined her for a while in Aberdeen, and then, finding life with her too confining, boring, and contentious, moved further down the street to live by himself. But soon he was anxious to remove himself from her vicinity altogether; he was enabled to do so by the gift of his sister, whom he was now also harassing for whatever she could spare. He returned to Aberdeen in the summer of 1790, extracted more money from his wife, causing her to involve herself in debt, and ran off to France, to Valenciennes, where his sister had a house. To the latter he boasted that he had already possessed "one third" of the female population of the town, and that he was by general verdict accounted "très amoureux but très inconstant." Now Catherine Byron was put to the necessity of applying for help to his sister too; she had asked Mad Jack to borrow thirty pounds or so from his sister for her, but he replied that that was a thing he could never do; she begged his sister to lend her the sum and that it would be repaid by May. She was in dire need of it for her son and herself. Captain Jack, however, made plain his indifference to both son and wife in a letter to that same sister: Mrs. Byron "is very amiable at a distance, but I defy you and all the Apostles to live with her two months"; as for the boy, "I am happy to hear he is well; but for his walking, 'tis impossible, as he is club-footed." Five months later, reduced to dire want, Captain Jack died, August 2, 1791. Characteristically, he had left a will naming his three-year-old son "heir of my real and personal estate, and charge him to pay my debts, legacies and funeral expenses." All there was for young Byron to inherit from his father was debts.

Mrs. Byron, victim though she had been of Captain Jack's wanton raiding of what had once been her fortune as well as of his constant neglect and unfaithfulness, was inconsolable at his loss, and her cries of grief echoed through the streets of Aberdeen. With that ease of self-deception to which widows are prone, she wrote to his sister that she and her husband never had parted except through necessity; "notwithstanding his foibles, for they deserve no worse name, I ever sincerely loved him . . . I do not think I shall ever recover the severe shock I have received . . . If I had only seen him before he died! Did he ever mention me?"

She never did recover from her grief or her frustrated passion for her indifferent husband.

In the meantime she had been pouring all the pent-up love she held into care of her little boy; her prime concern was to come upon a cure for the incurable, his clubbed foot. She was convinced that if only she had enough money she could procure the shoe that would correct his lameness. Byron himself was already humiliated by his physical handicap, and while out with his nurse, Agnes Gray, rewarded another nurse who commiserated with him on his misfortune by striking her with the little whip he carried.

No longer in need to defend herself against the greed of her husband, Mrs. Byron plunged into greater debt to move from her cramped quarters to a floor at 64 Broad Street and furnish it, so that her boy and his nurse might each have a room. What his mother may have overlooked in inculcating the narrowest kind of Calvinism was eagerly supplied by the energies of Agnes Gray. Catherine herself alternated wild expressions of love for her son—the greater now that he was fatherless—with violent fits of abuse, shouts that he took after his worthless sire, and frequent insults over his lameness.

When Byron was ten years old, the Wicked Lord Byron, his uncle, died. This was on May 21, 1798. On May 22, Mad Jack's son was informed that he was now the sixth Lord Byron.

At such an age and against such a background as had been his, this new elevation could not fail to be something of a disaster to the boy. It might be conceded that being born with a clubbed foot and having a mother who, without intending it, denied him any emotional security despite her enormous self-deprivations for his sake, were in themselves disasters enough for any child. But before succeeding to the title he had visited upon him a disaster more fatal still. It presented itself in a form hideously ironic: a succubus in the guise of a psalm singer.

May Gray had come to fill the position of Byron's nurse, the post formerly held by her sister Agnes and vacated when the latter married. Both girls were rigid Presbyterians, and May continued her sister's thorough reading of the Bible with her young charge, going again and again through

Mrs. Catherine Byron, the poet's mother, from a portrait by Thomas Stewardson.

the Old Testament, which fascinated the boy. But May Gray did more than that. When the lad was only nine she began coming regularly into his bed to manipulate his body in various sexual experiments. It may be supposed that at first through curiosity and excitement the child would naturally lend himself to these titillating adventures—and, being a child, rapidly became a slave to them.

May's nefarious power over him lasted for something like three crucial years. At length, however, he sickened of it. Small wonder, for it was a dominance maintained by a ritual complicated enough to have provoked the admiration of the Marquis de Sade. The lecheries in bed were varied during the day not only by readings in the Bible, but also by perpetual beatings so brutal that his bones ached; furthermore, she occasionally brought "all sorts of Company of the lowest Description" into his rooms. He was free of her only in his eleventh year when he was at last settled in a boarding school.

But the damage had been done. This prolonged nightmare, as it eventually came to be, had many terrible consequences. His sexual instincts were thus fully aroused at an incredibly premature age, ruling out the possibility of a normal development of them. Byron wrote later: "My passions were developed very early—so early, that few would believe me, if I were to state the period, and the facts which accompanied it." He himself attributed to those three years during which, as he put it, he had "anticipated life," his melancholy as an adult. What he never realized was that May Gray's viciousness had deprived his future of the probability of happiness in his relations with women. She had already set up for him a pattern of dissociating love from sexual experience. To his dying day he failed to understand that this had happened to him because, like all others who "make love" according to that pattern, seeking merely physical stimulation, he was never aware of all of which he had been cheated. With the exception of his sister Augusta, such was Byron's experience with every woman in his life. The absolute disgust which he felt for May Gray at eleven, though doubtless partially a moral revulsion, was also a foretaste of what he was destined to feel at the rapid conclusion of all but that one of his multitudinous affairs.

There was the further disillusionment, precociously imbibed, that a Bible-teaching, narrow Calvinist could at the same time be utterly depraved. His hatred for sham respectability and his penchant toward regarding all respectability as sham originate in his horror of what his nurse stood for.

These effects are the more pitiable because Byron by nature had more than a normal share of idealism, often suppressed as though he were ashamed of it. He was not born immune to deep affection. Indeed, the keynote to his character and his blundering is, perhaps, his profound need of love, of being loved.

Before the advent of May Gray he first experienced the emotion when he met Mary Duff, a distant cousin of his own age. His account of it in his journal, written during the days of his social whirl in London, is revealing: "I have been thinking lately a good deal of Mary Duff. How very odd that I should have been so utterly, devotedly fond of that girl, at an age [eight] when I could neither feel passion, nor know the meaning of the word." They had seen each other but briefly. Yet when he was sixteen and learned that she had been married, the news nearly threw him "into convulsions." Why? he wondered. They had not met again since early childhood; he had been "attached fifty times since." Yet he remembered everything about her, everything they said to each other, his "restlessness, sleeplessness," and his tormenting his mother's maid to write to her for him. He recollected, too, the pure happiness of merely sitting by her side. What is particularly interesting is that his lecheries with May Gray had become so impersonal, so mechanical, that he did not in any way connect them with warmth or affection, or even with sex. Speaking in retrospect of his love for Mary Duff he actually would say: "How the deuce did all this occur so early? . . . I certainly *had no sexual ideas for years afterwards* [italics mine]; and yet my misery, my love for that girl were so violent, that I sometimes doubt if I have ever really been attached since." (Byron was forever, in retrospect, electing a new candidate as the person he had loved most.)

By the time Mrs. Byron had discharged May Gray, a dividing line had already been drawn for him between love and sex. His emotional confusion as an adult is mirrored by his own use of the word *passion* for this ideal love for eight-year-old Mary, in which he knew sex had no conscious part. For the rest of his days he could feel that sort of "passion" (always with the exception of his great love for his sister) only for women unpossessed. After his sister had given herself to him, his love for her was, if anything, intensified; their mutual sin, he felt with some pride, damned them both, as befitted offspring of the doomed Byron tribe, and bound them forever in a Paolo-Francesca indivisibility. As for all the other women he "loved," when he eventually did take them to bed his affection swiftly gave way to boredom. To indulge the calculated excitements of the flesh, in which he had been initiated by his nurse, he spent a significant part of his life in fleeting alliance with creatures he could not help despising for surrendering themselves to him. For such women his personal beauty, his touching lameness, his sardonic tongue and charming manners, and his social position made it unnecessary for him to seek far. His almost feminine need of being loved he could hope to satisfy only with those with whom physical intimacies seemed improbable. He found, most of all, that satisfaction in friendship. Though he never knew this about himself, love lay in the realm of the physically inexpressible, and therefore, for so sensual a man as himself, the unattainable. Fulfillment of his sexual appetites brought only nausea and cynicism.

At the age of twelve, a year after he was rid of May Gray, Byron fell in love again, this time with a little girl slightly older than himself, his first cousin, Margaret Parker. From this idealized "passion," which gave him no rest or peace, he found relief in his first ventures into verse.

A lively picture of Byron's unhappy relationship with his mother at this time of his life has been sketched by Disraeli in his early novel, *Venetia* (1837). Many facts concerning the poet's life, of which the literary world was still in ignorance, were in the young novelist's possession through his famous father's circle. In the book Mrs. Carducis (Mrs. Byron), a "short and stout" woman of ruddy face, who dresses in a style combining "the shabby with the tawdry," comes to pay a first call upon her neighbor, Lady Annabel, with her twelve-year-old son, the young Lord Carducis (Byron). She orders him to make a bow to their hostess, and he obliges with "a sort of sulky nod." Soon she is complaining about him and the expenses his education has put her to. Lady Annabel politely expresses her conviction that the boy is always well behaved; his lips curl, and he half turns his back on the two women.

MRS. C.: Plantagenet, my dear, speak. Have I not always told you when you pay a visit, that you should open your mouth now and then? I don't like chattering children, but I like them to answer when they are spoken to.
HE: Nobody has spoken to me.
MRS. C.: (solemnly) Plantagenet, my love, you know you promised to be good!
HE: Well, what have I done?
LADY A.: (to put him at his ease) Do you like to look at pictures?
HE: (more civilly) I like to be left alone.

Presently his mother is objecting to his posture in his chair:

MRS. C.: Sit like a man.
HE: I am not a man. I wish I were.
MRS. C.: Plantagenet! Have I not always told you that you are not to answer me? ... He never does anything I wish. ... He does it to provoke me. You know you do it to provoke me, you little brat; now sit properly, sir. (Her face growing scarlet and menacing) Do you hear me?
HE: Yes, everybody hears you.
MRS. C.: (weeping) If only you knew the life I lead, and what trouble it costs me to educate that child! (Presently weeping torrents) He knows my weak heart; he knows nobody in the world loves him like his mother; and this is the way he treats me.

Refreshments are brought in. Between mouthfuls Mrs. C. appeals to him
to follow her example, now with cajolery, now with threats, until she works
herself into a rage. She dashes down the glass and, to the astonishment of
Lady A., rushes forward to give him "a good shake." Experienced, her agile
son pushes his chair between them. She chases him about the room; he
manages to escape her. Desperate, she seizes a volume nearby and throws
it at his head; he ducks and the book flies through a pane of glass. Now
she charges furiously. Frightened by her frenzy, the boy saves himself by
whirling a work-table in front of her. She falls over one of its legs, and
goes into hysterics. Her hostess helps her up while the lad stands in a corner,
pale and dogged. As she continues to weep, he says: "Mother, I am sorry
for what has occurred; mine was the fault. I shall not be happy till you
pardon me."

MRS. C.: (weeping profusely) No, yours was not the fault . . . I was in fault,
only I. There, Lady Annabel, did I not tell you he was the sweetest,
dearest, most generous-hearted creature that ever lived? . . . Oh my
dear Plantagenet, my only hope and joy! You are the treasure and
consolation of my life, and always will be . . . You shall have the
pony you wanted; I am sure I can manage it.

From all we know this scene reads like a transcript from life. Wildly
proud and already given to playing the little Lord Byron, he was forever
being subjected to public and private humiliation by her vulgarity and
uncontrolled temper. It is no wonder that all his life the one thing he came
to detest most was a "scene," and he would go to dangerous lengths in
avoiding one. He was as much nauseated by his mother's melodramatic
displays of affection as by her frequent outbursts of violence. A chief objective of his youth became to be where she was not.

In 1801 Byron entered Harrow. Life and literature both teem with
examples of adolescents forming ardent ties among themselves. It is normal
that the sudden access of an undefined need of attachment, at an age when
boys are shy of girls, should fasten itself on the materials available within
the limited precincts of a school. It is also usual that such attachments after
a few years either lose their heat or die. What is extraordinary about Byron
is the intensity and durability of the impassioned friendships he formed at
school. The strongest of these was with the Earl of Clare, four years his
junior. One of the first, Byron could say of it in his early thirties (1821):
"I never hear the word 'Clare' without a beating of the heart even now, and
I write it with the feelings of 1803–4–5 ad infinitum."
He was ever loath to discard the mementos of the past, and among

Byron at Harrow, artist unknown.
(Courtesy of the Royal Shakespeare Company, Stratford-upon-Avon.)

his papers was found an amusing Harrow letter from Clare to him, dated July 28, 1805, which said: "Since you have been so unusually unkind to me, in calling me names whenever you meet me, of late, I must beg an explanation, wishing to know whether you choose to be as good friends with me as ever. I must own that, for this last month, you have entirely cut me,—for, I suppose your new cronies. . . Though you do not let the boys bully me, yet if *you* treat me unkindly, that is to me a great deal worse. I am no hypocrite, Byron, nor will I, for your pleasure, ever suffer you to call me names, if you wish me to be your friend. If not, I cannot help it. I am sure no one can say that I will cringe to regain a friendship that you have rejected. . . . Therefore I beg and entreat you, if you value my friendship,—which by your conduct, I am sure I cannot think you do,—not to call me the names you do, nor abuse me. Till that time, it will be out of my power to call you friend. I shall be obliged for an answer as soon as it is convenient; till then I remain yours. I cannot say your friend."

This rather touching letter shows us Byron in a role characteristic of his Harrow days, the protector of his friends, usually several years younger than himself, from the brutalities of the older boys. On the back of it he inscribed the information that it was from "my *then,* and I hope, *ever* beloved friend . . . sent to my study in consequence of some childish misunderstanding." He added that the forgotten misconception was the only difference "which ever arose between us."

The last is not literally a fact. Another letter from Clare at Harrow makes it plain that Byron had taken umbrage at Clare's addressing him as "my dear Byron" instead of "my dearest Byron." In still another we read, between Clare's lines, Byron's pangs of jealousy; he had announced that he was presently "going abroad for six years," but soon their schoolfellow, John Russell, in fact went off to Spain; Byron had apparently been caustic at Clare's distress that Russell was leaving. Clare justifies himself: "How could you possibly imagine that I was more agitated on John Russell's account, who is gone for a few months, and from whom I shall hear constantly, than at your going for six years to travel over most part of the world, when I shall hardly ever hear from you, and perhaps may never see you again?" Byron, no doubt, had to content himself with this merely logical explanation, rather than the emotional one he must have hoped for.

But when Byron was twenty-one, some half dozen years later, Clare did him a great hurt. Byron was at last about to set out on his tour in 1809, and meeting Clare the day before his departure, asked him to spend an hour with him. "He excused himself; and what do you think was his excuse? He was engaged with his mother and some ladies to go shopping! And he knows I set out tomorrow, to be absent for years, perhaps never to return!

Friendship!" Byron was embittered at the moment, but his love for Clare was so great that he soon forgave him.

Within a matter of days of his 1821 entry in his diary concerning the beating of his heart at the mere sound of Clare's name, by coincidence he met him in Italy, after years of separation, on the road between Imola and Bologna. "This meeting annihilated for a moment all the years between the present time and the days of Harrow," Byron wrote. "It was . . . like rising from the grave, to me. Clare, too, was much agitated—*more,* in appearance, than even myself; for I could feel his heart beat to his fingers' ends, unless, indeed, it was the pulse of my own which made me think so." Byron was bound for Pisa, his old friend for Rome. "We were but five minutes together, and in the public road; but I hardly recollect an hour of my existence which could be weighed against them."

Only a week before his final illness in Greece, he wrote from Missolonghi to "My Dearest Clare," saying, "I hope that you do not forget that I always regard you as my dearest friend and love you as when we were Harrow boys together." These were stronger words of devotion than anyone had had from Byron for a long time.

After Byron's death his valet, Fletcher, Mary Shelley records, conveyed the information that in the delirium of his last moments Byron spoke of Claire (Clairmont), the mother of his illegitimate daughter Allegra. Those words were seized upon by Mrs. Shelley as proof that on his deathbed Byron was filled with remorse for his cruelty to Claire, whom, to be sure, he had treated savagely. Some biographers have made sentimental capital out of her interpretation. But the truth is that Byron never softened his intransigence toward Allegra's mother nor altered his conviction that she was "a damned bitch." Miss Moore, in *The Late Lord Byron,* has made a much shrewder guess in believing that the name Byron pronounced when he was dying was "Clare," rather than "Claire."

At Harrow there had been other attachments, if not quite so enduring as that of Clare, at least as sentimental and, for a while, as passionate—nearly all of them for boys much younger than himself: the Duke of Dorset; Earl Delawarr; John Wingfield; Charles Gordon; William Harness; John Claridge; James De Bathe; and Thomas Wildman, among others. When, for instance, Delawarr, three years his junior, felt affronted for some slight, Byron wrote him some expiatory lines in verse: Envy has malignantly "torn thee from my breast," but "in my *heart* thou keep'st thy seat" eternally;

> And, when the grave restores her dead,
>   When life again to dust is given,
> On *thy* dear breast I'll lay my head—
>   Without *thee! where* would be *my Heaven?*

The epicene tone of these verses is not unique among Byron's Harrow pieces. There is, for instance, his "Epitaph on a Beloved Friend," some boy "in cottage born": "For thee alone I liv'd"; now heartbroken he would join his friend in death;

> I'll make my last, cold, pillow on thy breast;
> That breast where oft in life, I've laid my head,
> Will yet receive me mouldering with the dead;
> This life resign'd, without one parting sigh,
> Together in one bed of earth we'll lie . . .

Adolescence forever victimizes with chaotic emotions, and the youthful poet no doubt genuinely felt all the anguish he sought to express in his lines. As for the details they record, it would be charitable to dismiss them as the product of a boy's overcharged yearning for affection. But no poet was ever more autobiographical than Byron, more prone to thrust his own experiences into his poems. And there is perhaps a little too much of his laying his head on some boy's breast, for the reader to take the expressions as meant only figuratively. One is almost forced to presuppose from the earthy bed which he longs to share with the dead boy an actual bed shared in a room. Certainly Byron's later exploits are consonant with that interpretation.

The world is familiar with the sort of intimacies encouraged before and after Byron's time by the very structure of student life at the English public schools. No doubt many of the boys who fell temporarily into the patterns of perversion all too common there left those patterns behind them on quitting school. No doubt, too, many did not—Byron, for one. For a child with a strong feminine streak in him—and a clubfoot—it would have been easy enough to fall in with a sexual code which, however furtively practiced, had the sanction of prevalence and even tradition. The Harrow boys, besides, inevitably thought of themselves as a picked lot, whose very standards required no reference to those of the common herd.

What that code and those standards were is baldly enough stated in a brilliant bawdy poem, of which it will later be necessary to say much, *Don Leon*.* This racy work, which G. Wilson Knight has proved beyond cavil is from the pen of George Colman the Younger, was written probably a decade after Byron's death, and has as its subject materials drawn from Byron's life. ("Don Leon" was intended to be understood as the same person as "Don Juan"—i.e., Byron.) Colman, himself a product of a public school —and later Oxford, which he had to quit for Aberdeen because of delinquency—was an intimate drinking-companion of Byron's at the time of the

---

* See Appendix.

latter's marriage, and clearly, from the contents of *Don Leon,* the recipient of the poet's most personal confidences, at a time when Byron, in his depression, most felt the need of such company. A man of the world and tolerant of the world's weaknesses, Colman has this to say of what went on in the British public schools:

> In vice unhackneyed, in Justine* unread,
> See schoolboys by some inclination fed,
> Some void, that's hardly to themselves confest,
> Flying for solace to a comrade's breast.
> In lonely walks, their vows of friendship pass,
> Warm as the shepherd to his rustic lass.
> Their friendship ripens into closer ties:
> They love. Their mutual vague desires arise.
> Perhaps by night they share each other's bed,

At this point we have one of those footnotes, learned and otherwise, in which *Don Leon* abounds, some of them apparently interpolated in later editions—the earlier printings having all disappeared—some probably penned by Colman himself. This one informs us that in France "they still put on youths a kind of straight jacket when they go to bed, with sleeves closed at the ends; the cuffs tied together or to the neck with tapes" to preserve the youngster's chastity.

> 'Til step by step, to closer union led,
> Like wantons, whom some unknown feeling charms,
> Each thinks he clasps a mistress in his arms.
> Impervious nature's sensual prickings goad,
> They own her dictates, but mistake the road.

It should be superfluous to state that the three years of May Gray's experiments with her charge's body may very well have made the boy the most susceptible of all his contemporaries at Harrow to their nocturnal sprees.

That this is no overinterpretation of Byron's friendships at school is further demonstrable by the evidence of the man who became his friend at Cambridge—the most profoundly loyal friend he ever had—and who, with not a jot of sympathy for Byron's continued interest in boys, maintained a deep unselfish love of Byron all his life, John Cam Hobhouse. Byron did not ever appreciate the fact that in the sturdy John Cam he had as great a friend as Hamlet had in Horatio. Until the very end Hobhouse was an Argus over his friend's reputation, and for decades after Byron's death

---

* De Sade's book.

remained the staunchest and most virile defender of the poet's good name. An honest man, he was clear-eyed about Byron's weaknesses, and even when disapproving of them was not censorious—because they were Byron's weaknesses. What he knew to his friend's discredit—and no friend knew as much or saw as much of Byron over the years—he did not reveal to others. But he did commit to his diaries and, when exasperated by the misinformation or ignorance of Byron's biographers, on the margins of their books, a number of jottings invaluable to us. For himself he penned a characteristically blunt comment which settles the nature of Byron's friendships at Harrow: "Certainly B had nothing to learn in the way of depravity either of mind or body when he came [to Cambridge] from Harrow."

There is another incontrovertible fact. Until his final days Byron, despite his countless affairs with women, continued to be attracted to good-looking boys.

His experiences at Harrow were the roots of a predisposition which continued to flourish, now and again, in his future years up to the last days of his life. They were also quite possibly a contributing cause to his marriage's ending in catastrophe.

3.

THAT HIS LATER ATTRACTION TO COMELY YOUTHS, A RECURRENT AND protracted adolescence, was an erratic outcropping of the sentimentalities and confused sensualities of his Harrow days is, in a paradoxical and curious way, testified to by an experience he had between terms.

The lines to Delawarr and the "Epitaph" were written, respectively, in February and March of 1803. In April of that year Lord Grey de Ruthyn leased from the impecunious Byrons for five years the ancestral home of the family, Newstead Abbey. In August Byron, who adored the place, and could hardly wait to achieve his majority so he might live there in seignoral style, came to stay on the grounds of the estate at the cottage of the caretaker.

Soon he had fallen in love again, this time with shattering thoroughness. Mary Chaworth of Annesley Hall, some four miles away, was the grandniece of the William Chaworth whom an earlier Lord Byron had killed in a duel. She was already engaged to marry a squire, John Musters. Nevertheless, Byron was so deeply smitten that his mother could not get him to leave the neighborhood and return to school for the new term.

In November, Lord Grey, a pampered young man, eight years older than Byron, arrived from his travels to take up residence at his new home, and pressed Byron, then nearing sixteen, to stay at the Abbey as his guest. By that time Mary Chaworth had blasted the boy with a devastating rejection of him. It was then too late to go back to Harrow until after the winter holidays for the following term. Miserable and brooding over Mary, Byron gladly accepted Grey's invitation. At first the young nobleman and his guest were very close companions and went shooting pheasants on moonlit nights.

Byron was still at Newstead Abbey at the end of December. Suddenly he left, vowing never to see Lord Grey again. Though a certain amount of mystery beclouds the event, one fact is clear: during their intimacy something dramatic happened, "which," Hobhouse cryptically observes in a marginal note, "certainly had much effect upon his future morals." That, as Marchand suggests, it was some sort of "sexual advance" which soon disgusted the boy is indisputable enough from the evidence of Byron's own letters. To make matters more difficult for him, his mother had taken a great fancy to Grey, and Byron had to resist her attempts to heal the breach between them. "I am not reconciled to Lord Grey, *and I never will*," he wrote to Augusta, his sister, on March 26, 1804. "He was once my *Greatest Friend*, my reasons for ceasing that Friendship are such as I cannot explain, not even to you, my Dear Sister . . . but they will ever remain hidden in my own breast. They are Good ones, however . . . He has forfeited all *title to my esteem*, but I hold him in too much *contempt* ever *to hate* him."

Two possible accountings for the break offer themselves. Either Grey attempted to alter what had been to Byron a welcome comradeship by making an unexpected attempt at physical intimacy, and so ended the friendship —a theory toward which I incline—or else they had been on such terms already (as Hobhouse's note might be taken to imply) and it was the specific nature of Grey's advances that shocked Byron into leaving the Abbey at once. If the verses already written to friends at Harrow are remembered, it becomes necessary to reject the conclusion of Byron's biographers that it was Grey who initiated Byron into epicene relationships. If Grey was his first instructor, then Byron's biographers must believe that there had been intimacies between them, first acceptable to the boy, before some particular attempt horrified him into running away.

It is not only because of the earlier Harrow poems that I reject that conclusion, and think that Byron had run at Grey's first physical aggression. The "contempt" he began to feel for the young nobleman quickly developed into violent detestation. In November he was writing Augusta again to complain about his mother: "all our disputes have been lately heightened by my one with that object of my cordial, deliberate detestation, Lord Grey de Ruthyn. She wishes me to explain my reasons for disliking him, which I will never do. . . . She also insists on my being reconciled to him, and once she let drop such an odd expression that I was half inclined to believe the dowager was in love with him. But I hope not, for he is the most disagreeable person (in my opinion) that exists. He called once during my last vacation; she threatened, stormed, begged me to make it up, 'he himself loved me, and wished it;' but my reason was so excellent—that neither had effect, nor would I speak or stay in the same room, till he took his departure. . . . If I am to be tormented with her and him in this style, I cannot submit to it. . . . If you too desert me, I have nobody I can love but Delawarr. If it was not for his sake, Harrow would be a desert."

It is to be noted: at this time, whatever his hatred for Grey because of some single act, he was dearly loving Delawarr, who was then only thirteen. I believe it was the simple fact that Grey was an adult, whom he had therefore somewhat respected, which nauseated Byron. To a boy of sixteen a young man of twenty-four is a mature man. It was not in Byron's nature ever to desire from adult men any inflamed or sentimental attachment. Hobhouse's words, therefore, may mean only that his experience with Grey certified Byron's addiction to boys and a sexual aversion to male adults.

The imposing fact is that among a very wide circle of friends and acquaintances acquired during his brief lifetime there is not a single instance of a male adult who was inverted. His strong feelings against Grey were not forgotten. On the whole, anyway, he much preferred the society of women. In February of 1814, during the height of his being lionized in London, he wrote in his journal: " 'Man delights not me,' and only one woman —at a time. There is something to me very softening in the presence of a woman—some strange influence, even if one is not in love with them —which I cannot at all account for, having no very high opinion of the sex. But yet,—I always feel in better humour with myself and every thing else, if there's a woman within ken." During the same month he also wrote: "The more I see of men, the less I like them. If I could but say so of women too, all would be well." Five years later he was confiding to the Countess Guiccioli that he had "always despised" the company of men. This professed avoidance extended particularly to literary men (with the exceptions of Shelley, Scott, and Moore). Two years later, he was saying that he did not "draw well" with them; "I never know what to say to them after I have praised their last publication."

4.

ACTUALLY, HIS FALLING IN LOVE WITH MARY CHAWORTH, WHICH PRE-ceded Grey's invitation to live in the Abbey, was an experience which was to leave a far deeper and more lasting impression upon him than did the

Lord Byron upon leaving Harrow.

unfortunate one with Grey. She was eighteen, almost three years older than Byron, beautiful and captivating. Though engaged to marry John Musters, and regarding her fifteen-year-old admirer as no more than a gauche schoolboy, she did flirt with him and encourage his visits. No doubt she found his chatter more entertaining and stimulating than the talk of her fox-hunting fiancé.

That summer Byron was steeped in the sentimental lyrics of Tom Moore, published two years earlier as the work of one "Mr. Little," who, according to Moore's preface, "died in his one-and-twentieth year." Byron had most of them by heart. They were full of hints of purple passion, abounding in phrases like "Sweet seducer!" "bosom flushing," "the burning glance," "amorous night," "cheeks of flame"; the tone of the volume may be surmised from a quatrain, "To Phyllis":

> Phyllis, you little rosy rake,
>   That heart of yours I long to rifle:
> Come, give it me, and do not make
>   So much ado about a *trifle!*

Such and similar lines were enough to inflame the boy Byron's erotic imagination. "I believe all the mischief I have ever done or sung," he eventually told Moore, "has been owing to that confounded book of yours."

He luxuriated in being near Mary Chaworth, and rode over from the caretaker's cottage at Newstead to spend every day with her. He was offered a bed at Annesley Hall, but declined it and returned every night to Newstead —until finally he changed his mind and announced that on the ride back the night before he had met a ghost, and would now willingly accept the proffered hospitality. After that he continued to sleep under the same roof which sheltered his beloved, probably torturing himself with visions of her proximity.

Of course, everything about the situation was impossible—above all, the crucial difference in their ages and the fact that she was in love with Musters. It is pathetic that this last chance the boy had to uproot what May Gray had implanted in him—as he might have succeeded in doing, for he was truly in love with Mary Chaworth—was doomed to an acrid conclusion for him.

They made an excursion to Matlock where, because of his lameness, he was put to the misery of looking on while she danced with men she had not met before. But there were happy hours riding by her side, or listening to her at the keyboard. At times he could not conceal from himself that she was in love with her fiancé; then he would revert to the petulant schoolboy, sit in moping silence "pulling at his handkerchief," or exhaust his frustration by firing his pistol at the door leading to the terrace. At such times he must have been a bore to her; the roughness of his manners and his chubbiness would only serve to remind her of his juvenility—though when the fit of vanity struck him, he would assure her that he knew himself to be "a good looking fellow."

Tom Moore, into whose custody Byron's memoirs were later confided, and who therefore had the privilege of reading them as often as he liked before they were consigned to the flames after their author's death,* was in the position of being able to recount graphically the terrible disruption of Byron's idyl at Annesley Hall. Mary's maid had apparently been chiding her for leading on poor Byron, and "he either was told of, or overheard, Miss Chaworth saying to her maid, 'Do you think I could care anything for that lame boy?' This speech, as he himself described it, was like a shot through his heart. Though late at night when he heard it, he instantly darted out of the house, and scarcely knowing whither he ran, never stopped till he found himself at Newstead."

It was not only as a child that Byron suffered excruciating pain because of his clubfoot, when a series of medicos prescribed torturing contraptions in a vain effort to correct his marked lameness. All his life walking was an agony for him because of the way in which the soles of his feet turned inward. He sustained terrible humiliations as a youngster from the taunts of other boys until, by his fierce participation in school sports, he won their respect. But this unintended derision of Mary's he never forgot. Many a woman thereafter expiated that affront. Yet against the perpetrator herself he held no grievance and, though it was a knife in him, he humbly accepted her verdict. He never got over Mary Chaworth, and the image of that unfulfilled love haunted his days. Circumstance, as is its way, was not to allow Byron's vision of her to remain uncontaminated, and he, in his less attractive moods, would speak coarsely of her. But she remained his ideal love. The proof will be found in one of his genuinely moving poems, "The Dream," written some months after his wife left him in 1816. It is significant that at a time when his thoughts were occupied almost exclusively with the bitterness of the separation, his poetic imagination should have carried him back more than a decade to the days at Annesley Hall.

In the poem he pictures Mary and himself standing on a hill near the house; though both of them were young, hers was the "one belovéd face on earth." He hung upon her very breath, he existed only in her presence; she was his life, the source of all his thoughts, and at

---

* Doris Langley Moore's brilliant *The Late Lord Byron* (1961) gives a complete account of that unforgivable destruction.

> A touch of hers, his blood would ebb and flow,
> And his cheek change tempestuously—

although his heart was too young to understand the cause of the agony he felt. But she participated in none of these emotions. And as they stood there, she sighed—not for him, for she was already in love with someone else. Eventually they parted, and she married the man she loved only to find misery in her marriage (as indeed Mary did). The poem presently shifts to the scene of Byron's own wedding. He is standing at the altar with his own bride at his side. Suddenly, in the midst of the ceremony, he loses consciousness of where he is; he repeats mechanically the words expected of him without knowing what he is saying; his thoughts are fixed upon Annesley Hall, the old mansion and its familiar hall, and she "who was his destiny," comes back to haunt him.

There is something tragic in this confession, which makes it all too clear that there was never much chance for the success of Byron's marriage. Confession it truly was. Byron later told Medwin that at his wedding he had "trembled like a leaf, made the wrong responses," and after the ceremony called his wife by her maiden name. Basing his comments on the burned memoirs, Moore remarks that in them Byron "describes himself as waking, on the morning of his marriage, with the most melancholy reflections"; he wandered about the grounds alone, still miserable; at the ceremony "he knelt down—he repeated the words after the clergyman; but a mist was before his eyes—his thoughts were elsewhere [on Mary, we may presume]; and he was but awakened by the congratulations of the bystanders to find that he was—married."

So long after her rejection, he could feel this love for the girl. No doubt at sixteen he had looked to the fulfillment of that love to put forever behind him his revolting experiences with May Gray as well as those homosexual affections of Harrow which, at that age, haunted his Calvinistic conscience. Lord Grey's advances, coming on the heels of that rejection, would inevitably have been the more horrifying.

5.

DURING THE EVENTFUL YEAR OF 1803, WHEN BYRON WAS FIFTEEN, HIS mother took a small house at Southwell, twelve miles from Newstead, to establish within easy reach of the Abbey he loved so well a home for her son during the holidays. But bored with the place, he soon went off to

Newstead, as we have seen, to live in the caretaker's cottage. In 1804 he was back at Harrow, and when he came to Southwell for the Easter interim he began in earnest to cement a relationship which was to be one of the most fateful in his life, that with his half sister Augusta, the daughter of Captain Jack's first marriage to Lady Carmarthen, and some five years Byron's elder.

It will be remembered that Catherine Byron, when pregnant with the poet-to-be, brought the little girl with her on her return to England for her accouchement, and left the child with Augusta's grandmother. By 1801, though full of curiosity about his half sister, Byron had not ever seen her. We do not know precisely when they first met. Presently there was some exchange of letters between them, but the earliest extant is that written at Southwell on March 22, 1804.

In it the boy apologized for his long silence and continued with unconscious humor, as he assumed for his sister the role of his Lordship: "I hope you will consider me not only as *a Brother* but as your warmest and most affectionate *Friend,* and if ever Circumstances should require it your *protector.* Recollect, My Dearest Sister, that you are *the nearest relation* I have *in the world both by the ties of Blood and affection.* . . . P.S. Do not forget to knit the purse you promised me." He also sent his regards to their cousin, son of the sister who had been generous to Mad Jack and Mrs. Byron, Colonel George Leigh of the Tenth Dragoons, with whom Augusta was in love, and whom she presently married.

Four days later he wrote once more, assuring her that nothing could induce him to become friends again with Grey, and a week later he thanked her for the gift of the purse and begged her to write him letters that would *"fill twenty sheets of paper"* to mitigate the ennui he felt at Southwell. That summer he inaugurated a series of long complaints to her about his mother and her *"diabolical* disposition"; the more he saw of her the more he disliked her; "no captive Negro, or Prisoner of war, ever looked forward to their emancipation, and returned to Liberty with more Joy" than he would, on returning to school, "to escape from this maternal bondage." In the fall he wrote bitterly: "She flies into a fit of phrenzy, rakes up the ashes of my *father,* abuses him, says I shall be a true Byrrone, which is the worst epithet she can invent."

Byron's own words on the wretched hours he spent with his mother are substantiated by Moore's recollection of the memoirs: "In speaking of his own sensitiveness, on the subject of his deformed foot, he described the feeling of horror and humiliation that came over him, when his mother, in one of her fits of passion, called him 'a lame brat.'" Moore speaks again of "the loud hurricane bursts of Mrs. Byron"; "It is told, as a curious proof of their opinion of each other's violence, that, after parting one evening in a tempest of this kind, they were known each to go privately that night to the apothecary's, inquiring anxiously whether the other had been to purchase poison, and cautioning the vender of drugs not to attend to such an application, if made." The violence was often physical enough; "poker and tongs were, it seems, the missiles which Mrs. Byron preferred, and which she, more than once, sent resounding after her fugitive son."

Southwell became more endurable when his young lordship made the acquaintance of the Pigot family, and through them the Leacrofts, the Housons, and others of their small circle. Elizabeth Pigot, who was several years older than he, has sketched vividly her first encounter with him. It was at a party his mother gave. He was so shy that Mrs. Byron had to send for him three times before he could be made to join her guests. "He was then a fat bashful boy, with his hair combed straight over his forehead." The next day he and his mother called on the Pigots; his conduct was formal; there was small talk about the theatre at Cheltenham; Mrs. Byron got up to go and her son made a ceremonious farewell bow. Elizabeth, a merry girl, referring to the character of Gabriel Lackbrain in the play they had been discussing, said, "Goodbye, Gaby." That broke the ice. "His countenance lighted up, his handsome mouth displayed a broad grin, all his shyness vanished, never to return, and, upon his mother's saying, 'Come, Byron, are you ready?'—no, she might go by herself, he would stay and talk a little longer; and from that moment he used to come in and go out at all hours, as it pleased him." After that day he and Elizabeth became good friends, and she was soon the recipient of his confidences. His letters to her show him thoroughly enjoying the correspondence they maintained for a number of years.

On returning to school, Byron, reacting from his shock over the Mary Chaworth affair, threw himself with greater warmth than ever into his Harrow friendships. He also continued his feverish reading. He had always been an omnivorous devourer of books, and like most people who read for pleasure, not duty, he read without system or order. In the long run such people manage to read vastly more than their more systematic or pedantic brothers. Looking back on those days he later said, "Till I was eighteen . . . I had never read a review. But, while I was at Harrow, my general information was so great on modern topics as to induce a suspicion that I could only collect so much information from *reviews*, because I was never *seen* reading, but always idle and in mischief, or at play. The truth is that I read eating, read in bed, read when no one else reads." By his twentieth year, as witnessed by the books he had listed as already read, his reading had been prodigious in Greek and Roman writers, English and French literature and philosophy, the law, oratory, divinity, and "novels by the thousand." The *Anatomy of Melancholy* was one of his great favorites.

His bitterness over the Mary Chaworth disillusionment had so hardened him that when Augusta saw him in 1805 for the first time in a year, she was shocked to find his temper and disposition "so completely altered" that she barely recognized him.

In August 1805 Mary married her John Musters. An eyewitness gave Moore a circumstantial picture of Mrs. Byron's attempt to wound her son: "His mother said, 'Byron, I have some news for you.'—'Well, what is it?'— 'Take out your handkerchief first, for you will want it.'—'Nonsense!'— 'Take out your handkerchief, I say.' He did so, to humour her. 'Miss Chaworth is married.' An expression very peculiar, impossible to describe, passed over his pale face, and he hurried his handkerchief into his pocket, saying, with an affected air of coldness and nonchalance. 'Is that all?'—'Why I expected you would have been plunged into grief!'—He made no reply, and soon began to talk about something else."

The schoolboy, about to enter Cambridge, was fast becoming a sophisticate, a man of the world.

6.

AS LORD BYRON HE FELT THE NEED OF BEING URBANE WHEN HE ARRIVED at Trinity College, Cambridge, two months later. But he parted with boyhood most reluctantly. "When I first went up to College," he later reminisced, "it was a new and heavy hearted scene for me . . . It was one of the deadliest and heaviest feelings of my life to feel that I was no longer a boy." In many ways he was never to cease being a boy. What he was missing, of course, was his Harrow friends and the sudden cessation of his role as their loving and loved protector.

"I took my gradations in the vices with great promptitude, but they were not to my taste; for my early passions, though violent in the extreme, were concentrated, and hated division or spreading abroad. I could have left or lost the world with or for that which I loved, but, though my temperament was naturally burning, I could not share in the commonplace libertinism of the place and time without disgust. And yet this very disgust, and my heart thrown back upon itself, threw me into excesses perhaps more fatal than those from which I shrunk."

Paradoxically, he remembered it of all periods of his life as "the most romantic." These were the days when he enjoyed the friendship of Edward Noel Long, who had come up from Harrow with him to Trinity—and of one other person, the object of a "violent, though *pure,* love and passion."

He could not live without being loved, and almost immediately after coming to Trinity College, Byron began there a passionate friendship which superseded all the Harrow affections in intensity and idealization. The shock over Mary Chaworth and that so different one over Lord Grey and his loneliness had prepared the ground for one of his recurrent deep devotions to some boy, such as was to become habitual with him for most of his life. It was the same October of his arrival at Cambridge that he first heard John Eldeston, a choirboy in the college chapel. The lad was too years younger than himself. They rapidly became fond of each other, and soon Edleston presented his friend with a pledge of their loyalty to each other, a cornelian in the shape of a heart.

Whatever the suppressed feelings on the part of both may have been, there can be no doubt that this "passion" was, as Byron described it, a "pure" one, with all the heat that went into it—a distinction that only a dyed-in-the-wool Freudian will think not worth the making. In the midst of dissipations he held it up with his love for Mary Chaworth as the two uncontaminated attachments of his youth. He seems also to have felt that Edleston's ideal love preserved him from some portion of that host of vicious experiences inviting a young man at Cambridge and London. Colman in *Don Leon* thus sums up the relationship: as manhood neared, the poet "sighed for some kindred mind" with whom there might be a mutual exchange of confidence. Such a one he found at a chapel service:

> Among the choir a youth my notice won,
> Of pleasing lineaments named Edleston.
> With gifts well suited to a stripling's mood,
> His friendship and his tenderness I wooed.
> Oh! how I loved to press his cheek to mine;
> How fondly would my arms his waist entwine!
> Another feeling borrowed friendship's name,
> And took its mantle to conceal my shame . . .
> Strong was my passion, past all inward cure,
> And could it be so violent, yet pure?
> So questioned I myself: What lights this fire?
> Maids and not boys are wont to move desire;
> Else 'twere illicit love. Oh! sad mishap!
> But what prompts nature then to set the trap?
> Why night and day does his sweet image float
> Before my eyes?

When at Harrow, *Don Leon* says, he stood "upon the brink of infamy," half willing, half afraid. It was Edleston who saved him.

Byron's own words testify to the fact that Colman did not exaggerate.

He had taken Elizabeth Pigot into his confidence about this great friendship. It had been flourishing for a year and a half when he wrote to her from Cambridge to talk of "the hero of *my Cornelian* (who is now sitting *vis-à-vis* reading a volume of my *Poetics.*)" Edleston "has left the choir, and is stationed in a mercantile house of considerable eminence in the metropolis. You may have heard me observe he is exactly to an hour two years younger than myself. I found him grown considerably, and as you will suppose, very glad to see his former *Patron.* He is nearly my height, very *thin,* very fair of complexion, dark eyes, and light locks."

Byron himself, who was to wage a lifelong battle against a tendency to corpulence, was able to report that he too was at least *"thinner"* and had lost two pounds since he was last at Southwell.

Five days later he was writing to her again: "My life here has been one continued routine of dissipation ... At this moment I write with a bottle of claret in my *head* and *tears* in my eyes; for I have just parted with my *'Cornelian,'* who spent the evening with me. As it was our last interview, I postponed my engagement to devote the hours of the *Sabbath* to friendship:—Edleston and I have separated for the present, and my mind is a chaos of hope and sorrow. Tomorrow I set out for London. . . .

"I rejoice to hear you are interested in my *protégé;* he has been my *almost constant* associate since October, 1805, when I entered Trinity College. His *voice* first attracted my attention, his *countenance* fixed it, and his manners attached me to him for ever. He departs for a *mercantile house* in *town* in October, and we shall probably not meet till the expiration of my minority [Byron was writing in July 1807, when he was nineteen], when I shall leave to his decision either entering as a *partner* through my interest, or reside with me altogether." At present Edleston would prefer "the *latter.*" "I certainly love him more than any human being." Aware of his own volatility, Byron is half-surprised that time and distance have had not the least effect on his usually "changeable disposition. In short, we shall put . . . *Pylades* and *Orestes* out of countenance, and want nothing but a catastrophe . . . to give *Jonathan* and *David* the 'go by.' He certainly is perhaps more attached to *me* than even I am in return." At Cambridge they met every day "without passing *one* tiresome moment, and separated each time with increasing reluctance. I hope you will one day see us together. He is the only being I esteem."

When Byron found someone who could love him, his first reaction was always like the traveler lost in the desert who comes unexpectedly upon an oasis. The very humbleness of his not daring to be sure that Edleston would consent to live with him ("He shall have his choice") points to the depth of what he felt, for humbleness is a posture in which he is almost never to be seen. The plan for sharing lodgings, it turned out, was never fulfilled; two years after writing these letters he was embarked on travels to foreign lands. When he returned it was to learn that Edleston was dead.

The gift of the cornelian heart was never forgotten. In "The Cornelian" he recreated the scene of its presentation:

> He offer'd it with downcast look,
>   As *fearful* that I might refuse it;
> I told him, when the gift I took,
>   My *only fear* should be, to lose it ...

The lines were probably written at Cambridge. There is a companion piece called "Pignus Amoris" [Pledge of Love]:

> ... this toy of blushing hue
> I prize with zeal before unknown,
> It tells me of a Friend I knew,
> Who loved me for myself alone ...

Byron's contemporaries Shelley and Keats had premonitions of an early death, which in the event proved only too true. In a like fit of depression, Byron wrote "The Adieu," in which he bade farewell to all that was dear to him, and in that category Edleston ranked high:

> And thou, my Friend! whose gentle love
>   Yet thrills my bosom's chords ...
> Still near my breast thy gift I wear ...

Byron was not a liar, and there is no reason to doubt that this love remained a "pure" one; but the scene of the giving of the cornelian and the language in which he speaks of his friend make it clear enough that Edleston was a youth of effeminate nature. It may be supposed that it was the completeness of his submissiveness to Byron's stronger temper which caused Byron, sure that he was loved at last for himself, to prize him so passionately.

With much reasonableness Marchand has suggested that one of Byron's best-known and best-written lyrics, "There be none of Beauty's daughters," was composed for Edleston; certainly its verses perfectly match both situation and feelings of the poet's devotion to Edleston, which began when he first heard the choirboy sing, and there may, therefore, very well have been more meant by the opening line than the world has supposed—a backward glance at Byron's disillusioning experiences with women:

There be none of Beauty's daughters
With a magic like thee;
And like music on the waters
Is thy sweet voice to me . . .

So the spirit bows before thee,
To listen and adore thee;
With a full but soft emotion,
Like the swell of Summer's ocean.

It would be rash, however, to conjecture from this lovely lyric that it was in reality the association with music which first enraptured Byron with Edleston. Like many men of letters, Byron was a Philistine in that art. When, for example, during the time of his being lionized in London, he dined at the Princess of Wales's in 1814, he was bored to death with the musicale which followed; there were performances on the flute and at the pianoforte which he could hardly suffer, until the engrossed expressions of the audience (some of whom surely, were experiencing what he was never to know) struck him as so ridiculous that he was forced almost to strangle himself with his handkerchief in his effort to smother his laughter. Not long after that soirée he was assuring Lady Melbourne that his friendship with Lady Forbes was based on a "mutual hatred of music." In 1821 he jotted in his diary: "like music"—as though to remind himself of what he ought to feel; no music lover would think of making such an entry. Whatever appeal music may have occasionally had for him was the sentimental and irrelevant one of evoking memories: a month later, at Ravenna, he heard a street organ playing a waltz which he remembered to have "heard ten thousand times at the balls in London." In 1823 he made his fullest statement on the subject to Lady Blessington: like Zuleika Dobson, he knew nothing about music but knew what he liked; he was, he said, glad of his ignorance, "for a perfect knowledge might rob it of half of its charms. At present I only know, that a plaintive air softens, and a lively one cheers me. Martial music renders me brave; and voluptuous music disposes me to be luxurious, even effeminate." This not uncommon attitude reduces the sublimest of the arts to the level of a shot of whiskey or an aphrodisiac. One can imagine the indignation of Byron, whose idol was Alexander Pope of the chiseled couplet, if the same criteria were applied to the reading of poetry. It was, then, not the music which he first heard Edleston sing, any more than it was the ditties which he had enjoyed hearing Mary Chaworth play, which involved his emotions. Rather, the music enveloped each of these loved ones in a rosy aura.

In July Byron and Hobhouse left England for a tour of exotic countries. While they were abroad mail from England spoke of stories being spread in London concerning Edleston's "indecency." Now twenty, the former choirboy was probably being propelled into the perilous paths to which his effeminate disposition was likely to have driven him.

The effect of these rumors was to sober Byron into a realization that it would be wiser for him to give up Edleston on his return. His love for him, nonetheless, remained unimpaired.

While the travelers were sailing from Greece to Malta, Edleston died on May 11, 1811. Though Byron was back home in July, it was not until October that he received the letter Edleston's sister had written to tell him of the boy's death. He had already steeled himself to the necessity of keeping Edleston at a distance, but this news was a great blow. He at once wrote to Hobhouse to say how deeply he was affected, and a week later he admitted that he was ashamed to feel the crushing effect Edleston's death was having upon him. At Cambridge for a visit, he was reminded at every turn of the choirboy and their happy days together. Never a moral hypocrite and well aware of Hobhouse's disapproval of such friendships, he added that he knew he was risking Hobhouse's contempt—"but you cannot despise me more than I do myself."

To another friend, who had never heard of Edleston, he wrote in his misery: "I have been again shocked with a *death,* and have lost one very dear to me"; to another he confided that Cambridge could only be full of sad memories for him: "I believe the only human being, that ever loved me in truth and entirely, was of, or belonging to, Cambridge."

As always, he found relief in composing autobiographical poems. Concealing Edleston's identity under the female name of Thyrza, he vented his grief. In "To Thyrza" he recollects their Cambridge days, now that "affection's heart-drops" are gushing from him; once their tears of love had mingled,

> Ours too the glance none saw beside;
> The smile none else might understand;
> The whispered thought, the walk aside,
> The pressure of the thrilling hand;
> The kiss that left no sting behind
> So guiltless Passion thus forbore;
> Those eyes bespoke so pure a mind,
> That love forgot to $\begin{Bmatrix} \text{plead} \\ \text{ask} \end{Bmatrix}$ *for more . . .

---

* These are the alternative readings in Byron's manuscript of a highly revelatory line. For publication he altered it to read: "Ev'n passion blushed to plead for more." I believe that no one has noted the connection between the title of this poem and a remark in his preface to *Cain,* a work written years later, in which

It is not surprising that, even without regard to the title, this and its companion poems should for so long have been construed as addressed to a girl. Upon no other poems did the women who persecuted Byron with their aggressive attentions so completely fasten their sentimental concentration; they felt that if the poet held the loss of such a maiden as Thyrza irreparable, they, each in her turn, might satisfactorily fill the void in his heart. For all that, he did all he could to encourage the false attribution. He told Claire Clairmont, for instance, that Thyrza was a girl he had seduced and who had borne two children to him; she had been anxious to marry him, but he had refused because of her low station; he went abroad and she committed suicide; her death weighed upon him heavily, but even that had not altered his conviction that she had been unsuitable as a wife for him because she was lowly born. Mary Shelley, on the other hand, believed Thyrza a female cousin; from Byron's own lips Mrs. Shelley had heard of his misery at Thyrza's death and how he had been left disconsolate; after so many years she had witnessed his recollection of the "acute despair" which had fathered the Thyrza poems and the poem on the broken cornelian heart which the "girl" had given him.

That keepsake he had asked Elizabeth Pigot to guard for him; on October 28, 1811, he had written to her mother asking for its return because "the person who gave it me, when I was very young [he was all of twenty-three in 1811] is *dead*," and it was the only memento he owned "of that person." When the cornelian heart was returned it arrived broken. He thereupon wrote "On a Cornelian Heart Which Was Broken," in which he compares its shattered state to that of his own heart.

In addition to the six poems already mentioned as inspired by Edleston, he wrote others. "Away, Away, Ye Notes of Woe" was occasioned by hearing music Edleston had once sung. Another poem is also called "To Thyrza"; in it he reflects bitterly on his unawareness while he was abroad of Thyrza's death; the grief here memorialized is honestly felt. The strains of sorrow continue in "And Thou Art Dead, As Young and Fair," wherein he sorrows over his inability, because he was away, to keep even one vigil over the loved one's bed,

> And show that love, however vain,
> Nor thou nor I can feel again.

---

he says that he had read Gesner's *Death of Abel* at the age of eight; "of the contents I remember only that Cain's wife was called Mabala and Abel's Thirza." The reader may decide if any significance attaches to Byron's bestowing upon Edleston the name (according to Gesner) of one of the first women to inhabit the earth.

His inability to obliterate the memory of Edleston is to be read again in "If Sometimes in the Haunts of Men." There is also a passage, of which we have yet to speak, in *Childe Harold* in memory of Edleston.

During his life Byron singled out a number of individuals as the being who had loved him best. But none of them inspired him to write as many as these eleven pieces to Edleston. And it is a fact that the boy's death left him inconsolable for a long time—the more so that he could not confide his grief in anyone else. However deplorable the poetic quality of all of these poems (with exception of "There be none of Beauty's daughters"), they reveal some of the sincerest love and grief to be found in Byron's poetry.

7.

BEFORE HE WAS EIGHTEEN, ON HIS ARRIVAL AT CAMBRIDGE HE STARTED, in the spirit approved there, by laying in a supply of four dozen bottles of wine. Less than a month after his first term had begun, his head was "confused with Dissipation which tho' I hate I cannot avoid." In London for the Christmas holidays a month later, he was already out of funds, and began the first of a long series of entanglements with moneylenders, which eventually drew him into debt for a staggering sum. That too was more or less *de rigueur* for a young nobleman.

When the new term began in January 1806, he did not return to Trinity. Temporarily separated from Edleston at the time, Byron was sufficiently disturbed by the strength of that tie to prove to himself in town that he was masculine enough, by a swift procession from the bed of one available woman to the bed of another, not even reluctant to call upon the services of a notorious French procuress "who assisted young gentlemen in their youthful pastimes." These expensive recreations, something of an answer too to Mary Chaworth's rejection by showing what a poor lame boy could do in the way of depravity, were varied with other exercises in masculinity: lessons in fencing from the celebrated master Henry Angelo and in boxing from the ex-champion prizefighter Gentleman Jackson. He did not leave London until April, and when the summer holidays came around he was unable to remain there long, as he wished to do; shortage of funds forced him against his inclinations to join his mother at Southwell.

There his perscrutations of his sexual potency continued unabated among the village girls. As usual, he was tempted to celebrate his conquests in verse. The record of one such exploit is to be found in his flippant lines "To a Lady Who Presented to the Author a Lock of Her Hair Braided with

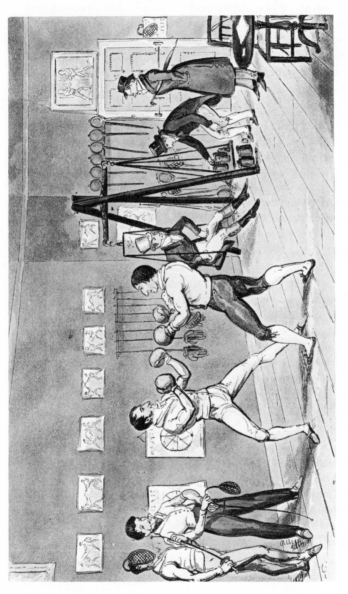

"Instructions from Mr. Jackson at his Rooms in Bond Street," drawn and engraved by I. R. and G. Cruikshank; from P. Egan's *Life in London*. (Courtesy of the British Museum.) "Gentleman" John Jackson, called by Byron "Professor of Pugilism," an ex-champion prizefighter, taught Byron boxing, visited him often during the summer at Brighton, was invited to Newstead Abbey, and was still sparring with him the year of Byron's marriage.

His Own and Appointed a Night in December to Meet Him in the Garden";
he asks the girl to change their rendezvous to her bedroom, for "There we
can love for hours together"; the request being granted, if his abilities should
"fail to please," he will be content to freeze in the garden the following
night. Another affair was with a certain Mary, to whom he wrote lines re-
joicing in how often they have done "what prudes declare a sin to act."

His well-developed cynicism was further fed by the complaisance of the
damsels at Southwell. He told Hobhouse that it was in that place that he
learned how far self-interest could drive some people; one of the families
there "winked at" the favors their daughter granted him in the expectation
that he would be entrapped, despite the difference in their stations, into
marrying the girl. Byron's comment on the affair, in a letter to Elizabeth
Pigot, derisively extends boundless thanks to the village lasses of "every
description" at Southwell; his gratitude was exceeded only by his *"contempt"*
for he was all the time quite aware of "the design of all parties," and only
pretended to add fuel to their aspirations. It is chilling to consider that an
eighteen-year-old could have been so cold-blooded an opportunistic libertine.
Life had obviously already warped his nature.

His superciliousness toward the sexual game, which he was playing to
the limit, can be read in several poems of this period. In the flip "To the
Sighing Strephon," he brags of having "lov'd a good number," for there is
"pleasure, at least, in a change"; although he enjoys kissing a girl, he has
not been so foolish as to forget, when his lips and those of various girls have
often met, "that still there was *something beyond.*" In "Egotism" he chuckles
at the knowledge that if "some sage *Mammas*" think him "a youthful Sinner," their daughters say, "You must not check a *Young Beginner!*" It must
have pleased him to know that the Southwell circle could not fail to be
shocked by such lines as those extolling the delight of boy and girl viewing

> . . . each other panting, dying,
> In love's *extatic posture* lying,
> Grateful to *feeling,* as to sight.

The italics were intended to emphasize the wickedness and *double entendre*
in case anyone was too prim to grasp them at first reading.

Embarked on his career as a young Casanova, he suddenly became
conscious of the inconsistency between such a role and his propensity to fat.
His struggle against it began in earnest. In 1806 he was tipping the scales
at 212 pounds, a formidable weight for a youth below average height. For
the next twelve years he followed a severe regimen which included strenuous
exercise, fasting, dieting, reducing drugs, and wearing "seven Waistcoats and
a great coat" while running and playing at cricket. On August 20, 1807, he

was enthusiastically telling Clare that his old schoolfellow would never recognize him now that he weighed only 151 pounds, a loss of 51 pounds in six months. By 1809 he had put on 8 more pounds, but on July 15, 1811, he was only 137½ pounds, a weight he more or less maintained for the next seven years, until in Venice he became weary of the battle. But for those twelve years he had imposed upon himself a martyrdom such as he felt was owing to a trustee of beauty.

On his return from his travels abroad, the poet Rogers gave a dinner to him in the fall of 1811 so Byron might meet him and Tom Moore; Thomas Campbell was also present. Byron's respect for these older practitioners of his art was gratifying, but at table problems arose for Rogers. "When we sat down to dinner, I asked Byron if he would take soup? 'No, he never took soup.'—Would he take some fish? 'No, he never took fish.'— Presently I asked if he would eat some mutton? 'No, he never ate mutton.'— I then asked if he would take a glass of wine? 'No; he never tasted wine.' —It was now necessary to ask him what he *did* eat and drink; and the answer was, 'Nothing but hard biscuits and soda water.' Unfortunately, neither hard biscuits nor soda water were at hand; and he dined upon potatoes bruised down on his plate and drenched with vinegar. . . . Some days after, meeting Hobhouse, I said to him, 'How long will Lord Byron persevere in his present diet?' He replied, 'Just as long as you continue to notice it.'— I did not then know, what I now know to be a fact, that Byron, after leaving my house, had gone to a Club in St. James Street and eaten a hearty meat supper." Poor Byron! Anyone who has valiantly undertaken the death struggle with obesity will not require much imagination to understand why, after watching the others stowing the food away, he should have felt himself so starved on leaving them that he had to yield to his hunger. Hobhouse, who had not the problem, could afford to be sardonic.

It was at Cambridge in 1807 that Byron began the most important of his friendships. But their closeness did not develop at once. John Cam Hobhouse, the son of an M.P., hated him for two years, as Byron phrased it, because his young lordship "wore a *white hat* and a *grey coat* and rode a *grey* horse," but forgave him when he learned that Byron was a poet.

In 1807 Byron left Trinity College for the Christmas holidays, and never returned except in the summer to take his M.A.

In January 1808, when he was twenty, he was posing as the archsophisticate to a distant relative, Robert Charles Dallas, whom he assured that he was "already held up as the votary of licentiousness. . . . In morality I prefer Confucius to the Ten Commandments, and Socrates to St. Paul. . . . I have refused to take the sacrament, because I do not think eating bread or drinking wine from the hand of an earthly vicar will make me an inheritor of heaven. . . . I believe . . . death an eternal sleep, at least of the body."

That final reservation is significant. For all these brave words, Byron was never able to shed his early Calvinistic training and was certainly never an atheist.

In February he was gleefully informing his old Southwell friend, the Reverend John Becher, that he was taking medicine because of debilitation from "*too much love*"; he had been sacrificing too liberally at the "altar" of his Paphian goddesses; at present he had a sixteen-year-old, blue-eyed girl for a bedfellow, who, like him, was "nearly worn out" from their love sports. The next day, to Hobhouse, he admitted that he was a frequenter of prostitutes and was, in consequence of excessive visits, under a doctor's care for debility; the night before he and a friend had attended the Opera Masquerade, where they had supped with a ballet master, seven harlots, and a bawd behind the scenes. He was thinking of "buying" some of the ballet master's pupils: they would make a marvelous harem.

8.

HIS FIRST VOLUME, *Hours of Idleness*—THE AUTHOR DESCRIBED AS "George Gordon, Lord Byron, a Minor"—was published. His friends having taken offense at the livelier poems he had written—despite their weaknesses, they expressed the best of his talents, the wit which was to blossom in *Don Juan*—he had suppressed those pieces or revised lines. What remained was either sentimental or dull, when not pompous. The volume also contained an unfortunate preface. The poems were, the author conceded, "the fruits of the lighter hours of a young man who had lately completed his nineteenth year." Poetry, however, was not to be his "primary vocation"; he had composed only to divert himself when bored or indisposed; this book would be his "first, and last attempt." It was unlikely that he, as a nobleman, "should ever obtrude" himself "a second time upon the Public."

The implied plea for leniency from the critics availed him nothing with some of the more important critical reviews when couched in the language of such arrogance. To anyone who took poetry seriously—one shudders to think of what John Milton would have said to all this—it was insufferable that his young lordship should condescend to poetry as something hardly worth his attention. Though the *Critical Review* praised some of the worst poems, and the *Anti-Jacobin Review* thought the volume gave "strong proofs of genius . . . and a benevolent heart," and the *Monthly Literary Recreations* urged him to abandon his intention of writing no more verse, the prestigious *Edinburgh Review* of January 1808 gave him a sound trouncing. The poems, the critic said, never rise above a dead flatness. "As an extenuation of this

NAZARETH COLLEGE LIBRARY

offence, the noble author is peculiarly forward in pleading minority . . . All that he tells about his youth is rather with a view to increase our wonder than to soften our censures. He possibly means to say, 'See how a minor can write! This poem was actually composed by a young man of eighteen, and this by one of only sixteen!' . . . So far from hearing, with any degree of surprise, that very poor verses were written by a youth from his leaving school to his leaving college, inclusive, we really believe this to be the most common of all occurrences; that it happens in the life of nine men in ten who are educated in England; and that the tenth man writes better verse than Lord Byron. . . . He certainly . . . does allude frequently to his family and ancestry—sometimes in poetry, sometimes in notes." The review went on to remind him that having a regular number of feet in a line and rhyming the final syllable does not constitute the art of writing poetry. Some liveliness and some fancy are also called for, and some originality of thought. It is one thing that a youth of sixteen cannot be expected to be original, it is another that a young man of nineteen should publish his unoriginal effusions. One expects poets to be egotists, but within limits. "Whatever judgments may be passed on the poems of this noble minor, it seems we must take them as we find them, and be content; for they are the last we shall ever have from him. He is, at best, he says, but an intruder into the groves of Parnassus: he never lived in a garret, like thorough-bred poets. . . . Therefore, let us take what we get, and be thankful. What right have we poor devils to be nice? We are well off to have got so much from a man of this lord's station, who does not live in a garret, but 'has the sway' of Newstead Abbey. Again, we say, let us be thankful; and, with honest Sancho, bid God bless the giver, nor look the gift horse in the mouth."

Byron's first reaction was feeling "cut to atoms" by this review; it "has completely demolished my little fabric of fame." Hobhouse later remembered that Byron was so deeply wounded that he was near suicide, but the good John Cam may have been speaking figuratively. For Byron wrote him on March 14, 1808, that all seemed to be over with him; for the last five days he had been confined to his room, taking quantities of laudanum; but though his health was in ruins (not, of course, because of the review), he still spoke of himself as the great lover; there were two girls, one already his "property," and the other soon to be his, too, when he was on his feet again; both awaited his amorous ministrations the first day he felt equal to them.

If Byron was thus really trying to destroy himself in an effort to forget the *Edinburgh Review,* it was not for long, however. His fierce pride, at once a besetting weakness and the source of much inner toughness, soon came to the rescue. In the long run he would have cause to be thankful for the attack, for its present result was the unveiling of the best part of his talents. The "savage review," he said, ". . . knocked me down—but I got up again. Instead of bursting a blood-vessel, I drank three bottles of Claret, and began an answer." That answer was *English Bards and Scotch Reviewers,* which so well tapped his fury that after composing the first twenty lines he began to forget his disappointment and feel instead the exhilaration of creation.

The gap between the general ineptitude of *Hours of Idleness* and the many flashes of brilliance in *English Bards and Scotch Reviewers* is astounding. He had digested the writings of his beloved Pope and Pope's school to better than good effect, and on the purely poetic side the volume indicates that had he been born a century earlier he would have given Pope a run for his money. Compounded of paradox, Byron, who before long would figure as the brightest star in the firmament of poetry, was at his poorest when writing the oratorical claptrap that won him his greatest acclaim. His best talents were those which in an earlier, the eighteenth, century were held at a premium: strong wit, sharp satirical perception, and a bubbling sense of fun—none of which was encouraged by the prevalent melancholy and/or rapture fashionable in his own time.

Though he was publicly to stand at their head, he had small use for the poetry of his best contemporaries and liked only those moderns who wrote under the shadow of the Augustans. His mature judgment of Keats, for example, was worse than that of Keats's most hostile critics; Byron said that his lines were "a sort of mental masturbation." In *English Bards and Scotch Reviewers* he already scores the leaders of the romantic movement, some of his daggers, in truth, being only too well aimed. Wordsworth, who had been indignant at the *Edinburgh Review's* treatment of Byron, now had little cause to congratulate himself on that score, for the youth he had defended to Charles Lamb now sat in judgment of him; by "precept and example" Wordsworth shows, Byron writes, that "verse is merely prose," his own being void "of all but childish prattle"; in his tale

> of Betty Foy,
> The idiot mother of "an idiot Boy". . .
> [He] each adventure so sublimely tells,
> That all who view the "idiot in his glory,"
> Conceive the Bard the hero of the story.

Robert Southey is admonished to cease writing—"A bard may chaunt too often and too long"; if this one persists in writing his interminable epics "the babe unborn" will rue it. Coleridge is not spared either and, as though he had never published "The Ancient Mariner" or "Kubla Khan," is nicked for his early and, it is true, absurd "To a Young Ass":

> So well the subject suits his noble mind,
> He brays, the Laureate of the long-eared kind.

Nothing in this production did Byron have greater cause to regret than his excoriations of Sir Walter Scott, who had voiced his objections to the *Edinburgh Review* for its severity, and who, despite the unprovoked savagery of Byron's attack on him here, was to become one of the kindest and most generous of his admirers; the young castigator hopes that "The Lay of the Last Minstrel" may indeed "be the last!" and calls his romances "stale." Even Tom Moore is not exempted, though Byron had adored his lyrics and had been indebted to them and would remain so; yet unexpectedly our poet reverts to the Calvinism he was never to overcome, and speaks of this "young Catullus," whose song is sweet but "immoral"—

> Grieved to condemn, the Muse must still be just,
> Nor spare melodious advocates of lust.

There are attacks on many scribblers whose names would now be meaningless to the well informed, and passages on current politics no longer of interest. But even here his footnotes are droll very often, as for instance his words on Prime Minister Cavendish, Duke of Portland: "A friend of mine being asked, why his Grace of Portland was likened to an old woman? replied, he supposed it was because he was past bearing. His Grace is now gathered to his grandmothers, where he sleeps as sound as ever."

Years later Byron, who could be very honest with himself, was sorry he had written "the greater part" of this satire, both in its critical and personal parts; "the tone and temper are such as I cannot approve." These regrets, however, were voiced at a time when he had become famous for his worst work, and before he had rediscovered his great gift for the sort of satire he first penned in this book and some pieces excluded from his first volume.

The poets he praises are all inferior to the great ones he damns; who ever reads Samuel Rogers, William Gifford, Thomas Campbell, or Cumberland now? But among their number is one to whom our present study will be much indebted, George Colman the Younger, future author of the *Don Leon* poems, whom Byron had not yet met, though he was later to become his crony.

While he was working on the satire, Byron's dissipations continued. He kept one of his women at Brompton, and dressed her as a boy when they went to Brighton together, introducing her as his brother. A noblewoman who happened to be at the seaside resort at the time, had some suspicions of what was going on and remarked to the poet's "brother" that he was riding a pretty horse. "Yes," was the answer, "it was *gave* me by my brother!" A grim piece of humor is said to have attended this masquerade: the "brother" had a miscarriage at a family hotel in Bond Street.

This girl may or may not have been the Miss Cameron whom he bought for a hundred guineas from a procuress, "Madame D," the first night he saw the young tart. No matter how much smitten at any given time, Byron, however, always stipulated for a bed of his own to retire to after his lovemaking.

Of one of these women he wrote Hobhouse that she had only two faults, both of which he found unforgivable in a woman: she could read and write. Allowing for the attitudinizing, one becomes increasingly familiar with the fact that he could not abide an intellectual woman. He considered "a female wit" a "dangerous thing," and when it came to what Gilbert calls that singular anomaly, the lady novelist, he ran quickly to obscenity in describing one of the most famous; after saying that he found Maria Edgeworth "a pleasant reserved old woman," he went on to accuse her of keeping a pencil under her petticoat, where other instruments should have access, and of feeling, like all such women, absolutely without imperfection just because no man had ever taken her to bed.

While he was at Brighton, Byron bet John Hay one hundred guineas he would remain a bachelor. He was to lose the bet in less than seven years.

Lord Grey's lease of Newstead terminated in June 1808, and in September Byron went there to superintend repairs. Hobhouse joined him. On October 7 he wrote his mother that he intended in future to live "as much alone as possible. When my rooms are ready, I shall be glad to see you: at present it would be improper, and uncomfortable to both parties." He was going to Persia, he told her, no later than May and she would be able to live at the Abbey until he returned. He had drawn up his will, and he had arranged that in case of accident she should have "the house and manor for *life,* besides a sufficient income. So you see my improvements are not entirely selfish." This was less a token of filial love than a warning and mitigation that he would never live with her again under the same roof.

Actually he dared not risk more money than was required to make a few rooms habitable, though on them he did not stint. He had already acquired William Fletcher, who was to remain his valet for the rest of Byron's life; he added to his staff of servants several girls and Robert Rushton, a good-looking son of a nearby farmer; he had, too, the beginnings of a menagerie, without a semblance of which he was always to find it impossible to live—a pet bear he had purchased during Cambridge days and his Newfoundland dog Boatswain.

An invitation to dine came from Mary Chaworth Musters; he accepted, and was unprepared to find his "boyish flame" for her still burning, except that now it held no hope. When her two-year-old daughter was brought in, he was humbled into silence for the rest of the evening; the sight of the child had given another twist to the knife still lodged in him.

Hobhouse had to leave in November, and Byron spent part of his days at Newstead moping, but not all of them. He was serious in his plans for a jaunt abroad. He told himself that his chief reason was to escape "temptation's snare," for to be near Mary Musters was to be in view of Paradise yet to be shut out forever. In the meantime there was a pretty housemaid, Lucy, with whom he was sleeping, and the handsome Rushton, with whom he was intimate. Lucy is said to have been very jealous of his attentions to the boy; apparently losing her head, she dreamt that Byron would marry her and that she would become Lady Byron. She apparently did not know her master very well. From a letter to Hobhouse we learn that he had made her pregnant and had infected Rushton with the cowpox. The next month he altered his will to leave £50 a year to Lucy and another £50 to the illegitimate child she bore. She later married and ran a public house at Warwick.

9.

ON JANUARY 22, 1809, BYRON BECAME TWENTY-ONE. HE HAD OCCA-sionally thought of taking a prominent part in politics, much to his mother's gratification, once he assumed his seat in the House of Lords. But it was not to be. When the anticipated event occurred on March 13, after infuriating preliminaries, the House, as often, was almost empty.

English Bards and Scotch Reviewers finished and his seat in the Lords formally occupied, he began to draw up an itinerary for travel. While he was waiting for Hanson, the family solicitor, to provide the money, he went back to Newstead for some fun with a group of old cronies, including Hobhouse, Charles Skinner Matthews, and Wedderburn Webster. Matthews, who was "uncommonly handsome" and extremely diverting, had become a particularly good friend. "He was not good tempered," says Byron, "nor am I—but with a little tact his temper was manageable . . . I was willing to sacrifice something to his humours, which were often, at the same time, amusing and provoking." While Byron was away Matthews had occupied his rooms at Cambridge; the tutor had warned him "not to damage any of the moveables, for Lord Byron, Sir, is a young man of *tumultuous passions.*" Matthews found the admonition hilarious, and "whenever anybody came to visit him, begged them to handle the door with caution." When

Hobhouse published a volume of verse named *Miscellany,* Matthews thereafter referred to it as the *Miss-sell-any.* One of his amusing quirks was dining in out-of-the-way places; he was fond of one coffeehouse in the Strand because he paid an extra shilling to *"dine with his hat on.* This he called his *'hat* house,' " and used to expatiate on the pleasures of dining with his head covered.

Byron's recollection of his own farewell party at Newstead is graphic. His cellar was well stocked, and he had rented some monks' robes from a masquerade warehouse. "We were a company of some seven or eight, with an occasional neighbour or so for visitors, and used to sit up late in our friars' dresses, drinking burgundy, claret, champagne, and what not, out of the *skull-cup,** and all sorts of glasses, and buffooning all round the house, in our conventual garments. Matthews always denominated me 'The Abbot,' and never called me by any other name in his good humours, to the day of his death." Hobhouse relates that one night, as he proceeded down the Long Gallery where there stood a stone sarcophagus, he heard a groan emanating from the coffin. On going closer he was confronted by a cowled figure, which rose to its full height and blew out Hobhouse's candle. It was, of course, Matthews.

There was some interruption of harmony in the celebrations when Webster and Matthews, who were normally good friends, had a quarrel over a joke (Webster, it will later be seen, can surely have had no sense of humor), and Matthews threatened to throw him out of a window. Webster, taking great offense, informed Byron that he would leave the next morning because of the insult, and his host pointed out in vain that "the window was not high, and that the turf under it was particularly soft." It was of no use, Webster left.

Somebody accidentally rubbed against one of Matthews's white silk stockings before dinner one day, and apologized. " 'It may be all very well for you, who have a great many silk stockings,' Matthews rejoined, 'to dirty other people's; but to me, who have only this *one pair,* which I have put on in honour of the Abbot here, no apology can compensate for such carelessness; besides the expense of washing.' "

When the festivities were ended at Newstead, Hobhouse and Matthews decided as a whim to walk together the one hundred and forty miles to London. En route *they* quarreled, and marched half the journey (the second half) without exchanging a word. Now and again they would pass and

---

* The Newstead gardener had dug up a skull of giant size and well preserved, which Byron decided must have belonged to some "jolly friar or monk" in the days when the Abbey was the house of a religious order. Byron had it mounted as a drinking cup.

repass each other. When Matthews reached Highgate he had only three-pence halfpenny left, and that he spent on a pint of beer; without their speaking Hobhouse passed him for the last time on the road. In London they made up their difference.

On May 22, 1809, Matthews wrote his own account of the party at Newstead. It was necessary, he said, to be on the alert there. "Should you make any blunder.—should you go to the right of the hall steps, you are laid hold of by a bear; and should you go to the left, your case is still worse, for you run full against a wolf!—Nor, when you have attained the door, is your danger over; for the hall being decayed, . . . a bevy of inmates are very probably banging at one end of it with their pistols; so that if you enter without giving loud notice of your approach, you have only escaped the wolf and the bear, to expire by the pistol-shots of the merry monks of Newstead . . . For breakfast we had no set hour . . . though had one wished to breakfast at the early hour of ten, one would have been rather lucky to find any of the servants up. Our average hour of rising was one . . . Between seven and eight we dined; and our evening lasted from that time till one, two, or three in the morning. The evening diversions may be easily conceived."

Rumor was not dilatory in conceiving. And *Childe Harold,* when published, would lend its support to converting those "diversions" into Roman orgies. For in an apostrophe to Newstead, Byron would speak of the "Paphian girls" who had afforded amusement. There was, of course, for Byron's pleasure the servant Lucy, and the boy Rushton installed in a room adjoining the master's bedroom; it is possible that some of the other maids were open quarry for the guests. On that subject Matthews is mischievously suggestive; he speaks of the monks' garbs, the crosses, beads, and tonsures which "often gave variety to our appearance, and to our pursuits."

Hobhouse had been more than willing to accompany Byron on his tour, but at the moment he was on bad terms with his father and had not the money. Although deeply in debt, Byron offered to advance the necessary amount.

Waiting in London with Fletcher and Rushton for Hanson to complete his financial arrangements, Byron became infuriated. He had made Fletcher responsible for superintending the boy's morals. Fletcher, who had lost no time in himself becoming a client of the city's whores, had his own notion of helping a country boy and had introduced Rushton to one of the bordellos. To worsen matters, he had coached the lad in a lie to cover them both, but the prostitute's address was found on Rushton in Fletcher's own illiterate hand. Their master was outraged at this "diabolical" corruption of an "innocent stripling." Small doubt that Byron, who posed before the world all his life as a rake, and was pleased enough with his own exploits among the strumpets of town, would hardly have been so incensed if his own feelings for Rushton had not been involved. He immediately sent Fletcher back to Newstead and the boy to his farmer-father.

It was only in exceptional cases, however, that Byron could feel resentment; his temper soon cooled, and when funds seemed ready he recalled both valet and page and set out for Falmouth with Hobhouse, Fletcher, Rushton, a German who had been recommended for his entourage, and old Joe Murray, who had been the servant of the fifth Lord Byron.

Awaiting the next ship, he found the seaport conducive to copulation, he wrote Matthews, and despite his recent indignation with his servants was thinking of carrying off some of Falmouth's daughters of joy to compare with the specimens he anticipated meeting in the East.

But before sailing, creature of moods that he was, he wrote to Francis Hodgson, another friend: "I leave England without regret—I shall return to it without pleasure. I am like Adam, the first convict sentenced to transportation, but I have no Eve, and have eaten no apple but what was sour as a crab." What he could not foresee was that if he was leaving England little known, he was to come back to it to bask in glory and fame.

The *Princess Elizabeth* sailed for Lisbon on July 2, 1809, with Byron tingling with expectation. The skipper, appropriately for our poet, bore the name Captain Kidd. The passage was tranquil enough but Byron was quite seasick.

10.

FROM LISBON, WHERE HIS PARTY DISEMBARKED, HE WROTE PLAYFULLY, on July 16: "I am very happy here, because I love oranges, and talks bad Latin to the monks, who understand it, as it is like their own,—and I goes into society (with my pocket-pistols) and I swims the Tagus all across at once, and I rides on an ass or a mule, and swears Portuguese, and have got a diarrhoea and bites from the mosquitoes. But what of that? Comfort must not be expected by folks that go a pleasuring." He was a brilliant swimmer, and it is typical of him that he should speak so casually of a formidable feat in swimming the Tagus against wind and tide. He was to be enormously proud of swimming the Hellespont, but that, of course, though requiring less prowess where he crossed it, was rich in literary association; not so the Tagus.

Across country through Elvas, the travelers made for Seville, where they took cramped lodgings in a house of two spinster ladies. They stayed three nights, and on their leaving, one of these ladies gently upbraided Byron for not having accepted her invitation to join her in her bedroom. She was, she informed him, due to marry an officer in the Spanish army. In the sentimental fashion prevalent in Europe, she cut off a lock of his hair—one wonders how men and women in those days had any hair left to cut —and presented him with one of her own, three feet long, which he forwarded to his mother to keep for him.

At Cadiz he found that intrigue was "the business of life; when a woman marries she throws off all restraint." He was as much enchanted with the beauty, large black eyes, and fine figures of Spanish belles as he was astonished at their freedom of manner. "If you make a proposal, which in England will bring a box on the ear from the meekest of virgins, to a Spanish girl, she thanks you for the honour you intend her, and replies, 'Wait till I am married, and I shall be too happy.'"

In the memoirs later burned, Moore read a summary of another encounter: "For some time I went on prosperously both as a linguist and a lover, till at length, the lady took a fancy to a ring which I wore, and set her heart on my giving it to her, as a pledge of my sincerity. This, however, could not be:—any thing but the ring, I declared, was at her service, and much more than its value—but the ring itself I had made a vow never to give away." The lady grew angry; Byron did too; the affair ended.

Of course the travelers had to see a bullfight, and went to Puerta Santa Maria for that purpose. Both Britishers were sickened, as is common with the tourist, at the spectacle of the disemboweling of the horses.

On August 3 they sailed on the *Hyperion* for Gibraltar. From there Byron sent Joe Murray and Rushton back to England, the former because he was too old to travel, Rushton because Turkey would be dangerous for a boy. To Rushton's father he wrote: "I allow you to deduct five-and-twenty pounds a year for his education for three years. . . . Let every care be taken of him. . . . In case of my death I have provided enough in my will to render him independent. He has behaved extremely well."

At Gibraltar, John Galt saw Byron for the first time, at the library of the English garrison. "His physiognomy was prepossessing and intelligent, but ever and anon his brows lowered and gathered—a habit, as I then thought, with a degree of affectation in it . . . but which I afterwards discovered was undoubtedly the scowl of some unpleasant reminiscence; it was certainly disagreeable, forbidding, but still the general cast of his features was impressed with elegance and character."

On August 16 the *Townshend Packet* sailed for Malta with Byron, Hobhouse, Fletcher, and Galt as passengers. In the business of getting baggage aboard, Galt remarked, "his lordship affected . . . more aristocracy than befitted his years, or the occasion; and I then thought of his singular scowl, and suspected him of pride and irascibility. The impression that evening was not agreeable, but it was interesting. Hobhouse, with more of the commoner, made himself one of the passengers at once; but Byron held himself aloof, and sat on the rail, leaning on the mizzen shrouds, inhaling, as it were, poetic sympathy, from the gloomy rock, then dark and stern in the twilight. . . . He spoke petulantly to Fletcher, his valet; and was evidently ill at ease with himself and fretful towards others."

Galt, a novelist traveling for his health, had no idea of one of Byron's paradoxical traits, his extreme shyness in the company of strangers. He noted, however, that "there was something redeeming in the tones of his voice," when, after indulging a mood of "sullen meditation," he next spoke to Fletcher. Galt concluded that he was capricious rather than ill-natured. The third day out, Byron suddenly became playful. But he spent only one evening being companionable with the other passengers, the evening they anchored at Cagliari. "For when the lights were placed, he made himself a man forbid, took his station on the railing . . . and there, for hours, sat in silence, enamoured, it may be, of the moon. . . . He was a mystery in a winding-sheet, crowned with a halo." This last touch Galt meant in earnest; everyone who ever approached Byron, he says, was aware of an "incomprehensible phantasma" hovering about him. Occasionally he would emerge from the cloud, but "his dwelling was amidst the murk and the mist, and the home of his spirit in the abysm of the storm, and the hiding places of guilt." This is the soon-to-emerge Byronic hero for which Byron himself would sit as the model.

At Cagliari, Sardinia, the English ambassador, Hill, invited his fellow countrymen who had disembarked, to dinner, and after that to the theatre. Out of deference to Byron's rank he withdrew with him to a separate box more in view of the audience. Later Hill escorted the visitors to the town gate, where Byron "thanked him with more elocution than was precisely requisite." Hobhouse and the others were amused. When Hill departed, Hobhouse rallied his friend on his excessive pomp. But Byron, who "fancied that he had acquitted himself with grace and dignity," quickly became annoyed and had words with John Cam, who walked on ahead. "Byron, on account of his lameness, and the roughness of the pavement, took hold of my arm, appealing to me, if he could have said less" after the hospitality extended them.

Galt became one of Byron's earliest biographers, though he could speak with authority only on this and later brief passages of time he spent in Byron's company. But what he saw and heard he could recreate sharply enough. It is true that as a writer he tended to poke "fun at his subject"; we know that Hobhouse and Byron had many a laugh over Galt's own coxcombry. But Galt's admiration for Byron as a poet was limitless. And it is a fact that for a mere youth Byron was given to make undo fuss about his rank.

The packet reached Malta on the last day of August. A little over a week later Byron met a Mrs. Constance Spencer Smith, who, despite her youth, had been involved in a conspiracy against Napoleon and had luckily managed to escape via a rope ladder from the custody of the French police. Byron's many bed companions, when women, had all been of the servant, peasant, bohemian, or prostitute classes. An innocent-looking creature with large soulful eyes, Mrs. Smith was the first woman of social position, both by birth and marriage, who gave him to understand that she was approachable—a message she managed to convey almost at once.

Thus encouraged, the youth, unaccustomed to the seduction of a lady, made slow progress, though he spent much time with her, toward personal intimacies—indeed, got no further than an arrangement to elope with her to Friuli. At the last moment they learned that Friuli was in the hands of the French, and so they postponed their love affair for another year. He had managed to leave Spain with his heart and his yellow diamond ring still in his own possession, but he surrendered them both to her at Malta. According to several of his lyrics his love for her still warmed him for several months, but by January of the next year his new erotic interests at Athens altered his feelings. His lines, "The Spell Is Broke," were the epitaph. Next September, faithful to their appointment, Mrs. Smith was at Malta, wrote to him twice, and waited through the winter. It was not until the following May that her lover-to-be would arrive and then only to terminate the relationship. By the following year he was describing her as a woman of dubious reputation and was sure that the "baubles" he had given her were by that time decorating the fingers of half of Hungary and all of Bohemia.

On September 21, 1809, Byron and Hobhouse continued their journey on board the *Spider*. In eight days they were at Prevesa, whence they made their way to Jannina, capital of Ali Pacha who ruled Albania, Epirus, and part of Macedonia. The British consul told Byron that he and Hobhouse were the first Englishmen he had ever seen there. Ali was away with his army, but, as Byron told his mother, "He had heard that an Englishman of rank was in his dominions, and had left orders . . . to provide a house, and supply me with every kind of necessary *gratis*." Byron bought a number of richly decorated Albanian robes at fifty guineas each.

Next, the two went to visit Ali's eldest son Mouctar, but he was not at his palace. However, they were gravely entertained by Mouctar's son Mahmout, a boy of ten, who asked Byron "how I came to travel so young, without anybody to take care of me." Afterward Byron also met Mahmout's brother, Hussein Bey, a child of nearly the same age. "They are totally unlike our lads, have painted complexions like rouged dowagers, large black eyes, and features perfectly regular. They are the prettiest little animals I ever saw." Mahmout hoped to see him again. "We are friends without understanding each other."

Setting out after Ali Pacha, they arrived after nine days, on October 19, at Tepelini, just as the sun was setting upon a vista Byron pronounced unforgettable. He found the dress of the Albanians the "most magnificent in the world." The soldiers, slaves, horses, the coming and going of couriers, the palace buildings—he found all of the scene entrancing. The next day they were introduced to Ali Pacha, Byron having outfitted himself with a staff uniform and a magnificent saber. Ali, the Sultan's Vizier, was "sixty years old, very fat, and not tall, but with a fine face, light blue eyes, and a white beard." Though kind and dignified in manner, his real character is that of "a remorseless tyrant, guilty of the most horrible cruelties."

Ali welcomed the Englishmen in a marble-paved room in the center of which a fountain played. Making Byron sit at his right hand, "he said he was certain I was a man of birth, because I had small ears, curling hair, and little white hands." He asked Byron to consider him as a father. "Indeed, he treated me like a child, sending me almonds and sugared sherbet, fruit and sweetmeats, twenty times a day. He begged me to visit him often, and at night, when he was at leisure." Byron had three audiences with Ali; he found the Albanians "brave, rigidly honest and faithful; but they are cruel, though not treacherous . . . They are, perhaps, the most beautiful race, in point of countenance, in the world; their women are sometimes handsome also."

Byron was mightily pleased that Ali had ascribed his small white hands, delicate ears, and curling hair to his noble birth, and dwelt upon the flattery in letters to his mother. Further experience, however, caused him to recast his view. It is open to question whether Ali's actual motive was deference to rank. Pederasty was notoriously endemic in the Turkish world.

When a few years afterward George Colman the Younger became Byron's drinking companion, he must have been the recipient of a vast outpouring of personal confidences, for *Don Leon* contains an enormous amount of Byron's personal affairs that almost no one else at the time knew anything about. Byron, of course, never got over the adolescent habit of exaggerating his own vices when he had an appreciative audience, and he may even have gone so far as to assure Colman that the prime reason for his travels to the East was a desire to visit countries where, unlike England, "Cupid's wings were free." At any rate, the hero of *Don Leon* says: he will "seek the Turk" for

There none can trespass on forbidden ground:
There venial youths in every stew are found,

And with their blandishments inveigle man,
As does in Christian lands the courtesan.

Byron and Hobhouse saw such establishments in Albania.
Don Leon's hero travels with a friend to Byzantium; there

> I sought the brothel, where, in maiden guise,
> The black-eyed boy his trade unblushing plies;
> Where in lewd dance he acts the scenic show—
> His supple haunches wriggling to and fro:
> With looks voluptuous the thought excites,
> While gazing sit the hoary sybarites . . .
> Yes, call it monstrous! but not monstrous where
> Close latticed harems hide the timid fair:
> With mien gallant where pederasty smirks,
> And whoredom, felon-like, in covert lurks.

A friend is with him (Hobhouse, of course) and Byron-Leon, knowing the former's distaste for such goings-on, feigns horror at the spectacle. But

> This mask of horror served my purpose well—
> Resolved to do what yet I feared to tell.

After a while the friend returns to England (as Hobhouse eventually did), leaving Byron-Leon free to allow no barriers between himself and his pleasure.

All this is true in spirit to what was to happen to Byron in the Turkish world. But there are a few minor details concerning Hobhouse, which Colman was not in a position to know. Unsympathetic toward the feminine streak in Byron's makeup, sturdy John Cam certainly was; Colman was wrong in supposing Hobhouse in total ignorance of Byron's alliances with pretty boys. To begin with, while the two were traveling together, Byron had already showed his friend an intimate journal he had kept of his early life, which Hobhouse prevailed upon him to destroy, for reasons not hard to surmise. Moreover, Hobhouse's own diary and his jottings in the margins of books on Byron make it plain that he was familiar with his friend's proclivities and many of his acts.

On leaving Topelini for a more extended view of the Peloponnesus (then generally called the Morea), which they had barely seen, they were given letters by Ali to another son of his, Veli Pacha, Vizier of the Morea. On their way to Patras, they returned to Jannina, arriving on October 26.

The impressions from his tour thus far crowding upon him, Byron sat down at Jannina on October 31, a day fateful to his fame as a poet, and began to write *Childe Harold,* the first of his long quasi-autobiographical poems.

His letter to his mother from Prevesa, dated November 12, gives a lively account of his more recent adventures: "Two days ago I was nearly lost in a Turkish ship of war [obligingly provided by Ali for their trip to Patras], owing to the ignorance of the captain and crew, though the storm was not violent. Fletcher yelled after his wife, the Greeks called on all the saints, the Mussulmans on Alla; the captain burst into tears and ran below deck, telling us to call on God; the sails were split, the mainyard shivered, the wind blowing fresh, the night setting in . . . I did what I could to console Fletcher, but finding him incorrigible, wrapped myself in my Albanian capote (an immense cloak), and lay down on deck to wait the worst. . . . Luckily the wind abated, and only drove us to the coast of Suli, on the main land, where we landed." He went on: "Not a week ago an Albanian chief . . . after helping us out of the Turkish galley in her distress," fed and lodged them all, and refused compensation with the words: "I wish you to love me, not pay me."

These were words of a kind Byron was not likely to hear in England, and they struck a forceful chord in his deeply affectionate nature.

After Patras the next significant stop was at Vostizza, where he stayed with Veli's governor, Londos. An event occurred one night which burned itself on the poet's memory; it was his first intimation of what some Greeks felt after several centuries of Turkish domination. Young Londos was playing checkers with a doctor from town, who began to talk of a fellow Greek who two decades earlier had tried to organize a revolt against the Oriental masters. Though himself an official of the Turks, Londos suddenly jumped up, threw over table and checkers, cried out the patriot's name again and again, and wringing his hands burst into a torrent of fervent speech, while without shame he wept profusely. Without recovering his calm, he passed to a passionate recitation of the war song "Rise up, O Greeks!" (When the movement for Greek independence in 1821 began in some earnest, Londos was one of its earliest chiefs.)

After seeing Delphi and Parnassus, Byron and Hobhouse on Christmas 1809 reached Athens. They at once found lodgings at the house of Mrs. Macri, whose dead husband had been British Vice-Consul.

There were three daughters in the Macri household: Mariana, fifteen; Katinka, fourteen; and Theresa, twelve. Soon Byron was confessing that he was "dying for love . . . of these divinities." It was eventually Theresa, the youngest, who interested him most. He still had a rendezvous to keep at Malta with Mrs. Constance Spencer Smith, and until now had convinced himself, since he had never gone beyond the Platonic with her, that he loved

John Cam Hobhouse (age c. forty-five),
drawing by Abraham Wivell.

her. But the daily attendance of these three lovely, unsophisticated nymphs quickly put an end to his self-delusion about that woman of the world. For the present the three girls were beyond his reach, if only because of the barrier of language, and he himself was therefore safe from the disillusionment which was bound to follow conquest.

After three weeks of investigating Athens and its environs, the two friends decided upon a tour of other parts of the mainland. On January 25, 1810, they were back at the Macris. Hobhouse then went off by himself for a short trip while Byron stayed on. Writing his descriptions of Negroponte, the good John Cam, who loved Byron on this side idolatry, deplored the "absence of a companion, who, to quickness of observation and ingenuity of remark, united that gay good humour which keeps alive the attention under the pressure of fatigue, and softens the aspect of every difficulty and danger." By the time he returned, the second week in February, he found that his friend had formed a new tie to which he could only be unsympathetic, that with a fifteen-year-old boy, Nicolo Giraud.

When in early March the travelers boarded the *Pylades* for the long-planned expedition to Constantinople, it was something of a wrench for the poet to leave his idealized young Theresa. It was to her that he wrote one of his most popular lyrics:

> Maid of Athens, ere we part,
> Give, oh give me back my heart! ...

To a correspondent in England he communicated his admiration for the Greeks and Turks. The differences between Englishmen and Turks were negligible: the former have foreskins, the latter none; "we talk much and they little"; in England the fashionable vices are whoring and drunkenness, in Turkey sodomy and smoking; Englishmen prefer a girl and a bottle, the Turks a pipe and a compliant boy. In this same letter, he again recounted Ali's conviction that "I was a man of rank, because I had *small ears* and *hands,* and *curling hair,*"—in charity let it be remembered that he was only twenty-two—and he went on to say that he liked the Greeks, who "are plausible rascals with all the Turkish vices," but without Turkish courage. All of them, however, are beautiful, "very much resembling the busts of Alcibiades;—the women are not quite so handsome." (Anyone familiar with Athens today must wonder where all that beauty has disappeared to. The Greeks are the most disarmingly warm and hospitable people in the world; they have, too, fine, open, large and wide-spaced eyes. But of their ancient classic beauty little is left.)

At Smyrna on March 8 both men were made to feel at home at the house of the British consul; they stayed a month. Presently John Galt turned up and learned that they were waiting to sail on the frigate *Salsette* for Constantinople. He thought Byron changed, less cordial to Hobhouse and fonder than ever of his own opinions. At a large dinner party he felt again that Byron was overdoing the role of young lordship. When an officer of the *Salsette* differed, with a strong show of logic, from Byron's opinion of the late Pitt, Byron felt "rebuked," because he had not been agreed with, and turned sullen. Galt deplored that a man of such genius should allow himself temperamental whims. He also noted that Byron spoke no more of passing beyond the Ganges, but seemed disposed to let chance carry him where it willed.

In April the *Salsette* at last set sail. When Byron quitted Smyrna, Mrs. Werry, a woman who had been his hostess, though in her late fifties wept copiously and cut a lock of his hair for remembrance. On the journey to the Turkish capital there was time to wander over the plains where Troy had once stood. From there they went overland to the Dardanelles and crossed back to the European shore by boat. Byron, eager for the triumph, and Elkenhead, a lieutenant of marines on the *Salsette,* tried swimming to the Asian side. After being in the icy water an hour they were forced to desist by the fierceness of the current. Trying again both men on May 3 managed the fabled swim across the strait. "The whole distance, from the place whence we started to our landing on the other side, including the length we were carried by the current," Byron noted, "was computed by those on board the frigate at upwards of four English miles, though the actual breadth is barely one. The rapidity of the current is such that no boat can row directly across, and it may, in some measure, be estimated from the circumstances of the whole distance being accomplished by one of the parties [Elkenhead] in an hour and five, and by the other [Byron] in an hour and ten minutes. The water was extremely cold from the melting of the mountain snows. . . . The only thing that surprised me was that, as doubts had been entertained of the truth of Leander's story, no traveller had ever endeavoured to ascertain its practicability."

He wrote some amusing stanzas "After Swimming from Sestos to Abydos" to celebrate the event: Leander was wont to cross the stream nightly, the tale says; if in December—

> . . . when the wintry tempest roared
> He sped to Hero, nothing loth,
> And thus of old thy current poured,
> Fair Venus! how I pity both!

The roguishness is made more explicit in a letter: "I doubt whether Leander's conjugal affection must not have been a little chilled in his passage to Paradise."

Still aboard the frigate, he wrote a letter to Hodgson which is remarkably unprophetic: "I am tolerably sick of vice, which I have tried in its agreeable varieties, and mean, on my return, to cut all my dissolute acquaintance, leave off wine and carnal company, and betake myself to politics and decorum." Never was a resolution less kept. On his return to Athens he would soon drown the memory of the intention in greater libertinism than ever, and once he was caught in the swirl of London lionizing on his return to England, he would only accelerate the tempo of his erotic involvements.

11.

THE FIRST SPECTACLE HE BEHELD AT CONSTANTINOPLE HE LATER INcorporated into *The Siege of Corinth:* outside the walls of the Sultan's palace he saw two lean dogs, "gorging and growling" over a human carcass; they had stripped the flesh from the skull as you would peel the skin of a fig.

Within a few days he went into a shop to buy a few pipes. There was present another Englishman, who has left a narrative as to what followed. Byron's Italian, which he spoke to his guide, at that time was only middling, and his guide's Turkish was even poorer; the shopkeeper could not make out Byron's wishes, so his fellow countryman offered help. Byron shook his hand and expressed great pleasure at meeting another Britisher abroad. They presently wandered through the streets together, the stranger pointing out sights of interest. The stranger tells us that the special circumstances "established between us, in one day, a certain degree of intimacy. . . . I frequently addressed him by his name, but he did not think of enquiring how I came to learn it, nor of asking mine. It was natural that, after . . . all that passed between us on that occasion, I should, on meeting him in the course of the same week at dinner at the English ambassador's [the meeting place of the English colony], have requested one of the secretaries, who was intimately acquainted with him [probably Stratford Canning, an ex-Etonian who had played against Byron at cricket], to introduce me to him in regular form. His Lordship testified his perfect recollection of me, but in the coldest manner, and immediately after turned his back on me. It was not, therefore, without surprise, that, some days after, I saw him in the streets, coming up to me with a smile of good nature in his countenance. He accosted me in a familiar manner, and, offering me his hand, said, 'I am an enemy to English etiquette, especially out of England; and I always make my own acquaintances without waiting for the formality of an introduction. If you have nothing to do, and are disposed for another ramble, I shall be glad of your company.'" Byron's charm, when he was in good humor, was irresistible, and the other readily agreed.

Adair, the English ambassador to Turkey, was about to return to England. The day of his public audience with the Sultan was announced, and the Englishmen in town were invited to accompany him to the Seraglio. This same anonymous acquaintance of Byron's tells us that a procession was to form on leaving British headquarters; the ambassador had drawn up a list of the order to be followed. Canning, secretary of the legation, was to ride next to Adair—he was to take over the ambassador's powers on Adair's departure from the country; after them were to come Byron and the Consul-General. While the Englishmen were lounging about waiting for the signal to go, Byron picked up the list of the procession, immediately threw it back on the table, and marched into the next room, where he went up to Adair to express his astonishment that "as a peer of the realm, his name should not have been put in the list next to the Ambassador's." Adair assured him that no disrespect had been intended, but that the place next to his own belonged to Canning and could not be assigned to anyone else. Byron replied with some heat that, in such a case, he was not coming along. "To this Mr. Adair replied, in a tone of cold civility, that his Lordship was, of course, at liberty to act as he thought proper; whereupon Lord Byron wished his Excellency a good morning, and hastily left."

Our anonymous Englishmen saw Byron almost daily during the several months of his stay at Constantinople. "At that time it was impossible to foresee that every action of his life" would acquire importance. "The eccentricities of his manners and mode of living already distinguished him from other men."

Adair, just the same, invited Byron to his final audience at the Seraglio, but warned him that no one would be assigned a special place. Relenting his former bad temper, Byron promised to follow Adair's servant, maid, ox, ass, or any of his chattels, and on July 10, says Canning, "he redeemed his pledge by joining the procession as a simple individual, and delighting those who were nearest to him by his well-bred cheerfulness and good-humoured wit." Byron, himself unimpressed, "attracted greatly the Sultan's attention, and seemed to have excited his curiosity." Years later the Sultan insisted that the beauteous Englishman who had formed part of that audience could only have been a woman dressed up as a man.

For Hobhouse sight-seeing in Turkey was not an unmitigated pleasure. Some of it upset him because of its sheer beastliness: the lascivious dances executed by boys in the winehouses of Galata, for example, and the howling and lunatic screaming of dervishes near Pera. By early July it was agreed that Byron would return to Greece and John Cam would begin his homeward journey via Malta. In a letter to Hodgson Byron observed that by July 2 it would be a year since they had left England; "I have known a hundred instances of men setting out in couples, but not one of a similar return. . . . I am confident that twelve months of any given individual is perfect ipecacuanha." But there was no break between him and Hobhouse, whose friendship was the most stable thing in his life, even if he did not always sufficiently value it. The innuendo that he had had enough of his traveling companion was due to a special reason. He reacted quite differently to what shocked his friend, somewhat because of his lively sense of the ludicrous, but even more because of his own confused inner promptings. He was beginning to feel irked at having, out of deference to Hobhouse's sensibilities, to masquerade his own desires. He apparently had also begun to think he was forfeiting opportunities for certain experiences, tempting in their novelty, which he would willingly have sampled—and safely so, far away, as he was, from the censure of fellow countrymen.

Later Byron was to write in his journal that Hobhouse "don't know what I was about the year after he left the Levant; nor does any one." But John Cam, if he did not know all the facts, was well qualified to surmise what Byron was up to during his own absence. After Byron's death, he himself annotated Moore's biography with the wry comment: "He has not the remotest grasp of the real reason which induced Lord Byron to prefer having no Englishman immediately and constantly near him" in the East.

Byron, however he chose publicly to defy convention, never thoroughly forgave himself for his hankering after vice—no true pagan he!—and probably half-dreaded his imminent freedom to follow his whims. Instead of being carefree, he was greatly depressed aboard the *Salsette* when it sailed from Constantinople in July. One day he picked up a small Turkish dagger he found lying on a bench, removed it from its sheath, studied the blade, and murmured: "I should like to know how a person feels after committing a murder."

When the boat touched Keos, the friends took leave of each other, Hobhouse unabashedly in tears.

At Athens, Byron went again to live briefly at the Macris. His purpose was to go off to the Peloponnesus once more. Meeting in town an old friend from Cambridge, Lord Sligo, he found it inconsistent with good manners to refuse his offered company for part of the journey, much as he would have preferred being alone. "I am woefully sick of travelling companions, after a year's experience with Mr. Hobhouse," he wrote his mother. At Corinth he and Sligo separated.

On his earlier stay with Londos at Vostitza he had met Eustathios Georgiou, a Greek adolescent. Arriving in that city again, he once more saw the boy, who now swore that he was anxious to follow him to England or to any other part of the globe. This new infatuation proved more of a nuisance than a pleasure.

As they were about to set out for Patras together, his "dearly-beloved" Eustathios presented himself on horseback, his "ambrosial" curls falling down his back, and, to Byron's stupefaction, a parasol in hand to protect his face from the sun. His young friend thus equipped, they traveled to their destination, where they had a furious quarrel. For a moment Byron's better judgment assured him that they had better part. He confessed to Hobhouse that he had never tried so hard to please anyone and with so little effect, though he had been most careful to say and do nothing which could give offense to the spoiled creature. He told the lad that he was sending him back to his father. This provisional adieu was accompanied, Byron wrote, with more kisses than girls exchange at a boarding school, and with enough embraces to ruin any male's reputation in England.*

But the next day Eustathios was repentant, called on him three times, and they made up. Byron agreed to let him accompany him to Athens, and provided him with a green shade to replace the absurd parasol. All this he told Hobhouse partly out of a desire to shock his sober friend. The heat was frightful; he was diverting himself by swimming and riding; when these palled there was Eustathios to bicker with and a couch to "tumble on." He was, in short, losing no time plucking forbidden fruits now that he was free of his friend's deploring shake of the head. He so little minded scandalizing him from a safe distance by telling him of his exploits that he asked Hobhouse to pass on his account to Matthews, whom he knew to be eccentric enough to be amused at anyone else's crotchets. For Hobhouse himself he added what was hardly to be construed as a compliment: now that John Cam was gone, he had been transformed in Byron's eyes into the best of companions.

Accompanied by Strané, the English consul at Patras, Byron and Eustathios went on to Tripolitza, where Ali Pacha's son, Veli, had his palace. Lord Sligo had already been there. Ali, it will be remembered, had given Byron letters to this second son, and the poet was assured of a welcome. He

---

* As this work was going to press I read J. B. Priestley's highly interesting and recent *The Prince of Pleasure and his Regency* (New York: 1969). Mr. Priestley, admitting a disinclination "to examine and then digest the huge mass of print" on the subject of Byron and his marriage, finds it impossible to accept the notion that Byron was "really homosexual," even though there does exist some evidence that "at certain times" Byron "indulged in homosexual pastimes." When he did so indulge, Mr. Priestley says, "it was on a low level" and devoid of "emotional involvement."

was happy to accept the gift of a fine horse from Veli, but his reception was rather warmer than he could have wished. Veli had to leave almost immediately on military affairs and invited him to join him at Larissa. Byron was taken aback. He knew that his host had rejected Sligo's request to accompany him as far as the Danube, and had ordered Sligo to take another route. Byron stressed his own purpose of going in the direction of Albania, not Larissa, but Veli would not hear of it. It was only appropriate that old men like Strané, for instance, should join Veli's father, Ali; but young men should remain with Veli—old men should be with old men and youth with youth. (Veli had a beard down to his middle.) Complimenting Byron on his beauty, he hoped they would remain close-bosomed friends for life. Was it not right that, as young men, the two of them ought to live together? Throughout this elaborate and public courtship, the purport of which was clear enough, Strané could only listen goggle-eyed. Byron contrived to accept the honeyed words gracefully, but he did not enjoy Veli's habit of encircling his young guest's waist with his arm and squeezing his hand. Nevertheless, he was sufficiently flattered not at once to abandon the possibility of going to Larissa.

But a new problem developed with Eustathios. Suddenly Byron learned that the boy was subject to epileptic fits. Without them his temperamental changes of mood had been difficult enough. After witnessing a few of these attacks, Byron sensibly sent him back to his father.

Later in August Byron was again in Athens. Now his life took a violently new turn. His delight in Theresa Macri was poisoned. No doubt his recent uninhibited intimacy with Eustathios provided a cause for his altering his attitude toward her. What he was conscious of, however, was an indignation with the stand taken by Mrs. Macri. She stipulated that he must either marry her daughter or else at a suitable fee (the custom) buy her as his concubine. The woman, he wrote Hobhouse, must have been insane to imagine he would have married Theresa. He was referring to her being not of his rank. Besides, he wryly noted, these days he had much better diversions.

The better diversions he rapidly discovered when, to escape the strained atmosphere at the Macri house, he rented new quarters at a Capuchin monastery just below the walls of the Acropolis.* Here lived the Abbot and six pupils. Excitement began within only minutes of his being introduced to these "sylphs," as he called the boys. One, Barthelmi, immediately sat beside

---

* The monastery grounds at that time included the Choragic Monument of Lysicrates. The monastery is gone, of course, and a street bordering the little square is now named after Byron, and given over to stores selling shoes, eggs, fruit, and so on.

the new tenant and kissed him on the cheek. Reproved by another for for-
wardness, Barthelmi retorted that he would repeat the kiss. At this Byron
laughed and the ice was broken. Before long his life was one riot with the
boys, day and night.

But his particular friend among them was a sixteen-year-old already
known to him, Nicolo Giraud, of French descent, whom he had made friends
with during his first stay at Athens, while Hobhouse was off journeying by
himself. Now Nicolo became his teacher in Italian, but was also his " 'amico'
and the Lord knows what besides." Most seriously he assured Byron that he
wished to follow him wherever he was minded to go, to live with him, and to
die with him.

Don Leon fills us in on the relationship. Colman depicts Byron as having wooed Nicolo with gifts when first they met, and to have busied himself
with developing the boy's mind. Nicolo was so lovely to behold that he
"Gave pleasing doubts of what his sex might be."

For hours Byron-Leon would sit watching that charming face, or hanging over him during his noon siesta to chase away the insects.

> How oft at morn, when troubled by the heat,
> The covering fell disordered at his feet,
> I've gazed unsated at his naked charms,
> And clasped him waking to my longing arms.

How often the poet protected the beloved youth from the winter's blasts;
how often did he teach him how to swim; the days fled in happiness,

> Spent half in love and half in poetry!
> The muse each morn I wooed, each eve the boy,
> And tasted sweets that never seemed to cloy.

Let someone skilled as Oedipus in solving riddles decipher the poet's puzzle:
How can one salt and one fresh stream flow from the same source? Why
should one fresh spring fertilize his brain with poetic inspiration,

> And why, anon, like some Artesian fount,
> Would oozings foul e'en from my entrails mount,
> Salacious, and in a murky current wet
> The urn beneath with interrupted jet?

Colman proceeds to take notice of the three Macri girls. They were
indeed beautiful; Colman has not forgotten the "Maid of Athens" lyric. The
poet perceived their loveliness but did not feel "their charms." Here is

appended a piece of gossip in a footnote: one of Byron's servants at that time is said to have spread the story that the poet consulted an English doctor visiting Athens about "a relaxation in the *sphincter ani* with which the boy Giraud was troubled."

It was Giraud's beauty, *Don Leon* says, which enabled Byron to overcome the fears of what other people might say, and he thus extols the lad:

> Receive this faithful tribute to thy charms,
> Not vowed alone, but paid too in thy arms.
> For here the wish, long cherished, long denied,
> Within the monkish cell* was gratified.

Like Rousseau our hero resolves to "confess his secret thoughts":

> Is there an idiosyncracy prevails
> In those whose predilection is for males?
> I know not: but from boyhood to the hour
> Which saw my wish accomplished in that tower,†
> One thought undying ever would intrude
> In pleasure's moments . . .

The road he took may be compared to that taken by spendthrifts who, going to pawn their goods

> where the brokers use
> A double entrance, will the back one choose.

It is here necessary to make some attempt to understand Colman's motives in writing *Don Leon*. Undeniably a ribald work—though its great wit, pithiness of expression, and scorn of four-letter words surely place it on a higher level than many a "forthright" novel of our own era, such as is hailed a masterpiece since the court decision on *Lady Chatterly's Lover*—it has been dismissed by the few scholars who have heard of it as beneath notice, with the exception of G. Wilson Knight, who fittingly describes Colman as "the most indecent poet of high quality in our literature." Colman's entire career as the most successful dramatist of his generation constantly exhibits him as an enemy of moral hypocrisy. As a recipient of Byron's confidences during a crucial period of the poet's life, and as a man who shared Byron's hatred of pretense, he must have seen an ideal subject in presenting ruthlessly, even brutally, the basic truths about Byron's moral dilemma, as a powerful means

---

* At the Capuchin monastery.
† Room of the monastery.

of blasting once more that sanctimoniousness which has always been fashionable in Britain. He must have been sickened by the interminable cant being whispered behind Byron's back by the self-righteous when Byron went into permanent exile after the collapse of his marriage, and renewing itself with zest after the poet's death. It is now clear, despite the unwillingness of scholars to affirm the obvious, that there had been incest between Byron and his sister, and Lady Byron preferred to allow that to be understood as the reason she left her husband—though even when she did, the evidence was overwhelming that she was dissembling the truth about her separation. Most of all, it must have been intolerable to Colman, detesting sham as he did, to be one of the very few people in possession of the central fact motivating Lady Byron's severing relations with her husband; the others who knew the truth were unwilling to allow it to come to light, first of all because you just could not do that to a lady, and also it would in those days have done more damage to Byron's already clouded reputation than did the lie being perpetrated and perpetuated. Lady Byron was contriving to figure as Byron's victim with a skill approaching brilliance, publicly charging nothing, but behind the scenes organizing the clamor of her supporters, who were, ignorant of what Colman knew, having a fiesta at the expense of Byron's name. The truth may not have been pretty, but since it was the truth Colman felt it ought to be known. He knew about the incest and he knew about Byron's homosexuality, and he saw clearly the connection between Byron's experiences before marriage and the act that ended it. *Don Leon,* for all its indecency, is brilliant. But loosely organized as a whole, it makes some important errors in chronology and a few in details. But, also, basically it tells the truth, as proved by Byron's letters and journals as well as Hobhouse's observations. It is unnecessarily Freudian to say that Colman composed it to justify secret vices of his own; there is no evidence for that. He was a satirist by long training, and he preferred to tell the truth as he knew it in a hearty style reminiscent in spirit of Smollett. If his poem does dwell at length on Byron's attraction to boys, it is on grounds psychologically sound enough. He slowly but convincingly is preparing us for the fact which explains the debacle of Byron's marriage.

To continue with *Don Leon.* If, the poems says, our hero's affections were fastened upon Nicolo Giraud, the affair, after all, took place in a Turkish world; he was but following the custom of the country. Once he had seen a beautiful Ganymede of fifteen attending the Turkish Governor, a Grecian youth publicly known as the Governor's "catamite." Was it criminal to do what the Governor was doing? In those lands everyone "from the Grand Signor down to the Tartar" indulges in sodomy. Even a Turkish husband, when bored with his wife, has learned "to vanquish when her back is turned."

Byron-Leon attempts to raise self-justification to the philosophical plane by considering the doctrines of Malthus and the evils of overpopulation. Any method of lovemaking which diminishes the birth rate is therefore a social good. With an eye now firmly fixed on the chief cause of Lady Byron's refusal to rejoin her husband once she left him, the author sees no crime in sodomy with man or woman:

> The poor wretch, denied a wife's embrace,
> Appeases nature in another place.
> In sterile furrows why not sow his seed?

Moreover, God created each man with tastes different from others. For example, Britain's Ambassador to Turkey:

> Adair delights his manhood to display
> From window casements, and across the way
> Wooes some sultana's fascinated eyes,
> Convinced the surest argument is size.

This was the man who had refused Byron's demand that he be placed second to the Ambassador in the procession to the Seraglio. A footnote to these lines tells us that Adair, while at Constantinople, "is known to have carried on an amorous parley across the street with a Greek lady by dumb signs; a significant one was the display of his poenis in a plate on the sill of the window." Eventually onlookers witnessed the comedy and "divulged the ambassador's innocent [!!] practices." Next cited is the case of a bishop who buggers "the foot guard grenadiers."

The poem passes to a view of other perversions to show how widespread they are. Extensive attention is paid to the crime of incest; there are also notes on that subject, one six pages long. We are reminded that "Incest was common enough at Rome"; that "Pericles cohabited with his son's wife"; that the practice was prevalent among the Indians; that the Duke of Cumberland got his sister Sophia with child; that Marguerite, Queen of Navarre, slept with her brothers. Copious footnotes show that contemporary England afforded examples aplenty: a Mr. Craven begot a child upon his illegitimate daughter, who lived with him as his concubine; a Joseph Preston raped two of his daughters, one eleven and the other sixteen; a woman had two children by her father; a blacksmith habitually violated one daughter and impregnated another; a Miss Dixie was often violated by her father. There are lines in the poem extending for more than two pages on Lesbianism among the Romans and the French; there are passages devoted to flagellation, irrumation, fellatio, cunnilingus, voyeurism, etc. The full intent of these tangential pages is obvious enough: Colman was exposing vice rampant to defend his friend against the charge of being an extreme case.

And so the poem continues with the assurance that Odysseus' wife Penelope, after her husband's return at last to Ithaca,

> Grasps in her hand all night the staff of life,
> And e'en in sleep to lose that bauble fears,
> For which she sighed, a widow, twenty years.

This passage could very well have been aimed at Lady Byron as reproof for her secret reason for leaving Byron:

> Oh! England, with thy hypocritic cant,
> To hear the bench declaim, the pulpit rant,
> Who would not say that chastity's pure gems
> Had shed their lustre o'er the muddy Thames?
> That self-condemned, decried, ineffable,
> Innominate, this blackest sin of hell,
> Had fled dismayed to some Transalpine shore,
> To sully Albion's pudic cliffs no more?

The footnote to the last couplet derides the British habit of calling Italy "the hotbed of poederasty." There is enough "arsenerasty" in England to deflect the accusation from abroad; "no class of English society has been exempt from the stain." A footnote has already been allotted to the scandal involving William Beckford, author of *Vathek:* Lord Courtenay, then seven years old, visited Beckford's celebrated house when the latter was still young; the boy was missed from his room one night and found in bed with his host; the King was of a mind to hang them both, but because of their lofty station their relatives were able to save them. In the present note Colman lists cases drawn merely from the opening months of 1833: a seventy-year-old vicar accused of sodomy; another accused of the same; a colonel and a merchant, both Londoners, involved in the raping of boys; a seventy-year-old clergyman taken for assaulting a lad of seventeen; a member of the House of Lords found guilty of indecent assault upon a policeman; another man of fashion accused of similar conduct with a youth.

There follows an attack on the "Bow Street bloodhounds" (prototypes of the modern detectives who go to all lengths to catch the homosexual in the act) who arrest some poor creature "with flap unbuttoned . . . caught in some tap room." How do those virtuous citizens who are horrified at the existence of such inverts know that the youths may be guilty of a lesser crime than seducing an innocent girl? "Perhaps he [one such invert] was ill favoured, humpbacked, shy," or too poor to afford a brothel's fee. (This passage could have been composed to mitigate the scandals which had been circulating about Edleston prior to his death.) The lines now summon the examples of Barley Row and Vere Street* as further proof that homosexuality was prevalent enough in Britain.

Since Colman had a particular reason for proving that what Byron was doing with his Nicolo Giraud at Athens was far from uncommon among Englishmen, he speaks of the soldiers' barracks at dawn:

> See where the huddled groins in hot-beds lie,
> Each fit to be a garden deity!

Not all the Messalinas of England, though devoting days and nights to the task, could manage

> To keep the martial priapism down.

Flogging and punishments will be of no avail for, says Colman, in a wicked pun,

> The soldier's post is ever at the breach.

As for sailors, away on the seas for six months at a time, not even the heaviest lead

> Could keep their manhood in quiescent state.

---

* The story of the male brothel on this notorious street will be found in *The Phoenix of Sodom or the Vere Street Coterie* (London, 1813), copy in the British Museum. It was written by a lawyer calling himself Holloway. The house was kept by a James Cook, himself no sodomist. When Cook was taken to Newgate he offered to reveal the names of his clients, many of whom were noblemen and wealthy citizens of London. Too many prominent persons were involved and he was not permitted to name them. The brothel was fitted up with various accommodations: "Four beds were provided in one room;— another was fitted up for the ladies' dressing room . . . —a third called the Chaple [*sic*], where marriages took place, sometimes between *a female* grenadier, six feet high, and a petit maitre not more than half the altitude of his beloved wife. . . . Men of rank, and respectable situations in life, might be seen wallowing either in or on beds with wretches of the lowest description . . . It seems many of these wretches are married; and frequently when they are together, make their wives . . . topics of ridicule; and boast of having compelled them to act parts too shocking to think of " The place was raided in July 1810, and twenty-three men were arrested.

Schoolmasters are constantly exposed to temptation; at Eton, it is said, there was one master who

> all his scholars knew
> By their posteriors better than their face.

Legislators are not outside the ranks of those who practice the vice which Byron shared with Giraud, however heinous the British law holds it to be. Noblemen and distinguished scholars, identified by name, have been charged with it; some have been sentenced to death; some have committed suicide because of the disgrace. Yet across the Channel it is thought only a minor trespass and is rather laughed at.

Presently Colman reaches the climactic section of his poem, Byron's marriage. Everything he has said has been intended to contribute to clearing the mystery surrounding Lady's Byron's behavior after leaving her husband. Until our own narrative has arrived at the separation of the Byrons, we take leave of *Don Leon*. At that time we shall find it strongly reinforcing the evidence.

12.

THAT COLMAN DID NOT EXAGGERATE BYRON'S DEEP PERSONAL INVOLVE-ment with Nicolo there is powerful circumstantial testimony. To skip, for a moment to the following year: when he was back in England, on August 12, 1811, Byron drew up directions for his will; the very first person singled out for a bequest is Nicolo, to whom he left "the sum of seven thousand pounds sterling, to be paid from the sale of such parts of Rochdale, Newstead, or elsewhere, as may enable the said Nicolo Giraud . . . to receive the above sum on his attaining the age of twenty-one years." This was not only a very large sum; it was also by far the largest he designated for anyone. Rushton, for instance, was to be given £50 a year for life and an additional £1,000 at twenty-five.

In the meantime, after referring to his new diversions at the monastery in a letter to Hobhouse of August 23, 1810, he spoke of planning to take Nicolo on a tour with him; it was even possible, he said, that John Cam would see the boy in England. He had been busy the better part of the day in conjugating the Greek verb *aspazo*—"I am making love." He could have wished Hobhouse at the monastery to enjoy the fun, but he remembered that his friend was too crabbed to enjoy it; he was having a better time without Hobhouse's supervision, he said; but, he assured him, he loved him just the same.

While returning to the monastery one day he had an experience that has since become famous, for it inspired him later to write *The Giaour*. It had to do with a girl discovered in an illicit love affair; there seems to be grounds for believing that Byron was the lover in the case. Later he asked Lord Sligo to put down all that he knew about the matter. This is Sligo's account, which though "strange," was, as Byron said of it, "not very far from the truth." The new governor had "barbarous Turkish ideas with regard to women. . . . In compliance with the strict letter of the Mohammedan law, he ordered this girl to be sewn up in a sack, and thrown into the sea. . . . As you were returning from bathing in Piraeus, you met the procession going down to execute the sentence. . . . On finding out what the object of their journey was, and who was the miserable sufferer, you immediately interfered; and on some delay in obeying your orders, you were obliged to inform the leader that force should make him comply; . . . you drew a pistol, and told him, that if he did not immediately obey your orders, and come back with you to the Aga's house, you would shoot him dead." The man went with Byron, who partly by threat, partly by bribery and entreaty won the girl's pardon on condition she leave Athens. That night Byron dispatched her to Thebes, where she found asylum.

A few days later Lady Hester Stanhope arrived at Athens and met Byron. She was disgusted that he had fought the police for a common woman, as she put it. He himself was well bred, but his face bespoke a life of vice, and his eyes were too close set. She was not impressed at his being a poet, for anybody, she felt, can "write verses."

By mid-September, with Nicolo, Byron was off again to the Peloponnesus. En route to Olympia he caught a fever. By September 25 he had been in bed three days, was very weak, no longer plump, and with not one whore to fondle him out of the ten he has had, he told Hobhouse. On October 2 he reported a relapse. With great tenderness Nicolo had waited on him twenty-four hours a day until the poor boy was sicker than ever his friend was. Two days later Nicolo was in a critical condition and he himself dazed from his late siege—Byron now playing the nurse. Debilitated though he was, he was still parading as a devil of a fellow. John Cam was asked to inform Matthews that he had had more than two hundred different and complete experiences of sexual gratification in Greece, so that now he was weary of them.

When the pair returned to Athens in mid-October, Sligo was shocked at Byron's wasted appearance. One day Byron stood before a mirror and said to him: "How pale I look! I should like to die of consumption." His old Cambridge friend asked why. "Because then," Byron replied, "the women would all say, 'See that poor Byron—how interesting he looks in dying!' "

While they went swimming together, his conversation turned, for some reason or other, upon his aversion to his mother. He pointed to his naked leg and exclaimed, "Look there! It is to her false delicacy at my birth I owe my deformity, and yet as long as I can remember, she has never ceased to taunt and reproach me with it. [He ascribed his clubfoot to his mother's corsetings when she was pregnant.] Even a few days before we parted, for the last time, on my leaving England, she, in one of her fits of passion, uttered an imprecation upon me, praying that I might prove as ill formed in mind as I am in body!" That had been, though he had no idea such would be the case, indeed the last time they parted, for he would never see his mother alive again.

His schoolfellow also remarked upon his rigorous program, despite his recent illness, for keeping his weight down. He took three Turkish baths a week, drank only vinegar and water, and seldom ate more than a little rice.

In November he sent that true son of Britain, Fletcher, home because of his valet's "perpetual lamentations after beef and beer," and his "bigoted contempt for every thing foreign." By the end of the month Byron was again in a black mood; he wrote Hobhouse that he had sampled every kind of pleasure, as he wished Matthews also to know, that he had nothing more to anticipate from life, and was toying with the idea of putting an end to a boring existence.

But none of his moods was of long duration. His diversions at the monastery continued their round with unabated zest on his part. These were briefly interrupted by short expeditions in the company of several archeologists, a German and two young Danes, with one of the latter of whom, "a pretty philosopher," he "contracted an alliance." In Athens his games with the monastery boys were varied with companionship of visiting foreigners. There were dances, dinners, and innumerable erotic bouts for all of them. The Macri sisters were once more on the *tapis,* though with what degree of intimacy it is not clear. Byron was specific enough on how he and his compatriots in town (a number had appeared) had shared the persons of many Greek and Turkish women—and how all of them, himself included, had contracted gonorrhea. His health was totally impaired, and he had also a cough and continuous pains in his side. It looked as though, before concluding his twenty-second year, he might after all achieve his ambition of destroying himself on the altars of Venus.

On January 14, 1811, he assured his mother that he was through with being an author. The verse he had written since leaving England would have to be published, if ever, posthumously, for scribbling was "a disease I hope myself cured of." On his return he was going to lead the life of a recluse—a thoroughly bad guess.

Eight days later he was twenty-three. He dallied in Athens, but on April 22 he at last sailed with Nicolo from Piraeus on the *Hydra.* Much more than half a year late for his rendezvous with Mrs. Smith, he disembarked at Malta, and in a series of difficult interviews made it clear to her that he no longer desired her. The heat was infernal on the island and he had another attack of fever.

While waiting for a ship to England he jotted down some reasons why his mode of life must change: (1) at twenty-three the best of life was over; (2) travel had confirmed his conviction that mankind was contemptible: (3) he could anticipate nothing that could pleasure him; (4) with advancing years he was sure to become more peevish because of his lame leg—in another life he expected to have *two, if not four* legs by way of compensation; (5) his affairs at home [chiefly his debts] and abroad were disheartening, and (6) he had outlived all appetites, including the desire to be a famous poet. Before the year had ended he would, in fact, be en route to becoming the most famous poet of his century.

His purpose in bringing Nicolo to Malta was to place him in school there. When Byron left the island, the parting with this boy who, he was again naturally sure, also loved him better than anyone else ever did, was extremely painful. He extracted a promise from Nicolo to write him at least once a month. It is likely the boy kept his word. Four years later he was still writing affectionately from Athens, but never received a reply. Though Byron on his return to England drew up a will leaving him £7,000, he omitted him from his will of 1815, the year of his marriage.

On June 2, 1811, Byron sailed from Malta on the *Volgate*. Aboard ship he began dreading the prospect of sharing Newstead with his mother; he wrote her a long letter asking that his rooms be ready for him, and warning her that he intended only a short stay at the Abbey. To Hodgson he wrote that he more regretted leaving Greece than he had England; his prospects were disagreeable; he was solitary without wishing to be social and his body was enfeebled by illnesses. "The first thing I shall have to encounter will be a lawyer, the next a creditor, then colliers, farmers, surveyors. . . . When I have a little repaired my irreparable affairs, away I shall march, either to campaign in Spain, or back again to the East."

13.

•

THE *Volgate* PUT IN AT SHEERNESS ON JULY 14. AFTER A BRIEF STAY IN London, Byron stopped at Sittingbourne to see Hobhouse, who to please his father had joined the militia. From there, via London, he went for a few days to revisit Harrow, the site of so many cherished memories. Back to London again, he was plagued by insoluble financial problems.

On August 1 a servant arrived from Newstead to urge him to proceed

there at once: Mrs. Byron was very ill. He set out as soon as he could—
he had not seen his mother since he left for the Continent more than two
years earlier—but on the road he met Rushton, who had been sent after the
first messenger to tell him that Mrs. Byron was dead. Her death at the age
of forty-six is said by Moore to have been due to a fit of rage brought on
"by reading the upholsterer's bills."

Suddenly Byron was aware of "a thing very little known," as Thomas
Gray had written, "which is, that in one's whole life one can never have
more than a single mother. . . . Every day I live it sinks deeper into my
heart." There was the added guilt of his having postponed seeing her again
until it was too late.

The night after he reached Newstead, Mrs. Byron's maid, passing the
room where the body lay, found him sitting by the bed in the dark and
weeping. He may have been thinking of the tremendous sacrifices his mother
had made for him since his boyhood to enable him to live in some style.

His grief was aggravated by the news of another death which he felt
deeply: his old Cambridge friend Matthews had come to a hideous end in
his early twenties. This, the wittiest and gayest of his chums, had been found
dead tangled among the weeds of the river Cam, where he had gone swimming on August 3. In a panic over these mounting sorrows, Byron wrote to
Scrope Davies begging him to come down and see him. Hobhouse had been
desolated by Matthews's death and Byron was much moved by John Cam's
sorrow. "Come to me, Scrope," "I am . . . left almost alone in the world."

With Hobhouse in the army, it was natural that Byron, feeling "some
curse" was hanging over him and everything connected with him, should
have wished to see Davies rather than sanctimonious Hodgson. Five years
older than Byron, Davies was caustic, witty, and all the more amusing because of his stammering. Byron thought him one of the cleverest men he
knew, with tongue of ever-ready wit. He had been one of the monks at the
Newstead party, and was a heavy drinker and gambler. Byron tells a droll
anecdote of him. One day, before the poet had achieved majority, friends at
a gambling house vainly urged Davies, who had lost a large sum, to quit
and go home. But he was, as often, too tipsy by that early morning hour to
move, and they left him behind, gravely worried about him. The next afternoon with aching heads and empty pockets they called at his lodgings, and
found him asleep; "a Chamber-pot stood by his bed-side, brim-full of—
Bank Notes! all won, God knows how, and crammed, Scrope knew not
where; but THERE they were, all good legitimate notes, and to the amount
of some thousand pounds."

At his mother's funeral Byron was now too much shattered to follow
the corpse. "He stood looking," Moore records, "from the abbey door, at
the procession, till the whole had moved off;—then, turning to young Rushton, who was the only person left besides himself, he desired him to fetch

the sparring-gloves, and proceeded to his usual exercise with the boy. He was silent and abstracted all the time, and, as if from an effort to get the better of his feelings, threw more violence, Rushton thought, into his blows than was his habit."

Moore was unfamiliar with Mrs. Byron's self-deprivations in behalf of her son, but he is fair in summing up their relationship: "Notwithstanding her injudicious and coarse treatment of him, there can be little doubt that she loved him and was proud of him." She was always confident that he was destined to fame, and the attack in the *Edinburgh Review* distressed her far more than it did him. She eagerly watched for every mention of him in print, and she collected into a volume all the literary notices that had appeared of his two volumes, with her own marginal annotations.

What Moore failed to observe was the irony which deprived her of a victory she was entitled to. It is pathetic that she should have died almost on the eve of his suddenly bursting into literary glory with the publication of *Childe Harold*. On the other hand, to have learned, as she would inevitably have learned, of the dissoluteness in London society into which he immediately thereafter plunged, might very well have given her the coup de grace.

Byron's venting his grief by sparring with boxing gloves was not dissimilar to his behavior, years later, when Shelley's remains were burned on the beach at Leghorn. When the pyre began to die, Byron stripped to the skin, went into the sea, and swam far out.

Byron had already heard that a close Harrow friend, John Wingfield had died in May. With death foremost in his thoughts, on August 12 he drew up directions for the will already mentioned; besides the large bequest to Nicolo and the sizable one to Rushton, he remembered Fletcher, Joe Murray, Hobhouse, and Davies; he asked that his body be buried in the vault of the garden at Newstead "without any burial ceremony or burial services whatever, and that no inscription save my name and age, be written on the tomb or tablet."

On August 20 he suddenly took up the threads of friendship with his sister again. Augusta had written a letter of condolence after his several years' neglect of her. Now he directed that should any successor to the title think of removing his body from the Newstead vault, they should thereby forfeit the estate, which would then go to Augusta and her heirs. When he communicated with her, he twitted her for increasing the number of his Majesty's subjects—she was eventually the mother of seven, one of them her brother's child—and mentioned lightly his two years of travel. Since she had never seen Newstead he invited her there. He himself would marry if he could find anyone "inclined to barter money for rank within six months."

Augusta answered him from her home at Six Mile Bottom in her characteristic style—long-winded, rambling, running over with words under-lined—and full of warmth for her half brother: "I feel so *very* happy to have the pleasure of hearing from you that I will not delay a moment in answer-ing it, altho' I am in all the delights of *unpacking*." Her eldest daughter had been unwell, but was now "in a fair way to be *herself* again." Davies had told Augusta "she was exactly the sort of child *you* would delight in." It would be wonderful to set out at once for Newstead and show him the children. "I can't tell you *half* the happiness it would give me to see it and *you;* but dearest B., it is a long journey." Since he had promised to visit Davies, "*pray do,* you can so easily come here." It had been so long since they had seen each other. "I have indeed *much* to tell you; but it is more easily *said* than *written*." He may have heard "of many *changes* in our situa-tion since you left England; in a *pecuniary* point of view it is materially altered for ye worse . . . I have not time to write half I have to say."

One wonders how much she knew or surmised about her brother, for she added: "I am so very glad to hear you have sufficiently overcome your prejudices against the *fair sex* to have determined upon marrying." How-ever, she was most anxious that "any future *Belle Soeur* should have more attractions than merely money, though to be sure *that* is somewhat necessary."

In his answer to her he joked about Davies's misrepresentations con-cerning his love for children; the truth was he abominated the sight of them; "I have always had the greatest respect for the character of Herod." He could not promise to visit her, because he had business in Lancashire. After that if he could not persuade some wealthy dowdy "to ennoble the dirty puddle of her mercantile Blood," he would return to the East.

He wrote her again the next day. He had heard something of her hus-band's quarrel with the Prince of Wales, and the attendant blighting of the Leighs' fortunes. He was full of pity. He reminded her: "in all Situations, you have a brother in me, and a home here." He begged her to visit him before Christmas. She would be entirely free at Newstead; the place was so extensive "that two people might live together without ever seeing, hear-ing, or meeting,—but I can't feel the comfort of this till I marry . . . My wife and I shall be so happy,—one in each Wing."

The next day she wrote again. "At last a *bright thought* struck me." The Leighs were planning a trip to Yorkshire in the fall; she could pay him "a visit *en passant* . . . But I fear you would be obliged to make up your mind to receive my *Brats* too . . . I shall be daily expecting to hear of a Lady Byron." Marriage was bound to make him happier, "PROVIDED *her Lady-ship* was the sort of person to suit you; and you won't be angry with me for saying that it is not EVERY *one* who would; therefore don't be too *pre-cipitate*. You will *wish me hanged,* I fear, for boring you so unmercifully, so God bless you, my dearest Bro."

To this he answered that when he discovered a wife "rich enough to suit me and foolish enough to have me, I will give her leave to make me miserable if she can. Money is the magnet; as to Women, one is as well as another, the older the better, we have then a chance of getting her into Heaven."

His next letter emphasized the solitude in which he lived: he was fencing, boxing, swimming, and running a great deal to keep fit and to induce sound sleep. To appease hunger he was chewing tobacco.

Though it pleased him to think himself a solitary, he began, he told Hodgson in September, "to gather my little sensual comforts together." Lucy, the maid who had borne his illegitimate child in 1809, he now "extracted from Warwickshire," and he hired other girls. He had, too, the beginnings of a menagerie once more: several tortoises brought from Athens, a hedgehog, and a mastiff.

In mid-October he left for a visit to Cambridge, but the memories of Edleston, of whose death he had only recently learned, haunted him everywhere. At the end of the month he was in London, where the first two cantos of *Childe Harold* were in press. Though heavily in debt, he had given the copyright to his distant relative, the toady Dallas, who had arranged for John Murray to publish it. Murray and Dallas had both been beleaguering him to omit and alter various passages, for reasons political, religious, and moral. To some of these demands he acceded. For instance, he deleted a passage referring to William Beckford and his perverted pleasures—later published as "To Dives, a Fragment." There were also some additions, including lines on Edleston.

Suddenly he was concerned about the highly autobiographical flavor of his poem; he had perhaps revealed, certainly had hinted, too much. He told Dallas that he intended to deny all connection with Harold. But the precaution was vain; he would become famous just because everyone saw his Harold as a self-portrait.

14.

PUBLICLY DISILLUSIONED WITH MANKIND, JADED BY PLEASURE, PROUD as Lucifer, preferring to conceal inner tenderness beneath a cloak of disdain, and only too patently cherishing some deep-lying sorrow which he scorned to reveal—such was the exciting portrait Byron had drawn in that poem. It became the model for the so-called "Byronic hero," whom the world would hungrily await meeting again and again in a series of narrative poems from his pen. Though men generally found him companionable, the sardonic was the face he chose to present to the public at large—and, usually, in private to his women. It is, indeed, the Byron which his personal records show he frequently thought himself to be.

Accounting for this "Byronic" character is not an uncomplicated task. The clubfoot with which he was born; his mother's unpredictable alternation of violent abuse and tearful affection—he preferred her abuse; his inheritance of the title at the age of ten, when it was bound to unbalance him; his native magnanimity and pride of place so much at odds with enforced penny pinching in his youth; his constant worry and vanity over a natural tendency to fat, so ironically inharmonious with the beauty of his face—these and many allied circumstances would seem to offer themselves rationally, as the origins of the "Byronic" traits.

Nevertheless, Byron and the Byronic hero seem to a degree also an extension of Charles von Moor. Charles von Moor is only a literary creation, the central character in *The Robbers*, a hodgepodge of a play written before 1779 by the boy Schiller. Nevertheless, it is a very real question as to whether Byron, and therefore the Byronic hero, might not have been quite different if *The Robbers* had not been translated into English (1792) and become immensely popular. Disillusioned with mankind, proud as Lucifer, preferring to conceal inner tenderness beneath a cloak of disdain, and cherishing a deeply-lying sorrow—that is the basis of Charles von Moor's character. The added ingredient in Byron's heroes is that, although always susceptible to the charms of some damsel, they are jaded by pleasure. (As for the difference between von Moor and Byron in the flesh, the former was not lame and showed no interest in boys.) Charles von Moor personified the lofty soul whose sensibilities have been trampled upon by society, and who therefore chooses to conduct a one-man war against it. (After *Childe Harold* Byron's heroes were often robbers by profession, too.) The antisocial hero of Schiller's unedifying play was a sort of German Robin Hood, without a touch of his English prototype's merriment—a sort of personal avenger of the world's wrongs—who suffered all the more just because his hatred of injustice and hypocrisy had driven him, in violation of his own delicacy and sensitivity, into a life of crime.

Von Moor came to the conclusion that man was false and perfidious, of the "crocodile brood," with tearful eyes and heart of steel. The Robber, once a "gentle lamb," became a tiger, his spirit panting for freedom. Throughout his career as a marauder, he has always suffered with the sufferer. To him life was a drama, "bitter enough to bring tears into your eyes, while it shakes your sides with laughter." While all living things went forth to bask in the sun, the Robber alone had to "inhale the torments of hell out of the joys of heaven." He alone was "the outcast," he alone the "rejected." His days of lost innocence would never return. "Never will their delicious breezes cool my burning bosom!"

This character, invented a few years before Byron was born, a fictional creation well known to the public before Byron began to write, provided the quintessential elements of the Byronic hero—who, for Byron's readers, and partially for Byron himself, would become essentially Byron too.

When young Schiller created Charles von Moor, he could hardly have imagined, of course, that he was creating the outlines for a far more important person, George Gordon, the sixth Lord Byron. Who can gauge the power of fashion upon any given era? Who can put a finger on the point where life ceases to copy the models set by the arts, where purely native factors begin to determine a man's emotions or way of life? To what extent was it because he was uniquely himself and to what extent was it because the Provençal poets had set the pattern, that Dante loved Beatrice the way he did? The same question may be asked concerning Petrarch and Laura, Boccaccio and Simonetta. Why did men start climbing the Alps and risking their necks for the fun of it, only *after* Rousseau discovered that the Alps were sublime? To what extent did Byron live and feel the way he did because of his own experiences and nature, and to what extent were some of his experiences and part of that nature shaped because he felt himself to be the living embodiment of the von Moor-type hero? *

At any rate, the world of fashion in which he moved in London must have been well aware of his resemblance to the type. How thrilling for the women to meet The Robber in the flesh instead of in the pallid pages of a book!

Byron had undeniably advertised himself in his poem as fitting Lady Caroline Lamb's description of him as mad, bad, and dangerous to know. The early stanzas of *Childe Harold* spoke of the hero as "shameless," "given to revel," and occupying himself chiefly with "concubines and carnal companie," and having without remorse run "through Sin's long labyrinth." "Sore sick at heart," he had fled from his scenes of vice (i.e., in England) to go abroad; sometimes "the sullen tear" would rise to his eyes, but it would there be "congealed" by his pride. The self-portraiture was substantiated by references to what Childe Harold had left behind when setting forth on his travels—a "sister whom he loved," his mother, his lands and houses, and

---

* See his two references in a long footnote he wrote for *The Corsair*. He compares his hero to the pirate La Fitte, and says: "The chief of this horde, like Charles de [*sic*] Moor, mixed with his many vices, some transcendant virtues." Further on he again calls La Fitte, with his "noble traits," a "modern Charles de Moor."

tempting dames whose bodies, fit to pervert the sanctity of a hermit, "long had fed his youthful appetite."

There were, besides, references to two other matters about which the public could know nothing and was therefore free to hypothesize. There was first a "fair Florence" in the stanzas. She was actually the Constance Spencer Smith of the Malta epoch. In *Childe Harold* the story was modified to be consistent with the portrait of a blasé hero. She is spoken of as surrounded by suitors for her favors, yet her attraction was only to Harold. Little did she guess, the stanzas say, that though apparently made of marble, Harold had had more than a little experience in spreading "snares licentious far and wide"—which, when transposed as applying to Byron himself, was a declaration not calculated to render him less alluring to feminine hearts. If Harold did not take advantage of Florence's desire for him, in the long run what matter?

> When all is won that all desire to woo,
> The paltry prize is hardly worth the cost.

Here was the young roué's gauntlet flung down for female readers to pick up and, in the contest, prove him wrong.

There was a second reference in *Childe Harold* which Byron, always tempted to autobiography in his verse, could not abstain from including, though hardly anxious that anyone decipher it. Near the conclusion of the second canto, the poet pauses to lament the passing of a "loved and lovely one," who—and the statement was capable of wide interpretation—"did for me what none beside have done." Recently death has taken from the poet all it could: "the parent, friend [Matthews], and now the more than friend [Edleston]." Lady Caroline, like most of Byron's readers, naturally must have assumed that this third lamented loss was a girl whom Byron deeply cherished. It was only a very few friends who knew that the "more than friend" was no girl, but the former choirboy at Cambridge.

It was at this time that one of the most important friendships of his life had its beginnings, that with the poet who had so much influenced his boyhood, Tom Moore. It began unpromisingly enough. There had been a rather absurd contretemps between Moore and Jeffrey, editor of the *Edinburgh Review:* as a result of that magazine's critique of his 1806 volume Moore, even though he had only once discharged a gun—and then nearly blew off his thumb—felt honor bound to challenge the editor to a duel. The opponents met, but the police, having been warned by Moore's friends, rushed upon them and seized their pistols; according to the gendarmerie, Jeffrey's pistol turned out to have been unloaded. This almost-skirmish was much laughed over, and Byron in his *English Bards and Scotch Reviewers* poked fun at it. When Byron's name appeared on the title page of the new edition of the satire, Moore sent him a letter opening the way for a duel with him. But Byron was still abroad, and did not receive the quasi challenge. On his return Moore sent a second letter; but having married in the meantime, Moore declared that he would now be satisfied if Byron could offer an acceptable "explanation." His lordship answered proudly: though he at no time had felt hostile to Moore and admitted that his remarks on the affair had been based on squibs he had read, he was in the position of being able neither to retract nor apologize; he awaited Moore's decision on the next move. Moore replied that he was satisfied with Byron's explanation, and concluded, "We Irishmen, in business of this kind, seldom know any medium between decided hostility and decided friendship: but, as any approaches to the latter alternative must now depend entirely on your Lordship," he would let the matter rest until he heard from Byron. His lordship's response to that was not encouraging: he was still prepared to give Moore the opportunity to arrange a duel; as for closer acquaintance, "Was I to anticipate friendship from one who conceived me to have charged him with falsehood? . . . I should have felt proud of your acquaintance, had it commenced under other circumstances." Annoyed at Byron's tone, Moore suggested that they cease corresponding. At this Byron softened, and hinted that since there was no longer any difference between them, "I shall be most happy to meet you, when, where, and how you please." Moore at once sought out his friend Rogers, and Byron suggested meeting at the dinner where he would eat only mashed potatoes drenched in vinegar.

Moore was much impressed with Byron's personal beauty, gentleness of voice, and politeness of manner. "Being in mourning for his mother, the colour, as well of his dress as of his glossy, curling, and picturesque hair, gave more effect to the pure, spiritual paleness of his features." The spiritual paleness, Moore had no way of knowing, may very well have been due to a steady diet of vinegar.

Soon Byron was inviting him to go down to Newstead with him, Hodgson, and Harness, a young friend, "the earliest and dearest I ever had from the third form at Harrow to this hour." Byron's "dearest friend" seemed, by this time, to number something like a dozen. Moore was unable to go.

Harness, two years younger than Byron, was lame, too, but, unlike his friend, had been a weakling at school. Byron had saved him from many a persecution by the bullies. A misunderstanding had ended mutual communication during Byron's last year at Harrow. In 1808 he wrote Harness a charming letter deploring the disruption of their friendship and assuming all the blame; he also told him, "The *first lines* I ever attempted at Harrow were addressed to *you*." Always under the influence of momentary emotion

Byron in 1814, portrait by Thomas Phillips.
(Courtesy of the Nottingham Public Libraries.)

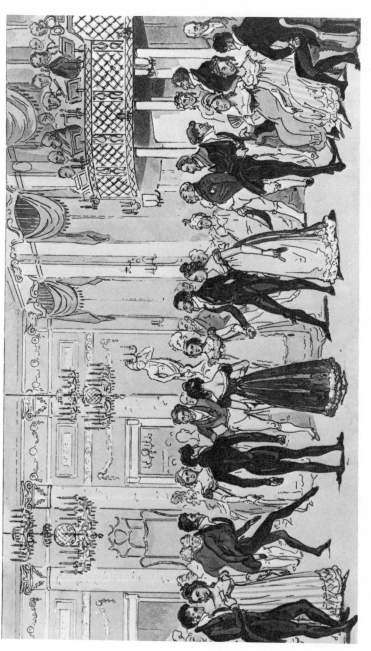

"Highest Life in London . . . among the Corinthians at Almack's," drawn and engraved by I. R. and G. Cruikshank; from P. Egan's *Life in London*. (Courtesy of the British Museum.)

Byron had intended dedicating *Childe Harold* to him, but refrained lest it injure Harness as a clergyman, as which he was ordained in 1812.

Hodgson, seven years Byron's elder, became his friend in 1807; he, too, was preparing for the church. In his will of 1811 Byron remembered him handsomely. Though leading a dissolute life, Hodgson tried to convert Byron to orthodox Christianity. Byron had retorted: "I will have nothing to do with your immortality; we are miserable enough in this life, without the absurdity of speculating upon another. If men are to live, why die at all?" If those who have never heard of Christ may be saved, of what use Christianity? If, to be saved, one must know Christ, how could God "damn men for not knowing what they are never taught?"

Despite these differences and Hodgson's hypocrisies, Byron was fond of him, as well as of Hodgson's clergyman friend, Robert Bland. Bland had been away from England and asked Hodgson to keep in touch with Bland's mistress so he could send regular news of her. When Bland returned, his kept woman refused to see him; he wrote a frantic letter to Byron accusing Hodgson of stealing her affection. Presently, as Byron told the tale, Bland was challenging an officer of the Dragoons over a common whore—as the Dragoon admitted her to be—but Bland was determined to marry her. During Bland's absence from the country, Hodgson had abandoned his own mistress and wished to marry Bland's. She, however, had turned him down, too, preferring to be kept by the Dragoon. Bland began to run amok at the situation; Hodgson was drowning his own sorrow in drink. Byron, having met the woman, estimated her value at seven shillings. He was asked to carry Bland's challenge to the Dragoon, but managed by tact to quiet the fuss. Now Hodgson was beating his breast for having slept with a woman whom his good friend Bland had confided to his care. One can understand Byron's feelings in saying to Harness about all this: "So much for the sentimentalists, who console themselves in their stews for the loss . . . of the refined attachment of a couple of drabs! You censure *my* life, Harness,— when I compare myself with these men, my elders and betters, I really begin to conceive myself a monument of prudence—a walking statue—without feeling or failing; and yet the world in general hath given me a proud pre-eminence over them in profligacy. Yet I like the men, and, Gods knows, ought not to condemn their aberrations. But I own I feel provoked when they dignify all this by the name of *love*—romantic attachments marketable for a dollar!"

15.

NEITHER A CLERGYMAN NOR PREPARING TO BE ONE, BYRON MIGHT therefore in all justice compare his moral stature favorably with that of these two men. But he was not precisely leading the life of an anchorite. When Harness and Hodgson came to stay with him at Newstead for Christmas it is true that they saw nothing to justify the stories of Byron's orgies there. During the day he was busy with late revisions on *Childe Harold*, they with their own work; at night Hodgson continued to marshal his best arguments for the conversion of his host. His guests were ignorant, however, of what went on during later hours when Byron joined his private little harem.

In addition to his old favorites, Lucy and Rushton and several other servants, Byron now had in his employ a Welsh girl, Susan Vaughan, with whose charms he was for a brief while smitten. When he left for London after the Christmas holidays, she wrote him a series of letters reminding him of his parting kiss, which she still felt on her lips, of the fact that he had been her first lover, and how even in the presence of Fletcher's little son (for whom she was acting as nursemaid) he had come into her bedroom to kiss her and fondle her breasts. During his absence in London, Lucy and Rushton, jealous of Susan, were highly antagonistic to her, and she reported to her master that they were spreading stories about Byron's intimacies with her; she also hinted that Lucy and Rushton were going to bed together, while she herself vowed that she would remain faithful to him.

Stung by the possibility that both Rushton and Lucy were betraying him, Byron wrote to the boy reprimanding him: "Susan is to be treated with civility, and not *insulted* by any person over whom I have the smallest controul . . . I am truly sorry to have any subject of complaint against *you*. . . . I see no reason for any communication between *you* and the *women*." Rushton at once let him know that dear Susan was bestowing her favors elsewhere, and painted himself as the victim of her intriguing. It is, of course, not possible to ascertain where the truth lay in these various accusations; what is clear is that Rushton's word and affection counted more than Susan's. Byron replied to him with great kindliness: "If any thing has passed between you *before* or since my last visit to Newstead, do not be afraid to mention it. I am sure *you* would not deceive me, though *she* would. Whatever it is, *you* shall be forgiven. I have not been without some suspicions on the subject, and am certain that, at your time of life, the blame could not attach to you . . . I do not remember ever to have heard a word from you before *against* any human being." This tender leniency of Byron's toward the boy under the circumstances speaks eloquently of the confusion of the sexual pull in Byron's life.

For at once Susan and another girl were dismissed. "The women are gone to their relatives," he wrote Hodgson, "after many attempts to explain what was already too clear." He could only wonder at his folly "in excepting my own strumpets from the general corruption . . . I have one request to make, which is, never mention a woman again in any letter to me, or even allude to the existence of the sex."

Before going abroad he had a number of times attended the transactions of the House of Lords without taking part in them. After casting about for a subject for his own first speech, he decided upon that of the rioting weavers of Nottingham. Unable to find employment, they had been smashing the machines which they held responsible for their distress; the troops which had been sent to suppress them had only augmented the violence. In February the Tories of the House of Commons had passed a bill condemning to death anyone found guilty of breaking the weaving frames; the Whigs in the Lords were inclined to delay action on the bill rather than to attack it. Such was the position of Lord Holland, whose assistance Byron sought.

When he arose to speak on February 27, 1812, though he had written out his speech and practiced a sophisticated manner, Byron forgot his preparations in the excitement of actually delivering his maiden address. "I spoke very violent sentences with a sort of modest impudence, abused every thing and every body . . . As to my delivery, loud and fluent enough, perhaps a little theatrical." For all this self-disparagement, it will seem to the impartial reader of that speech, that Byron had the makings of an eloquent, perhaps a great, orator. But his interest in politics quickly waned after making this speech.

He began by acknowledging the outrages committed by the weavers; but, he said their very perseverance "tends to prove that nothing but absolute want could have driven a large, and once honest and industrious, body of the people, into the commission of excesses so hazardous" to themselves, their families, and the community. Despite the activity of the military, the police and the magistrates, no one has been caught in the act of destruction. Nevertheless, he went on caustically, several "notorious delinquents" have been detected clearly guilty of "the capital crime of poverty" and of the nefarious charge of "lawfully begetting several children" whom the times disqualified them from maintaining. These unemployed men foolishly supposed that the "well-being of the industrious poor" was of more moment "than the enrichment of a few individuals" by implements of trade which had thrown them out of work. "These men never destroyed their looms till they were become useless." They have been derided as a mob, "but even a mob may be better reduced to reason by a mixture of con-

ciliation and firmness, than by additional irritation and redoubled penalties."
It is just such a mob "that labour in your fields and serve in your houses,—
that man your navy, and recruit your army," which have enabled Britain
to defy the world and which "can also defy you" when driven to despair.
Without regard to the injustice of this bill and its impracticability, "is there
not blood enough upon your penal code, that more must be poured forth
to ascend to Heaven and testify against you?" Moreover, how is the bill to
be carried out? Can a whole county be jailed? Are gibbets to be erected
in every field? And will the starving man who has braved bayonets be
frightened by gibbets? "When death is a relief, and the only relief" the
country affords him, will he be subdued by such a bill? "But suppose it is
passed; suppose one of these men, as I have seen them,—meagre with
famine, sullen with despair, careless of a life which your Lordships are
perhaps about to value at something less than the price of a stocking-frame
. . . —suppose this man—and there are ten thousand such . . . —dragged
into court, to be tried for this new offence, by this new law; still, there are
two things wanting to convict and condemn him . . . —twelve butchers
for a jury, and a Jeffreys for a judge!"

With that fine flourish Byron sat down. No wonder Burdett, who came
to hear it, pronounced it "the best speech by a *lord* since the Lord knows
when." Grenville and Holland also complimented Byron, when they got
up to speak. Privately Holland was not impressed; he granted the speech
its wit and imagination, but found it affected and illogical, not conforming
to Parliamentary standards of eloquence. But Byron seems not to have
spoken in vain, so far as the peers were concerned. He was appointed to a
committee which amended the bill by changing the death penalty to a fine
and imprisonment. Commons, however, voted the amendment out.

Byron concluded, despite his earlier dreams, that politics were not for
him. Besides, fate soon decided that his career must be that of a poet. *Childe
Harold* was published early in March 1812. "I awoke one morning," he
records, "and found myself famous."

Women of London society began throwing themselves at the head of
the bad and dangerous man depicted autobiographically in the poem. They
were eager to attend parties where he was expected, and they used their arts
upon their hosts and hostesses to inveigle a place next to him at dinner
tables. He had many a cause for being as much vexed as flattered, but in
no instance more so than that which Lady Falkland provided.

Before going off on his tour Byron had made a friend of Captain
Charles Cary of the Royal Navy, ninth Lord Falkland. He had been dismissed from his ship for too much "circulation of the bottle," but had
been promised reinstatement. In March 1809, excessively high in and with
spirits, he met a friend at a coffeehouse, a Mr. Powell, and cried out merrily

that he perceived the latter was drunk again. Powell responded with something Falkland, already far gone in drink himself, found so offensive that he began to bastinado his friend. A challenge ensued; at the duel Falkland was mortally wounded. Lady Falkland bore a posthumous child, to whom Byron was named as godfather. Though low in funds, Byron inserted five hundred pounds into a cup at the Falkland home so that the widow would not discover his generosity until he had departed.

Now in the blaze of his success he heard from her. She had talked herself into a strange obsession: she had read his new volume and wrote him that the Thyrza poems contained in it were all composed for her, as was also the Farewell he had penned to Mrs. Smith. Had he asked her to marry him earlier she probably would have declined, she told him, but now, if he believed that he could make him happy, let him come to her, and she would be his. But he must remember: she must have all his love, he must give up his vices and wicked acquaintances, and embrace a quiet life as the father of Falkland's children. The letter was accompanied by a lock of her hair. (Byron already owned a lock cut from her husband's head.)

He did not reply. A month later she wrote again to assure him that she understood that his silence was owing to his magnanimity. She had reread *Childe Harold* and now saw that she was also his beloved in the Spanish and Greek scenes; she knew herself to be the original of the Maid of Athens, too. No doubt he believed that with Falkland died her ability to love. Not so: she had long ceased to care for her husband before he met his end. Her very heartbeat was now only for Byron.

Her protestations continued until finally, early the next year, he arranged through his lawyer that an intermediary read her a letter in the presence of another person, in order to put an end to the nuisance. The plan had no effect. She refused to believe a syllable of his note. What had she done, she demanded, to lose his affection? Nobody could convince her that she had not been the constant theme of his despairing verses; it was only too clear that he had composed *Childe Harold* itself only to give her the choice of accepting or rejecting the offer of his hand. Even her older sons were reading the poems and recognized the references to their mamma.

At length she was forced to face the fact that she would not hear from him. She wrote him a farewell, saying that she now realized they were incompatible, and asking him not to write her—a needless precaution. She upbraided him for treating her like a "puppet," and hoped he had learned a lesson from the decision she had taken. Apparently he not only took a perverse pleasure in making himself wretched, but also liked to convert others to partnership in his misery. However, she concluded, with the sentimentalist's illogic, she would always feel the warmest affection for him.

He had never uttered or written a word to give her the slightest notion that he had at any time taken the dimmest personal interest in her, beyond coming to her aid when he could ill afford it, as the widow of his friend.

But he found a true friend in Lady Jersey, a great beauty, cultivated and a woman of taste and intelligence. She ruled her circle, he says, as the "veriest tyrant that ever governed Fashion's fools, and compelled them to shake their caps and bells as she willed it." She is reported to have observed: "Treat people like fools and they will worship you; stoop to make up to them, and they will directly tread you underfoot." Her high-handed treatment, later, of the hero of Waterloo was typical. As patroness of the balls held at Almack's, she laid down the rule that no one was to be admitted after eleven o'clock. Shortly after she introduced this limitation, Wellington appeared one night at the door seven minutes after eleven. She sent word by an attendant: "Give Lady Jersey's compliments to the Duke of Wellington, and say that she is very glad that the first enforcement of the rule of exclusion is such that hereafter no one can complain of its application. He cannot be admitted."

Byron never ceased to be grateful to her as one of the only two women (the other being Mme de Staël) "who ventured to protect me when all of London was crying out against me on the separation and *they* behaved courageously and kindly."

His first place of resort in London those days of fame was Holland House. But soon he was in demand everywhere.

It was at Lady Westmoreland's that Lady Caroline Lamb first saw and snubbed him. But a few days after that while she was in the company of Lord and Lady Holland she allowed herself to be introduced to him. Her figure was too thin, slight, and not rounded enough to attract him that day, but he soon felt that all the classic beauties in her circle paled before her fascinating and unpredictable temperament. Presently he was calling daily at Melbourne House, where she and her husband had an apartment above the Melbournes, her husband's parents. Even then it took time for him to grow close to her, for he was alienated by the light-headedness and the great number of her friends whom he encountered at her parties, which were consecrated to the practice of new dances. Dancing, of course, was not for him; furthermore, he was abnormally shy in those crowds of fashionable women, for whose company his experiences with women of the lower orders had ill prepared him.

It was during his second visit to Melbourne House, on March 25, 1812, that he saw someone quite different from the ladies usually convened there, someone who was to provide the central drama of his life. On the way upstairs that day he stumbled on the steps and remarked to Moore, who was with him, that that was a bad omen. If only he had heeded it! he later had cause to reflect. "On entering the room I observed a young lady, more

simply dressed than the rest of the assembly, sitting alone upon a sofa."
Nothing would have seemed more wildly improbable to him at that moment than that this quiet, not too attractive girl up from the country, could
figure in any significant way in his life. It was odd, too, that he should have
met her before he had even begun his mad affair with her cousin's wife,
Lady Caroline—not to speak of his dangerous one with his sister. For she
was William Lamb's cousin, Annabella Milbanke, the girl Byron would
perversely hound into marrying him.

T W O

CARO

1.

THE OLD WAR IN PSYCHOLOGY between the opposing schools of heredity and environment could find material, as it could as well with Byron, for a battle royal over the case of Lady Caroline Lamb. One could prove her to have been a madcap by either inheritance or influence. Her mother, Lady Bessborough, had been rash enough in youth, and in maturity spent over two decades as the mistress of a handsome man much younger than herself, Lord Granville Leveson-Gower, even after he married her sister's daughter; nor did she let go when in the furtherance of his political career he proceeded to engage in innumerable liaisons and bestowed upon her the dubious pleasure of receiving his uncensored confidences on these affairs. She hunted him as unremittingly as Richard Brinsley Sheridan (who promised that on his deathbed he would be looking up at her through the lid of the coffin) hunted her. Her sister, the Duchess of Devonshire, was notorious for her enormous gambling debts as well as for her willingness to maintain with her husband a *ménage à trois,* the third corner of this isosceles triangle being her best friend, Lady Elizabeth Foster.

Caro was as ingenuous a girl as such a background allowed, until her marriage in 1806 to William Lamb. But the background did not encourage unsophistication. She was sent to Italy when only four "to be out of the way," and lived there alone with a maid until she was nine. Later, her grandmother Lady Spencer took charge of her, but was sufficiently alarmed by her fits of temper to consult a physician, who forbade that she be taught anything or see anyone lest her violence lead to madness. After that she was taken to her aunt's home, Devonshire House, and there with the other

Caroline Ponsonby, later Lady Caroline Lamb,
engraved by Francis Bartolozzi
from a painting by Richard Cosway, R.A.
(Courtesy of the British Museum.)

children, all of them neglected by their mothers, "served," as she recalled, "on silver in the morning and carrying their own plates at night," and believing that "the world was divided into dukes and beggars."

Lady Morgan, who knew Lady Caroline well, describes her as entirely fetching and of powerful imagination; she was "gifted with the highest powers, an artist, . . . a woman of society and of the world, the belle, the toast, the star of the day. She was adored but not content. She had a restless craving after excitement. She was not wicked, not even lax, but she was bold and daring." Members of the *haut monde* are notoriously generous in estimating the creative talents of their fellows, as though belonging to that circle endowed one with special gifts to begin with; Caro's writings are more hysterical than accomplished and her spelling and grammar would not do credit to a schoolgirl—but then, the nobility have ever held themselves above the requirements of spelling and grammar; her drawings have a certain touching quality characteristic of the primitive; but for the rest, one can go along with Lady Morgan's tributes to her for the most part. Imaginative, adored, restless, and daring she undeniably was—and not wicked—until her terrifying frustration over Byron later converted her into a mischievous hypocrite.

She fell in love with William Lamb when she was only fifteen. He was the favorite son of his brilliant and free-living mother, Lady Melbourne, but not the son of his official father, her husband. In keeping with her philosophy that once a woman had borne her lord an heir, she was at liberty to yield to her affections elsewhere, she had had one of her affairs with the Earl of Egremont, and William was the product of that liaison. Her fourth son, George Lamb, "was universally supposed" to be the son of the Prince of Wales. (He in turn married the Duchess of Devonshire's illegitimate daughter.) Adultery was a way of life in Caro's circle.

It is not true that her endless quarrels with William Lamb were due exclusively to her love of Byron, for their contentions began long before Byron and she ever met. Lamb, tall, strong of feature, and with dark flashing eyes was, in contradiction to his looks, a lazy though well-bred, disenchanted young man. How much his cynicism was owing to the gossip about his paternity is a subject for speculation. Ironically enough—Lord Melbourne's own son by his wife had died—he became the second Viscount Melbourne (in 1828); but the pittance of an allowance granted him by his "legal" father indicates that Lord Melbourne was quite aware that William was not his own son. No one could have prophesied that this same indolent, handsome young man was going to be Prime Minister of England when Victoria came to the throne.

William Lamb quickly won his girl-wife over to his own blasé values. He "cared nothing for my morals," Caro was to say; "I might flirt and go about with whom I pleased." Her husband had been well instructed by the example of his mother, whose indoctrination led him to observe with an unconcerned eye his wife's flagrant behavior with Byron. A thoroughgoing romantic like her would probably construe that indifference to mean her husband no longer loved her.

It is to be remembered that in the summer of 1814, when her affair with Byron was far from ended in her own heart, though her lover had long declared it over and done with, and all of London society knew it as a choice piece of scandal, she asked a neighbor at dinner, "Whom do you imagine I consider the most distinguished man I ever met?" and he replied, "Lord Byron," she shook her head and soberly said, "No, my husband, William Lamb."

The Lambs, living on the upper floor of Melbourne House, were inevitably somewhat dominated by William's urbane mother, who had had more than her share of amorous irregularities.

Such was the temper of the society now engulfing Byron. One night at Covent Garden he was momentarily annoyed to note, in a private box opposite, a notorious kept woman who, as he wrote in his journal, had been "actually educated, from her birth, for her profession," sitting beside her mother, an infamous procuress to the army. But his ill temper soon gave way to laughter when, looking about the house, he saw in the box next to him, "and the next, and the next," women of social position but tarnished reputation, a divorcée and her daughter, "both *divorceable*," and so on. He knew all their histories. "It was as if the house had been divided between your public and your *understood* courtesans." What was the difference, he asked, between one group and the other? Only that one class of whore might "enter Carleton and any *other house*," while the public strumpet was limited to the Opera and the bawdy house.

What set Lady Caroline apart from her social equals was only her indifference to their opinion. They managed their profligacies within the bounds of a certain outward *bienséance.* What they did was of no importance, so long as what they did had requisite style. She, on the contrary, delighted in fracturing the rules—though always with a half-guaranteed impunity because of her rank, her husband's indifference, and her powerful family connections. It is said that her voice would often rise to a shriek above everyone else's at dinner tables, and that she went out of her way to shock the people she knew. Hers is a recurrent pattern of conduct; when persons of the lower orders behave like that, members of Caro's station dismiss them as "common"; when the offender is of their own class, she is accepted as an interesting "eccentric." Caro has been labeled an exhibitionist, but that, like everything usually said about her by Byron's biographers, is an oversimplification. Other than Byron himself, she was the

William Lamb, Lord Melbourne,
portrait by Sir Thomas Lawrence.
(Courtesy of the British Museum.)

most complicated person figuring in his life. She may very well, with her impulsive nature, have been as disgusted as he was with the hypocritical pretenses of a circle as thoroughly corrupt as the Regent, who set its tone. A fatal difference between them, however, was that Byron, no matter how rowdy in his letters or how abandoned behind a closed door, was a stickler for a certain decorum among people of his own class—a reason that he spent the better part of his life enjoying himself with those of lower station. He could not bear public display, while she seemed to enjoy it, and was far more embarrassed by her Bohemianism than was her uncritical husband.

Certainly it is not necessary to pass judgment on her—at least, not for the first two or three years of their association; if it were, a fair one would be hard to arrive at. That she later became something of a viper toward Byron cannot be denied. It is disgusting to come upon her deliberate intrusion into Byron's difficulties when his wife left him, to see how Caro labored to make everything as bad for him as possible, to witness her two-faced dealings with those concerned, to read her treacherous betrayal of his confidences and her frantic attempts to avenge herself because of jealousy of Augusta and Lady Byron. Yet even here Byron shares the blame for his own callousness in having made her his confidante, especially concerning his incest with his sister. He knew, by the time he told her all, how unstable Caro was, and he, moreover, by then felt that he was through with her. Probably his need of being the Byronic hero in the flesh was stronger than his native decency. Caro was also a woman to whom lying came naturally—as some men claim it does to all women—and there was a streak of insanity in her excesses. But it must also be remembered that she had always been encouraged in them. Her excesses were the delight of her friends.

Her perpetually outraging the amenities resulted in her becoming to her lover by degrees a trial and then a vexation. Besides, once passion had burned itself out—and that never took long for Byron—it was unendurable for him to have the relationship prolonged. Exasperation drove him, whose nature was not cruel, to cruelty, once he felt trapped. But that made her cling to him the more violently. She suffered a great deal at his hands, partly, of course, through her own perversity.

Seen in their totality, her shortcomings were both prodigious and loathsome. Yet in the end it is impossible not to feel sorry for her. Women far more virtuous than Lady Caroline have, through frustrated love, like somnambulists found themselves perpetrating infamous acts in complete defiance of their deepest natures. And that Caro fell madly in love with Byron and even accepted, difficult to accept for any woman, all the predispositions fixed by his experiences at school and in the East, there can be no question.

Shortly after Byron's death she wrote a letter to Medwin on the heels of his publishing *Recollections of Lord Byron*. Unreliable himself, Medwin had declared that Byron had confided to him that Lady Caroline "had scarcely any personal attractions to recommend her," that her marriage to Lamb had been one of convenience and which permitted each complete freedom in matters amatory, and that because of her obvious partiality to Byron, he had more or less forced himself to pretend love for her. In order to stimulate an emotion he did not deeply feel, he kept "feeding the flame with a constant supply of *billets-doux* and amatory verses." He was, Byron is said to have told Medwin, "easily governed by women, and she gained an ascendancy over me that I could not easily shake off. I submitted to this thraldom long, for I hate *scenes* [that was certainly the truth], and am of an indolent disposition; but I was forced to snap the knot rather rudely at last."

Still oblivious of the figure she cut, Lady Caroline, though peppering her letter to Medwin with some exaggerations, nevertheless said enough of the essential truth to render her words touching. "It was when the first Child Harold came out upon Lord Byron's return from Greece that I first had the misfortune to be acquainted with him—at that time I was the happiest and gayest of human beings I do believe without exception—*I had married for love* and love the most romantic and ardent—my husband and I were so fond of each other that false as I too soon proved he never would part with me. . . . At Melbourne House where I lived the Waltzes and Quadrilles were being daily practised, Lady Jersey, Lady Cowper, the Duke of Devonshire, Miss Milbanke and a number of foreigners coming there to learn—You may imagine what forty or fifty people dancing from twelve in the morning until near dinner time all young gay and noisy were—in the evening we either had opposition suppers or went out to Balls and routs —such was the life I then led when Moore and Rogers introduced Lord Byron to me." She goes on to speak of the rose and carnation he brought her, and continues: "I have them still . . . Byron never could say I had no heart. He never could say, either, that I had not loved my husband. In his letters to me he is perpetually telling me I love him [i.e., her husband] the best of the two; and my only charm, believe me, in his eyes was, that I was innocent, affectionate, and enthusiastic. . . . I was not a woman of the world. Had I been one of that sort, why should he have devoted nine entire months almost entirely to my society*; have written perhaps ten times a day†; and lastly have press'd me to leave all and go with him—and this at the very moment when he was made an Idol of, and when, as he and you justly

---

* This is perhaps the first detail quoted from her letter which was an exaggeration of fact.

† Since almost all their interchange of letters is lost, there is no way of judging the truth of this. It might have been so. Byron was an indefatigable letter writer.

observe, I had few personal attractions. Indeed, indeed I tell the truth. Byron did not affect—but he loved me as never woman was loved." She enclosed for Medwin a stone-press copy of one of his letters to prove Byron's love. "His health being delicate, he liked to read with me & stay with me out of the crowd. Not but what we went about everywhere together, and were at last invited always as if we had been married. . . . I grew to love him better than virtue, Religion—all prospects here. He broke my heart, & I still love him."

2.

IT WAS LATE IN MARCH 1812 THAT THEY BECAME ACQUAINTED AND BY April they were lovers. As April wound into May their affair became more and more hectic. He was not the man long to suffer sitting contentedly and watch her practicing the new dances with her crowd of laughing friends. To his inflamed mind the harmless merriment was a mockery of his own lameness. As for that new importation from Germany, the waltz, which called for a proximity in the dancers unknown before, he felt as scandalized at it as the primmest of spinsters. In his satire, *The Waltz*, we may read what torturing salacious thoughts were his, as he looked on while his mistress was held in the arms of other men, and he sat on the side unable to participate:

> Seductive Waltz!—though on thy native shore
> Even Werter's self proclaimed thee half a whore . . .
> From where the garb just leaves the bosom free,
> That spot where hearts were once supposed to be;
> Round all the confines of the yielded waist,
> The strangest hand may wander undisplaced:
> The lady's in return may grasp as much
> As princely paunches offer to her touch . . .
> The breast thus publicly resigned to man,
> In private may resist him—if it can . . . .
> Hot from the hands promiscuously applied,
> Round the slight waist, or down the glowing side,
> Where were the rapture then to clasp the form
> From this lewd grasp and lawless contact warm?

No matter to what degree his physical deformity may have motivated the wrath, the observation remains that of a lecher; like all roués Byron stipulated for the standards of the harem in his women. At the time he met Caro, she seems to have been only a creature deriving maximum pleasure from dancing, to which her lithe and graceful form peculiarly fitted her. But it was inevitable that her lover should soon demand that she give up waltzing, and that she did humbly enough.

There were many scenes of violence. He was furiously jealous of her husband, and often pressed her to prove that she loved him better than Lamb. Once, when she hesitated to take an oath that she did, he stormed, and promised that he would make her pay for her reluctance by wringing her obdurate heart. Whether or not for that reason, wring her heart he presently did. For himself, he felt free, when they were out together, to pay court to other women. On one such occasion at her grandmother's, her distress was so uncontrollable that she bit through a glass she was holding.

It is clear from her later letters to Lady Byron, as well as from Lady Byron's memoranda, that Caro became quite familiar with her lover's earlier affairs with boys. His love entanglement with her was the first of any duration since he had left Nicolo at Malta. It has always been emphasized that her figure was unrounded and boyish; it is possible he was drawn to her for that reason. She was, moreover, fond of dressing as a page, wore that masquerade for a miniature painting, and appeared before Byron that way more than once. Dallas was sitting one day with Byron at a period when he was trying to avoid her; a boy brought him a letter from her—"a fair-faced delicate boy of thirteen or fourteen years old, whom one might have taken for the lady herself . . . I could not but suspect it was a disguise." Were all these antics but hysterical attempts to hold her lover by appeals to that other side of his nature? It is safe to assume, from her later writings, that Byron succeeded, because of her infatuation, in thoroughly corrupting her. Are two cryptic sentences in Medwin, which as biographer he plainly had no clue to himself, possibly further evidence? After a great quarrel, Byron told Medwin, Caro and he "made up in a very odd way, and without any verbal explanation. She will remember it."

(I believe it probable that Caro's penchant for dressing up as a page gave Byron the crucial idea for *Lara,* one of his highly successful narrative poems—it sold 6,000 copies at once—written in the late spring of 1814, when he had broken with her. Its hero is, of course, again highly Byronic, like his predecessors in *The Giaour, The Bride of Abydos,* and *The Corsair.* His bosom, like Charles von Moor's, is surcharged with past crimes. Like Byron himself, he has a pet death's-head in his study and suffers [as Byron did at the time] from terrible nightmares—Byron's being due, no doubt, to the approaching birth of the child who was the fruit of his love for his sister. Like Byron, Lara seems to hate mankind, is given to cynicism, and yet for all that owns a tender heart. He has a page who serves him faithfully and follows him everywhere. When Lara meets his death at the hands of foes, the page faints, and is revealed to be a woman. Looking back at Caro's obsessive love for him, was Byron in this covert manner doing some justice to the sincerity of her love?)

She did not lie in telling Medwin that Byron had first loved her for her gaiety. In her own way, too, Caro loved her husband, possibly no less than she loved Byron, though certainly without the passion—after all, it was Lamb who had established values for her. The knowledge that she did love her husband drove her lover half mad. His own perversity could not rest until he had altered her into a frenzied woman. He was probably the first man she knew who took no pleasure in yielding to her caprices and in generally spoiling her. Everyone else had. Perhaps it was that egocentricity in him which impelled her, in true feminine style, toward self-destruction in loving a man whose inner core could not be penetrated.

At this time, when she was beginning something like friendship with John Murray, Byron's publisher, she occasionally sketched for him traits of her own character. "What is the meaning of right and wrong?" she asks Murray. "All is but appearance." (A philosophy learned from her husband.) Again: "I hate to go slow . . . I run and gallop and drive as if for a wager." Indeed, she was wont to gallop even through the intertwined streets of London. "I never keep the windows shut, even in winter."

By May, London society was gossiping about the unpardonable openness of her affair with Byron. He was talking of going abroad again, and, to force her to choose between him and Lamb, suggested that she run off with him. Her mother, Lady Bessborough, and her mother-in-law, Lady Melbourne, did what they could to throw cold water on her feverish obsession —to no avail.

Curiously enough, out of this family attempt to interfere grew one of Byron's greatest (and, considering that the lady was Caro's husband's mother, outrageous) friendships, that with Lady Melbourne. In a letter to him, assuring him that, to her, a man of letters was but a man like other men and that she was a woman like other women, she drew a self-portrait: "Superior in nothing, I happen fortunately to be gifted with a fund of good nature & chearfulness & very great spirits—& have a little more *tact* than my neighbours." She added, "Once you told me you did not understand Friendship. I told you I would teach it you, & so I will, if you do not allow C. [Caroline] to take you quite away." He was to say of her that she was the "best, kindest, and ablest female I have ever known, old or young"; to Lady Blessington he confessed that although Lady Melbourne was old enough to have been his mother, she "excited an interest in my feelings that few young women have been able to awaken. She was a charming person—a sort of modern Aspasia, uniting the energy of a man's mind with the delicacy and tenderness of a woman's. She wrote and she spoke admirably, because she felt admirably. Envy, malice, hatred, or uncharitableness, found no place in her feelings. . . . I have often thought, that, with a little more youth, Lady M. might have turned my head, at all events she often turned my heart, by bringing me back to mild feelings, when the demon passion was strong within me."

A woman of the world she certainly was, and soon became the recipient of Byron's most intimate revelations. Raised to the level of mentor by him, she was equipped both by social position and intelligence to give him practical advice for moving in the circle to which they both belonged, but her experience hardly fitted her for a moral guide. Her son William, Caro's husband, said of her that she was a devoted mother, a good wife, and a remarkable woman—"but not chaste, not chaste." By the time Byron became her assiduous correspondent she was at sixty-two urbane, sharp minded, and even tempered.

His biographers are at one in admiring her benevolence toward him. Kind she certainly was, though there was more than a little left in her of the courtesan, for all her years, and Lady Caroline fairly hit the mark when declaring that her mother-in-law had, like so many of the young women, been infatuated with him from the beginning. We cannot, of course, help being grateful that their relationship resulted in his writing the letters he sent her, replete, as they are, with information we are glad to have. But I find myself revering her considerably less than others do. There is something nauseating in this woman's inviting him to confide in her matters most intimate, his peccadilloes and amours, and forwarding to her letters from his women, letters which were certainly never intended for her eyes. There is something too much of vicarious salacity in her receptivity to such confidences, such breaches of faith with others—even those most dear to him, and, sometimes, close to her. A woman of real dignity would have wished and known how to instruct him in drawing the line for the sake of his own self-respect. No doubt she often acted in his interest according to her best lights, but she was a cynic and encouraged him to be one, so that if he was often at his most witty with her, he was also at his least admirable.

By mid-May Byron was writing Caro that their two months of "delirium" must terminate. He could no longer bear seeing her looking so unhappy, and he suggested that if they took a month's leave of each other it might give them both some perspective. He talked of going off to Cambridge or Edinburgh for a while, as the easiest solution. But she was not to think that his feelings for her had altered or could alter; what he suggested was intended chiefly to make people stop talking.

In the midst of these fevers he had a fairly shattering encounter. He had gone with two friends directly from some party to witness the hanging of Bellingham, who had shot the First Lord of the Treasury. At the house where Byron had rented a post at a window for a good view, he arrived at around three in the morning on May 18 to find the place still locked for the night. While one friend undertook to awaken the household, Byron sauntered up the street arm in arm with the other. A beggar woman was lying on the steps of a doorway, and with some words of compassion Byron offered her a few shillings. Instead of accepting them, she roughly pushed his hand away, jumped to her feet with a shriek of laughter, and began in mockery to burlesque his lame walk. His friend could feel Byron's arm trembling as they hastily moved on.

Apparently it was on that same day that Lady Caroline left for the country, probably at her family's insistence. A few weeks later Byron's cousin and heir to the title, Captain George Byron (who will figure later in our story), the poet, and Hobhouse, who had resigned his commission in the army, all went down for a stay at Newstead, the object being what Hobhouse described as a "delirium of sensuality," involving the participation of at least one maidservant. Obviously Lady Caroline was no longer the focus of Byron's interest, though one of her pages arrived with letters from her. Nine days of Newstead and he was back in London. Before the month was over he had begun to see more than a little of the woman who was to be Caro's successor, Lady Oxford.

Because of him Lady Caroline was back in town, too, and renewing the frantic behavior which so unnerved her lover. It was during these days that she wrote him, "My remaining in Town and seeing you thus is sacrificing the last chance I have left. I expose myself to every eye, to every unkind observation. You think me weak and selfish; you think I do not struggle to withstand my own feelings, but indeed it is exacting more than human nature can bear, and when I came out last night, which was of itself an effort, and when I heard your name announced, the moment after I saw nothing more, but seemed in a dream. . . . Lady Cahir said, 'You are ill; shall we go away?' which I was very glad to accept, but we could not get through, and so I fear it caus'd you pain to see me intrude again. I sent a groom to Holmes twice yesterday morning, to prevent his going to you, or giving you a letter full of flippant jokes, written in one moment of gaiety, which is quite gone since. I am so afraid he has been to you. . . . Do not marry yet, or, if you do, let me know it first. I shall not suffer, if she you chuse be worth you, but she will never love you as I did. . . . How very pale you are! . . . I never see you without wishing to cry; if any painter could paint me that face as it is, I would give them any thing I possess on earth—not one has yet given the countenance and complexion as it is. I only could, if I knew how to draw and paint."

Her mother, concerned over the gossip, and seemingly unaware of how

Lady Caroline Ponsonby (Lady Caroline Lamb),
portrait by John Hoppner.
(Courtesy of the Right Honourable The Earl Spencer.)

far things had proceeded, pleaded with Hobhouse to use his influence with Byron and make him go off somewhere for a while. Hobhouse did his best, knowing the affair must end sooner or later in unpleasantness. He almost succeeded, but Lady Caroline decreed otherwise.

July 29 proved a day of nightmares to poor John Cam. He and Byron had arranged to visit Harrow in order to avoid a "threatened" call by Lady Caroline. Hobhouse arrived at 8 St. James's Street to carry off his friend. They were just going out at noon when resonant knocks sounded on the door. When they opened they saw a crowd outside watching eagerly; Caro stood in the doorway in a "strange disguise." All the servants knew she had come prepared for an elopement. Under the circumstances John Cam felt it his duty not to abandon his pliable friend. He therefore remained in the sitting room, while she ran into the bedroom to remove her masquerade. When it was off she stood revealed in a page's outfit. For the sake of decorum in the house she was prevailed upon to don the dress, hat, and shoes of a maidservant, and in these she appeared in the sitting room. Hobhouse lost no time in begging her to go away at once; she refused to do so. It must have been with the resignation of despair that Byron murmured, "We must go off together, there is no alternative." Here Hobhouse became stubborn and declared that he would not permit an elopement that day. Oddly enough, Lady Caroline gave in on that point, but declined to leave the house. When Hobhouse tried reasoning with her on the necessity of her going, she cried that blood would be shed. Indeed it would, he countered, if she insisted on staying; Byron agreed to that. Then, declaimed Caro, the blood spilled should be hers. She tried to seize a court sword lying on the sofa, but Byron intercepted her. Presently she grew calmer and promised to leave if Byron would see her before the week was ended. He was ready to agree to anything if she would but leave. Now a new problem presented itself: if she were to enter her carriage she would have to change to suitable clothes; if, on the other hand, she changed clothes at Byron's she would at once be recognized when she was on the other side of the door. Luckily Hobhouse had asked a hackney coachman to wait in the street, and he now offered her the use of that vehicle. She could drive to his lodgings and change there. She was willing, provided Byron accompanied her, but Hobhouse, after his interview with her mother, refused to have them together in his rooms, and was deaf to her entreaties. Finally she stipulated that Byron at least accompany her in the coach. John Cam ran across the park and was waiting as the hackney drew up. He saw to it that Byron quitted the coach at the corner, and he had the coachman drive her to the doorway, himself conveyed Caro up to his rooms, left her to dress, went back to the street, and walked Byron to a coffeehouse, came back to his own house, where he found the lady properly clothed, and urged her to go at once to the house of some friend. Soon a note arrived from Byron, saying he wished to see her before she departed again from London. She delivered an answering note to her host, and persuaded him to accompany her in a coach to Mrs. Conyers at Grosvenor Gate; before he left her she wrung a promise from him that he would not try to prevent Byron's seeing her again.

Byron soon admitted that had Hobhouse not been there he most assuredly would have been drawn into an elopment he did not wish.

Her communication of August 9 clearly implies that he was still seeing her, and on the most intimate terms, for she then sent him some of her pubic hair with an inscription describing herself as next to Thyrza (whom she may or may not have known to be a boy) "Dearest & most faithful." The letter accompanying this unusual gift makes it appear that he had agreed to send in exchange hair from the neighborhood of his genitals. She had asked him not to send any blood with his hairs, yet if blood means love she would prefer now to have it. As for her own, "I cut the hair too close & bled much more than you need—do not you the same & pray put not the scizzors points near where quei capelli grow . . . pray be careful." Why, she asked too, did he not keep Newstead and take her there with him, where they could "have lived & died happy"? She vowed she would "kneel & be torn" from his feet before she would ever give him up.

Three days later she erupted again. On the morning of August 12 her mother tried to talk her into going with her to the country house of the Bessboroughs, where William Lamb would join them, and whence they should all leave for Ireland. While she was pleading with Caro, Lord Melbourne came in and upbraided his daughter-in-law for her outrageous flaunting of public opinion. She threatened to run to Byron then and there; he impatiently told her to go and be damned—adding that he was sure Byron would not take her in. Her mother rushed out of the room to find Lady Melbourne, whose tact could be counted upon. When they came back to the room Lady Caroline was gone. Her mother ran to her carriage and drove up and down Parliament Street in the hopes of meeting her daughter. When that proved fruitless she went with Lady Melbourne to Byron's. He was merely astonished, and rather more frightened than they.

He gave his word that he would find her and bring her to Melbourne House. A threat and a bribe to the coachman who had delivered to him a message from her, and she was located at a surgeon's house in Kensington, from which place she was headed for Portsmouth and the first ship sailing out from there. With no funds, she had sold the rings she happened to be wearing to pay for her tickets. Pretending to be her brother, Byron carried her off by main force, convinced her that for her mother's sake she must return to the Melbournes, and sent her there. Her husband and his parents quickly forgave her, and she was touched by their kindness.

Lady Bessborough, sick at heart, returned to 2 Cavendish Square. Her housekeeper, a redoubtable woman, has left a graphic account of the consequences in that home. She at once wrote to Lady Melbourne: "Madam, we was all most dreadfully allarm'd last night at Lady Bessboro being found at the bottom of her Carriage in a fit with great difficulty the footmen got her out & oh Madam think of my Horror when I saw her poor mouth all on one side & her face cold as marble we was all distracted she continued senseless . . . if she is to undergo many more such very miserable days as the few last it will Quite kill her. I have written to Lady Caroline but fear she is lost to all feeling even for such a mother."

Enclosed with this one was her letter to Caro, and she talked fearlessly: "Cruel & unnatural as you have behaved you surely do not wish to be the Death of your Mother. I am sorry to say you last night nearly succeeded in doing so." After retailing Lady Bessborough's condition when found in the carriage, she continued, "Oh, Lady Caroline, could you have seen her at that moment you surely would have been convinced how wickedly you are going on . . . even her footmen cryed out *Shame* on you for alas you have exposed yourself to all London you are the talk & [*sic*] every Groom & footman about the Town. A few months ago it was Sir Godfrey* & now another has turned your Head & made you forget what a Husband you have what an angel Child besides makeing you torture all your kind relations & friends in the most cruel manner. Your poor father two was heart broken . . . [He] would not let me send for you he said the sight of you would make her worse. You have for many months taken every measure in your Power to make your Mother miserable & you have perfectly succeeded but do not quite kill her . . . Oh lady Caroline pray to God for streanth of mind & resolution to behave as you ought for this is Dreadful. I feel by sending this I offend you for ever but I cannot help it."

It is ironic that poor Caro should have been the recipient of all this disapproval on the one occasion when she did nothing worse than attempt to run away from her emotional complications. Her actions prove she was desperate. Lord Melbourne complained to the Prince Regent that Byron had bewitched the whole family, "mothers and daughters and all," and was making a fool of Melbourne too; Caroline was mad, her parents almost the same. The Prince thereupon exploded to Lady Bessborough: "I never heard of such a thing in my life—taking the Mothers for confidantes!" (Byron's correspondence with Lady Melbourne evokes just such shock for the very reason.) This was all that scandalized the lecherous Regent, and Lady Bessborough herself admitted to Lady Melbourne that she found it impos-

---

* Sir Godfrey Webster, with whom Lady Caroline had had her first fling at adultery.

sible to "get away from Ld. Byr., when once he began talking to me—he was part of the time pleasant & talking of other things—but he did tell me some things so terrifying & so extraordinary!!" She wondered if "a shocking notion the Prince had of B. could be true," but dismissed it as "too diabolick."

If we are to believe Caro, the letter of which she sent a copy to Medwin and which she said Byron wrote her, would have been penned the day of this flight of hers. If it were possible that he did write it—which I do not believe to be the case—it would serve as a document to prove how readily the pen in hand can betray a correspondent into false sentiment. Accepted as by him, it would indicate that his feelings for Caro were considerably confused—part love, part exasperation at her forcing him into situations he loathed, and part relief at the prospect of seeing the last of her. That is, if he did write it. The letter, a fairly long one, poses an interesting puzzle:

> If tears which you saw and know I am not apt to shed,—if the agitation in which I parted from you,—agitation which you must have perceived through the *whole* of this most *nervous* affair, did not commence until the moment of leaving you approached,—if all I have said and done, and am still but too ready to say and do, have not sufficiently proved what my real feelings are, and must ever be towards you, my love, I have no other proof to offer. God knows, I wish you happy, and when I quit you, or rather you, from a sense of duty to your husband and mother, quit me, you shall acknowledge the truth of what I again promise and vow, that no other in word or deed, shall ever hold the place in my affections, which is, and shall be, most sacred to you, till I am nothing. I never knew till *that moment* the *madness* of my dearest and most beloved friend; I cannot express myself; this is no time for words, but I shall have a pride, a melancholy pleasure, in suffering what you yourself can scarcely conceive . . . I am about to go out with a heavy heart, because my appearing this evening will stop any absurd story which the event of the day might give rise to. Do you think *now* I am *cold* and *stern* and *artful?* Will even *others* think so? Will your mother ever . . . ? 'Promise not to love you'! ah Caroline, it is past promising. But I shall attribute all concessions to the proper motive, and never cease to feel all that you have already witnessed, and more than can ever be known but to my own heart,—perhaps to yours. May God protect, forgive, and bless you. Ever, and even more than ever, Your most attached, Byron. P.S.—These taunts which have driven you to this, my dearest Caroline, were it not for your mother and the kindness of your connections, is there anything on earth or heaven that would have made me so happy as to have made you mine long ago? and not less *now* than *then,* but more than ever at this time. You know I would with pleasure give up all here and beyond the grave for you, and in refraining from this, must my motives be misunderstood? I care not who knows this, what use is made of it,—it is to *you* and to *you* only that they are *yourself* [*sic*]. I was and am yours freely and most entirely

to obey, to honour, love—and fly with you when, where, and how you yourself *might* and *may* determine."

Professor Marchand, who has had no superior as a Byron scholar, thinks that "there is little reason to doubt the sincerity of Byron's statement of his feelings at the moment." Scholarship distrusts all subjective judgments, and for some reason or other, all aesthetic reactions are likely to be held by scholars as subjective. Yet to me it is astonishing that anyone can have read Byron's letters without forming an unshakable conviction that not a sentence of that letter could have been composed by Byron.

Miss E. C. Mayne, some time ago, "hestitatingly" offered the supposition that though in Byron's handwriting, the letter was possibly forged by Lady Caroline to represent what she dreamed Byron ought to have written her. Frances Winwar was more emphatic: she was fairly convinced that Caro was the author, and wrote it in Byron's hand "for everyone to see"; "rejected, despised," she would show the world "how much he still loved her." I not only endorse this judgment, but affirm that this was never a letter by Byron; it could have been written only by Caro.

The slovenly syntax and general vagueness of meaning are certainly unlike Byron. Though given to underlining words in his letters, he usually did so, except in boyhood, to enforce a point of wit; here there is something schoolgirlish about the superfluous emphasis. The whole tone, in fact, is feminine, which was never true of any letter Byron wrote in his majority. The phraseology is purely Caro's (e.g., "I care not who knows this, what use is made of it"). I have attentively read her novels, and I find that this letter contains phrases to which she was addicted. The heroine of *Glenarvon* (who is Lady Caroline herself) is always *agitated* about one thing or another or in a state of *agitation:* the lovers are, in that novel, constantly ready to *give up all here,* even *all beyond the grave*—such phrases, one feels, Byron would have held stomach-turning. Moreover, however wicked he delighted in feeling himself to be, he, like Hamlet, was never willing to surrender his soul's immortality. Concerning that he did not jest.

About the handwriting there is no difficulty. Caro became quite skillful at imitating his hand. She was able to deceive Murray, his publisher, who by that time had seen so many of Byron's manuscripts, with a letter she pretended he had written, and the purpose of which was to extract from Murray a miniature Byron had left in his keeping. Subsequently she admitted to the forgery.

But without regard to style, the contents of the letter brand it as spurious. It is almost laughable that he should be represented as concerned about Caro's duty to her mother or himself giving a moment's thought to her feelings, for he despised Lady Bessborough, and almost never referred to her except in terms of derision—his favorite name for her was "Lady Blarney." Nor was he the hypocrite to call his mistress a "most beloved friend"—not, after their uninhibited physical intimacies. He would never have spoken of having "a pride, a melancholy pleasure in suffering" anything, no matter what he felt. He certainly would never have asked her whether she "*now*" thought him "*cold* and *stern* and *artful.*" He would have loved any woman to think he was. And he certainly would not have fallen into the conventional piety of "May God protect, forgive and bless you."

If Lady Caroline did, as I am convinced, play the forger here, it is one of the most pathetic things we could know about her.

The case may be considered complete if it is remembered that on this same hectic day she is known to have written him a letter, addressing him as "Dearest Lord Byron," and confessing that there could be no excuse for the harebrained escapade in which she had just indulged. In it she begged him not to tell anyone what she had done unless he wished to ruin her, and assured him that she would neither write nor ever see him again. She was about to leave for Ireland. Surely, had Byron written the letter she later claimed was his, it hardly matched in any way the contents of hers.

They had one of their many "final" meetings, and in early September she left for Ireland with her husband and mother. Her cousin, Lady Harriet Leveson-Gower, whom they visited en route, found poor Caro wasted, "pale as death," and in a state bordering on dementia.

Breathing easier, Byron wrote Lady Melbourne that she too might relax now that her tormentor was separated from her by the sea, and vowed that he was through with her daughter-in-law. Indeed, he had no desire "to make love" again unless obliged to. Three days later he was telling her that he was attached to another—of all people, her niece, Miss Milbanke, whom he esteemed above all women he had yet met, and to whom he had once hoped to propose marriage, though it was now too late for that.

As for Lady Caroline, he promised Lady Melbourne that if by December he did not disenchant Dulcinea then he "must attack the windmills, and leave the land in quest of adventures." In the meantime he was writing "the greatest absurdities" to Caro in order to keep her gay—all the more so because her last letter had reminded him that but eight guineas would bring her back to London.

Lady Melbourne thought that perhaps the romance might be allowed to cool off into friendship. His answer was, "No—it must be broken off at once, and all I have left is to take some step which will make her hate me effectually."

Caro now implied in a letter that she might release him if he would answer this question: Could he live without her? He did not reply. After reporting that too to her mother-in-law, he declared that if he was to marry it must be within three weeks; meanwhile he was doing all he could to fall in love—the candidates being a girl of the lower orders, an Italian opera singer, a Welsh seamstress, his agent's wife and daughter—and a picture of Napoleon's wife.

On September 25 he admitted to being occupied with his Italian singer, who spoke no English and who, being already married, was saving him the bother of getting married. His only objection to her was her prodigious love of food; at table she gorged herself on everything in sight; he disapproved of a woman's allowing herself to be seen eating or drinking unless a lobster salad and champagne. Luckily this mistress was attached to her husband; she therefore naturally liked even more one to whom she was *not* married. In Caro's recent communication, she dwelt on the attraction men felt for her. What woman, "not absolutely disgusting," could not say as much? Any woman can evoke a man's love. The problem was to keep a man so!

Soon he was deep in an affair with Lady Oxford, at whose house in the country he was staying. His excuse: "I cannot exist without some object of love." Did Byron ever pause to define the word for himself? In October he admitted to Lady Melbourne that he proposed playing off this new mistress against the old as a way of getting rid of Lady Caroline. Poor Caro! Hearing that he was involved with someone else, she wrote to him, half-pleadingly, half-angry, and in response received from him this admonition: "Correct your vanity, which is ridiculous and proverbial, exert your caprices on your new conquests and leave me in peace." To this she sent a message express: "Only for God sake [*sic*], Byron, explain yourself. What have I done—if you are tired of me say so, but do not, do not treat me so." The irony was that Lady Oxford and she were presumably good friends, and had maintained a correspondence on "learned" subjects, for Lady Oxford prided herself on being something of a bluestocking. Innocently Caro wrote to her, not knowing Byron was staying at her house, "My dearest Aspasia, only think Byron is angry with me! Will you write to him, will you tell him I have not done one thing to displease him, & that I am miserable . . . I will write no more—never teaze him—never intrude upon him, only do you obtain his forgiveness." Lady Oxford did not reply directly. Then Caro learned who her rival was; she threatened to commit suicide as well as to kill Byron and his new light-o'-love. From Tipperary she also wrote Lady Melbourne, lamenting the failure of her attempt to escape from all of them: "Oh that I had not been weak enough to return when Lord Byron brought me back, that I had never returned—but . . . such an exit I will make from this scene of Deceit & unkindness that I shall expiate even my atrocious conduct. . . . Lord Byron has *now* seald my destruction, and it shall follow . . . I never have, I hope, I never have accused Lord Byron to you—he or you best know why he behaves ill to the woman he so lately professed to love. His love for another is no crime, but I neither expected nor can bear insult, hatred suspicion & contempt."

For his part, Byron asked her mother-in-law to make it clear that he absolutely refused to see Caro again. He had found a woman he was perfectly content with, and who seemed content with him. What they both wished was to be left alone.

On the same day, November 9, he sent Caro a letter, part of which she was later to incorporate into her novel *Glenarvon*. Lady Oxford never answered Lady Caroline's ingenuous plea for her help; instead, she apparently dictated this note to her new lover and, with a consummate touch of female malice, sealed it with her own seal, which she of course knew was entirely familiar to Caro; it showed Cupid in a chariot drawn by two horses. The cruel letter, as Caro transcribed it for her mother-in-law, read (the hysterical punctuation being plainly hers, not Byron's): "Our affections are not in our power—mine are engaged. I love another—were I inclined to reproach you, I might for 20 thousand things, but I will not. They really are not cause of my present conduct—my opinion of you is entirely alter'd, & if I had wanted anything to confirm me, your Levities, your caprices, & the mean subterfuges you have lately made use of while madly gay—of writing to me as if otherwise, would entirely have open'd my eyes. I am no longer your lover—I shall but [*sic*] never be less than your friend—it would be too dishonourable for me to name her to whom I am most entirely devoted & attached."*

The heartless letter drove her close to that insanity which later overtook her, a condition from which, because of her violence and waywardness, she was never far distant. Speaking of this letter at a later time Lady Caroline claimed that Byron had sent it because he "knew it would destroy my mind and all else—it did so—Lady Oxford was no doubt the instigator. What will not a woman do to get rid of a rival? She knew that he still loved me. ... I was brought to England [from Ireland] a mere wreck."

In the meantime she had written to Lady Oxford, and that same night the latter had received a letter from her full of "unanswerable questions." Byron could not decide whether she was really mad or only mischievous. A comparison of this letter with Caro's last to him and another to Lady Melbourne (who did not scruple to send it on to him) forced him to conclude that Caro was not only the most inconsistent but also the most "absurd,

---

* In her novel, *Glenarvon*, Lady Caroline made a composite of this letter and the letter from Byron quoted preceding this one. It begins: "I am no longer your lover," and includes a caddish sentence Byron never thought of: "I shall ever remember with gratitude the many instances I have received of the predilection you have shown in my favour."

selfish, and contemptibly wicked of human productions." He would have preferred remaining her friend; she herself averred that if she could not be loved she chose to be detested.

In mid-November Caro threatened to appear at Eywood, Lady Oxford's house. By November 16 she and her mother were back in England, and she announced that she would write to Lord Oxford, in which case, Byron was sure Lord Oxford would write to William Lamb. "If so—there will be a pretty scene; we had some difficulty to prevent this once before. . . . He [i.e., William Lamb] is tolerably obstinate, and it would be as well not to bring it to the proof."

Brocket Hall in Hertfordshire had been in the possession of the Lambs since the days of William's grandfather, Sir Matthew, and when Caro was there once more in December, she staged a pathetically futile revenge. On the grounds she erected a pyre containing copies of Byron's letters to her, a miniature portrait of him, one of his publications, his ring and other mementoes, dressed up some village girls in white, and had them dance around the flames as she ignited the fire, while, herself in a page's uniform, she recited verses composed for the occasion:

> Is this Guy Faux you burn in effigy?
> Why bring the Traitor here? What is Guy Faux to me?
> Guy Faux betrayed his country, and its laws.
> England revenged the wrong; his was a public cause.
> But I have private cause to raise this flame.
> Burn also those, and be their fate the same . . .

Here she placed the basket of memories under an effigy of Byron.

> Burn, fire, burn; these glittering toys destroy . . .
> Ah! look not thus on me, so grave, so sad;
> Shake not your heads, nor say the Lady's mad . . .
> London, farewell! vain world, vain life, adieu!
> Take the last tears I e'er shall shed for you.
> Young tho' I seem, I leave the world for ever,
> Never to enter it again—no, never—never!

She did attempt to kill herself.

Nevertheless, soon after this auto-da-fé she was sending Byron a banker's draft for money she insisted she owed him. He was equally positive she did not, and returned it.

3.

LADY OXFORD, THOUGH THE DAUGHTER OF A CLERGYMAN, WAS REMARK-
able even in that age of license, for her libertarian life. She was well known
for her consecration to radical thought and reform, though she was rather
more devoted to the radicals and reformers than to the thought or the reform. Forty when Byron was twenty-four, she had had a great many lovers.
Her first was Sir Francis Burdett, with whom her husband, Edward Harley,
fifth Earl of Oxford, had had the indiscretion to leave her alone in the
country for a week. She confessed the transgression to her spouse, and because she was so completely frank he forgave her. Thereafter she felt she
had established a tradition for transgressing frequently with various liberal
leaders—one at a time, since she was a respectable woman—who fathered
upon her a succession of lovely children known in her circle as the "Harleian Miscellany."

Byron had frequently been seen at her parties during the summer of
1812. Toward the end of October he had gratefully accepted her invitation
to come to Eywood; the calm life there had been a welcome contrast to the
hectic capers of Caroline. He was not only able to relax in Lady Oxford's
tactful, undemanding surrender, but also took great pleasure in the company
of her beautiful young daughters.

Lady Oxford equally pleased with her beautiful young poet, had
observed to him, "Have we not passed our last months like the gods of
Lucretius?" She was a devotee of the classics. Byron had agreed and stayed
on. She assumed too much, however, in supposing that he was in total
accord with her politics, as he confided to Lady Melbourne, to whom he
relayed the information that she was given to tiresome sermons on her own
innocence, in which he did not quite believe. But on the whole, he was
diverted at Eywood and boasted of a rare "phenomenon": he had not yawned
once during the last two months. In December there was talk of their taking
a trip to Sicily in the spring.

But the relationship was not always Olympian in tranquillity. That
was not in Byron's nature to permit. The Princess of Wales, for instance,
had occasion to be witness to his testiness with his inamorata, and later to
find her in an anteroom weeping bitterly.

Suddenly he was again in communication with his sister, whom he had
not seen since before leaving on his Eastern tour. In March of 1813 he
wrote her: "I am going abroad in June, but should wish to see you before
my departure. You have perhaps heard that I have been fooling away my
time with different 'regnantes'; but what better can be expected from me? I
have but one relative, and her I never see."

In April it seemed as if Byron had made his contribution in adding a new member to Lady Oxford's "Harleian Miscellany," but the symptoms turned out to be false.

Meanwhile Lady Caroline had been doing what she could to break the comparative peace he was enjoying. She had her servants outfitted with new buttons on their uniforms, engraved with an alteration of the Byron motto, *Crede Byron*, to *Ne Crede Byron*. In January of 1813 she wrote him to say that she had broken all but the sixth and ninth commandments, and threatened to break them too. She continued to make scenes, and her hysterics had been brought to the attention of the Earl of Oxford's mother and unmarried sister, and they were quick to warn the Earl of what must be expected from his wife's "guest," whose cast-off mistress was so eager for trouble.

Caro herself was determined to use every avenue of approach to force Byron to see her again. She also insisted that it was necessary for her to see Lady Oxford too. Hoping to awaken again a romantic idea of her, she pressed him to let her have a lock of his hair as a memento; he sent her one of Lady Oxford's. Finally, to avoid becoming enmeshed herself, the mistress of Eywood counseled her lover to see Lady Caroline alone, and have done with the matter—as though it were possible ever to have done with Caro. Lady Bessborough personally lectured Byron for masquerading before Lady Melbourne as a "sober, quiet, Platonic" man, and then idiotically accused him of being deficient in "Romance." As for this poor befuddled woman, Byron ranked her as "next to a breast of veal, an earwig, and her own offspring, amongst my antipathies."

In his thoughts of abroad, he confessed being torn among three plans: to accompany Lady Oxford to Italy; to go off again to the Middle East with Sligo; or to join Hobhouse on a tour of Russia and the East. In the meantime he was hiring "doctors, painters, and two or three stray Greeks" then in England, as well as a former member of Napoleon's Mameluke Guard, and was measuring them for uniforms, shoes, and inexpressibles.

In April 1813 he was again vowing never to open a letter from Caro. He could feel only "detestation" and "utter abhorrence" of her; she had poisoned his whole future. "I know not whom I may love, but to the latest hour of my life I shall hate that woman." These sentiments he expected to carry to the grave. Despite her insistence, he wished to be spared seeing her again until they might "be chained together in Dante's Inferno." In a new letter, Lady Caroline opened with flattery, and closed by calling him "the greatest villain that ever existed."

Shortly thereafter, promising to haunt him with her ghost, she pressed once more for a meeting. On May 2 he sent an answer via her mother-in-law: if the opposition of her friends could not dissuade her from a meeting, he acquiesced "with reluctance." Aware that she thirsted for revenge, he believed her quite capable of carrying out her threats. "Perhaps I deserve punishment; if so, you are quite as proper a person to inflict it as any other." She had said she had the means to ruin him. He had saved her the trouble by having done it for himself. She had threatened to destroy him. That she was welcome to do and spare him the effort. His intention of leaving England was largely due to her persecutions and to the gossip she had been sponsoring. She had everywhere belied and betrayed him; yet in the end she had hurt only herself. He agreed to a meeting, then, provided Lady Oxford was no longer bothered. "The sooner it is over the better."

The meeting was in May. Lady Caroline's account of it is, as ever, vivid enough. "He asked me to forgive him; he looked sorry for me; he cried. I adored him still, but I felt as passionless as the dead may feel.— Would I had died there!—I should have died pitied, & still loved by him, & with the sympathy of all. I even should have pardoned myself—so deeply had I suffered. But unhappily, we continued occasionally to meet."

It is true that over the next few years her conduct would successfully deprive her of nearly everyone's sympathy as well as the pity, which surely she merits, of all but a few. There seems no doubt that her account of that meeting is honest enough. Despite the harshness of his letters, Byron by his own admission would do anything to avoid a scene—as would most men. Doubtless his distaste for her, too, as expressed to her mother-in-law was something of a pose. He was essentially kind and courteous with everyone face to face, and he may very well have been touched by the intensity of her love.

After that meeting, she assumed that he was going to carry out his announced purpose of going abroad, and she wrote him under that supposition: "You have raised me from despair to the joy we look for in Heaven. Your seeing me has undone me for ever . . . you love me still." His eyes and looks proved as much. How could he now give her up if she was still so dear to him? "Take me with you—take me, my master." Ah, but he was probably already gone from England. If only, she concluded, he had killed her before leaving!

Lady Oxford was not unaffected by these proceedings; she burst a blood vessel, was quite weak, and blamed her illness on Byron and his "friends in town." He foresaw that this was the beginning of the end, which, he knew, "would eventually be a great *relief*" to both her and himself.

At the end of the month she was in London too. The day before she arrived in town he could say, "I have no attachment within these two thousand miles," though, he added portentously, referring to the East, to which his thoughts were turning, "I feel some old ones reviving." Lady Oxford's presence in London he regretted; after all they had "fairly parted." Nevertheless, early in June he accompanied her, eventually to Portsmouth, the first piece of their projected journey to Italy. But Lord Oxford at last attempted a stand against the notoriety of his wife and her lover's public relationship; in short order the Earl was suitably placated by his lady; Byron, it was agreed, would for appearance's sake sail after they did. The poet returned to London.

On June 27 he wrote again to Augusta: "If you like to go with me to yᵉ Lady Davy's tonight, I *have* an invitation for you. . . . I will watch over you as if you were unmarried and in danger of always being so. Now do as you like; but if you chuse to array yourself before or after half past ten, I will call for you. I think our being together before 3ᵈ people will be a new *sensation* to *both*."

The next day the Oxfords departed for the continent. Byron never followed them. Such was, in effect, the end of his affair with Lady Oxford. He asked Lady Melbourne not to mention her name again during his remaining weeks in England—he was so sure of going off himself—and admitted feeling "more *Carolinish* about her" than he had anticipated.

William Lamb had now rejoined his wife, found her weeping, and demanded to know whether Byron had affronted her—at least, so Caro told the tale. This was all too ridiculous for her ex-lover to bear: "If I *speak* to her *he* is insulted; if I *don't* speak to her, she is insulted."

4.

CONTINUING HIS SOCIAL WHIRL, HE COULD NOT AVOID ENCOUNTERING her at various gatherings. On July 5 they met at Lady Heathcote's, where Caro enacted a choice piece of histrionics. Surrounded by a crowd of people, he asked her courteously, according to one version of what happened, whether there was anything he could do to please her. Her answer was to turn away without a word. Presently on the threshold of the room where supper was to be served they met again. She seized his hand and pressed a sharp tool against his palm, whispering that she meant to put it to use. He trembled lest she be overheard by the lady he was escorting and by other guests nearby, and walked, shaking, into the room. After the repast they arrived at the doorway again at the same instant, and he suggested that it would be wise for her to waltz now, so that no one might imagine she was refraining for his sake.

Her recollection of that terrible night follows a different sequence and is more dramatic: "He had made me swear I was never to Waltz. Lady Heathcote said, Come, Lady Caroline, you must begin, & I bitterly answered —oh yes! I am in a merry humour. I did so—but whispered to Lord Byron

'I conclude I may walze [sic] now' and he answered sarcastically, 'with every body in turn—you always did it better than any one. I shall have a pleasure in seeing you.'—I did so you may judge with what feelings. After this, feeling ill, I went into a small inner room where supper was prepared; Lord Byron & Lady Rancliffe entered after; seeing me, he said, 'I have been admiring your dexterity.' I clasped a knife, not intending anything. 'Do, my dear,' he said. 'But if you mean to act a Roman's part, mind which way you strike with your knife—be it at your own heart, not mine—you have struck there already.' 'Byron,' I said, and ran away with the knife. I never stabbed myself [as it was soon generally rumored]. It is false. Lady Rancliffe & Tankerville screamed and said I would; people pulled to get it from me; I was terrified; my hand got cut, & the blood came over my gown. I know not what happened after. . . . Still, in spight of every one, William Lamb had the generosity to retain me. I never held my head up after—never could. It was in all the papers, and put not truly."

The Satirist, which had ridiculed Byron's first volume but praised Childe Harold, devoted an article to the event, with the motto,

With horn-handled knife,
To kill a tender lamb as dead as mutton.

After mentioning "Lord B-n, Lady W-. and Lady C. L-b" as among the guests at the party, it went on to say: "Lord B., it would appear, is a favourite with the latter Lady; on this occasion, however, he seemed to lavish his attention on another fair object. This preference so enraged Lady C.L. that, in a paroxysm of jealousy, she took up a dessert-knife, and stabbed herself . . . 'Better be with the dead than thus,' cries the jealous fair; and, casting a languishing look at Lord B—, who, Heaven knows, is more like Pan than Apollo, she whipt up as pretty a little dessert-knife as a Lady could desire to commit suicide with, 'And stuck it in her wizzard.' The desperate Lady was carried out of the room, and the affair endeavored to be hushed up."

The fact is that Byron was not a witness to the bloodletting, and not until later in the morning did he learn that a scandal had occurred, and even then was not given the exact details. What they precisely were is not decipherable. Soon Lady Caroline was telling Tom Moore that all that had happened was that she had broken a scent or laudanum bottle, which gave her a small cut; some blood squirted on Lady Ossulston's gown, and that it was which gave rise to the tale of attempted suicide. Lady Melbourne, however, said that her daughter-in-law had gashed herself with a broken drinking glass and then tried to make a deeper cut with a pair of scissors.

If the general reaction was that this time Lady Caroline had exceeded the limits of the permissible, more, much more offense to good taste was in the offing. To her potential wildness there were actually no bounds. Lady Melbourne, full of foreboding, wrote, "She is now like a Barrel of Gunpowder." The talk of this melodrama penetrated even into the country. The Duchess of Beaufort declared that she would pity Lady Caroline if it were possible to forget how Lady Bessborough must be feeling about the incident. "These tales of horror strike me I assure you with aggravated terror in the country where only imperfect reports reach one. . . . The recollection of this poor l^y. Caroline & her afflicted friends will continue to haunt me night & day." One does not know, of course, whether the Duchess was more disturbed because of the afflicted friends or because she had not been able to get the actual facts straight.

5.

BYRON CONTINUED TO INSIST THAT HE WAS THROUGH WITH LADY Caroline; their love affair had been but an episode, and the episode was ended. Wishful thinking. For all the harassments, which were not to cease while he remained in England, he was soon reflecting that his temperament found satisfaction in danger, and in that respect Caro might have suited him well. Then he drew himself up short with the sobering thought: "But though we admire *drams* nobody is particularly fond of *aqua fortis.*"

He kept assuring himself that he loathed her, but was there not some regret that he should feel he *must* hate her? The need to be loved was deep in him, and he knew that, however mad, she loved him with a monomania.

One year after she had received his letter with Lady Oxford's seal, she wrote to Murray: "What I have suffered since, I hope will atone in part for all my guilt." She spoke of her husband as her "best and only friend, . . . one whose goodness no words of mine can describe." While the world continued to censure her, he had been superior to everybody in nobility of spirit and generosity. This was November 11, 1813.

On November 22 Byron was telling her mother-in-law that "C. has at last done a good-natured thing." He had asked for the return of Holmes's miniature of him which he had once given her, and which he now wished to give *"a friend leaving England."* (He did not mention that the friend was another woman, Lady Frances Webster.) Surprisingly, Caro had obliged.

This was a curious way to assure his breaking all contact with her. She, in any case, was never to be through with him. During the ensuing year, while he was intermittently courting Miss Milbanke, and having a succession of affairs with others including his sister, Lady Caroline did not slacken her delirious pressure on him, alternating resignation with wild demands, humbleness with fury. Once she would write him that they must meet no more, and, having heard some gossip about him and Augusta, begged him to tell her "to try & not dislike me." Next, she would salute him as "Mefistocles [sic]," Richard III, Valmont (of Les Liaisons dangereuses), and the wicked Duke of Orleans (well known to have been a flagrant pederast)—and then append that he also reminded her of Lancaster the educator and the actor Kean in the role of Othello, both remarkable for their ugliness—and after that promising beginning proceed to write him a passionate love letter, wherein she declared him to be without equal on earth.

About this time Byron was having bad dreams. "Such a dream!—but she did not overtake me. I wish the dead would rest, however. [Had the nightmare been about his mother?] Ugh! how my blood chilled,—and I could not wake . . . Am I to be shaken by shadows? Ay, when they remind us of—no matter. . . . I must not dream again; it spoils even reality."

Early in 1814 Lady Caroline was writing: "Lord Byron injures himself . . . by not knowing how to command his tongue. [She was referring to the notes and prefaces to his recent poems.] I sometimes think his own words too true—he has many flatterers but few real friends." She had not heard from him since he sent for the miniature. "No one names him to me now." She was determined not to show herself anywhere where there was a chance of meeting him. "I have suffered cruelly at his hands for whom I incurred such guilt. . . . Think what it is for a woman to bear who, from the language of idolatry and confidence, is all at once betrayed, taunted, exposed to all, and made hateful even to her nearest friends."

Lady Caroline, like Vladimir de Pachmann in our century, was always making her final farewells, and in March 1814 she wrote Byron: "Thanks for your goodness to me . . . Thanks too for your patience and forgiveness in many trying scences. Even thanks for your cruelty as it has humbled a very proud and vain character whom none but you dared contend with before."

A month later Lady Melbourne had wrung a promise from her that when she and Byron should happen to meet, it would be as with any two other persons in their circle who met casually. Lady Caroline agreed—provided that he behaved "properly." He felt, too, that there was no reason for their biting each other when they found themselves together under the same roof. Touched, he saw her several times again, secretly. The result: in the summer of 1814 she began to appear at his living quarters at the Albany, unannounced. It was inevitable that his pity should revert to disgust. Lady Melbourne urged him to keep her out. That was impossible, he replied; she came whenever she wished and he could not throw her out his windows. He felt himself her prisoner, and she knew no shame in hounding him this way. He began to resort to bolts and bars on his door, but she would walk in the minute his door was open.

Elizabeth, wife of the first Viscount Melbourne, Byron's favorite correspondent during the years of his difficulties with Lady Caroline and of his negotiations for marriage with Annabella, Lady Melbourne's niece. (Courtesy of the Most Honourable the Marquess of Lothian.)

One day when she had thus intruded, she found him not at home. A copy of *Vathek* was in evidence, and on its flyleaf she wrote: "Remember me!" When he returned and read her two words, he rapidly composed beneath them:

> Remember thee, remember thee!
> Till Lethe quench life's burning stream,
> Remorse and shame shall cling to thee,
> And haunt thee like a feverish dream!
>
> Remember thee! Ay, doubt it not,
> Thy husband too shall think of thee;
> By neither shalt thou be forgot,
> Thou *false* to him, thou *fiend* to me!

She never saw these verses until Medwin published them shortly after Byron's death.

Gossip was now generating on his intention of marrying. Caro wrote Murray that when the day of the wedding arrived, "I shall buy a pistol at Manton's and stand before the Giaour and his legal wife and shoot myself, saying . . . that as I must not live for him, I will die."

When in mid-September, Byron's engagement to Miss Milbanke was announced, instead of buying a pistol Caro sent him her best wishes: "Do you remember the first rose I gave you? The first rose you brought me is still in my possession . . . Now God bless you—may you be very happy. I love and honour you from my heart . . . as a sister feels—as your Augusta feels for you." (Was this last clause written in malice? At some time before his marriage, Caro knew that he had made his sister his mistress.)

To Murray she expressed too the hope that Byron would be happy; the wife he had chosen deserved the best he could give. "It is his last chance of keeping clear of what has too often led him astray." (In these mysterious words was she thinking of his boy loves?) Did Murray know, she asked, her cousin Annabella? "She is very learned and very good, and the top of her face is handsome." This may seem to be damning with faint praise, but in point of beauty Miss Milbanke hardly merited greater.

Shortly after his marriage to Annabella, Lady Melbourne took Caro at Byron's request to see them in Piccadilly. She thought the invitation cruel but she went. "I never looked up," she reported; "Annabella was very cold to me; Lord Byron came in and seemed agitated [that word again!]— his hand was cold, but he seemed kind." One is free to speculate on his possible reasons for wanting her to visit them.

She summarized for Murray Byron's chances for felicity: "He has not a noble heart." There was in it "a black speck" which would show itself in time. As for Annabella, of whom Murray had spoken with enthusiasm, she was pure, sensible, and intelligent, but as for playfulness! "It must be the dance of an elephant." For Byron, Caro says, misquoting Shakespeare, if his sins, like Lady Macbeth's, could be washed away by "all the syrups of the East and all the waters of the ocean," she herself might bow to her "sometime idol . . . in spight of wife and Six-mile Bottom [where Augusta lived]." The last phrase again implies that she knew of the incest.

Within not more than a year the marriage proved a failure, and after the separation Caro and he met once more in his chambers at the Albany before he left England forever. "As he pressed his lips on mine, he said, 'Poor Caro, if everyone hates me, you, I see, will never change . . . and I said, 'Yes, I *am* changed, and shall come near you no more.' For then he showed me letters and told me things I cannot repeat, and all my attachment went."

He had, in fact, already told her things and possibly shown her letters damaging to himself, and he had, before he went into exile, no suspicion that she was already engaged at the time of their parting in venomous work and the pursuit of his destruction. We have yet to trace the tangled love and hate which tortured her into contriving deadly mischief against him and helping to put him in his separated wife's power.

In this place it is apropos to consider her novel *Glenarvon,* part revenge, part adulation, part self-justification, and part self-immolation, which she had begun to write two years earlier (though she always claimed vaingloriously that she had composed it in a mere month). It appeared on May 9, 1816, when Byron was already in exile, and she had done all she could behind the scenes to ruin him. It is odd that the book has received scant notice from nearly all his biographers, even from Professor Marchand in his admirable three-volume work on the poet's life and career—but, then, the documents and letters pertaining to Byron are so extensive in quantity that no one can include everything. That *Glenarvon* is a trial to read is conceded, for no novel was ever more monotonously high pitched in tone. Its inflated emotionalism is as wearying as its repetitiousness. Yet for several reasons it is high time that it be given some particular attention.

First of all, it afforded Lady Caroline a chance to portray Byron as she either knew him or thought him to be. The character she gave him was assuredly the essential Byron he wished the world to believe he was. Beyond this, the novel is revelatory of her own obsession and his cruelty to her, of her rashness, of her husband's prolonged indifference. Most of all, one understands how Caro thought of herself as the romantic heroine without any notion of how absurd she was. Her self-portrait was softened by making her Calantha, who was everywhere known to be herself, whatever her flippancies, a staunch defender of her technical virtue; she is always on the point of committing adultery without ever actually surrendering her body to her lover.

One day at Coppet, Mme. de Staël asked Byron whether he was not the original of Glenarvon. "He answered cooly, *'C'est possible, Madame, mais je n'ai jamais posé.'* " But for all the exaggeration, there was more than a little truth in the portraiture; Glenarvon is certainly another Byronic hero—and therefore quintessentially the public Byron. The same year of its publication Claire Clairmont, mother of Byron's illegitimate daughter, wrote to him about the book: "Some of the speeches are yours I am sure they are: the very impertinent way of looking in a person's face who loves you & telling them you are very tired & wish they'd go." She had good cause to know.

Byron himself, in reading *Glenarvon* with his traveling companion, Dr. Polidori, "pointed out the places that were exact, and those that were gently painted."

As befitting a novel with such a hero, its three volumes are filled with Gothic trappings: somber rocks, broken colonnades and arches, and whistling winds. Glenarvon makes but a brief appearance in the first volume. When still a boy, his heart is already "but too well inclined" to misuse his rare natural gifts. In Florence he falls in love with a great beauty; in vengeance her husband kills her. The youth disappears at once—from Florence and the first volume until its concluding pages. (Was Caro hesitating as to whether she dare depict Byron at all?)

The scene shifts to Ireland. There we meet the orphaned daughter of the Duchess of Altamonte, Calantha (Lady Caroline), left to the care of her father, who pampers her. "Thoughts, swift as lightning, hurried through her brain:—projects, seducing, but visionary crowded upon her view: without a curb she followed the impulse of her feelings." Presently she falls in love with the Earl of Avondale (William Lamb). Everyone adores her; he succumbs too. They marry. He makes a perfect husband and is enslaved to her. Soon the oversophisticated society in which they move begins to undermine the purity of her thoughts. She is mad about dancing.

Glenarvon is suddenly heard from again as the author of a seditious pamphlet. Mrs. Seymour (Lady Bessborough?) denounces him as "a dishonour to his sex" and is furious to see "how you all run after him." Lady Mandeville (Lady Oxford) concedes, however, that though "his stature is small," his "eye is keen and his voice is sweet and tunable"; she warns Calantha that he is dangerous.

In the second volume Calantha, visiting an old castle, comes upon a youth leaning against a tree and playing a sweet melody on a flute "as if from a suffering heart." ... The proud curl of the upper lip reveals "haughtiness and bitter contempt," though an "air of melancholy and dejection" softens the harshness. In that flash of time Calantha knows she will forever feel the power of this young man. He is, of course, Glenarvon (Byron).

Abroad he has given himself day and night "to every fierce excess" until his sense of honor is debased. A rebel, he insists just the same upon being called by his title and is very "jealous of his rank." He has returned to Ireland with his page, O'Kelly. He has seen the dying and the dead and "the tear of agony" without emotion; he has known what it is to murder an enemy without compunction; he has been unmoved even by the tempests of nature. He prefers venturing forth on stormy nights to watch the "forked lightening [*sic*]."

Lovely Elinor, but sixteen, "the pride of her family, the wonder and ornament of the whole country," has forsaken her "hopes of heaven" to become his mistress, and follows him in the attire of a boy. What is to become of her when Glenarvon tires of her? "Did he love?—Never: in the midst of conquests, his heart was desolate; in the fond embrace of mutual affection, he despised the victim of his art." And everywhere new beauties attract his attention and yield to him. He soothes Elinor with promises while seeking to be rid of her. (Elinor is obviously also an extension of Lady Caroline.) Love with him is an art; a skilled flatterer, he knows how to conquer the female heart. However, his ability to please is exceeded by "the venomed lash of his deadly wit."

At a dinner Calantha and Glenarvon at last meet formally. Her husband asks her if she is ill: she feels a rush of pain and joy at seeing this man, who takes no part in the conviviality. His "pale cheek and brow" show "disappointed hope"; his boyish air affects gaiety, but his laughter is forced. This is the same flute player she once saw. At his surpassing beauty Calantha trembles, but though fascinated she recognizes that he is evil, that his charm has something of the rattlesnake overpowering a bird.

That night she gazes upon the sleeping form of her husband, reflects on how long and well she has loved him, but realizes that when those eyes awake, "they will not look for me." She blames him for neglecting her and leaving her to her wicked thoughts.

The next afternoon Glenarvon plucks a rose and gives it to her, saying (more or less what Byron had said to Caro), "I offer it to you because the rose at this season is rare, and all that is new or rare has for a moment, I believe, some value in your estimation." He succeeds in winning over everyone in the party, even Calantha's aunt, Mrs. Seymour. Calantha is haunted by his image; she feels herself "on the very edge" of a "bottomless chasm." Now he has become the favorite guest, coming and going as suits his fancy. One day he sits next to her and assures her, "My only inducement in coming here was you . . . If you dance, when you dance, I shall retire." (This is in accord with Byron's early courtship.) Presently she is dancing to the admiration of all onlookers. During an interval he approaches her and hints that she is causing him much suffering. She turns away, and he cries, "Dance on then, Lady Avondale, . . . the easy prey of every coxcomb to whom that ready hand is so continually offered." He accuses her of dancing only to torment him. She insists he is wrong; he asks for the rose she is wearing in exchange for the one he gave her. The whole assembly watches as he presses the rose to his lips until "all its blushing beauties" are gone, and then casts it to "the earth to be trampled upon by many." The history of that rose is a prophecy of Calantha's fate.

Still in love with her husband, she nevertheless has violent scenes with him, aware that he prefers being blind to the misuse she makes of her liberty. Neglected, she feels that she has again found her lost happiness in Glenarvon. But if ardent one night, he is frigid the next morning. She blames only herself for imagining that he cares for her. One day in the library he comes upon her reading; he bends over her and begins to read the poetry, which is almost as "beautiful as his own," and recites the lines most stirringly. He takes her hand, brings it to his lips, and says, "Fly me . . . To look upon me is in itself pollution to one like you." (From here on Caro starts to ennoble and sentimentalize her own character.) He then begins to praise her husband, "He is as superior to me as Hyperion to a satyr." She admits loving her husband and that her love is returned more than she deserves. Glenarvon goes on: "I can never love again . . . for I am cold as the grave—as death; and all here," pressing her hand to his heart, "is chilled." He pities her for her infatuation with him—"poor little thing that seeks to destroy itself."

Later he tells her: "You love your husband . . . but if I wished it, your eyes already tell me what power I have gained;—I could do what I would."

He confesses that he hides a terrible secret. (By the time the novel was published Byron had told Caro about the incest.) When it weighs upon him his gestures are terrifying; he talks to the air, laughs "with convulsive horror," gazes "wildly around." After such moments he weeps, calls her his only friend, and speaks of happier days. One fatal day he seizes her with violence, demands her love, and cries, "You must be mine! . . . I love you to madness." He has but few years to live, he knows, and it is in her power not to shorten them. Admitting her passion for him, she begs him to "spare" her and to allow her to be his friend. He promises.

At home she is treated with coolness. Only Lady Mandeville (Oxford) is sympathetic. Glenarvon tells Calantha that he "must be obeyed. You will find me a master—a tyrant perhaps." He will tolerate no rivals. The only chains must be those of his bestowing. Mrs. Seymour angrily assures him that Calantha is too chaste ever to abandon Avondale. Glenarvon leaves in a temper, and sends Mrs. Seymour a letter Calantha has written him. Feeling betrayed, Calantha vows to end their relationship. When next they talk she demands the reason for his treachery. He answers that he was wounded, and wished the whole world to know she loves him. She declares herself free of him, but he smiles scornfully, says, "You shall be my slave. I will mould you as I like," and symbolically throws a chain around her. Now she is happy that he loves her so much.

Elinor, his cast-off mistress, appears at the castle to return a miniature he has given her so he can give it to Calantha. (This was no doubt inspired by Byron's asking for the miniature he destined for Lady Webster.) After Elinor gallops off, he remarks cynically that he more merits pity than Elinor: "She absolutely forced herself upon me. She sat at my door, and wept when I urged her to return home. What could I do? . . . It is not in man's nature to resist." (This certainly sounds very much like Byron on the subject of Caro's pursuit of him.)

By this time it is obvious that our author is determined her readers should be convinced that however indiscreet Lady Caroline Lamb may have been, she had never surrendered her virtue to Byron. There follow endless passages in which Glenarvon reiterates his knowledge that she is his slave and hints that he can take her when he likes. But he never does. He concentrates on trying to get her to elope with him. She fears that should he demand it she will have to go with him. Now Glenarvon opens to her "the dark recesses of his heart; deeds of guilt concealed from other eyes" he dwells upon "with horrid pleasure." (Byron's escapades in the Orient and Greece, which he seems to have told Lady Caroline, confident as he was that he could make her accept the duality of his nature? And, too, the incest? It will been seen presently that she knew a great deal of both matters.) He bids her not shrink, as she trembles at each relevation: "Proud, even of my crimes, shalt thou become, poor victim of thy mad infatuation; this is the man for whom thou leavest Avondale! . . . Weep, I like to see your tears; they are the last tears of expiring virtue."

He suddenly announces that he is quitting Ireland, and cries: "I must make you mine before we part: then I will trust you, but not till then. . . . Give yourself to me: this hour be mine." But his page, O'Kelly, interrupts them with the information that they are being watched and had better return to the castle. Calantha's virtue is saved again.

"Driven to despair—guilty in all but the last black deed that brands the name and character with eternal infamy," Calantha resolves to follow her lover. One by one he betrays to her the windings of his mind as well as the confidences others have entrusted to him. She learns of the terrible fate of another abandoned mistress, Alice; on the last night with this unfortunate girl Glenarvon was most tender; he gave her a sleeping potion; she awoke to find him fled. Later he sent men to tear his child from her. (It is interesting that although the novel was published before Byron's child Allegra was born, he was to behave somewhat similarly about the infant.)

Lady Margaret warns Calantha that Glenarvon "is little, contemptible and mean. He unites the malice and petty vices of a woman, to the perfidy and villany [*sic*] of a man." Finally convinced that she is now despised by everybody, Calantha flees from the castle. (The episode probably corresponds to Caro's flight from Melbourne House when she intended to leave the country.) Generally it is thought that she has eloped with Glenarvon.

Volume three finds her at a vicar's house nearby, where she has taken refuge (as Caro did in the house of a surgeon). Glenarvon finds her and takes her home (as Byron did Caro). He places her in the hands of Mrs. Seymour, saying: "I give to you what is dearer to me, far dearer than existence [as Byron surely never said to Lady Bessborough]." But when leaving he whispers to Calantha that he has been playacting to keep the family quiet; he will see her tomorrow. The next day, finding her weeping, he sneers: "Once you were pure and spotless; and then, indeed, was the time for tears; but not now!"

Glenarvon leaves for England and writes frequently in terms teeming with passion. He hopes they can elope in the spring. She may hear that he has been seeing her relative Miss Monmouth (Annabella Milbanke), but she cannot compare with his beloved Calantha; he swears he is not serious about the other young woman. Nevertheless, Lady Trelawney (Lady Melbourne) writes to Calantha's family that he has proposed marriage to Miss Monmouth and will probably be accepted. Calantha is not to know, for Glenarvon has shown Lady Trelawney her letters to him (as Byron had sent Lady Caroline's to her mother-in-law quite regularly), and she fears the girl's violence.

Suddenly all communications from him cease. Calantha writes him in gentle reproof for his silence. The next day she herself hears from Lady Trelawney that he declared "that a *grande passion* bores him to death. . . . Have enough pride to shew him that you are not so weak and so much in his power as he imagines." Calantha refuses to credit her. Wherever she goes, everyone cuts her. She continues to write him without ever being answered. At length there arrives the letter (which Byron admitted is more or less the letter he wrote Caro), announcing that he is no longer her lover and is attached to another; he calls her ridiculous and bids her exert her caprices on other people. "This letter was sealed and directed by Lady Mandeville [Oxford], but the hand that wrote it was Lord Glenarvon's."

Calantha thinks of suicide but fears death. All interest in life deserts her and she is overwhelmed by a sort of madness.

Glenarvon goes to stay with the Monmouths in the country (as Byron did with the Milbankes), and takes Lady Mandeville completely into his confidence (as Byron did Lady Melbourne). He jeers at Calantha's misery (as Byron did at Caro's).

The innocent Miss Monmouth, an only child, is at first suspicious of her suitor because of all the rumors current about him; but soon she finds herself fascinated by him like everyone else. Glenarvon lays siege to her heart and tells her that she alone can "reform him" (an argument which, in fact, Byron used to persuade Annabella to marry him). To reclaim a genius she admires seems to the unsophisticated girl "a task too delightful to be rejected." Suddenly he receives a letter which unnerves him, and he leaves for Italy.

Calantha's husband upbraids her for betraying his trust, though "they say you are not yet guilty." He decides that they must part. She swears that she is still guiltless of adultery, and reminds him of how much he loved her once. Though moved he is relentless. Realizing the harm she has done him, when he leaves the castle she follows him. Very ill, she arrives in a town at the inn where he is staying. She calls for him. Astounded that she is dying, he begs her to live, swearing he will take her back. It is too late. Calantha dies.

Grief-stricken, Avondale pursues Glenarvon bent on revenge, catches up with him in Ireland, and challenges him to a duel. But Glenarvon plunges a dagger into Avondale and severely wounds him. Glenarvon reflects: "I could have loved that man." He learns of Calantha's death and sails for England to be married.

Avondale dies of his wound. Glenarvon, now in the Royal Navy, is haunted by Avondale, whose shape comes toward him over the waves. He falls into a troubled sleep and relives the events of his brief life, and thinks of his betrayals and treacheries. At the third watch, Calantha's shade, "clothed in angelic beauty and unearthly brightness," appears before him, and speaks to him. She comes not to reproach him, but to save him. He asks, "Is Glenarvon dear even thus in death?" At these words, she becomes as pale as when last they parted, throws him a mournful look, and fades from sight.

After a battle in which Glenarvon inspires his men to victory, he takes ill, suffers delusions, and becomes absolutely mad. He plunges into the sea, but is rescued. Nevertheless, his end has come. As he closes his eyes in death, a loud and terrible voice seems to address him: "Hardened and impenitent sinner! the measure of your iniquity is full! . . . The axe of justice must fall!"

Thus, Lady Caroline, confusing herself with the Almighty, finally meted out just deserts to the Byron she hated and loved to the end.

How did William Lamb take this public exposure by his wife of her own shame—disgraceful enough even though Calantha was depicted, no doubt to the titters of members of their circle, as having technically avoided adultery? Lady Caroline tried to pretend to friends that he had enjoyed the novel very much. The truth is that, though her actions had not so moved him, he was crushed by the novel.

He had never been told a word about the undertaking during the two years she had labored over it, and was still in ignorance while others were hearing of its impending publication. Just before she sent it to be printed, Lady Jersey, one of the few true friends Byron still had, publicly snubbed her; Lady Caroline also had a dreadful scene with Lord Melbourne. Last to hear the news, William Lamb learned it the day before the novel appeared. He warned her: "I have stood your friend till now—I even think you ill used; but if it is true this novel is published, and as they say, against us all, I will never see you more."

It was too late. The book was out next day, and she presented him with the small richly gilt volumes, whose title page shows Love meditating upon a burning heart, with the motto: "*L'on a trop chéri.*" He read, was doubtless horrified, but continued to stand by her. If he did not divorce her, though he had every provocation to do so, it was, David Cecil suggests, because he felt guilty over his own earlier indifference to the life she had been leading. She herself summed up their relationship: "When I laugh, play, ride, and amuse him, he loves me, in sickness and sorrow he deserts me." All parties bore a share of the guilt.

For Byron Lady Caroline had a copy splendidly bound and stamped with his coronet and initials; on the flyleaf she inscribed a key to the characters. But she could not summon the courage ever to send it to him.

Besides, the sudden intervention of Hobhouse may have caused her to think twice. In May 1816, when Byron was already on the Continent and the novel had not been out long, John Cam wrote to Lady Melbourne threatening to counter *Glenarvon* by publishing letters Lady Caroline had written to her lover. Not at all intimidated, Caro herself answered him: She possessed, she assured him, in Byron's own hand a solemn declaration that he had burnt all she had written him. "Let him publish the tenth part of a single line in any letter I ever wrote him . . . and if I die for it I vow to God I will on the instant publish not only his, but the whole exact journal I have kept of my acquaintance with him." What more, she demanded, could she possibly have to lose now? Hobhouse was apparently silenced.

Soon she was asking Murray what Byron had to say of her novel. All there was to repeat was what Byron had said to Mme de Staël upon being questioned by her as to what he thought of the portrait Lady Caroline had drawn of him in her book: "*Elle aurait été plus ressemblante si j'avais voulu donner plus de séances.*" (It would have been more of a likeness had I been willing to sit for it longer.) On receiving Murray's reply Caro built another bonfire and burned on it every copy of her novel which she owned.

The book sold very well, but it received little notice from the press. The author could have been little gratified by the words of the *British Critic,* which knew that the author had made herself the heroine and that the hero was "a certain noble Lord." The critic wished to spare the public "the horror of reading one continuous series of vice and misery." It labeled the book as dangerous to the innocent because of "its scenes of seduction and adultery." Perhaps the author intended no evil "in thus publishing to the world her own shame," but "she appears to glory in her guilt." It was too dreadful to be assured that Glenarvon's character is a transcript of reality; the reviewer preferred to believe "such a monster were an illusion"—a man whose delight is "to seduce the innocent into guilt and then with cool and rancorous malignity to trample on the partners and victims of his crime." Divested of his malignancy, egocentricity and "theatrical misanthropy," what is left? "A languid, nerveless, insipid sensualist, who never said a good thing, nor ever did a wise one. Yet this is the creature, which is the idol of the female heart." Calantha herself is just a "very silly woman." In the novel "she expiated her crime indeed by death,"—but that, at least, does not correspond to the facts, for in actuality she, "we are informed, still lives."

If revenge was her chief motive Lady Caroline's publication of *Glenarvon* was perfectly timed. On its appearance Byron had left behind in England but few well-wishers. As the review indicates, the hounds were in full cry.

6.

AFTER THE PUBLICATION OF THE THIRD CANTO OF *Childe Harold,* she wrote to Murray, "Be not dazzled by his success. . . . Whenever he may speak of *himself* Lord Byron will succeed." He was no Homer, Dante, Milton, Spenser, or Tasso, she observed, who could write objectively. Above all, Murray was not to allow Byron's brilliance as a poet "make you forget what a rogue he is. . . . The sun may shine upon a bit of broken glass till it glitters like a diamond, but if you take it up you will only cut your fingers."

She began to drink far too often and too much, cognac by preference, and long-suffering William Lamb at length became disgusted with her. One day her maid overheard her insisting upon her right to come into his bed; she was, she reminded him, his lawful wife: why must she sleep alone? He answered angrily that he would be hanged before he would allow her to share his bed again, and urged her to retire quietly to her own. When she persisted, he cried: "Get along, you little drunken ——!" (We have been left to fill in the blank.)

Her quirks became increasingly intolerable. Once when the butler was arranging the table for a dinner party, she came in, observed what had been done, and remarked that the decor of the center lacked "expression and elevation." Agreeing with her ladyship, the butler continued laying the plate. Unexpectedly, she swept aside the ornaments, jumped on the table, and in its center assumed an attitude suggesting an épergne that did have expression and elevation. Alarmed, the butler ran into the library to fetch her husband. He dashed into the dining room, took her in his arms, admonishing her only with a gentle, "Caroline, Caroline," and carried her outdoors, where he spoke to her as though nothing extraordinary had occurred.

It would seem that the event which proved the one thing too much was a piece of violence exerted on a domestic. A boy, one of her pages, was given to throwing squibs into the fireplace to enjoy the explosion as the flames leapt; she had reprimanded him several times for the prank. One day as she was playing ball with him, the lad did it again. In a fit she threw the ball at his head. He screamed, "Oh, my lady, you have killed me." Her anger turned to terror, and she rushed into the hall shrieking, "O God, I've murdered the page!" The servants all heard her, as did passersby in the street. Another public scandal ensued. As she said in reminiscence of that day, "William Lamb would live with me no more."

The doctor was sent for to warn her about herself, and promised that if she continued her reckless behavior she might wind up in prison. At that she picked up a poker from the fireplace, and he himself had to flee.

In 1818 she wrote to Byron reminding him of how things had been between them six years earlier: "[In those days] I had the misfortune to consider you as the dearest friend I possessed on earth, when I had willingly died to serve you . . . you promised me . . . that whatever might happen, whatever my conduct might be, you would never cease to be my friend." She now begged his forgiveness. "I have sinned against every one on earth and against you—but from my soul I suffer for all I have done, and accuse no one but myself." Her husband, strange as it might appear, liked Byron, "and almost cries when he reads anything you have written."

If that was the truth—and one can never be sure about the truth of Lady Caroline's reports—William Lamb is more difficult to understand than his wife. If it is not the truth, then it merely proves that her affection for her husband was real enough, however odd, and that she wished Byron to think well of him.

Later that year she begged a friend of Byron's to tell her how he was, and whether he was ever going to return to England. "Though he has done so little to entitle him to happiness," she wished to hear only that he was happy and enjoying himself. She admitted he had been magnanimous to her. "He had the power to retaliate in such a manner that I could never have shown my face again. I was in his power. I have done every thing at every time to offend him most." Nobly he has refused to lift "up his sword to crush a fly."

The first two cantos of Byron's *Don Juan* were published on July 15, 1819. In this work Byron indisputably achieved his greatest stature, for at last he was writing in his own voice, with the energy, wit, and raciness which make his letters among the best in the language. Caro at once indulged in foolish competition with him. She published anonymously *A New Canto*, a highly ineffectual and confused would-be-satire of twenty-seven stanzas. It was absurd of her to think she could in any way diminish or share in his accomplishment with her own anemic verses. But here and there there are lines which are interesting as showing what was going on within her:

> A woman then may rail nor would I stint her;
> Her griefs, poor soul are past redress in law—.

She saw through Byron's pose of superciliousness:

> Mad world! for fame we rant, call names, and fight—
> I scorn it heartily, yet love to dazzle it.

The conclusion is malicious:

> For my part, though I'm doomed to write in rhyme,
> To read it could be worse than an emetic—
> But something must be done to cure the spleen,
> And keep my name in capitals, like Kean.

This sally, of course, made no impression on anyone. The next year this chameleon of a woman appeared at a masquerade at Almack's as Don Juan surrounded by a group of little devils—her pages, probably.

In 1820 there was talk that Byron was returning to England. Lady Caroline, under the misconception that Murray had gone to meet him, wrote to the publisher complaining that he had failed to give her an account of how Byron "looks, what he says, if he is grown fat," whether he is good natured or cross, still wears curls in his hair or, as rumor has it, now prefers to comb it straight, and whether he proposes to remain long.

In 1821, in a fit of despondency, she said of herself, "I am like the wreck . . . of a gay merry boat which perhaps stranded itself at Vauxhall or London Bridge." And in a surviving draft of a letter to a friend, she says that Byron ought to be the last man in the world to vilify her. If the public knew how he had treated her, that "might indeed harm him," but she had no intention of betraying him. (She had already managed to do that very well to Lady Byron.) *Glenarvon* may have been stupid and in bad taste, but it was not malevolent. Everyone, before its publication, was urging William Lamb to part from her, and Lord Melbourne ordered her out of his house. Was she not more worthy of pity than to be the object of universal reproof? She then makes several completely truthful allegations: "I have been insulted, my letters shown, my words misrepresented, my gifts offered and worn by such a woman as Lady Oxford." She herself, she concludes, may be guilty of much, but for Byron there could be no excuse.

Two years earlier there had occurred a trifling event which was later to blossom into an undignified, if brief, affair of hers. Edward Bulwer (the future Bulwer-Lytton) was a schoolboy of fifteen when he heard of a kind act of hers at some private races. According to him, she "set a noble example of humanity and feeling; when a poor man being much hurt, she had him conveyed to her carriage and interested herself most anxiously in his recovery." He wrote some verses on the subject and sent them to her. Pleased with them, she wrote his mother asking her to bring him over to Brocket. She took a fancy to him and painted a picture of him "as a child seated on a rock in the midst of the sea, with the motto under it, *Seul sur la terre.*" After that she saw little of him until 1824, when he was twenty.

It was in April of that year that Byron died in Greece. The news of his end was some time in reaching England. By ill luck, on July 12, 1824, while Lady Caroline was riding with her husband just outside the park gates of Brocket they met the cortège bearing Byron's body on its way to Hucknell Torkard. She fainted, and immediately lapsed into grave illness.

In the fall of that year, Bulwer, a pseudo Byron like all the literary young men of his generation, innocent but posing as blasé, was invited to Brocket for a week. His imagination was stirred by the thought that his hostess was a woman who had immolated herself on the altar of love for Byron, his own hero. At Brocket he at once fell under her spell. She was about forty at the time, and he later said of her that she "looked much younger than she was, thanks perhaps to a slight rounded figure and a childish mode of wearing her hair." Her laugh was delightful and her voice musical, despite her "artificial drawl, habitual to what was called the Devonshire House Set." She "never failed to please, if she chose to do so." He found her conversation fascinating, rapidly changing, as it did, from deep feeling to infantile nonsense; "it sparkled with anecdotes of the great world," then would become "gravely eloquent with religious enthusiasm" or shot through with "metaphysical speculations—sometimes absurd, sometimes profound," and all spoken in a soft, slightly lisping voice. She showed him a letter of Byron's which said, "You are the only woman I know who never bored me." No one was permitted to say a word against the dead poet. She herself spoke much of him and always without bitterness; her verdict on him was that on the whole he had been "lovable and noble."

Daily young Bulwer, in closer and closer intimacy with her, and convinced that she loved him, anticipated her giving herself to him. She even allowed him during his visit to wear the ring Byron had given her, though out of reverence for his hero and because "it was so costly," he refused to accept it when she offered to make him a gift of it. She sent him back to Cambridge with promises that his passion for her would be fulfilled.

During the next year its fires became more fervent, as it is likely to become, when a pair are sentimentalists, via correspondence. When she became ill again, she sent for him. He sat by her bedside and she was most tender.

On Christmas of 1825 he came again—only to find that he had been supplanted. Another youth, Russell, illegitimate son of the Duke of Bedford, had already achieved pride of place—and was wearing Byron's ring! (Among her last letters, those to Lady Morgan, Lady Caroline declared that in her love her husband stood first, her mother second, Byron third, her son fourth, and last, her *"petit* friend Russell . . . because he stood by me when no one else did.") Young Bulwer decided to leave Brocket at once, wrote her a note saying so, but the next morning received an urgent summons to her room. "She entreated me to forgive her, threw her arms about me and cried. Of course she persuaded me to stay."

But no evidence lacked that Russell was her "idol of the moment," and the other's vanity was deeply wounded at his having to accept her continued indifference. When she found Bulwer in tears, she mocked him with flippancies. Smarting under all the attention Russell was receiving, he presently was told that he must think of himself as her son, not her lover. He left "more in love with her than ever"—as young men are wont to be with the unattainable—but embittered.

This painful experience he made the subject of a youthful novel, *Rupert de Lindsay,* which he never finished. That same year his future wife, Rosina, met Lady Caroline at a party, and thereafter became inseparable from her. In January of 1826 Rosina wrote a friend that Lady Caroline "is the most fascinating, bewildering, attractive creature I ever knew—one of whom the more I know of her the more convinced I am she has been more sinned against than sinning." Luckless Bulwer! It was an evil chance, as Michael Sadleir observes, that he should choose for his wife "a girl who had passed through the irresponsible and youth-despoiling hands" of Lady Caroline, and therefore take unto himself "a poison which could never be eradicated." But that is another story.

7.

AFTER THE *succès* *de* *scandale* OF *Glenarvon,* WHICH LAUNCHED IT
into several printings in quick succession, in England and abroad, Lady
Caroline fancied herself as a novelist. She published a second novel, *Graham
Hamilton,* and in 1823 a third, *Ada Reis,* in which she reverted to a depiction of Byron. Surprisingly, John Murray, into whose good graces she
had insinuated herself, published it. Perhaps Murray had hoped for sizable
sales such as *Glenarvon* had had. He certainly had not in view his friendship for Byron or Lady Caroline's literary gifts, for none are to be seen in
Ada Reis. If he hoped for financial rewards he was doomed to disappointment, for the book had few readers, and has been totally ignored since—
even by Byron's biographers.

But its author was obviously unable to banish Byron from her mind,
even though he had by 1823 for seven years already banished himself.
Indeed, he was still so much of an obsession that in this novel she tried
portraying him in two different characters. Of course in the name of the
hero, Ada, she blatantly made use of the Byronic association; the literary
world well knew that it was the name he had given his daughter by Lady
Byron. Her intention was fortified by her description of her Ada as the
"Don Juan of his day." For some reason, however, having introduced a new
character, Count Condulmar, halfway through the first of the three volumes,
she then decided to concentrate upon him her vindictiveness against her
former lover.

Ada is made Reis to the Bey because of bravery; a man of vigorous
mind, at times rising to the sublime, he is "fond of low company." His
passions, "ungovernable beyond all control" betray him often "to the very
verge of madness." He is stubborn and violent, speaks Turkish and Greek
fluently (a reminder of Byron's travels) and receives universal attention—
from no one more than from himself. In his writings "upon that subject
he expatiates at the greatest length. He cannot for a moment cease to
commend himself." His auburn hair hangs "in curls over his fair brow
and neck" à la Byron; his smile is irresistible, his voice most melodious. He
acknowledges being a "strange compound of every excellence and every
vice." When offended, he becomes almost lunatic in violence, and his "dark
soul" rushes through his lips and pours forth in execrations. (Byron's version of Byron.) In his autobiographical account (i.e., Byron's poems) "for
pages together he does nothing but boast of the advances made to him by
the fair sex." According to him, many of them died for love of him.

Bianca bears Ada an illegitimate daughter, Fiormonda; after killing

Bianca and her husband, Ada abducts the child and raises her without religion. After numerous adventures, during a storm at sea Fiormonda, now a young woman, persuades her father to rescue a youth who has been shipwrecked. This is Count Condulmar, a Venetian, who also becomes Byron (the public was well aware that Byron had spent some years in Venice); he is "nearly as great a traveler" as Ada. They all sail for the New World. Condulmar sings to the girl of "bloody deeds" and "lawless love" and seems to labor under a burden of grief. Fiormonda falls in love with him. Like Glenarvon, he knows "how to excite every feeling and passion." His treatment of her varies from kindness, neglect, to admonition; sometimes he appalls her "with the dark look of sullen anger," then reassures her with "a lover's smile." His power over her is soon unbounded. Like Glenarvon and Byron he tells her he will "tame" her, and that he is destined to be her master.

Ada settles in grand style at Lima; Fiormonda has many suitors, but meets Condulmar secretly. The Duke of Montevallos asks for her hand, but sees that she loves Condulmar who, however, is now paying court (as did Byron) to an Italian singer. Fiormonda urges the Duke to go away, for the guilt she harbors would only mar his name. Condulmar, meanwhile, is having an affair as well with an immoral princess (Lady Oxford?), who does all she can to subject Fiormonda to "as much mortification as possible."

He now avoids Fiormonda and in public makes a point of proclaiming his power over her. When he speaks to her it is with scorn. He says, "Nothing can be more fatiguing than a permanent attachment." (Byron's opinion.) He drinks too much; one night in his cups, in the presence of the Duke, he announces that the chaste Fiormonda is his mistress, that she gave herself to him "almost unsolicited," and that now his feelings for her are of contempt.

The third volume, wherein Lady Caroline's feeble talents strained for the sublime, takes a sudden turn into diabolics in the style of *Vathek*. Condulmar is revealed to be actually the son of Zubanyánn (Satan?). Separated from his daughter by certain events, Ada is told by Zubanyánn's servant that he can see her again if he will drink drops of a special poison. At present Fiormonda is with Condulmar in a chamber of gold and a palace of riches. Ada drinks and dies. He is carried off, by a majestic black bird, to Zubanyánn's palace in "the unhappy valley." A new Dante, Ada journeys through Hell, meeting various persons; he is to rule in Hell as a king. Among the inhabitants of Inferno is a guiltless woman who through gossip lost her character; another (spokeswoman for Lady Caroline?) explains that her punishment is to see the shades of those once dear pass her by with indifference, to know that all her thoughts and actions are misrepresented. Ada is taken before Condulmar and his queen, Fiormonda. The Devil's voice is heard declaring a short respite for everyone. Each of the multitude begins to commit anew his old crimes—except Fiormonda.

Seeing her resist him now, Condulmar woos her again, pretending his past cruelty was only a test of her constancy. Fiormonda forgets Condulmar's cruelty and wickedness, and love for him overcomes her again. Praying for support, she is saved and borne out of Hell to the world. She is taken care of by Indians, and later converted by a missionary to Christianity. She lives the remainder of her life alone in repentance for past offenses.

Lady Caroline was a master of self-delusion.

She herself figures in a number of nineteenth-century novels, after she had inaugurated the tradition. In Thomas Henry Lister's *Granby* (1826) she is portrayed without malice as her admiring circle had known her, in the person of Lady Harriet Duncan, who, it is said, makes an odd wife for her sensible, pleasant husband. At a party she is discussed:

Mr. Trebeck: "She is certainly an amusing piece of sillyness [*sic*]."

Lady Elizabeth: "She is absolutely charming—quite a grown-up child." When Lady Harriet enters, she glides in "with a step half languid, half alert, between a walk and a run." Introduced to a young lady, she says, shaking her warmly by the hands:

> I think I shall like you—if I don't I'll tell you—you will like me, I know—new people always do.

Does the girl believe in phrenology? consider music to be the food of love? improvise in Italian? Does their host know *Christabel?* He does not, and asks what it is about. Her reply:

> I cannot exactly describe it—but do read it—it's singularly original and shows a delicate sense of the beauty of things.

If she were a man, she would choose only a woman of commanding intellect,

> She should have a great deal of imagination . . . tremblingly alive to every little shade of sentiment—yet firm and powerfully minded.

Inspired by Byron's life, Disraeli's *Venetia* inevitably also portrays Lady Caroline, here as Lady Monteagle. During the period when she is having an affair with Carducis (Byron), he is at one of her gatherings. Though busy with her guests, she never allows her eyes to leave him for a moment, while he sits disconsolately apart from everyone on a couch. She dreads his silent rages, and joins him at the first possible moment:

LADY M.:   Dear Carducis, why do you sit here? You know I am obliged to speak to all these odious people, and it is very cruel of you.
CARDUCIS: You seemed to me to be extremely happy.
LADY M.:   If I think you are in one of your dark humours, it is quite impossible for me to attend to these people.

He bids her attend to them, if she prefers them to him.

After she learns that he is interested elsewhere, she makes a scene so violent that he never enters Monteagle House again. She repents and overwhelms him with letters, which next to scenes, he most abhors. Her letters vary from the indignant to the passionate, the reproachful to the pathetic, and they arrive daily. He eventually greets them with silence. She begs for a final interview; he agrees, but leaves town the day before the rendezvous. One day his valet announces the arrival of a boy from the Abbey. The lad is shown up, lights are brought in, the valet leaves, and Carducis bids the boy speak. As soon as he opens his mouth he is recognizable as Lady Monteagle. He tries to avoid another scene, and lies about where he has been. She cries:

> The sublime, the ethereal Lord Carducis, condescending to the last refuge of the meanest, most commonplace mind, a vulgar wretched lie! . . . I know you . . . And I will let every body know you . . . I may be spurned, but at any rate I will be revenged.

He yawns. She continues her tirade. He whistles. After a pause she loses all control of herself and throws herself into a chair. He picks up a book and begins to read. Gradually her hysterics subside into sobs and sighs. She springs up, grasps his arm, falls to her knees at his side, and exclaims tenderly, "Carducis, do you love me?" He answers coolly that she knows he likes women who are quiet; he cannot abide scenes; her presence is a torture. He reminds her that at their last meeting she banished him forever. Finally, he contrives to get her to leave by promising to call on her next day.

Disraeli's presentation of Byron's and Caroline's interrelationship is far less convincing than his picture of Byron's wretched experiences with his mother; he does justice neither to Lady Caroline's obsession nor Byron's complicated feelings of attraction and repulsion toward her. In his *Vivian Grey* Disraeli again portrayed Lady Caroline, this time even less faithfully, as Mrs. Felix Lorraine, seducer of men.

8.

THOUGH HE NEVER COMPLETELY BROKE WITH HER, WILLIAM LAMB finally separated himself from his wife and took a small house in town. In August 1824 she went to Paris with one maid, but soon returned. She was permitted to come back to Brocket, but when she arrived her husband left. He would, in short, still do anything for her except live with her.

In her last few years she gradually lapsed into insanity, and had to be shut up at Brocket under the care of two women. One day, for no reason, she snatched her doctor's watch from his hands and smashed it.

In December 1827 she fell ill of the dropsy and was brought to Melbourne House. By January she knew it was her end. When she died on January 26, less than four years after Byron, it was in her husband's arms.

The obituary notices were much kinder than they had been to her lover. The *Gentleman's Magazine* paid her the doubtful compliment of being "a woman of masculine character"—never was characterization less apt—and conceded that she "possessed considerable literary acquirements" —a gift she certainly never owned. The *London Gazette* felt that "the mistresses of poets" must be dealt with leniently; Lady Caroline was "gifted and warm-hearted"; no one "had less malevolence in all her errors. She hurt only herself, and against herself only were levelled her accusations"—a generalization, as we are to see, which was much less than the truth. Rumor has it that this obituary was written by William Lamb himself.

Whether it was or not, we do know that William Lamb, future Prime Minister of England, after her death would say moodily: "Shall I meet her in another world?" We are not told precisely whether he uttered these words because of a guilty conscience, because he was thus expressing hopeful anticipation, or because he was voicing a depressing dread.

Byron, engraved by H. Meyer,
from a drawing by G. H. Harlow,
and published in January 1816.
(Courtesy of The National Portrait Gallery.)

THREE

AUGUSTA AND OTHERS

1.

ON JUNE 28, 1813, LADY OX-
ford sailed from England without
Byron—not entirely to his regret.
His sister Augusta had just come
to London; he had not seen her
since going abroad himself four
years earlier. On July 8 he wrote
to Moore: "My sister is in town,
which is a great comfort—for, never having been much together, we are
naturally more attached to each other." This was three days after Lady
Caroline's bloodletting scene, the scandal of which might have made any
other man revel in the joys of celibacy, at least for an interval.

Yet if by that same July 8 he had not already gone to bed with
his sister, it cannot have been much later that he began to do so, for a
scant nine months thereafter, on April 15, 1814, Augusta gave birth to a
daughter, Elizabeth Medora, who was beyond much question Byron's child,
and who herself testified that after her midtwenties she never doubted that
she was.

There is no need of either exculpating or arraigning Byron in this
matter. That incest is less uncommon than the world prefers to pretend the
case histories of psychiatrists have made evident. Byron's apologists remind
us that Augusta was but a half sister, that they were reared apart from each
other and thus had not that variety of familiarity of a brother-and-sister
relationship which comes from being brought up together. True enough.

153

But it is to miss Byron's makeup to overlook the fact that what tended to drive him into sexual involvement with Augusta was the very fact of its incestuous nature. If the Lamb and Oxford affairs indeed left him without a wish for a breather, he had only to choose among the countless women ready to fling themselves at him, for he was still being lionized everywhere. But he had not yet himself capped the Byronic hero with a perhaps *unpardonable* sin. Of course, he had tried. He had sampled boys, but that had behind it the classic examples of Greece and Rome; in the East it was still a way of life, and in Britain was common enough in the schools. He had sampled girls, prostitutes, women of various classes—according to middle-class values in England he was there behaving only like the rake of the fashionable world—and adultery—no objection to that in his circle, so long as the rules were observed. Incest—that was a real shocker.

Part of the Byronic character was his pleasurably gloomy conviction that to be a Byron was to be doomed. Augusta was a Byron too and, though she had no inclination to consider herself doomed, he graciously extended the privilege to her. Their affair sealed that doom and, in his eyes, set them apart from others in a union of tragic guilt, a new and more cursed Paolo and Francesca. In gratitude for her sharing the guilt (which she seems not to have felt herself until the persecutions of Lady Byron), he remained convinced forever after that Augusta was the only one who truly loved him and whom he truly loved. For the rest of his life with no small satisfaction he hugged to himself the treasured knowledge of their mutual sin—though hugged it not entirely secretly. He knew that his ever-increasing public always saw him as the hero of his narrative poems, and from that time on his stories contain hints and more than hints of incest committed by the hero.

Not much later that same year he began to write *Zuleika,* whose title he eventually changed to *The Bride of Abydos*—it sold 6,000 copies the first month—about the love of a brother and sister, set again in the East with a hero who was, like the preceding Giaour, a robber. Further reflection counseled altering the relationship of hero and heroine, but he did not bother to change the beginning and thus kept close enough to incest to satisfy his own feelings as well as to titillate the public.

The Pacha Giaffir orders his Nubian to fetch his daughter Zuleika from her bower. His son, Selim, admits to Giaffir that he has invaded his sister's chamber while she slept, and has spent hours with her reading and reciting poetry. The Pacha upbraids him for his effeminate pastimes and sneers at his failing to participate in battles. The Pacha has no love for the boy, and resolves to keep a watchful eye on him. His daughter Zuleika, however, he adores. Like Augusta and Byron, Zuleika and Selim are apparently half sister and brother, offspring of the same father but different

mothers. Zuleika appears, beautiful and pure. Her father tells her of a
highly connected wooer whom he expects her to marry. Zuleika begins to
weep and the Pacha rides off to the wars. Selim, lost in thoughts of Zuleika,
gazes out through the lattice grate. His sister is unable to guess his thoughts—

> Equal her grief, yet not the same
> Her heart confessed no cause of shame.*

She is hurt that he has turned away from her, and scatters attar of roses to
attract his attention. She offers him flowers, sits at his feet and cries:

> Oh, Selim dear! oh more than dearest!
> Say, is it me thou hat'st or fearest?
> Come, lay thy head upon my breast,
> And I will kiss thee into rest.

She knows that their father does not care for him, but can Selim forget her
love? She takes an oath that she will never marry the husband who has
been chosen for her without Selim's consent or command. She could never
bear to part from him:

> Years have not seen, Time shall not see
> The day that teareth thee from me.

Even when death comes, parting all others, it

> shall doom for ever
> Our hearts to undivided dust.

Hearing her vow, Selim emerges from his trance, and exclaims,

> Now thou art mine, for ever mine,
> With life to keep but not with life resign,
> Now thou art mine, that sacred oath
> Though sworn by one, hath bound us both.

He swears her to secrecy. It is at this point that Byron must have decided
that his original purpose of having them half brother and sister, like himself and Augusta, would not go well with the public, for Selim now hints
that he may not be Giaffir's son. Zuleika, however, unfamiliar with her
author's change of plot, continues to think of Selim as her brother; thus the

---

* My quotations are from the manuscript versions of the poem, often more
revealing of Byron's original intentions than the published copy.

note of incest is prolonged. She hates the night because they meet only during the day;

> With thee to live, with thee to die,
> I dare not to my hope deny:
> Thy cheek—thine eyes—thy lips to kiss—
> Like this—and more than this;
> For, Allah! sure thy lips are flame.

Innocent of the illicit nature of her emotion, she asks why their love must be kept secret. Why not tell their father? His worst anger could not cause her to revoke her oath. She sees her father returning, and Selim leads her back to her tower, promising to see her at night. We need not follow the story further: suffice it to say that, the author's plans having changed, Selim turns out to be his father's nephew, the leader of a pirate crew.

In his journal, Byron wrote on November 14 of that year, "Last night I finished my 'Zuleika.' . . . I believe the composition of it kept me alive from the recollection of—'Dear sacred name [Augusta's], rest ever unreveal'd.' At least, even here, my hand would tremble to write it."

Three weeks after this poem was published he began *The Corsair*, and had finished the first draft in ten days. The day of its publication 10,000 copies were sold, and 15,000 more were purchased in a month. This is the work in which his fascination with Schiller's *The Robbers* is made explicit in a long footnote at the conclusion. Again the hero has patently autobiographical traits. Conrad, a pirate chief, first appears in a cave which, like Selim's, is his private abode; his men know that he gets moody when they intrude upon him; he is a man of "loneliness and mystery." Like Byron—when on a diet!—he eats but little. Over his pale forehead, too, the "curls in wild profusion" fall, and even his stature is akin to Byron's:

> to the sight
> No giant form sets forth his common height.

(Here our poet in self-justification appends a significant footnote containing quotations from Sismondi and Iomandes. From the former he cites the case of the celebrated Eccelino who "étoit d'une petite taille," and from the latter that of Genseric the Vandal, conqueror of Rome, who was of "statura mediocris.") There was a "laughing devil" in Conrad's sneer, as in Byron's in a drawing room. In this ridiculous narrative there are a few overtones, and those faint, of Byron's love for his sister—as, for instance, when we are told that this man of sin has one virtue, his love for Medora, a love "unchangeable—unchanged"; his heart, he tells her, is

> Without one hope on earth beyond thy love,
> And scarce a glimpse of mercy from above.

But *The Corsair* has one important connection with Byron's own story. At the time he was writing it Augusta was already carrying their child, and when that child was born she was christened Medora.

Lara, begun a few months after Medora's birth, contains a passage which, in describing the hero, reflects upon his sinful capacities: he had it in him to do

> what few or none would do beside;
> And this same impulse would, in tempting time,
> Mislead his spirit equally to crime.

That month, when Medora was three weeks old, Byron addressed to his sister one of the several poems entitled "Stanzas for Music"; it was not published until after his death. It echoes the conviction he held, in the midst of countless other love affairs, that Augusta was his only true love: [manuscript version]

> I speak not—I breathe not—I write not that name—
> There is grief in the sound, there is guilt in the fame . . .
> We have loved—and oh, still, my adored one we love!
> Oh the moment is past, when that Passion might cease.—
> We repent, we abjure, we will break from the chain,—
> We will part, we will fly to—unite it again! . . .
> The thought may be madness—the wish may be guilt!
> Forgive me, adored one!—forsake, if thou wilt;—
> But I cannot repent what we ne'er can recall . . .
> And stern to the haughty, but humble to thee
> The soul in its bitterest moments shall be . . .
> And thine is that love which I will not forgo
> Though the price which I pay is Eternity's woe . . .

This is not only the fullest statement in his poetry of his devotion to his sister but also the clearest declaration of his inability, despite Calvinistic prickings of the conscience, to regret the sin.

In later works the theme of incest continues. It is not necessary to cite all the examples. But in *Parisina,* for instance, written when he had been married a year, the theme is undisguised, though on this occasion between a young man and his father's wife. Of such forbidden love the poet has this to say:

> The hearts which feel its fiery sway:
> Of guilt, of peril, do they deem

> In that tumultuous dream? . . .
> With many a lingering look they leave
> The spot of guilty gladness past:
> And though they hope, and vow, they grieve
> As if that parting were the last.

In this poem the heroine thinks of her lover as Byron had written of Augusta, "A name she dare not breathe by day." It is interesting, too, that at first Byron thought of calling his hero's mother Medora.

In April 1816, his marriage in ruins, Byron wrote the "Stanzas to Augusta," possibly the last lines he ever composed in England. She was with him those final days before he went into exile. In these verses he calls her, in the midst of total loss and hatred, his "solitary star," illuminating his night;

> There's more in one soft word of thine
> Than in the world's defied rebuke . . .

Like a tree bent over a monument she has protected him, shedding her "weeping leaves" over him;

> But thou and I shall know no blight
> Whatever fate on me may fall . . .

Because of her love earth is not desert even to him.

In the play *Manfred,* composed shortly after his going into exile, the Faustian hero has loved a woman "of all earthly things" the only being he could love—

> As he, indeed, *by blood was bound to do**—
> The Lady Astarte, his—

Presumably he is about to add "sister," but the entry of the Abbot that instant spares the audience the shock of hearing the relationship made explicit. However, the fact was already made clear by innuendo earlier in the drama:

> My blood! the pure warm stream
> Which ran in the veins of my fathers, and in ours
> When we were in our youth, and had one heart,
> And loved each other *as we should not love.* [italics mine]

---

* Italics mine.

He is addressing Astarte's spirit and goes on to exclaim: heaven is "Where thou art not—and I shall never be" because "my embrace was fatal!" Again he cries that it was "The deadliest of sin to love as we have loved." Manfred's sense of being doomed and his pride in being doomed because of his passion for his sister is a covert confession. It is a mirror of what Byron was feeling about himself and Augusta.

In his *Cain,* the hero perforce, being of the first generation after Adam, has as wife his sister, who has borne him a son and daughter. It is remarkable that throughout the work, Adah, Cain's wife, calls him "brother," rather than "husband," as if to stress the idea of incest. If Byron was thinking of Augusta he for once expressed his sister's limitations:

> my Adah, my
> Own and beloved, she, too, understands not
> The mind which overwhelms me.

With the authority of the Biblical situation behind him, in *Cain* Byron boldly defends physical love between brother and sister. Adah is attempting to win her brother-husband from Lucifer's influence:

ADAH: Cain! walk not with this spirit.
     Bear with what we have borne, and love me—I Love thee.
LUCIFER: More than thy mother, and thy sire?
ADAH: I do. Is that a sin too?
LUCIFER: No, not yet:
     It one day will be in your children.
ADAH: What!
     Must not my daughter love her brother Enoch?
LUCIFER: Not as thou lovest thy brother Cain.
ADAH: Oh! my God!
     Shall not they love, and bring forth things that love
     Out of their love? have they not drawn their milk
     Out of this bosom? was not he, their father,
     Born of the same sole womb, in the same hour
     With me? Did we not love each other? and
     In multiplying our being multiply
     Things which will love each other as we love
     Them?

In short, viva incest! In the last lines of the play Byron makes stronger mankind's indebtedness to Cain and Adah's mutual love, for the dead Abel "who lieth there was childless." That is, we owe our very existence to the carnal love of that brother and sister.

Byron had at last written his full justification of his union with

Augusta. Nevertheless, he took scant interest in the child Augusta bore him. After his death, when that child, Medora, was a young woman, Augusta, as we shall see, took even less.

Among the oddities of Byron's conduct is that he should have given the name Adah, bestowed upon his legitimate daughter, to Cain's wife.

2.

IT BEING SETTLED IN 1813 THAT HE AND AUGUSTA WERE NOW BOTH tragically doomed because of their mutual sin, Byron addressed her as "My dearest," and in his journal wrote: "No one except Augusta cares for me"; again: "I can't deny her anything." Five days before their child was born, he referred to Augusta as *"her* I love (God knows too well, and the devil probably too)."

He never regretted what they had done. How could he have? For their love affair had accomplished the heretofore impossible, a delightfully new sensation, Byron's ability to shock himself. In his mind he turned the matter over and over with fascination, almost objectively—if one can conceive of him as being objective about anything. It was a pleasure to know that he could never do anything which could more outrage the Calvinism deep within him. On August 22, 1813, when he had already slept with his sister, he allowed himself the satisfaction of hinting to Tom Moore a new depravity without telling him anything: "I am at this moment in a far more serious and entirely new, scrape than any of the last twelve months— and that is saying a good deal." (In his biography of Byron, Moore was enchanted with the brotherliness of the poet to Augusta; Hobhouse, aware of the facts, annotated his copy of Moore's book with the comment, "My dear M you know nothing of the matter.") Nor, after several fumbling attempts to confide in Lady Melbourne, did Byron fail presently to make clear to her the nature of his dealings with Augusta.

And what did the incest mean to Augusta herself? Of all the people connected with Byron I find Augusta to be the most undecipherable. Before I had made my studies in depth I was willing to endorse the judgment of Byron's biographers that she was simply a fool. And a fool's feelings and motives are sufficiently difficult to make out. From 1813 through the next few years she certainly seems to be exceedingly foolish and superficial and, like Hamlet's mother, to have desired above all else to keep everybody happy, no matter what the moral cost. It is probably the case that cowardice is a leading cause of wickedness, and she was certainly a coward. For, during the bitter period of the winter of 1816, when Annabella, having left Byron, refused to rejoin him, Augusta turned out to be a treacherous spy on her brother, faithfully reporting everything to the enemy; and after his exile she was elaborately two faced in her dealings with him, so that nothing in Byron's life seems now more pathetic than his complete faith in her and unawareness of how his beloved sister, the being he loved more than any other, continued to betray him. Her cruelty, moreover, to their daughter almost surpasses belief.

Most biographers agree that she was not beautiful, but for anyone studying Holmes's miniature of her and Hayter's drawing of her, that will be hard to believe. She had her brother's great eyes and, though utterly feminine, his chiseled features; deceptively, she must also have looked intelligent. In addition to her good looks what she certainly shared with him was a love of fun. It was a great solace to him to have found someone with whom he would laugh unrestrainedly. The "Guss" which he had dubbed her soon, with good cause, became converted to "Goose."

In her choice of a husband she had been most unwise. She was the sort of girl to find the military uniform beyond resisting, and, falling in love violently with her first cousin, Colonel George Leigh, whose father had opposed the match, she had been married to him in 1807. But the colonel had turned out an impossible spouse, a spendthrift and a quarreler, who had thus far fathered three daughters upon her, with more offspring to come. This though he was largely husband *in absentia* from Six Mile Bottom, their home near Newmarket; he could not bear missing the races wherever they happened to be run. Augusta, inept in financial as in all other concerns, was constantly in debt, and had been forced to apply for help a number of times to her brother.

Within a few years she was to exhibit a total want of character when it was her ill luck—and, through her, her brother's—to fall under the domination of Lady Byron, his wife, so that, for all her love, she became a traitor to him. Now it was no doubt her weak-willed desire to please that was as great a factor as any in her giving herself to him. If incest held a dangerous fascination for him, it held none for her; while he was in England she seems hardly to have noticed that aspect of their attachment. In the sophisticated circle in which her rank destined her to move, piety was hardly consistent with good taste, but she was given to distributing copies of the Bible. In fact, she was completely lacking in moral sense, that moral awareness which was so lively a part of Byron's makeup that he had constantly to punish it. It is likely that anxious to pleasure her "baby" brother, she felt none of the excitement of sinning he experienced nor any of his deep-lodged guilt. The gaiety of his company was, moreover, a welcome relief from the cares and anxieties of Six Mile Bottom.

Augusta Leigh, Byron's half sister,
drawing by Sir George Hayster. (Courtesy of the British Museum.)

Byron had been talking of leaving for the Continent again. By mid-August he and Augusta of course knew that their lovemaking was to bear fruit. He suddenly told Lady Melbourne that he would take his sister with him. But later in the month Augusta left London and returned home. Soon Byron was confessing their love to Lady Melbourne, who now understood his reason for desiring to flee England with his sister. She firmly advised against such a move. In September, still unsettled in mind, he briefly visited Augusta at Six Mile Bottom, probably with the objective of convincing her of the folly of their going abroad together—she had suggested Sicily—though the tie between them was stronger than ever.

It would be unfair to assume that all the passion was on his side. From their joint movements during the next few years, it is clear that she offered no resistance to his love. Indeed in the autumn of 1813 she sent him the following message to London: *"Partager tous vos sentiments ne voir que par vos veux n'agir que par vos conseils, ne vivre que pour vous, voila mes voeux, mes projets, & le seul destin qui peut me rendre heureuse."* (Which unpunctuated boarding-school French signifies: "To share all that you feel to see only by your eyes to act only on your advice, to live only for you, those are my vows, my ambitions, and the sole destiny which could make me happy.") This is total surrender, and no doubt Augusta felt less culpable—if indeed she felt any qualms—expressing her love in French. Enclosed in this letter was a small package containing a lock of dark brown hair; inside the package underneath the lock, was written "Augusta." On the outside of the little package Byron wrote, "La Chevelure of the *one* whom most I loved+." (The + sign was used between them to mean kisses.)

3.

IT WAS IN THE MIDST OF THE UNCERTAINTIES HE WAS THEN CONFRONT-ing, made more confusing by the unexpected reemergence of Annabella Milbanke in his life, that he at length accepted a long-standing invitation to visit Aston Hall with James Wedderburn Webster, his old, foolish friend.

There must have been some significant compensations in the friendship of Webster, but what they could have been escapes one. Did Byron enjoy him as the unwitting clown among his acquaintance? It is hard to believe that, for he was not usually one to suffer foolish men patiently for any length of time. Yet this friendship was of some date. It took years for Byron to weary of him, as he at long last did. But even then it was unquestionably Webster's wife who supplied the complicating factor that soured the relationship.

A year younger than Byron, Webster used to accompany him when, at twenty, he practiced at Manton's Shooting Gallery; he was at Brighton, too, when Byron brought the girl he was keeping to that resort in boy's clothes; Webster, it may be remembered, was also one at the party gathered at Newstead for Bacchanalian revelry before Byron went abroad—when, less patient than their host, Matthews threatened to throw Webster out the window and the latter humorlessly departed from the Abbey raging with wounded vanity. The next year, while Byron was in the midst of his travels, Webster married the seventeen-year-old Lady Frances Annesley, daughter of the Earl of Mountnorris, and for some years luxuriated in matrimonial bliss.

In 1811, on his return to England, Byron ordered from Goodall the carriage maker a vis-à-vis, which presently he arranged to exchange for one owned by Webster. A few weeks later Webster decided against the agreement. Good-naturedly Byron then offered to buy Webster's carriage and canceled the order at Goodall's. When the carriage arrived, despite the accepted stipulation that Webster have it relined, it still bore a threadbare interior. For a moment Byron was angered and wrote his friend: "I always understood that the *lining* was to accompany the *carriage;* if not, the *car-*

riage may accompany the *lining*. . . . Two hundred guineas for a carriage with ancient lining!!! Rags and rubbish!" And since Webster had been pressing him to visit him, he added, "I am infinitely obliged by your invitations, but I cannot pay so high for a second-hand chaise to make my friends a visit."

This letter plunged Webster into "hysterics" when he replied, and Byron characteristically, on August 24, was writing him a kind, amusing note more or less apologizing for the tone of his last one, and making it clear that he was anxious not "to lose altogether your valuable correspondence. . . . Seriously, *mio Caro W.,* if you can spare a moment from Matrimony, I shall be glad to hear that you have recovered from the pucker into which this *Vis* (one would think it had been a *Sulky*) has thrown you." He promised surely to come in the winter to Aston Hall, where he would be another Lucifer gazing on the felicity of a new Adam and Ave.

In November he told Hobhouse that Lady Webster "is very pretty, and I am much mistaken if five years hence she don't give him reason to think so . . . I really thought she treated him, even already, with a due conjugal contempt. . . . At present he is the happiest of men, and has asked me to go with them to a tragedy to see his *wife cry!*" Byron's account of this first visit to Aston in a letter to Moore fills out the picture. As was his habit he was—"I won't call it singing"—applying some of Moore's lyrics "to what I think tunes, one morning"; Webster came in looking very grave and announced, "Byron I must request you won't sing any more, at least of *those* songs"; Byron stared, agreed to comply, but asked the reason. "They make my wife *cry* and so melancholy," Webster explained, "that I wish to hear no more of them."

Two weeks after the visit Byron was saying that Webster "will be a notable subject for Cuckold-dom in three years. . . . She is not exactly to my taste, but I dare say the Dragoons would like her."

And now, in the midst of his hectic relationship with Augusta, Byron was nominated godfather to a child the Websters expected. He accepted the responsibility, and suggested that if the baby be a girl they call her Georgina, even though Byron would do as a name "for a spinster." The child, a boy, was christened Byron Wedderburn, but died in infancy. Informed of the death, Byron "almost chuckled with joy or irony," if we may believe Webster, and said, "Well, I cautioned you, and told you that my name would almost damn any thing."

Webster was urging Byron to come again to Aston. After a short visit to Augusta, Byron accepted. Writing from Aston to Lady Melbourne on September 21, he reported that Lady Webster was in delicate health, her husband good natured and intelligent enough, but constantly inveigling his guests into admiring his wife, while at the same time frightfully suspicious of every man on the premises. Byron therefore hit on the expedient of avoiding looking at her when her husband was present and rapturously praising her when she herself was not. Webster expressed a desire to go again to Newstead, where he had been recently, because of his attraction to a "foolish virgin of the Abbey." His friend suggested that he go alone and leave Byron in charge of the Aston household in his absence—but of that plan Webster did not think much. Poor Byron was subjected to endless preachments upon his hostess's beatific qualities; her husband concluded one of his sermons with the remark that in morality she was "very like 'Christ' "!!! Byron himself thought the lady in fact so virtuous that it would be pointless to attempt making love to her. The truth is that he had for a while lost his taste for that sort of challenge because of his passionate involvement with his sister.

He would have none of the Doncaster Races, and while the Websters went to them he left Aston for a week. A letter to Tom Moore affords a lively vignette of one part of his entertainment there: "It is odd,—I was a visitor in the same house which came to my sire as a residence with Lady Carmarthen* (with whom he adulterated before his majority—by the by remember *she* was not my mamma),—and they thrust me into an old room, with a nauseous picture over the chimney, which I suppose my papa regarded with due respect, and which, inheriting the family taste, I looked upon with great satisfaction."

He asked the Websters to invite Augusta too for his return visit to Aston; Lady Frances obliged but Augusta could not come.

For all his wife's Christlike qualities Webster was now, with adulterous intent, busily pursuing a countess; she, as he put it, was "inexorable." Byron's advice was to let her alone: "She must be a *diablesse* by what you told me. You have probably not *bid* high enough . . . I would not give the tithe of a Birmingham farthing for a woman who could or would be purchased, nor indeed for any woman *quoad mere woman;* that is to say, unless I loved her for something more than her sex. If she *loves,* a little *pique* is not amiss, nor even if she don't; the next thing to a woman's favour is her *hatred.* . . . Get them once out of *indifference* . . . and their passions will do wonders."

Lady Melbourne was amazed at her correspondent's portraits of the Websters. Encouraged, he set out to amaze her further. When he warned Webster that if his chase of the countess became known there would be reprisals, this gauche Don Juan replied that he considered all women "fair game" for him because "I can *depend* upon L^y F's principles—she can't go wrong, and therefore I may." Why then, demanded Byron, was he so jealous

---

* Augusta's mother.

of his wife? Webster denied being jealous, but Byron enumerated instances. Suddenly attacked by an access of affection, Webster would publicly kiss his wife's hand, to her total indifference. She apparently expected Byron to try to seduce her and had prepared a fine defense against him. She was astounded when he failed to live up to his reputation and, Byron supposed, thought him "blind—if not worse." Whatever she did think, of course, she had no way of suspecting the true cause of his indifference.

On October 5, back at Aston, he was telling Lady Melbourne that Webster, having lost his countess, was in terrible temper. He objected to Byron's Italian books—such dangerous works as those of Dante and Alfieri —and insisted that Lady Frances "may not see them because, forsooth it is a language which doth infinite damage!!" Byron was still not interested in Lady Frances, pretty as she was.

But within three days the situation had changed. He was having extensive conversations with her and had got around to laying siege to her heart. He was in fact confident enough about his prospects with her to designate her as *Ph.* to Lady Melbourne. If words mean anything, he had reason to believe the lady was in love with him.

In the billiard room she asked him how a woman might let a man know she was fond of him when he seemed unaware. Thus encouraged, he wrote her a love letter, which he was pleased to see her placing next to her heart—just as her husband came into the room. She held her composure, even though the risk was great. "My billet prospered," he wrote, "it did more, it even (I am this moment interrupted by the *Marito,* and write this before him, he has brought me a political pamphlet in Ms. to . . . applaud . . . ; oh, he is gone again), my billet produced an *answer,* a very unequivocal one too, but a little too much about virtue." She spoke much of the soul, "which I don't very well understand . . . but one generally *ends* and *begins* with platonism." Thus our cynical poet was already anticipating the conclusion of an affair before it had begun. He hoped the spiritual nonsense would not last indefinitely, but felt obliged to "make the experiment." He experienced no compuction about being such a guest, and blamed what was happening on his host's silliness; if Webster insisted on chasing after "any little country girl" he met (Byron had little right to look down on anyone for that reason!) and even on boasting of it, despite his having a very pretty wife, he had it coming to him that another should be interested in what he underprized. Didn't he feel that every woman was *his* rightful prey? Trouble might come of this complication; Byron hoped not, but was prepared to face the music. In a 6:00 P.M. postscript he remarked that "*Platonism*" was in some danger. There was very nearly a scene—which he always loathed; the lady had been hysterical; she had wept and he had consoled her—a situation perilous to both had anyone come in. There was a further postscript at 10:00 P.M. He had been listening to Webster, who offered to wager that he could win " 'any given *woman*, against any given *homme* including all friends present." Byron and the other guests declined the bet.

Two days later he wrote Lady Melbourne from Newstead, whither he had gone with Webster for a short stay. Webster was congratulating himself on possessing a wife "without passion." Byron already had reason to doubt that. Lady Frances had answered his letter by declaring she loved him, though she would never be unfaithful to her husband. He assured her he would not "infringe" upon her conditions, a promise which caused her to burst out "into an agony of crying"—with her sister in the next room and her husband almost as close. She also managed to give him a note and receive another from him as well as a ring, before her husband's "very face," even though she said her prayers morning and evening, "besides being measured for a new Bible once a quarter." To tangle the possibilities for him, Webster had declared that his wife's disinclination to copulate is "beneficial to population." If that was an accurate description of the lady's temperament, which Byron doubted, he feared his own efforts would prove love's labors lost.

By this time Webster had asked him to lend him £1,000, and on October 10 Byron wrote to his solicitor to ask that that sum be sent to Aston. (Seven years later Tom Moore ran into Webster at Paris, and was told by Webster that he still owed Byron the money. Moore thought that he did not "seem to have the slightest intention of paying.")

Webster was soon in a new scrape. On November 11 there was something like a scene at dinner. Byron had taken a place at table between a fierce-looking bluestocking, Lady Sitwell, and Lady Frances's sister, Lady Catherine Annesley; Lady Frances, looking like Lady Caroline "when *gentle*," exclaimed that he was in the wrong place: he was to change with her sister. When Byron had obligingly shifted, Webster roared, "Byron, that is the most ungallant thing I ever beheld." Lady Catherine came to the rescue with, "Did you not hear Frances ask him?" The next morning Webster lectured him on the incident but was put down by the ladies.

It was decided that everyone was to go to Newstead for a visit. In front of Byron a contention arose over the room assignments; Lady Frances wanted her sister to share her apartment, Webster angrily maintaining that only a husband had that right. Though agreeing with him in principle, Byron felt quite uncomfortable at this public airing of private matters. He understood, however, that Lady Frances's purpose had been to assure him of her loyalty to him. Because of her gentleness and kindness to everyone and her never saying a stupid thing, he was now "totally absorbed in this passion," and even toyed with the idea of an elopement. She had said, "We cannot part." If they did run off together Webster would probably wish to cut his throat.

The hectic Platonism at Aston Hall, where he was staying longer than he had intended, prevented him from answering any of his correspondence—except to his mother-confessor, Lady Melbourne. Not having heard from him, Augusta thought he was angry because she had not joined him at Aston. He jotted a note to her: "I have only time to say that I am not in the least angry, and that my silence has merely arisen from several circumstances which I cannot now detail."

On the morning of October 14 Webster, before servants, attacked his wife and sister-in-law at breakfast for reasons neither knew, with the result that Lady Catherine was on the point of leaving. By now Byron was utterly fed up with him and felt fully justified in trying to get into Lady Frances's bed, if that could ever be managed. "He may convert his antlers into *powder-horns* and welcome," since he had threatened such violence if any man seduced his wife. Losing his temper for once, Byron retorted that he would be willing to put these warlike phrases to the test any time—an outburst which he immediately saw as stupidly inviting suspicion.

The whole party now went to Newstead. One day he and Lady Frances found themselves alone. She said to him: "I am entirely at your *mercy . . .* I give myself to you." But she could not bear to face the consequences of becoming his mistress, and concluded, "Now act as you will." He asked Lady Melbourne: "Was I wrong? I spared her." (At this date it is merely astonishing that Byron and his contemporaries, no matter how blasé, could seriously believe that the woman was to be "spared" or not spared, and that, roué though he was, he still understood so little of what Lady Frances, having said what she did say, expected.) Lady Melbourne had asked how far he was prepared to go: as far as a duel and a divorce, was his answer. He was sure he loved Lady Frances—probably because he had not taken her to bed. She had refused to elope with him for his own sake. Everyone at Newstead suspected them now, and Webster never left his wife's side; it was some comfort to her lover that she was not sleeping with her husband and had not done so for some time. Her present anxiety had made her frailer than ever; she ate practically nothing. Despite her standing upon her virtue she, incomprehensibly to Byron, continued to caress him, but he found it hard to "confine" himself to the "laudable portion of these endearments." She also wrote him a passionate letter: "Promise to love me and not let my circumstances separate your heart from mine . . . I love dearly—I more than love—but *never* will survive my fall. . . . I invoked every blessing upon you for not taking advantage of my *imprudent,* my unguarded situation." She asked him not to despise her; she never knew before what it was to adore anyone, and until then could have appeared before her God "perfectly pure and unspotted."

The guests quitted Newstead on October 19. Webster, though he had been very cold to Byron, accompanied him to London—to sign papers for the loan of the £1,000. Before parting, Lady Frances, promising they should meet in the spring, begged him to be faithful to her for one year. Her husband presently remarked that her distress upon saying au revoir to Webster for only a week had so overwhelmed her that it was obvious that she simply doted upon him.

She could not refrain from writing to Byron. Within a day or so she was composing an eighteen-page letter to him, full of tears, sorrow, and spirituality. As her letters continued he was callous enough to send them on to Lady Melbourne with the excuse that his love for the lady was in earnest and that he desired the older woman's opinion of her; he was prepared to sacrifice everything for this new love—except, patently, granting it the privacy which real love instinctively demands. Nevertheless, he could not resist pointing out that she used two words, *effusions* and *soul* "rather oftener" than one could wish to meet outside popular novels. He would have been willing to return to Aston; Webster had extended another invitation, but in such a tone as made it impossible to accept.

Not having heard from him in three days, she wrote him an anguished letter toward the end of October, expressing her fear that he had already discarded her and intended to betray her to the world. She asked him for a likeness of him. Lady Caroline had already been asked to surrender two portraits of him, one of which went to Lady Oxford, the other to Augusta, and was now called upon to give up a third, by the artist Holmes.

One of Lady Frances's letters rather surprised him, for in it, having remarked on how easy it was to deceive people, she passed on to a consideration of Webster's attitude: *"May he be always deceived!"* In this particular case, she judged, deception was not a crime, for it insured the husband's peace of mind. In late November she was sent off to her husband's relatives in Scotland; writing or receiving letters was for the time impossible.

Byron fancied himself still enamored of her and even pondered having an open understanding with Webster, if only because it would hasten bringing the affair to a head. The result of such a confrontation would certainly be a duel, which he would find not unwelcome. If he were killed, it would at least make a dramatic end for him, and all women would treasure his memory. Lady Caroline would "go wild with *grief* that *it did not happen about her*," and Lady Oxford would say he deserved it for not following her to Cagliari. Augusta would be "really uncomfortable."

However, as the days passed his passion cooled. By January 10, 1814, he had heard from Lady Frances that they could not meet until the spring.

"By that time it is impossible she should not be altered"—Byron's women aged in no time at all! Even if she were not, he would waste no more time on "theories" and Platonisms. He was weary of placating her fears and being the object of her coquetry. She would soon find a "less indulgent" preceptor, for whom he paved the way. About that he felt no guilt, for he had been only her fool. Three days later he told Lady Melbourne that he was thinking of Lady Frances no more. "If people will stop at the first tense of the verb 'aimer,' they must not be surprised if one finishes the conjugation with somebody else." What had he to look back on as the reward of his attentions? "A few kisses, for which she was no worse."

4.

IN THE LATE SPRING OF 1815 TWO OF BYRON'S LOVERS WERE IN BRUSSELS flirting with the susceptible Duke of Wellington, Lady Caroline and Lady Frances. To Caro, Byron wrote an unkind letter hoping that she was "as happy with the regiment" as he was with his recently wed wife, Annabella. As for the "saintly" Lady Frances, the St. James Chronicle suggested in its issues of August 3, 5, and 8 that her flirtation with the great military hero was far from innocent. On February 16, 1816, Webster sued the paper's proprietor, Charles Baldwin, for libel. Mr. Campbell, speaking in court for the plaintiff, said that Lady Frances "had always preserved an unsullied reputation" until Baldwin had printed his "false, scandalous and malicious libels charging her with having been guilty of adultery" with Wellington. Fifty thousand pounds damages were asked. Mr. Serjeant Best stated his case: "Mr. W. Webster was a gentleman of fortune, and was allied to many Noble Families; his wife, twenty-four, the daughter of the Earl of Mountnorris, was "endued with great beauty—but her beauty was lost sight of by those who knew the virtues she possessed." Wellington had visited the Websters in the environs of Brussels, but he was "never in his life alone with Lady F. Webster." Her husband had now to return to England, while his wife lived with her father. When the English arrived in Paris after Waterloo, the Earl of Mountnorris had had occasion to travel to Belgium in the company of Webster. At this juncture Lady Frances was seven months advanced in pregnancy, and it was not until "she was in that situation" that she ever "had an opportunity of speaking" to Wellington. The St. James Chronicle said on August 3 that when, after the battle, Wellington "came to visit the wounded—perhaps the wounded heart was meant." Said Mr. Serjeant Best, the meaning of this obviously was: "all he went back to Brussels for, after the victory, was to indulge in adulterous intercourse." On August 5 some doggerel was printed under the title of "Brussels 1815." It read:

In the letter *W*, there's a charm half divine,
War, Wellington, Wedderburn Webster, and wine.

The paper went on to say that the "fortunate lover" (Wellington) had offered to pay Webster £50,000 to keep the matter quiet, but that it was already too late. On August 8, it was further declared, "A very beautiful woman of Irish extraction [i.e., Lady Frances] is said to be a party in the amour at Brussels."

Baldwin's defense by Mr. Serjeant Lens was that the publisher was not himself the author of the slander; he had merely reported what was being said. Lord Chief Justice Gibbs indignantly attacked the viciousness of the libel as well as the injustice visited upon the Websters. The verdict found £2,000 for the plaintiff. When Byron heard from Murray of the conclusion of the suit, he replied: "You see by it the exceeding advantage of unimpeachable virtue and uniform correctness of conduct." Therewith he also composed one of the most celebrated of his lyrics, "When we two parted." When published in 1816, it omitted a final stanza later printed by Gore:

> Then fare thee well, Fanny,
> Now doubly undone,
> To prove false unto many
> As faithless to one,
> Thou art past all recalling
> Even would I recall,
> For the woman once falling
> Forever must fall.

It is well that this stanza never appears with the poem, for without it the lyric shows Byron at his best. These last lines not only murder the music and mood of the preceding stanzas, but they are also an unpleasant reminder that it is the rake who is always the most censorious of women's morals. Moreover, Lady Frances may still have been guiltless of adultery. Characteristically of such men, Byron considered stain enough that her reputation had been called in question, no matter how unjustly.

That same year Webster decided to burst upon the public as a poet himself with a volume published in Paris, *Waterloo and Other Poems*. In the past he had contented himself with scribbling political pamphlets, much to the embarrassment of all connected with him, and to the foolishness of which Byron had been captive audience at Aston. It is not at all beyond possibility that the title of this volume and the long poem itself were an attempt to capitalize on the scandal connecting his wife with Wellington; that would have been quite consistent with this ridiculous man's character. The book bore a motto from *Childe Harold* and the "Advertisement" apologized for the contents while, at the same time, trying to win distinction for Webster by dragging in his friendship with Byron; it spoke of the "Beauties, which the Gigantic Talents and mighty Genius of my friend Lord Byron have given to the World—which the present age have [sic]—never can equal." An idea of the quality of Webster's verse may be gleaned from a concluding passage after many stanzas denouncing Napoleon and gloating over his exile to his "Ocean Rock":

> Insects of a Day! Creatures of an hour!
> Dare ye deem other of your short liv'd pow'r?
> E'en the dull Bat that flits on leathern wings
> Is previleg'd [sic] beyond ye mortal things!
> It still may flit—and buz [sic] away its day . . .

Our poet helpfully provided a note for this rare line: "Day, is of course used here to express the date of existence—for in point of fact the Bat's Day is the Night." Addison's Ned Softly had nothing on Webster.

Among the shorter pieces are lyrics—"To Phoela," "To Corinne," "The Parting," "On Love" (a subject on which he always considered himself an authority), etc., and a gem entitled "Lines on Lord B—ns Portrait." This could have been the miniature Byron had required of Lady Caroline:

> Such thy form, o! B—n, but say what art,
> May paint the colors of thy noble heart . . .*

Concerning this masterpiece Byron said that the "poesies" of his old friend contained "an epitaph on his bull-dog, and another on myself." His further opinion he expressed in some doggerel:

> I turn'd a page of Webster's "Waterloo";
> Pooh! pooh!

For some reason Byron was impelled in the autumn of 1818, from Italy, to get in touch with Lady Frances once more after she had not heard from him in a long time, despite the way he had sat in judgment of her. He sent the letter via Augusta, whom he "particularly" begged to see this missive "safely delivered," and to forward to him the answer, if any.

From Ravenna he later told Murray that poor Augusta had been hounded by the attention of his former mistresses, much to her confusion.

---

* These lines should make one reflect on how impossible it is to evaluate a rhyme independently of the rest of the verse. "Art" and "heart" seem here to have achieved the nadir of the banal; yet how different is the effect they create when employed by Blake in "The Tiger"!

Among others Lady Frances had "marched in upon her." It never occurred
to him that his request that Augusta deliver his letter to Lady Frances might
have had something to do with her unwelcome incursion. He saw only that
it was odd that so many of his "loves" should become interested in his sister
now that he was in exile. These "calamities" had made Augusta "afraid of
her shadow." What he did not know was that by this time she lived under
the constant worry over the gossip of their incest, which was being whispered
by everyone in her circle. No doubt those old loves of his were resolved to
find out what they could on this subject for themselves, and marching in on
her was as good a method of taking her by surprise as any other. It could
not have required much sagacity to know that Augusta was not clever enough
to defend herself against well-aimed questions.

In 1822 Byron was visited at Genoa by Webster himself. He and his
wife were now separated, too, but not divorced. Nevertheless he was already
planning to marry Lady Hardy, widow of a naval officer. He had come to
Genoa just to see her, and when she left town he followed in pursuit of
her, not, however, without advertising in the *Genoa Gazette* for "an agreeable companion in a post chaise." Byron wrote Lady Hardy that Webster
considered himself badly treated by her, and thought her a "cold Calypso,"
who had led astray her amorous suitor without giving him "any sort of compensation"; Byron approved of her method. As society operated in England,
a woman who allowed her suitor to become her lover would eventually discover that he had turned into a tyrant. (Byron could testify to that.)

He also wrote to Hobhouse to say that he had been seeing "that little
and insane" Webster, who, having been knighted, was now Sir James. He
found little change in him except that his face "rather more resembled his
backside" than ever. When they met, after the passage of years, Webster
had exclaimed on how well his friend was looking, but unfortunately added,
"You are getting fat." His battle with weight was a sensitive subject to
Byron, who muttered to Edward Trelawny, present at the moment, "I can
hardly keep my hands off him."

Later that year Webster, now bent on making up with his wife, was
back in Genoa to seek Byron's intercession. With grim irony at the absurdity
of the situation, Byron honestly did try, but with no success. Webster then
made a brief trip to Paris, where Lady Frances resided, and ran off with one
of his wife's children—as Byron put it, "by mistake it is supposed for one of
his own." The police took Webster in charge, and Byron came to his aid
with ransom money.

5.

TO RETURN TO BYRON'S PERIOD OF DISILLUSIONMENT WITH LADY Frances, after the visit of the Websters to the Abbey in the autumn of 1813. Suddenly the girl, now a disenchanted woman, who had denied she could ever care "any thing for that lame boy," appeared on his horizon again. Mary Chaworth had married her John Musters, who was now dividing his time between hunting and philandering. On December 24, 1813, she wrote Byron that if he were coming into her neighborhood again he must call on her, and he would find "a *very old* and *sincere friend* most anxious to see him." She signed herself "Mary." By January 8, 1814, she had written again, and he described her to Lady Melbourne as "my old love of all loves." He more or less resolved to go see her, though he anticipated a "melancholy interview." They had not met for years; all this while Musters had been chasing after "all kinds of vulgar mistresses." Byron forwarded this second letter to Lady Melbourne, desiring her advice on the proposed meeting. He explained that she had been spoiled, rich, simple, intelligent, but without any particular gifts; but she was dear to him for memory's sake.

Mary's third letter elaborated on the pleasure of seeing again "the *friend* of my *youth*." Though the world might condemn her for taking these steps in approaching him, she could rely upon his discretion, she felt—little guessing how everything was confided to Lady Melbourne—and that he would destroy her letters—which he did not do. Their correspondence, she said, must terminate, but before it did, she wished him to understand, in extenuation of her writing him first, that she had been very ill. He would be astonished if he saw the changes in the once-happy creature he used to know. She was pale, thin, and depressed; the little she had seen of the world had filled her with disgust for it.

Rumor furnished him with a pretext for altering his plan to go. He heard that she was about to become reconciled to Musters, and he declared it foolish to make a journey of 150 miles just to be "a witness of ye reunion." But she was not minded, after all, to end writing to him, and she sent off almost daily a letter to her now-celebrated friend, with much detail of her sicknesses, aches, and pains. She said that both of them had been luckless in their parents, a situation which had, in her case, more or less forced her prematurely into marriage. All he had heard of her husband's barbarous behavior was true. As for her old admirer, his reputation, as she had heard, was that of a man utterly unprincipled in his dealings with women, but she wished him to know that she had defended him against the slander—which, for his own part, he thought indiscreet of her in her present circumstances. He answered her letters with the assurance that she need not refrain from

Mary Chaworth,
miniature, artist unknown.

saying anything she wished; only, he pleaded, let her expunge in the future all references to health.

She had also heard of his proposal of marriage to Miss Milbanke and of her rejection. She thought that no catastrophe: her own opinion of marriage was that it extended little hope of happiness to either party. She had been told of Lady Caroline's great public scene; though she thought such conduct indicative of an unsound mind, she pitied her.

The reappearance in his life of Mary must have cost him considerable inner turmoil. Few people of imagination can calmly resist the temptation to reopen communication with a childhood sweetheart who had thoroughly engulfed thought and feeling as Mary had young Byron's. His letters of early 1814 show him battling with himself and trying hard but unsuccessfully to be guided by his cynicism. "Nothing," he told Lady Melbourne, "can deprive one of the past." Perhaps he would undertake the trip anyhow, but if he should find the Musters reunited he would make no effort to reestablish a friendship with Mary.

On January 11, he was telling himself that "in present circumstances" (his love for Augusta and his renounced hopes of ever sleeping with Lady Frances), all he could feel for Mary or anyone else would be friendship; the passion he had known with his sister would make an affair with anybody "insipid." But he was not at all sure that seeing Mary again "would not bring on the *old attack* on *me*." It was the "same sickly friendship" which he felt reviving between them both. (All this month he had been hearing regularly from Lady Caroline, whom he steadfastly refused to answer.) In the middle of the month he planned on going to Newstead, and he intended while there to see Mary, though he could not think that "any good" could result. On January 17 he set out for the Abbey—with Augusta. There was a heavy snow, and he made the excuse of bad roads for not going the short distance to see Mary. The truth was that he was too happy with Augusta to break the charm of their being secluded together, like the hero and heroine of one of his Eastern tales. Mary, to encourage him, wrote that a return of her husband was impossible, and she talked of coming to London in the spring. Augusta urged him to see her, and Lady Melbourne encouraged him to do so, too, convinced that any other attachment he could form might cancel the dangerous one to his sister. He temporized. Mary continued to write to him as a "beloved brother"; he himself was sure that he could never mean more to her than that. Moreover, what he felt to be her indiscretion in writing to him at all irritated him. He greatly respected appearances; since Musters seemed to count on his wife's returning to him, Byron thought he would be blamed if the reunion failed to come off, as if he had dissuaded her.

So he left Newstead without seeing her. Her letters followed him; he replied infrequently. In April she sent him some violets and made a purse for him. She doubted he would remain a bachelor; through a friend corresponding with Annabella Milbanke she had been hearing a great deal about him. Often she looked back with regret at the way she had treated him when they were young. This was the month in which Elizabeth Medora was born, and it therefore is not surprising that he was in no hurry to answer Mary.

In mid-July she was in London with a friend. He made negotiations over the sale of Newstead his excuse for leaving town and running off—with Augusta—to Hastings, without having seen Mary. Soon she found reasons for coming for the sea-bathing to Hastings too. Unhappily for her hopes, Byron, warned of her coming, escaped with his sister just in time to miss her. On August 20, 1814, she wrote him from the seaside that after all his "professions of regard," his long silence was humiliating; living at Hastings House, where he had recently stayed, her thoughts were all the more centered on him, even though she suspected he had quit the place to avoid her.

While she was at Hastings, Musters paid her a brief visit. Torturing herself over Byron's reluctance to know her again and worried about her husband, she suffered a serious nervous collapse. She was brought back to London, only a few streets away from Byron, and was thought to be in some danger of dying. It took her months to recover. There was some poetic justice in the fact that the thoughtless girl who had caused the boy Byron so much suffering and left so indelible a distrust of women upon him should, as the wheel turned, have been shunned by him when she felt she had great need of him. Nevertheless, there is no hint that any such revenge was in his mind or that he sought to wound her pride. He had been truly tempted to take up the threads of their friendship, but was deterred by many considerations—a real fear that his adolescent love of her would return if they met, his genuine preoccupation with Augusta and the child who was on its way, and, of course, his dislike of getting into a public situation with a woman who might become reconciled with the husband from whom she was separated. But, surely, one of his chief motives was that he now, for various reasons, was in earnest about getting married, had been paying court to Miss Milbanke, and before 1814 was out had been accepted by her. In his determination to straighten himself out, he wished no further involvements.

Annabella, when Lady Byron, met Mary in town at the house of Lady Caroline the next year. She wrote to Augusta about Mary: "She asked after B. Such a wicked-looking cat I never saw. Somebody else [Lady Caroline] looked quite virtuous by the side of her."

The Musters came together again in 1817, when Byron was already living in Venice. Five years later, during the rioting of Nottingham workers, Mary, while her house was being ravaged, took shelter with her girls in the shrubbery. The experience proved a shattering one to a constitution already debilitated; she fell into a decline, and died in February 1823, a year before Byron met his end in Greece.

6.

BYRON NEVER WILLINGLY HAD A LOVE AFFAIR WITH A YOUNG WOMAN on the platonic level. Nevertheless, among his innumerable conquests of women of his own generation or younger, those of Lady Frances and Mary Chaworth were not the only instances of an amatory skirmish that failed to end in bed. One of the more interesting cases during the hectic year of 1814 was that of Henrietta d'Ussières.

We have only her own words to sketch in her background, and since, though quite naïve and innocent, she was equipped with a ragingly romantic imagination, such as the times much encouraged, one must be on guard against taking her too literally. It is a little hard, for example, quite to credit her tale of meeting Napoleon in her early teens. On his return from Italy she ran to the parade grounds near Lausanne, defying parental prohibitions, and just escaped being run over by one of Buonaparte's men on horseback. Acting quickly, Napoleon saved her from death. Lifting her up from where she had fallen, he talked to her, not with his celebrated look of ferocity, but smilingly, like a friend.

She says she was the daughter of a fanatical disciple of his fellow Swiss, Jean-Jacques Rousseau. A devotee of liberty, he allowed his children to run wild day and night, naked and barefoot, in every kind of weather. Though Rousseau hardly intended that sort of thing for girls as well as boys, d'Ussières made a practice of throwing his children, from the time they were two, from a great height into a six-foot pond to teach them to swim. They were allowed to read as they pleased, but without instruction. Yet, for all his love of freedom, he was a tyrant to his family. One day Henrietta was informed that she was to marry an old, hideous man. She fled home, spent three days in a wood, but was found by her father when he was out hunting. She was given the choice of marrying the man he had chosen or of being banished from home at the age of fifteen. When she persisted in refusing to marry, she was placed in the care of an English merchant's daughter and went with that family to England.

She began writing to Byron in the spring of 1814, continued to write despite his silence, was extraordinarily determined to achieve her objective which, she said, was simply to receive one line of his handwriting. Granted that, she promised, she would cease troubling him. He was in no haste to oblige. In May she was telling him that being sure of his goodness, she realized that only "powerful motives" could have prevented him from sending what she asked. Angry he could not have been, for then he would have sent her a cold note to show he was offended. If he truly did not wish to hear from her any more, let him send back her last letter with a servant to tell the clerk at the penny-post-office in Mount Street to inform her so. If, however, she continued to have no word from him, she would take that to mean she was to continue writing—which for her would be the greatest of pleasures. She stressed the fact that her feelings were purely Platonic. With Lady Frances fresh in memory, that would hardly have encouraged Byron.

Next came a declaration which must have struck him as ironic. Assuming with the rest of the world that Thyrza had been a girl, she said she wished to become another Thyrza, whom she too loved and whose death she deplored. Who was Thyrza's successor to be? She declared that her ambition, after all, was too modest to enable her to conceive herself in that role, so she had been busy imagining the lucky girl's features. Had Thyrza lived she would naturally have become Byron's wife; the girl being created in Henrietta's fancy was therefore his wife-to-be.

Byron still responded nothing. He was fairly soaked by cataracts of female enthusiasm mixed with pleas for Platonic alliance, and he could hardly spend his days replying to the myriads of women who laid siege to him. This correspondent, moreover, was more persistent and annoyingly ardent than most. She wished to be his sister. What would her reaction have been had she known how un-Platonic his love for the sister he had actually was? She did not desist, wavering in her letters between fear she had angered him and reassurance that he was too noble to be vexed at her devotion. Next she suggested he put a notice in *The Courier* merely stating, "B— forgives." That would make her deliriously happy. Daily she read the columns of that paper, but he remained stolid. Perhaps he disapproved of *The Courier?* She herself disliked it. Then let him address one line to her in care of a Swiss banker in London; all she wished to hear was that he forgave her. If he refused this request, she might have to storm his doors at the Albany, or wait on his doorstep. To soften his resistance she said she wished only to serve him quietly and unobtrusively, keeping his papers in order, making ready whatever kind of fire he preferred: "No cracking of doors— I should always come on tiptoe." She could picture him near the window composing his "angelic verses." If only Thyrza were still alive—how she would love her too!

Her persistence finally wore him down, and he wrote her on June 17, despite his desire for peace during this troublesome year. When a servant brought his letter to her, she was penning another of her own. She opened his message and palpitated with joy at his goodness. And he was not angry!

The sequel was her answer to his questions, the account of her own history. But she coyly avoided being precise about her age or her present vocation. She had overheard people he knew talking about him and his works. Did Byron therefore think her a lady's maid? a companion? Let him reflect: she could have heard this talk at the opera or theatre; for all he knew she might be a lady herself.

The following letters besought his permission to visit him. She had heard the Albany was a dwelling for bachelors; if she came there unexpected, what if she ran into some of the lodgers—a woman in bachelors' quarters? If it became known she had gone to Lord Byron's chambers, she would have to drown herself in the Serpentine. She soon decided that the hope of seeing and hearing him was all that could matter; she now simply wished him to say whether her invasion should be during the day or in the evening.

Later in June she gained the admission she had so long coveted. At first Byron was gracious as only he could be. They chatted at ease about a thousand things. Then, without transition, he transformed himself into the cynical rake. He offered her terms for sleeping with him.

Terrified, she fled home, and wrote him a feverish letter. That first half-hour she had been so happy—until he became someone other than Lord Byron. Did she deserve such a wretched future as must be hers if she had accepted his proposition? She had imagined that the tale of her misfortunes would have aroused his pity, not the bestial in him.

We do not know whether Byron apologized, but she forgave him, and was soon suggesting a second meeting. Unfortunately, she chose a date without consulting him, a day when Piccadilly was crowded with hosts of the curious out to catch a glimpse of the King of Prussia, the Emperor Alexander, Marshal Blücher and other notables of the Allies. Standing out from the mob both by height and awkwardness—to both of which her letters admit—frightened and unsure, she had a dreadful time of it making a path for herself. She became lost in side streets and began to weep bitterly, while the ragtag people stared at her. A man, "half-gentleman, half-beggar," followed her and, tapping her arm, offered to "take care" of her. By good luck a kindly middle-aged couple, seeing her confusion, led her to the back entrance of the Albany. When she rang, Byron's valet, Fletcher, told her that his Lordship could not be seen, for he had with him a number of men friends. She asked to be allowed to wait and to beg Byron to see her. Meanwhile she stole into a pantry. An attentive reader of the Gothic school, she reflected, "Had I been in a *subterraneous, a ruined Chapel, a cave strewn with skulls and reptiles,* sepulchral lamps, etc.—but a Pantry!! a Pantry flanked with mops and brooms!" When Byron did appear among the mops and brooms, he thought the situation merely funny. "You laughed," she accused him, "when I was ready to cry."

Her next suggestion was that they meet at Grosvenor Chapel. He did not come. She began anew to beg for a letter. He wrote none—which fact did not deter her from adding to the bulk of letters Byron kept, never heeding requests of the women in his life when they realized they had said too much on paper, to destroy their correspondence—and thereby enriching the Byron papers in the John Murray archives at 50 Albermarle Street. When he married, she asked, would he name his daughter after her? All this while that the tempestuous Henrietta wrote, she never imagined that his putative marriage was soon to become a real one.

Then she learned of it. At one blow her hopes were cut off, whatever they may secretly have been. She was not a girl to desire intrigue. She sat down to compose her farewell, eight pages which are still tear stained. Why had he not told her of his betrothal? She must, of course, never come to the Albany again—that room so dear in its every detail to her memory—his chair, the silver urns, the crucifix, the parrot, the bookcase. She asked to be forgiven for having troubled him, and begged for his compassion. Did he think that Augusta might permit her to correspond with her—say, in a dozen years—"we'll then be very old"? She blessed and kissed his hand that would receive this final letter, and prayed to be remembered without severity.

If Miss E. M. Symonds (whose work was completed by Peter Quennell) had not conscientiously plowed through the Byron papers at 50 Albermarle Street some three decades ago, no one would ever have heard of Harriet d'Ussières.

7.

OF THE COUNTLESS WOMEN WHO HAD DRIFTED AND WERE YET TO DRIFT into and out of Byron's life—he once reckoned his conquests in four figures —the story of none is droller than that of Elizabeth Francis. An inflated version told by Teresa Guiccioli, with whom she became friendly years later, was given in *My Recollections of Lord Byron,* where a whole chapter is disproportionately devoted to Elizabeth. Through the Marchesa Origo, Professor Marchand had access to Eliza's manuscript account of her experience, and it is to him that we are indebted for the actual facts.

Byron was already engaged to marry Annabella Milbanke when he received a letter dated October 21, 1814, from one who signed herself "Your young admirer & enthusiastic friend Eliza." There was nothing in it to alarm him with the likelihood of a new intrusion in an already overcomplicated life—at a time, moreover, when he was sincerely anxious to simplify it and reduce it to some order. His unknown correspondent, giving an address near

Bristol, seemed interested chiefly in rhapsodizing on his poetry and its effect on her.

Actually his "young admirer" was about the same age as himself, twenty-six. According to her narrative, she appeared on October 24 at the Albany. Fletcher answered the bell, and she asked him to tell his master that she was the lady who had written him three days earlier. (There must have been others who fitted that identification.) Fletcher returned with his Lordship's requirement that she state the purpose of her visit in writing.

Near tears, she was finally admitted to Byron's presence. Moving from the fireplace, where he was standing, to behind a large desk, he courteously invited her to be seated. In answer to his queries she sketched the neediness of her family: her father, formerly partner in a bank, then alderman, finally mayor of his town, had fallen into bankruptcy. Byron guessed her to be only seventeen; she confessed to twenty-five. It was, in fact, her youthful appearance which had blocked her attempts to find employment. He took out his checkbook and chatted pleasantly with her while he made out a check, folded it, and handed it to her. She remained some two hours, talking with him about novels and other literary topics. She fancied herself a poet, and when she at last rose to go he agreed that she might bring her verse for him to read. Outside, she was deeply moved to find that the check was for £50.

His not-really-so-young visitor allowed Byron a day's respite, after which she called again at the Albany, poems in hand. This time she managed to get him to promise that he would look at other of her compositions. He shook her hand; it was like a wave of electricity shooting through her. When she called the next day he was polite about her work, and she was entranced that he knew how much she had suffered. She asked him to call on her, but her heart sank when he told her frankly that he was soon to be married. Noting her confusion, he sent her home in his carriage, accompanying her as far as the house of his friend Kinnaird.

Shortly after that, Byron was off to the country to see Annabella—after a stop en route at Augusta's. During his absence from London for more than a month Eliza allowed her attraction to him to develop into a fixation; she wished to see no one else. On his return, she came to visit him again. This time he was kinder than ever. On her entry he held out both his hands in greeting, and expressed his regret that they had not met earlier. (Was he already in dread of his approaching marriage after a stay with Annabella and her family?) He asked her to come again in a day or so. On that occasion she timidly hoped that he would introduce her to his wife after he was married. That hope he extinguished at once: his bride-to-be was not a suspicious girl, but there were those who could evoke jealous thoughts in her about his friendship with Eliza. When she was leaving, they held hands

again. This time she observed that his eyes were not dark, as she had supposed, but large and gray—it was the long sweep of his lashes which made
them seem black. Later in life she declared they were the most beautiful
eyes she had ever seen.

Her two succeeding attempts to see him were frustrated by his preoccupation with lawyers. When she at last could see him his manner and voice
were unexpectedly cold. He hardly looked at her. Three days later he was
kinder and managed to hint that only his coming marriage stood in the way
of yielding to his desires; if he let down the barriers he imposed upon himself, he could work only mischief for her. After that he reverted to chilliness.
But when, sighing profoundly, she turned around at the door, she saw
that he was looking at her with passionate love written all over his face.

We are, of course, relying on Eliza's own words for this. But she seems
to have been an innocent, if highly romantic, young woman. The very fact
that she did not scruple to put down details unflattering to herself entitles
her to some measure of credence. Of course, smitten with him as she was,
she may have read in his countenance what she wished to find. On the
other hand, it is equally credible that the Byronic hero was doing justice
to a dramatic situation. Also, he might have been filled with anguish at the
idea that here was another girl he might have slept with, whom he was
letting slip through his fingers.

At any rate, Eliza rushed home and dissolved in tears. More than a
week passed without a sign from him. At length she determined to storm
the fortress and tell him he was deceiving himself in thinking she was in
love with him. Whatever she had hoped for from this interview, she could
hardly have been gratified at the way it evolved. She murmured to him that
she would come no more. At that he told her she was wise. She was so
obviously stunned by that, that he took her hand and said that had they
met more frequently friendship might have converted to something else.
When she ventured to say she had not imagined there was any danger of
that, he retorted that the danger would have been all his. Now all she
wished was to get out of his rooms, but her trembling was so violent that
she was about to fall. His arm sustained her. When she felt a little better,
she tried to disengage herself, but he held her about the waist and clung
to her hand. Her head was lowered and she felt him brush aside her curls
and kiss her neck. Virtuously she wriggled to be free of his grasp, but he
drew her passionately to him. She cried to be released—never could she
have anticipated his behaving this way. He asked her to be neither angry nor
alarmed, protested with emotion that she was entirely safe with him, threw
himself into a chair, and pulled her to him. She allowed him to hold her
on his knee a moment, both arms tight about her waist. He kissed her
cheek feverishly and then tried to kiss her lips. Declaring she had to go now,

she tried to rise, but he clasped her with a kind of frenzy, his face distorted with passion. However, she was able to calm him with a few gentle words, and he let go of her. He would not for the world, he said, upset her, and asked if she would come again. She replied that she must not. He agreed that she was right to refuse, but urged her to come just the same. She moved toward the door, but was arrested by the tone of his voice, which was bidding her stay a little. Did she remember to take all her papers? She had brought none that day. He came to her, took her in his arms, begged her to come again, but she still refused. Once again at the door, she turned to look at him; he seemed so grief-stricken that she flung herself into his arms once more. "Another wild embrace, and with a desperate effort I tore myself for ever from the truly noble Lord Byron."

Though she knew Eliza's own account and freely quoted from it, Teresa Guiccioli preferred to repaint the picture of that final interview: "Lord Byron soon perceived the danger of these visits. . . . How many young men, in a similar case, would not without a scruple have thought that he had only to cull this flower which seemed voluntarily to tempt him? Lord Byron never entertained such an idea." In order to end the danger for her, "he went so far as to try to appear less amiable. For the sake of destroying any hope, he assumed a cold, stern, troubled air." When he had convinced her that she must for her own sake cease coming to the Albany, "she left his house having ever been treated with respect . . . and the young man's sacrifice only permitted one kiss imprinted on the lovely brow of her whose strong feelings for himself he well knew."

Aside from the falsifications here, contrary to what we know about Byron's behavior with young women, it may seem odd that the Countess Guiccioli, who during the closing years of Byron's brief life was to establish a record as the woman he kept longest as a mistress, should depict as an extraordinary and heroic "sacrifice" that her dead lover had not seized the opportunity to deflower Eliza. It should be remembered that she was not only a hypocrite herself, but wrote and thought as an Italian. There would be few of her fellow countrymen, women as well as men, who today would not find it strange that Byron did not "take advantage" of the situation. Italians generally assume that if a young woman is willing to be alone in a room with a man, there can be only one possible conclusion before she leaves it.*

---

* I was recently asked by a Venetian, an ugly dwarf of a man, whether it was true, as he had heard, that sometimes in the United States and in England a normal young man will spend the night alone under the same roof with a young woman without his sleeping with her. When I told him that this happened often

8.

AUGUSTA GAVE BIRTH TO HER BROTHER'S DAUGHTER, ELIZABETH MEDORA
Leigh, on April 15 of that turbulent 1814. Ten days later he wrote to Lady
Melbourne to justify himself for a relationship she was still urging him to
break: "Oh! but it is 'worth while.' I can't tell you why, and it is not an
'Ape,' and if it is, that must be my fault." (The "Ape" has been explained
as referring to the age-old superstition that the child born of incest would
be a monster; Byron's use of quotation marks around the word indicates that
Lady Melbourne may have made, in her light way, such a prophecy.) "It
is utterly impossible," he continued, "I can ever be so well liked elsewhere,
and I have been all my life trying to make someone love me." He tried to
soothe his confidante by adding that he and Augusta would "grow good,"
and that they were good *now,* and should be for the next three weeks or so—
one imagines only because of the physical limitations placed upon Augusta
after childbirth.

On December 14, 1814, Augusta wrote him (the +s are kisses):

> My dearest B+
>   As usual I have but a short allowance of time to reply to your *ten-
> dresses*+ but a few lines I know will be better than none—at least *I* find
> them so+ It was very very good of you to think of me amidst all the
>   +   +
> visitors, & c. & c. I have scarcely recovered [from?] *mine* of yesterday—
> La Dame did talk so—oh my stars! but at least it saved me a world of
> trouble—oh! but she found out a likeness in your picture to Mignonne
> [i.e., Medora] who is of course very good humoured in consequence+
> I want to know dearest dearest B + your plans . . ."

It was signed, "Ever thine."

Her passion for her brother is evident; as regards her child, then eight
months old, she sounds normal enough—the mama pleased to hear that the
baby looks like its father. Her later treatment of the girl, however, was so
unnatural and unfeeling that it fairly cancels the impression Augusta at
first creates of being pathetically inept. Byron's attitude toward Medora
is quite mysterious too. Considering the to-do he made about some of his
illegitimate children, notably Allegra, it seems very odd that none of his

---

enough among friends—that in our countries men and women were often good
friends—he looked sincerely bewildered, and exclaimed: "Then what's wrong
with American men and Englishmen?"

multitudinous letters after the one to Lady Melbourne, a few days after Medora's birth, makes any reference to the child of his great love—at least none of the letters which have been published. Nor did he make any provision for her in his will, though he may have felt that the handsome bequest he was leaving Augusta would be used for the welfare of their child. Such turned out to be far from the case. It is above all very odd that, with the passionate and undying love he felt for his sister he should have shown no interest at all in their daughter—unless he confined what he had to say in letters to Augusta which she may have preferred to burn. As will shortly be seen, when Medora was in trouble with Henry Trevanion and wrote Augusta a letter confessing the facts, Augusta's first move was to burn the letter. She may have done the same with letters of Byron's which referred to their child. The bulk of Byron's correspondence is so huge that one is likely to overlook all the letters that may have been destroyed or are still unpublished.

On the other hand, beyond the brief reference to Medora as an infant, already quoted, there are no letters from Augusta to him that have to do with their child. While it is not beyond possibility that such letters existed and he destroyed them for reasons similar to hers—or simply to protect Augusta—that is quite difficult to believe. Byron—we are grateful—tended to save every scrap of correspondence he received, if it had the smallest emotional overtone, even those letters which he had been expressly asked to destroy. It is hard to conceive of him parting with any which had to do with the love child Augusta bore him.

In any case it is equally strange that Byron's biographers have also shown no interest in Medora. Generally, she has been merely mentioned *en passant* during a discussion as to whether Byron had really been his sister's lover—as though the evidence were not sufficiently overwhelming! I know of only one work on Medora,* a book written by Charles Mackay and published in 1870, and that is based upon her autobiography, which itself seems to have aroused no one's curiosity. Although her story properly begins after Byron's death—she was still a child when he died—and therefore might be said to lie outside the limits set for the present biography—I have considered

---

* Between the writing of the above passage and the publication of the present work Peter Gunn's *My Dearest Augusta* (New York, 1969) has appeared, and in it (pp. 236–52) there is an account of Medora, differing in some details from my own. Since Mr. Gunn does not indicate the source of his information and his "Short Bibliography" lists nothing which might be that source, I am at a loss to explain the discrepancies. My own narrative, as I have indicated, is largely derived from Medora's autobiography.

it worth examining, so that it may at last appear on the record; it is, after all, part of the Augusta-Byron history. For the years covered by her autobiography, my own account is based upon the manuscript of her terribly moving narrative.

The beginnings of Medora's appalling career lie outside the autobiography. For some unknowable motive—unless it were the simple one of wishing to have one daughter the less on her hands—the ever-impecunious Augusta when Georgiana, her eldest daughter, had reached seventeen, was set upon marrying her to the girl's third cousin, Henry Trevanion of Cornwall, second son of a family not particularly exalted. Augusta was allied to some of the leading families in England and moved in the circle of the royal court; she certainly could have arranged a more advantageous match. The reason she advanced was a wish to make the young people happy. If that was the truth, her judgment proved to be as poor in this instance as was habitual with her. A rumor which it is not necessary to credit, told to Byron's grandson by his father, the Earl of Lovelace, had it that Trevanion had been Augusta's lover and that, moreover, she had promised him each of her daughters to sleep with once they were of age to do that. The grandson, ever bitterly Lady Byron's partisan and therefore hostile to Byron and Augusta, made the strangely prejudiced comment that it was "impossible to be absolutely certain of the falsehood of these charges." Augusta's unreasoning fondness for Trevanion and subsequent indifference to Medora, his victim, as well as Trevanion's own weakly lecherous conduct with two of her children, of course, would seem to lend weight to the scandalous allegations.

By 1825 Augusta had a large family to take care of. In a letter to Lady Byron, she recounts how four of the children at home were ill and her two boys at school were down with the measles. This letter eventually came to *"a proposal of marriage* to Georgey! . . . The young Man is studying the Law . . .—exceedingly clever & in other respects the only person I know *worthy* of Georgey—I had known his Family as relations before my Marriage . . . we renewed it [our intimacy] only about 2 years ago—& I asked after the *Hero* of my present tale among a groupe [*sic*] of other CHILDREN forgetting how years must have made them into men! . . . I've seen much of him since from liking him & finding him so far superior to the *common herd,* but without the slightest idea that Georgey was likely to attract him or indeed any body—She is such a *quiet* being . . . The present state of things is that the Father at a distance of 300 miles, is approving . . . but doubting whether there will be *de quoi* to enable them to marry at present." She professed horror of long engagements, foresaw no likelihood of any improving change in the financial situation, and was "strenuous for the thing being brought to pass as soon as possible." Her husband, Colonel Leigh, when he was home, opposed the match, but his disapproval did not daunt

Augusta. She was anxious to raise £2,000 at once, particularly since an aged aunt of Trevanion's, from whom he had expected help, was now senile and could not be coerced into giving any money. This blatant appeal for Annabella's help did not fail of its objective. Lady Byron was not averse to lending financial assistance when it was likely to give her a hold on anyone connected with her late husband's incest.

Despite Colonel Leigh's protests the marriage took place in 1826 at St. James's—without his attendance. Besides Augusta and the man who gave the bride away, there was present only Medora. Augusta declared that she would not have parted with Georgiana "to ANYONE in the world . . . with such perfect confidence *as* to Henry Trevanion. I have seen him *dáily hourly* for 3 months," and his character "has only *risen* in my estimation!" No one could ever have been a worse judge of character.

Henry's father had promised him £900 a year but lowered it to half that sum, so that the young man also felt compelled to borrow money from Lady Byron; Augusta plunged deeper into debt than ever to pay for the marriage expenses. Henry, it turned out, was too delicate of health to enter the law. At this point we turn to Medora's autobiography. Unfortunately, we do not know what she looked like—beyond Augusta's report that someone had found her at eight months looking just like Byron.

She was not yet twelve when the wedding took place, and for the following years was often in the company of Georgiana and Henry, who were far from happy because of the shortage of funds. In 1829 Lady Byron put at their disposal a country house near Canterbury for Georgiana's approaching accouchement; fifteen-year-old Medora went with them. On their leaving Six Mile Bottom, Augusta warned Medora that she must exert herself to overcome her patent dislike of Henry and do all she could to please him—above all "to cease ridiculing him as I had been in the habit of doing." The girl promised to mend her childish ways.

Because of her sister's illness she was left alone a great deal with her brother-in-law. (Hobhouse was told that they spent much time reading the Bible together.) Just how far she interpreted her mother's admonition that she must please Trevanion as much as she could, we cannot guess. At any rate he ended by seducing her and, as Medora phrases it, he "effected my ruin." She was only fifteen, but soon discovered that she was *enceinte*. Henry implored her to tell Georgiana the truth; it was best that both of them throw themselves "upon her mercy." Georgiana was herself but twenty, yet blamed herself for having placed her sister too much "in Henry's way." A strange education Augusta's girls had received! It was agreed that Augusta, without mention of what had happened, be asked permission for Medora's going abroad with them.

Several months later they took her to Calais. Her distress forced a premature birth; the boy, when born, was taken away under the charge of the officiating doctor. Three months later the three returned to England, the couple to the house of an aunt, Medora to Six Mile Bottom, where her mother remained in ignorance that her daughter was no longer virginal. With Augusta's encouragement, Henry came almost daily to see Medora; since the house was sorrowing over the death of another sister, her mother wished her to go to balls and have a lively time.

Thus left constantly in Trevanion's company, early in 1831, when she was seventeen, the girl "for the second time" found herself "likely to become a mother." This time Henry asked her to confide in Augusta; he wrote a letter which she copied and signed, invoking her mother's aid. Augusta burned the letter at once, but at first was compassionate. In March 1831 the girl was again sent off into the country with Georgiana and Henry. Either this child was stillborn or else Medora had a miscarriage—it is not clear from her autobiography.

Three months later Colonel Leigh suddenly appeared in a carriage with a stranger to take her away. "I then believed, *though I had been told the contrary by my sister and her husband,* that Colonel Leigh was my father. I wished to spare him the knowledge of my shame. We were never, any of us, taught to love and honour him. But strange to say, I was his favourite child." She could influence him as no other member of her family could when he had one of his fits of violence.

Allowed ten minutes of private conversation with Henry, she was pressed to promise him that "I would escape as soon as possible from my mother, and run away with him." Obviously they all supposed that she was about to be conveyed home to Six Mile Bottom. Georgiana said she would immediately procure a divorce from Henry so that her sister might marry him if she chose to do so.

Poor Medora was being taken, not to her home, but to a lunatic asylum —a house in which the windows of her room were nailed down and the door was also chained and bolted from the outside. (Hobhouse in his Journal for July 1, 1831, says that he had been told the whole "sad" story. "What a fate!" he reflects, "and what a retribution!" That remark itself is meaningless unless one grants that Hobhouse knew Medora to be Byron's child. It also implies that Augusta told him some cock-and-bull story about her daughter's sanity.)

During her stay in the asylum Colonel Leigh came to see her three times and Augusta only once. An aunt sent her some religious books for edification—strange diversion for a reputed lunatic! Two weeks after her arrival, through the window she beheld Henry driving by; after that for a fortnight he appeared in the street almost daily. She found notes from him sewed in her linen when it came back from the wash.

One day the woman of the house told her she was free to go if she wished. Wasting not a minute, she left, and found Henry outside waiting for her.

They fled at once to the Continent. For two years they lived in Normandy as man and wife under the name of Aubin. By then her health was so poor and she had had so many miscarriages that she was convinced she could never bear another child. It would seem that this was the reason she expressed a desire to separate from Henry. He made no difficulty. She wrote to Augusta that she wished to enter as a boarder in a convent in Brittany. For a long time her mother neglected to reply; when at length she did it was to offer Medora a mere £60 a year on which to live.

Medora left Trevanion, entered the convent, but soon discovered that she was again pregnant; she naturally felt compelled to quit the convent. From that time on, she says, "I never was but as a sister" to Henry. After eight months she gave birth to a little girl, to Henry's "great joy." She and he went to live with their child at an old chateau in a deserted spot "in great poverty." Henry gave himself up wholly to religion and shooting, I to my child. We never met alone and seldom met at all." (It must be admitted that this was a way to avoid pregnancy.)

Sixteen months later he returned to England to procure some money. When he was back at the chateau, he tried to win her to his passion, but "two years' experience had enabled me to know how to resist."

In the spring of 1838, when she was twenty-four, she developed tuberculosis; the doctor gave her but a few months to live. He was so kind that she confessed to him her whole story, begging his help to free her of Trevanion, whom she knew to be worthless. With the physician's counsel she wrote to her mother and an aunt, describing her straits. The aunt, Lady Chichester, sent her £5, her mother nothing. Leaving Henry, Medora went to a neighboring town, whence she pleaded with Augusta to grant her £120 a year, "the smallest sum I could live on in a very cheap place." Her mother promised it, and then forgot about her promise.

After a year and a half Medora felt forced to sell the reversion of £3,000 which had been allotted by Augusta and Lady Byron as provision for Medora after Augusta's death. For some months she and Augusta continued to write each other with affection, but with almost no material aid coming from England. Medora then applied to Lady Chichester to persuade Augusta to surrender the Deed of Reversion which was in her keeping, so it could be sold. She also counted on Lady Byron's using her influence with Augusta to the same end. Colonel Leigh had been all for sending Trevanion to prison for his misdeeds; now it was proposed that he be thrown into debtors' prison for failing to pay Lady Byron the debt he had contracted with her. Disgusted with the plot, Medora thought it only decent to warn Henry.

It was in August of 1840 that Byron's widow, Lady Byron, who had lived with him for only one year before leaving him, entered Medora's history actively by writing her a most affectionate letter which enclosed money and promised to protect her and her child—a communication which was received "joyfully." Lady Byron then expedited a physician to bring Medora to Tours, where she and her niece met. The two women and the child went on to Paris. At Fontainebleau Lady Byron explained to the younger woman *"the cause of the deep interest she felt, and must ever feel"* for Medora. (Lady Byron had bided her time in realizing this interest.) *"Her husband had been my father."* It must have been deliciously satisfying to Lady Byron to inform Medora that her parents had been brother and sister; that was at least one dividend of the vast revenge she never ceased to plan and exact because of Byron's love for Augusta. Greater dividends were in store, and to insure them she seemed now to spare nothing to win her niece's love. Medora, innocent of what the future held, was only too happy "to repay by my affection and devotion any pain she must have felt for circumstances connected with my birth and her separation from Lord Byron. [The world had generally been misled to believe, as a result of Lady Byron's subterranean efforts, that the separation was due to the incest.] Her only wish, she said, was to provide for me, according to Lord Byron's intention respecting me, and according to my rank in life. She evinced much anxiety for my health and comfort, expressed indignation for all I had suffered, spoke of the comfort I would be to her [Lady Byron had her own daughter, Ada], and of the necessity that I should be a devoted child to her." Medora melted at her aunt's goodness, at her ability to forgive and forget the great wrong done her, the wrong of which she was the personification—(though, indeed, there had hardly been any wrong done to Lady Byron since the act had been committed before she accepted Byron's proposal of marriage). All this generosity and magnanimity easily persuaded Medora to accede to her aunt's wish that she remain with her. They stayed some ten months in Paris, and in May 1841 came to England. (If there was one thing Lady Byron could do it was to wait as long as necessary to spring.) There Lady Byron showed her Byron's letters relative to the separation. Apparently more attached to Medora then ever (the softening-up process, which had already worked splendidly with Augusta), Lady Byron declared that her niece must stay with her always, and that if she ever went away it would kill her. Medora was more than grateful, even though it was true that sometimes her aunt's "temper caused me great misery."

There had for some time been a suit in Chancery to obtain possession of the Deed of Reversion from Augusta, which had remained with the latter. Lady Byron (by now alienated from Augusta, whom for years she had made a point of loving most dearly as well as torturing upon the rack for her sin) was apparently lending her support to the claims of her niece. In May 1842 the suit was settled, and although the Deed was surrendered to Medora, the decision was in Augusta's favor, so far as the money was concerned. Medora, who felt that she had been "sacrificed in her mother's interest" (Augusta's connections at the royal court were powerful), now wished to leave England, and asked for her aunt's help. "She again continued, as ever, saying that it was for her to provide as Lord Byron would have done, &c. &c." (Such provision Annabella could well afford; born an heiress, she had become considerably richer by her marriage to Byron.) Now quite ill, Medora was ordered on medical opinion to the south of France. Lady Byron insisted that she must have a woman to live with her abroad, and engaged a maid, whose stipulated avocation was to spy on her mistress. In July 1842 Lady Byron volunteered to give her niece an allowance of £150 a year as well as the wages of the handpicked servant. She had told the woman about Medora's past, and the maid kept remarking to Medora that she would have preferred being "with a lady whose conduct had ever been irreproachable." Tiring of this refrain, Medora told her that she had better find another post, "as my life and past history were not such as she could wish."

Placated by this blunt declaration, the woman announced herself anxious to serve Medora and assured her of her devotion. Medora had reason to believe that £150 a year would be insufficient for subsistence at Hyères, then a favorite Riviera resort, where she was bound, and was prepared to find some employment there to supplement the promised income. Without offering to increase it, Lady Byron firmly forbade her trying to work: women in their rank simply could not work for a living. For all this delicate regard for the *comme il faut* for a person of rank, it was to the servant that Lady Byron paid Medora's allowance and from whom she required an exact accounting of all her niece's expenditures.

Before they left England the maid offered a suggestion which was later to become the source of poor Medora's final sufferings. She left with her aunt's housekeeper a box containing letters and papers to be given Lady Byron on her return to Moore House; and with Ada, Lady Lovelace, Lady Byron's daughter, the Deed of Reversion, which was to be locked up with the papers of the Lovelace family. (Considering Lady Byron's assiduity in amassing archives to the detriment of the characters of her late husband and his sister, it is not farfetched to suppose that this suggestion of the servant-spy may very well have originated with Lady Byron herself.) These deposits Medora was glad to make as proof of her love for Lady Byron and her complete trust in her. Nevertheless, Lady Byron at no time acknowledged the receipt of the box, even though she had already asked Medora to will all her papers to her.

Upon the servant's instigation Medora asked her benefactress to employ also the maid's husband to accompany them to France. Lady Byron agreed. (Two spies are better than one.) The three left England with Medora's little girl on Friday, July 22, 1842.

When they reached Hyères, Medora was already out of money. Lady Byron in her letters was always affectionate, and instructed her to procure teachers for the child and to hire carriages for driving; she was, in short, to live in a manner becoming her illustrious lineage. Medora did all she could to economize, but her aunt suggested moving to a cheaper place. The servant "got certificates as to the rent being far from unreasonable, from the mayor of Hyères." The allowance was always quite late in arriving. In December Lady Byron "expressed dissatisfaction, and accused me of rendering all the money arrangements as vexatious as possible to her." Suddenly Lady Byron announced that after the first of January she would no longer pay the wages of the manservant.

No money at all arriving, Medora was pressed by both servants to go to Paris. A retired captain of the British army, De Barallin, who had taken pity on her plight, offered to accompany her and the child and advance whatever sums were needed for the journey out of his own fairly empty pocket. Grasping at this straw, Medora left for Paris in March 1843, and wrote her aunt from there in explanation of the change she had made. She received no reply. A Miss Davison visited her and told her that it would be necessary for her to beg forgiveness of Annabella. (Lady Byron always managed such little negotiations, when unpleasant, if not through lawyers, then through friends devoted to her as a martyred woman.) The servants wrote to Lady Byron too. Medora still had no answer to her letters, though Annabella wrote to the servants, accusing them of having seconded the removal to Paris, and of having failed in the offices to which she had appointed them. She also took the trouble to write to the proprietor of Medora's hotel to apprize him of the facts of Medora's history. Things must have been more than uncomfortable for Medora, but she was able to find lodgings elsewhere.

Early in May a Dr. King was in Paris to see her for Lady Byron. He had brought word that she was to "resign to her all control over my self and child." Medora—she was still only twenty-nine—declined. King, when she interviewed him, was authorized to offer her £300 a year if she would agree to all the stipulations. But she refused to sign the agreement. King kept pressing her: "Sign, sign, you great fool!" But she stood her ground.

She wrote to Messrs. Wharton in England, asking them to forward her Deed to her at Paris. They would give it to no one but herself or a designated messenger. Since her maid was going back to England to collect her husband's salary in arrears, Medora gave her the authority to retrieve the Deed as well as the box of papers left with Annabella. But when Medora consulted the British Embassy at Paris and the men there had read the maid's letters from England, they strongly advised against allowing her emissary to get her hands on the Deed.

Captain De Barallin, whom Mackay describes as a veteran "who had received several severe wounds at Waterloo," had all this while been a true friend, asking no questions when, as she says, he rescued her from "the very brink of starvation." Nevertheless, she confided in him the grim details of her experience. When the British Embassy urged her to conciliate her aunt as the best solution of her problems, the Captain seconded the advice. Though his income was meager, he brought her to England from Paris, still at his own expense, on the natural assumption that the sum would be made good by her family. She, however, must have been more worried at the possible outcome of her journey, for to her recent letters her mother had never returned a word.

When, during the summer of 1843, they reached London, they were notified that Lady Byron, known to her admiring and compassionating friends as a saint whose days and nights were given to acts of familial philanthrophy despite the monstrous treatment she had borne at the hands of the incestuous pair, was determined, notwithstanding all those protestations of motherly affection, "to have no further intercourse" with Medora. The kind Captain did what he could for Medora with the lawyers, but with so little luck that he found no one even willing to reimburse him for his outlay. Having already spent more than he could afford, he was compelled to return to France. Poor Medora was faced with utter destitution. Thus, Lady Byron's long-range revenge against her dead husband, his erring sister, and the fruit of their incest, was complete, managed with a finesse which is the endowment of only really good women.

It is worth stating here that when Byron married Annabella he settled on her, as Hobhouse put it, all he had—£60,000—and that she since had inherited a great deal of money, and was now a wealthy woman. So beneficent a creature, after having declared that parting with Medora would cause her death, might possibly have thought that her husband's child, reared according to her rank to no employment, ought to be granted at least a small portion of what was to be eventually hers after her aunt's death. But that, of course, would have tarnished the revenge.

(Mrs. Harriet Beecher Stowe, in her uninformed defense of Lady Byron, speaks of the "unfortunate child of sin, born with a curse upon her, over whose wayward nature Lady Byron watched with a mother's tenderness.")

Medora called on Augusta, but was told at the door that her mother was "not at home" to her. After a long campaign of browbeating, threats, and terrorization mixed with affection and endearments, Annabella had brought the weak-willed Augusta to heel, to a full admission of her sin, and a willingness to gratify Annabella's every whim—not excluding the

Augusta Leigh,
miniature by James Holmes.

treacherous handing over to her of Byron's letters from the continent which he sent his beloved sister all unsuspectingly, as Augusta received them, one by one. Now that Byron was long dead and Lady Byron had wrung from Augusta everything else she could have wished, and had reduced her from a merry, if harebrained, to a dull, frightened woman, they had, by 1843, been estranged for well over a decade. Had Annabella succeeded so well with her sister-in-law that Augusta had come to dread the sight or thought of her child of incest? How else is one to account for her having become so unnatural a mother?

Medora's autobiography has nothing more to say of her desperate pass. She disappeared from London that same year, and died soon thereafter— we may be sure, in great wretchedness.

Mackay, her sole biographer, adds a few details where her own account has left off; he speaks of a letter she had written at this time to her mother, but says, "It is of such a nature, that, after mature deliberation, we have deemed it both expedient and proper to exclude it from these pages."

It happens that the Morgan Library owns that letter. I believe it has never been published before this. It makes a fitting close to Medora's tragic story:

August 13, 1843
3 Church Row, St. Pancras

My Mother

The motive that led me last night to seek what I have long since hoped to be spared, to meet once more, you, I so tenderly loved, was not as you have given me the right to do, to accuse you and reproach you, nor yet to seek to awaken your pity for the misery I owe alone to you.

Since I was made to understand you could never have loved me, the child of your guilt, in whom you have seen but a means to satisfy your ambitions, a sacrifice to be made to those you feared, then to throw on the world, destitute, homeless and friendless, I have expected and sought nothing from you, but [am] now compelled to seek aid and protection from all who will give it. I once more remind you I am *your child*—The world & strangers will tell you in harsher terms all you owed me [,] do owe me—could I have felt I was writing to a mother, I would have said much, now I can only beg you by the memory of my father, the brother to whom you, & the children you love and enrich by my destitution owe all—no longer to forget and neglect what you still owe

Your child
Elizabeth Medora Leigh

ANNA=
BELLA

1.

IT CAN BE PROPHESIED THAT A
writer whose work is à la mode will
quickly be "discovered"; his contemporaries will outdo one another
in their zeal to discover him too and
to sing his praises. Even authors
truly superior are not exempt from
this succumbing to the adulation of
such a writer. Shelley and Keats, both Byron's betters as poets by far, though
their following was small, agreed with the general verdict that Byron was
the greatest poet of their epoch; Shelley called him the Apollo of his day
and said that his was a genius "destined to lead and not to follow"; Keats
thought that, with Scott, he was one of the two literary kings of the day.
Though not thinking much of Shelley's poetry and less of Keats's, Byron
agreed with the latter in holding Scott to be the prince of living poets. Just
below Scott he placed other poets with considerable, if inflated, reputations
in his day, first Rogers and next Moore and Campbell; all of them, he was
convinced, were far superior to Wordsworth and Coleridge.

But in the midst of the clamor over his own verse, Byron did not
delude himself. To his journal he confided his contempt for "the mighty
stir" made over poets altogether; it was a symptom of effeminacy, degen-
eracy, and weakness. "Who would write that had anything better to do?"
he asked. For him action was what he really desired, not writing, "least of
all rhyme." He had "no great esteem for poetical persons," and sometimes
resented his own urge to compose. "I have just thrown a poem into the fire
(which it has relighted to my great comfort)," he recorded. "What the devil
have I to do with scribbling? It is too late to inquire." Nevertheless, if he

ever married and had a son, "I will bring up mine heir," he decided, "in the most anti-poetical way—make him a lawyer, or a pirate . . . If he writes too, I shall be sure he is none of mine, and cut him off with a Bank token." As for his own verse, though he was concerned about the "costume" and the local color of his narrative poems (his worst works), "I don't care a lump of Sugar for my *poetry.*" He told Hobhouse that his poems "are of the sort which like every thing of the kind in these days pass away & give place to the ancient reading," though he esteemed himself "fortunate in getting all that can now be got by poetry [,] a passing reputation for which there are so many competitors."

Overpraised in his own time, he underrated himself. His greatest weakness as a poet is his fatal facility, which makes his verse racy—no great merit in poetry—but its poetic quintessence far too thin. Nevertheless, even though the bulk of what he wrote in verse is not worth much—his letters are among the best in the language—a number of his lyrics have a fine, manly directness, and *The Vision of Judgment* and *Don Juan* are in a class by themselves. These are first rate and are likely to endure.

And what were Byron's thoughts of himself as a human being at the time of his early fame in London? On November 14, 1813, he wrote in his journal, with the disenchantment to be expected of the self-conscious romantic: "At five-and-twenty, when the better part of life is over, one should be *something;* and what am I? nothing but five-and-twenty—and the odd months. What have I seen? the same man all over the world,—ay, and woman too." He hoped to be near the Black Sea again by the spring of 1814, "provided I neither marry myself nor unmarry any one else in the interval." He admitted to knowing nothing of what he really wanted. Whenever he set himself seriously to desire a thing, he always attained it—and always repented afterwards.

It was one of the flaws of all the major Romantic poets, from which only Wordsworth was exempt, that they held that with the passing of early youth life commenced its decline. To them it was the undiscriminating enthusiasms of youth which were the most precious part of experience; to think was to be full of pain and despair. (It is interesting that the wheel has come full circle and the youth today of the psychedelic persuasions have come to the same conclusion.)

As a matter of fact, there was plenty of vivacity and capacity for simple enjoyment in the adult Byron.

The composer Isaac Nathan observed that so far from being morbid, Byron was extremely playful. Once Edmund Kean, whose acting Byron greatly admired, entertained them by sketching the face and body of a dancer at the opera with a piece of burnt cork upon the back of his hand; using his two middle fingers to represent thighs and legs, his nails the shoes, he wrapped a handkerchief about his wrist to serve as a turban; the performer thus fabricated began to dance with great abandon and assumed absurd attitudes. Byron was in a delirium of delight, applauded violently, and asked for an encore.

Hobhouse tells us, by the way, that after seeing Kean in *Hamlet* he and Byron came home "& sat up until 1 . . . drawing up rules for a club of which he & I are to be the only members."

Throughout his life Byron nurtured a devotion to animals; at times he owned a considerable number of them at once. Three days after the melancholy piece of self-examination just quoted, he had seen a hippopotamus which had, he declared, a "face like Lord Liverpool's" and a sloth with the "very voice and manner" of his own valet, Fletcher. "The tiger talked too much"; the elephant was so well behaved "that I wish he were my butler."

Those who met him during the years of fame in London commented upon nothing more frequently than upon the beauty of his voice. "The tones of Lord Byron's voice," said the novelist Amelia Opie, "were always so fascinating, that I could not help attending to them"; it "was such a voice as the devil tempted Eve with; you feared its fascination the moment you heard it." Jane Porter, author of *The Scottish Chiefs,* at a small evening party, was distracted from listening to the person talking to her by the sound of Byron's voice—she had not known he was present—"the most melodious Speaking Voice I had ever heard. It was gentle and beautifully modulated. I turned round to look for the Speaker, and then saw a Gentleman in black of an Elegant form . . . and with a face I shall never forget. . . . There was no scorn, no disdain, nothing in that noble countenance *then* of the proud spirit which has since soared to Heaven, illuminating the Horizon far and wide."

His tendency to put on fat was still, and was to remain, a problem. "When I *do* dine," he wrote in November of 1813, "I gorge like an Arab or a Boa snake, on fish and vegetables, but no meat. [In those days a man was free to develop his own unscientific notions of how to lose weight.] I am always better, however, on my tea and biscuit than any other regimen, and even *that* sparingly." It was his idea, too, that it was wise to take frequent drafts of vinegar. That may be the reason he was so often cold, even in autumn. He had "never yet found a sun quite *done* to my taste." At a social gathering, he sympathized with the guests who all "looked as if they were just unpacked, like *salmon* from an ice-bucket."

It was not only excess weight which ruffled his vanity. "My arms are very long for my height."

The lionizing of which he had been, and continued to be, the victim aggravated his inclination toward melancholy, and was making him more and more antisocial. "The more I see of men, the less I like them. If I could but say so of women too, all would be well. Why can't I?" At twenty-six his passions, he reasoned, had surely been fed enough. During the winter of 1813–1814 his journal shows that he rejected many invitations to go out into society. In December he said, "If I must fritter away my life, I would rather do it alone." He wondered of what use were dandies, kings, fellows of colleges, "women of 'a certain age'—and many men of any age—and myself, most of all!" Hobhouse warned him that he was fast becoming a *loup garou,* a solitary churl. He could not understand why the rational John Cam liked parties; they were all very well, "if one is in love, and wants to break a commandment and covet any thing that is there. . . . But to go out amongst the mere herd, without a motive, pleasure or pursuit—'s death!" For himself, "I hardly ever go out—and, when I do, always regret it." After two such gatherings, he reflected: "Nothing imparted—nothing acquired— talking without ideas . . . In this way half London pass what is called life." (In this way today much of London, New York, Paris, Rome, or any metropolis still does.) Even when with Augusta he could not help "yearning for the company of my lamp and my utterly confused and tumbled-over library." On April 10, 1814, he could add that he had not stirred out of his room for four days. Perhaps it is of some significance that these yearnings for solitude were vented during the months that Augusta was carrying their Medora; on April 10 the birth was expected daily. During this period, too, he had his teeth examined, and was told that he had been grinding them in his sleep and had chipped their edges.

2.

IN THE MIDST OF FAME, MELANCHOLY, HIS AFFAIRS WITH LADY CAROLINE, Lady Oxford, Augusta, the Platonic comedy with Lady Frances and his invasive young adulators like Henrietta and Eliza, a subject paramount to his thoughts was matrimony.

Later he was to tell Medwin that remembering his father very well, despite his own extreme youth when his sire died, he "had a very early horror of matrimony, from the sight of domestic broils." Nevertheless, upon his return from the East in 1811, he began to think of marrying, sometimes seriously, sometimes jokingly, sometimes with aversion. That year he told Augusta, "I shall marry, if I can find any thing inclined to barter money for rank within six months; after which I shall return to my friends the Turks." This was before the great to-do over *Childe Harold.* (Did a return to his friends the Turks mean a return to his love of boys, which could be freely indulged in the Balkans?) Again he wrote her: "I must marry to repair the ravages of myself & prodigal ancestry, but if I am so unfortunate as to be presented with an Heir, instead of a *Rattle,* he shall be provided with a Gag."

A year later he was telling Lady Melbourne, in the cynical style she expected, that love was no essential to matrimony; it is "done in a week" after the ceremony; besides, marriages are better founded on esteem and trust. To Tom Moore he wrote half-soberly, half-jocularly, during the summer of 1813: "My circumstances are mending, and were not my other prospects blackening, I would take a wife. . . . After all, we must end in marriage; and I can conceive nothing more delightful than such a state in the country, reading the county newspaper, etc., and kissing one's wife's maid." In the autumn he was of the opinion that no good ever came of marrying a young wife; "but a mistress is just as perplexing—that is, *one,*—two or more are manageable by division." He had been listening to two men boasting of the felicities of marriage; such creatures are foxes "who have cut off their tails and would persuade the rest to part with their brushes." "I never see any one much improved by matrimony"; all that men seem to acquire from it is to become "bald and discontented." If only the heir to the Byron title, his cousin, George Anson Byron, would marry, he himself would never think of doing so; "I should like nephews better than sons."

In January 1814 he wrote to Lady Melbourne in the strain to be expected of her pupil; if he married, his wife should be free to do as she pleased (he probably knew that Lady Melbourne had felt free enough); for himself, he should demand freedom of action; he had seen enough of love matches; what he wanted was someone who had her temper under control. On that same day he spoke more honestly to his journal—at the time he was toying with the idea of proposing to the younger sister of Lady Frances, Lady Catherine Annesley: "A wife would be my salvation. I am sure the wives of my acquaintances have hitherto done me little good. Catherine is beautiful, but very young, and, I think, a fool . . . That she won't love me is very probable, nor shall I love her. But on my system . . . that don't signify. The business . . . would be arranged between papa and me. She would have her own way, I am good-humoured to women, and docile; and if I did not fall in love with her, which I should try to prevent, we should be a very comfortable couple." If he did love her, he would only be jealous, and he feared his temper would lead him "into some of our oriental tricks of vengeance, or, at any rate, into a summary appeal to the court of twelve paces." Better, therefore, not to marry, "though I should like to have somebody now and then to yawn with one."

These pros and cons on marriage flourished during the period when it was still an open question as to whether Annabella Milbanke would, after all, agree to be his wife.

3.

SHE WAS THE ONLY CHILD OF EXTRAVAGANTLY DEVOTED PARENTS, WHO would have given her anything in the world she liked. Was it not symptomatic of a basic incompatability between Byron and her that she never in her life wished to own an animal, not even a cat or dog? There are no people on the globe who more dote upon animals than the British, and Byron was an extreme example. In Ravenna in 1820, for instance, he housed at one time a fox, a civet cat, two house cats, six dogs, a badger, a falcon, a crow, and a monkey.

Sir Ralph Milbanke had been happily married for fifteen years when his wife, then forty, gave birth to Annabella on May 17, 1792, who was to exhibit in perfection the powerful will which astrologers attribute to Taurians —a trait Byron little guessed she possessed until it was too late. Sir Ralph was a loyal husband to a loving wife, an amiable man, forever busy in Parliament with committees. His wife was a well-read woman who lived, first for her husband, and later even more for her daughter. More than conscious of her own rectitude, she nursed a holier-than-thou disdain of others, was censorious, loved scandal, and was deeply resentful of her husband's sister, Lady Melbourne, whose sophisticated and free life she never wearied of bitterly condemning. If Annabella was not precisely as arrogant as her mother, she was not discouraged from developing considerable self-importance, which, allied to her tendency to be pedantic, could be quite irritating.

This pedantry was already in evidence at the age of seven. She was asked if her father was not always right in his judgments, and the precocious child replied: "Probably not, sometimes right, sometimes wrong, as *we all are.*" By the age of eleven the pedantry was in full bloom; after attending a political meeting, she wrote to compliment the speaker for remembering every word of his speech and showing no stage fright; it had been a large "& in part a very respectable audience"; she concluded by declaring herself "an impartial Tory."

At thirteen she was composing blank verse in imitation of Young's *Night Thoughts;* it was an elegy for a dead friend. Under her mother's influence she was reading the religious writers, and by seventeen she was already a patroness of Joseph Blackett, the "cobbler-poet" whom Byron pilloried in *English Bards and Scotch Reviewers,* and whom Annabella thought better than Burns. She had read a good deal in drama and poetry, the Latin writers, and in her particular love, mathematics. She was addicted to writing her thoughts in a journal. Had Byron, who loathed intellectual women, been able to read the reflections of his bride-to-be at seventeen, he might very well have preferred to run for his life. For instance, the dread of death may

Annabella Milbanke in 1812,
miniature by Charles Hayter.

be due to two causes, she reflected; these causes, being directly in opposition to each other, should produce opposite effects. But such is not the case. "1. *From want of belief in a future existence.* The idea of annihilation is terrible. 2. From a firm belief in a future existence, and a confidence in our being placed there according to our merits." (Annabella was well aware of her "merits," and had a pretty clear conviction of where in the world to come she would be "placed." Byron's own thoughts on a Hereafter were summed up in this brisk fashion: "Who knows? He that can't tell. Who tells that there is? He who don't know.")

At eighteen, in 1810, she went to London for the season, accompanied for a while by her mother, though she would have liked, she said, to postpone her "entrance into the world," of which she had already formed a highly unfavorable opinion. She prayed to God to reinforce her against temptation and to help her be staunch in her religious duties and in "promoting the happiness of others." She had already, in short, all the qualifications for becoming that terror of her sex, a really good woman.

Country girl though she was, she was by no means impressed by the celebrities she met. The Duchess of Devonshire made this estimate of her: she was "good, amiable, and sensible, but cold, prudent, and reflecting. . . . She is really an icicle."

Though no beauty, Annabella was presentable enough, in addition to being an heiress, to have during the next few years a number of suitors. Augustus Foster, the Duchess of Devonshire's son, who was assiduous in attention during 1810, characterized her in a mixture of truth and error: "She is certainly too cold in her manners, and gives to reason too much empire over her mind, but she has good eyes, is fair, has right ideas, and sense, and mildness. I don't think she will ever be able to love very warmly." He judged by what he saw: a certain prettiness, coldness of manner, intelligence, and self-control. But she was far from being the icicle his mother thought her. Her love of mathematics, her pedantry and aloofness did not signify that within she did not own something of a volcano which was never allowed to erupt. The only way to explain her unremitting pursuit of vengeance against Byron and Augusta, even for years after Byron's death, is that she was acting in fury over her frustrated love of him and almost insane jealousy of his sister and a deeply wounding conviction that he had never loved her herself at all.

Foster proposed and was rejected. A similar fate met: the Hon. George Eden, twenty-six, barrister and Member of Parliament (he later became the Earl of Auckland); the Hon. Frederick Sylvester North Douglas, a Member of Parliament at twenty-one and heir of Lord Glenbervie; William John Bankes, a friend of Byron's; and others.

At a party of Lady Gosford's she found reason to complain of Bankes's behaving as though he owned her. When she rejected him, it may be said in light of his future, her instincts were serving her well. Bankes has received no attention from Byron's biographers, though he may be the clue to some of the poet's unrecorded activities at Cambridge. It was there that he and Byron became friends. Bankes, son of a prominent Member of Parliament, had the reputation of being a leader in the concocting of student mischief; he was also responsible for introducing Byron to the poetry of Scott. In two letters written in 1812 at the height of Byron's fame, I find Byron addressing Bankes in a tone fairly foreign to his correspondence, humbleness. In one he said: "Do not distress me by supposing that I can think of you, or you of me, otherwise than I trust we have long thought. You told me not long ago that my temper was improved. . . . Believe me, your friendship is of more account to me than all those absurd vanities in which, I fear, you conceive me to take too much interest. I have never disputed your superiority." On April 20, 1812, he wrote again: "I should be very sorry that any part of my behaviour should give you cause to suppose that I think higher of myself, or otherwise of you than I have always done. I can assure you that I am as much the humblest of your servants as at Trin. Coll.; and if I have not been at home when you favoured me with a call, the loss was more mine than yours." He signed himself "most affectionately yours"—an unusual subscription for him. There is an overtone in these letters, especially if Bankes's later experiences are taken into account, that he might have shared with Bankes at Trinity College some of such intimacies as he had had at Harrow. On September 28 of that year he said to Bankes: "When you point out to one how people can be intimate at the distance of some seventy leagues, I will plead guilty to your charge . . . I do assure you I am much indebted to you for thinking of me at all, and can't spare you even from amongst the superabundance of friends with whom you suppose me surrounded," and this was signed, "Ever your most affectionately." By the end of the year Bankes was preparing for a tour of the East himself, in regions familiar to Byron, who sent him letters of recommendation, and expressed hopes of joining him. In the East, the author of *Don Leon* hints, Bankes may have allowed himself to indulge freely in the vices which Byron had found so pleasant. At any rate, eleven years later, in June 1833, he was surprised standing at a urinal near Westminster with a soldier named Flower, both of them having their "breeches and braces unbuttoned at ten at night." Arrested, Bankes had numerous distinguished men at his trial to speak for him—he was something of a public figure, having been a Member of Parliament while still a youth; Wellington, Rogers, and a host of other celebrities testified that he had never been heard to utter a licentious word— as though that proved anything about his aberrations. He was exonerated and the case dismissed. But within another eight years, in 1841, he was apprehended a second time for indecent exposure. He soon disappeared from society altogether, and died in Venice in 1855. In rejecting him, Annabella was unknowingly sparing herself one grim future—though she managed to prepare for herself another almost as grim.

It was in the spring of 1812 that she met Byron. On March 22, three days before they first saw each other, she began to read the *Childe Harold* which everyone was talking about, in the copy Byron had sent Bankes; she recorded in her journal that the poet excelled most in the depiction of deep emotions—a subject on which she could hardly have spoken with authority yet. On March 25, when he was paying his second call at Melbourne House, after he had stumbled on the stairs on the way up to the Lambs' apartment —the "bad omen" of which he spoke to Moore at the time—he saw in the drawing room a simply dressed young woman sitting apart from the rest. This was Annabella. That day she wrote in her journal that Byron's mouth indicated a bitterness of spirit, though he seemed "sincere and independent." She noted his habit of covering his mouth with his hand when he was speaking. By nature he was sarcastic, she observed, though he made some effort to control this trait; just the same his lips constantly curled in contempt. To put her reflections in perspective, we should recall that that day there was waltzing among the visitors and that Byron, because of his clubfoot, was bitterly disabled from participating in the gaiety.

She also wrote her mother that she had met him, "the object of universal attention. Lady C. has of course seized on him, notwithstanding the reluctance he manifests to be shackled by her." (Byron and Caro were still new acquaintances on that day.) Some hours later, at another house, Annabella heard some disquieting stories about him, such as his telling a young man that he thanked Heaven because he had quarreled with his mother *"for ever."* (Mrs. Byron had died the preceding August.) Annabella concluded that he must be an atheist, even though *Childe Harold* showed he was capable of noble feelings. His features were good, but his upper lip was constantly raised in an expression of "impatient disgust."

So far she made no attempt to be introduced to him, particularly since all the women were throwing themselves at him. However, she said, she would have no objections to becoming acquainted with him.

She saw him a second time on April 13. On this occasion she was impressed with the "humanity of his feelings." He spoke to her with gratifying respect, and she admitted to her mother that his conversation was the most agreeable she had ever listened to. "He really is most truly an object of compassion. . . . He is a very bad, very good man. Impulses of sublime goodness burst through his malevolent *habits.*" A week later they met again at Lady Jersey's assembly.

Her mother was alarmed for her innocent daughter; in answer to her warning Annabella wrote on April 26 that the people who spoke ill of him did not know him; of course he had been excessively made much of, though she was sure he was levelheaded enough to understand that all this adulation was no proof of true friendship. She considered it her Christian duty not to deprive him of any satisfaction he might derive from knowing her! There was no cause for worry: "He is not a dangerous person to me."

Two-and-one-half years later she was to send him, after she had finally accepted him, this and early descriptions of her estimate of him. When he read them he was astonished that he had seemed so evil to her then. His excuse was that in 1812 he had not long returned from a distant land where everything was different, and that when she first saw him he was unhappy and "bewildered." He certainly had had no desire to excite all the curiosity of which he had been the object; he had had no idea that *Childe Harold* would create such a stir. The consequence was that he had been seized up into the center of a whirl; no wonder he had seemed "repulsive and cold" to her.

By May 1812 Annabella obviously had no objections to knowing him better. Through Lady Caroline, her cousin's wife, she submitted some of her verses to him. Byron answered Caro that the lines displayed fancy and feeling. "She certainly is a very extraordinary girl, who would imagine so much strength and variety of thought under that placid countenance?" However, he added, "I have no desire to be better acquainted with Miss Milbank [*sic*]; she is too good for a fallen spirit to know, and I should like her more if she were less perfect." His affair with Lady Caroline was by then in its hectic career. His Calvinistic conscience was laden with guilt over the license with which he had lived for years, and Annabella somewhat abashed him with her unqualified rectitude. But his words also show that he preferred the life he had been leading; he knew himself so much a sensualist that women like Annabella were not for him. The pity is that he did not hold fast to that knowledge during the next two years.

They continued to meet at various houses. Caro, not pleased that her cousin should give hint of being interested in Byron, on May 22 wrote her in admonition against making friends with those whose conduct was in violation of Annabella's admirable principles, no matter how interesting such persons appeared to be. It was dangerous to attempt befriending fallen angels, she warned—they cannot be saved. Caro did not exempt herself: it would be better for Annabella not even to be her friend. It was a mistake to have come from the country to London, where merely to be was to become tainted. The gravest dangers there were not the dancing and gossiping, but the geniuses to be met, the men of greater talents. Annabella's comment on this was dry enough: "very remarkable." By this time she was well aware that her cousin's wife was Byron's mistress.

By September he was discussing with Lady Melbourne her brother's daughter. They had been talking about the advisability of his getting married, and he said that the one woman he wished to marry was Annabella. He knew nothing of her fortune, but felt he would have enough for both; he knew almost nothing, too, about the girl herself, and was fairly sure she did not think much of him. Nevertheless, he had never seen a woman whom he so much esteemed. Five days later, September 18, he was admiring her for her amiability, cleverness and "high blood"; whomever he might eventually marry, "that is the woman I would wish to *have married*." Lady Caroline had told him, as had several others, that Miss Milbanke was engaged to marry Eden, and that is why he had seen no point in making his sentiments known to her. But if she were indeed free of promises to any man, it was she he would prefer to marry. If not, "the very first woman who does not look as if she would spit in my face," would be a candidate for a proposal.

The amazing Lady Melbourne, who wished above all things to be a close friend and confidante of the man who had cuckolded her favorite son —and who had not a word of blame for him, only for her daughter-in-law— had decided that the best way of leading Byron into the ways of respectability (which, of course, has never meant morality) was to marry off her niece to him. This remained her project all through the next two years until she achieved her end—during which period she was the recipient of his confidences on his many love affairs with Lady Oxford, his sister, and the rest. She was an odd mother and quite as odd an aunt. Her reputation is for complete urbanity; I read her as more the amoral, not quite human woman of revolting salacity than a philosopher who had learned to accept things as they are.

It was through her that Byron, early in October 1812, proposed marriage to Annabella. She did not accept him. Sometime around the same date she composed for her notebooks a "Character of Lord Byron." It was highly representative of her in tone. He was, she said, a man whose passions, triumphing over a very superior mind, were unenlightened by any belief in immortality. Yet there was much in him of the true Christian—his appreciation of goodness "in its chastest form" (i.e., Annabella?), and his detestation of whatever is degrading to human nature, proved that his moral sense was not annihilated. He was totally unselfish and his ideas of love and friendship were chivalrous. By a strange perversity he concealed his best qualities. But when indignation possessed him, he became malevolent. Thus, he was forever moving from good to evil, and from evil to good. He could be quite humble toward those with qualities he respected—like her own, one assumes.

Byron did not blame her for the rejection. "Such a woman" would hardly have wanted him; besides, his own heart "never had an opportunity of being much interested in the business." He thanked Lady Melbourne for her "efforts with my Princess of Parallelograms . . . ; she has not forgotten '*Mathematics*,' wherein I used to praise her cunning. Her proceedings are quite rectangular, or rather we are two parallel lines prolonged to infinity side by side, but never to meet." But he still admired her, and Lady Melbourne was to tell her that he was prouder of being rejected by her than he would ever be at anyone else's acceptance. Lady Melbourne was not to distort his meaning with one of her "*wicked* laughs." What he implied was that the hope of obtaining her had been extremely pleasing to her sad and "unmathematical admirer."

Annabella hoped they could be friends. That, he replied, must rest with chance; in any case, he told her aunt, even if she changed her mind now, they could never be more than friends because he had never been in love with her.

Within a month of her rejection he was congratulating her and himself on their narrow escape. It would have been "but a *cold collation*"; "hot suppers" were more to his taste.

In the meantime Lady Melbourne had not hesitated to give her niece a dressing down. It was going to be impossible for Annabella ever to find a husband worthy of her while she remained "on ye Stilts on which you are mounted." Why was the girl pretending that she wished to be married for reason, not love? Annabella replied that she was not on stilts, only on "tip-toe."

Months passed, and in February 1813 Byron assured Lady Melbourne that he would be happy to meet Annabella to prove he bore her no ill will; but it was not until May that they saw each other at a party. Neither made the effort to be friendly. By this time his affair with Lady Oxford was in its final days. He told Lady Melbourne that he rejoiced that her niece had been spared marrying him; his flight from Lady Caroline had plunged him into a deeper morass than in October of the year before he would have imagined possible. This summer Annabella saw Augusta with him for the first time, and was deeply impressed with his affectionate manner to his sister, proof that he was capable of gentleness.

Failing to draw him into friendship, Annabella at last, in late August, wrote to him herself. She told him frankly that she sought his better acquaintance. She wished him to know that from the beginning she was for and with him, understood that he was being both flattered and persecuted, and hence left desolate. With her usual moral superiority, she confessed to being interested in his welfare without being blind to his shortcomings; she honored him for his sense of moral rectitude, which she saw had remained pure even though "tried by the practice of Vice." She would have liked to attempt to wake his own virtues into a scheme of virtuous action. He had promised her aunt that he was going to try to behave in a way that Annabella would approve, and she now claimed that promise. He was not to permit himself to weary of goodness or "to be the slave of the moment. . . . Do good. . . . Feel benevolence and you will inspire it." With characteristic modesty she confessed knowing the happiness of arousing virtue in others, a power she owned only because that was the habitual line of her thoughts. (!) She hoped he would not mention this letter to her aunt, who, though she had been kind, would never understand her niece's motives.

Byron was annoyed, naturally, with her moral patronizing, as he made clear when he answered her a few days later, August 25, 1813. He had concluded that she was the one woman with whom he might have anticipated happiness; he had confided his hopes to her aunt; his utmost expectation had been that, getting to know her better, he might eventually progress to warmer feelings. But Lady Melbourne had somewhat gone beyond his intentions when she indicated to Annabella that he was making a proposal of marriage. It was true enough that he preferred Annabella to all others, but he had not been disappointed in her rejection "because it is impossible to impart one drop more to a cup which already overflows with the waters of bitterness." (Byron's pen, before he knew it, was depicting the Byronic hero again.) As to what she had heard of his conduct, it was all probably true enough, though possibly exaggerated. In the matter of being her friend, he would speak out with candor: "It is a feeling towards you with which I cannot trust myself."

Abashed by his tone, she answered briefly: she would trouble him no more.

Which was enough to win from him a repenting letter expressing his willingness to obey her and to allow her to set the terms of their future relationship. Three days later, she replied graciously: if she could lighten his despondency it would comfort her much—the angel! If he wished to find those who would serve him, he must seek them elsewhere than in the circle where he and she had met.

He repulsed the notion that he was despondent. "I look upon myself as a very facetious person. . . . Nobody laughs more . . . Your sweeping sentence on 'the circles where we have met' amuses me much when I recollect some of those who constituted that society. After all, bad as it is, it has its *agrémens.* The great object in life is sensation—to feel that we exist, even though in pain." He would be glad to hear from her, "but do not let me encroach a moment on better avocations." Being head over heels in love with his sister, with whom these days he was assuredly laughing enough, he was not particularly anxious to encourage Annabella to write him. Had she thought less of herself, she might have noticed that his letter was a gentleman's way of discouraging her from further communication.

But on September 16 she rejoined: "You may be *gay,* but you have not convinced me that you are *content*. . . . May I know your sentiments concerning Religion?"

His next letter, part Byronic hero again, part honest, was penned after a visit to the Websters. "I am glad that you know any 'good deed' that I am supposed ever to have blundered upon. . . . You don't like my 'restless' doctrines . . . If I must sail let it be on the ocean no matter how stormy—any thing but a dull cruise on a land lake." It was true enough that he was gay but not content. He admitted having been proud ever since boyhood. As for his religious views, he was bred among Calvinists, and hence had a dislike for what they stood for. Since then he had been in countries where bigotry and credulity flourished. He himself believed in God, and would be willing to believe in more. It was his distrust of believing men and women which had undermined his faith in revealed religion.

She replied to this on October 1 with a lecture on religion, and on how Christianity was the only faith in which moral precepts had been united into a system.

His preoccupation with the ridiculous Platonisms of Lady Frances as well as his constant thoughts of Augusta delayed his response for weeks, so that he was able to inform Lady Melbourne at the moment that correspondence between him and her niece had ended. After a month's wait, Annabella engaged on a treatise to prove that the cultivation of reason and of noble feelings must lead to a belief in Christianity and to the performance of good works. On November 10 he begged to be excused from a disputation with anyone so skilled in philosophic speculation as she. In their next letters they looked forward to meeting in London during the spring. In hers there was, if he chose to think so, even an overtone suggesting that her interest in him might be due to more than a desire to aid in his moral uplift.

In any case, on November 29 he wrote her for the first time with freedom and intimacy. "It is true I could not exist without some object of attachment." Yet he had not been entirely weak. In his search for his ideal woman, there had been but two he had found. "The first I was too young to have a prospect of obtaining." This doubtless was Mary Chaworth. "The *second*—the only woman to whom I ever seriously pretended as a wife [i.e., Annabella]—had disposed of her heart already [she had foolishly implied as much], and I think it too late to look for a third." He had been "scribbling" on *The Bride of Abydos* and promised her a copy. In it she would find some Mussulman words which would be his revenge for her "Mathematical and other superiority." He hoped they would meet in town. She was not to take fright at the prospect, for he would not add to the myriad number of her suitors. "I have taken exquisite care to prevent the possibility of that, tho' less likely than ever to become a Benedick." She had been the only Beatrice he had seen in many years but she, of course, "will not trouble to assume the part. . . . The worst that can be said is that I *would* and you *won't.*" (Byron's letters prove that he had at least an enchanting wit in common with Benedick; no one in the world was more unfit to be cast as a Beatrice than the Princess of Parallelograms.) If he should find his heart less stoical on the subject than he at present believed it to be, he would keep out of her way. He wanted her to understand that he suffered no pique at her rejection. He had only two women friends in the world, herself and her aunt, who was the best-hearted woman alive.

After that, Annabella may be exonerated if she secretly felt that another proposal was in the offing. She wrote to her good friend, Lady Gosford, her rapture at the thought that she might be the means of rescuing his immortal soul. She repeated his declaration that she and Lady Melbourne were the only friends of the sex he had; but she found his words on the state of his emotions inscrutable, and feared he had been doing something rash. (What would she have said had she known his sister was already carrying his child?) She was genuinely troubled now that he really believed she loved someone else, yet she did not see how she could convey to him the fact that such was not the case.

She fell ill and on February 10, 1814—Byron's fatal year—she wrote to him that their meeting in London would have to be postponed, for her parents insisted that she stay in the country to recuperate. In a roundabout way she hinted that she had been less than sincere with him, without making plain in reference to what matter. He asked for clarification. Her answer was just as ambiguous: she spoke of a person with whom she had once dreamed of sharing happiness and that dream had now ended. He was expected to understand that the person was himself, but he did not. At any rate, he professed ignorance of the identity of man and circumstances.

Their relationship remained at a stalemate, and Annabella filled her letters with other matters, including her favorite, Religion. He frankly admitted that it had never brought him any consolation. Why he had been born he did not know, whither he was to depart it would be futile to ask. Being the merest atom in the scheme of things, why should he fret? Did he not consider, she retorted, that an atom has its own worth in the eyes of God? After receiving this message of faith, he wrote in his journal on March 15, 1814: "A letter from Bella, which I answered. I shall be in love with her again if I don't take care." (Mercurial Byron! Augusta was in her eighth month of pregnancy with Medora.) He was now anxious to see Annabella again and wrote to say as much.

Since her parents would not hear of her going to London, even though her health was improving, the only chance of their meeting would be his coming to their home in Seaham. Lady Milbanke would have to agree to his being invited, and it took four weeks before Annabella had convinced her that it would be safe to ask him. Finally, on April 13, on the eve of Medora's birth, Annabella was able to say that it would be a great pleasure for all of them if he felt inclined to pay them a visit. There was the problem of what to tell her aunt. Would it not be enough for him to say that whenever he was minded to travel northward he intended to stop at Seaham?

But Annabella could not guess that he faced his own dilemma with her aunt, who was well informed about the incest and his other affairs, since she first had furtherd his suit of her niece. Might she not, in the light of Medora's birth, feel relieved that Annabella had rejected him?

On April 18 he wrote to Lady Melbourne asking, with some embarrassment, how she now regarded the union she had once encouraged— given the possibility that Annabella might consider it favorably. He would do nothing, he declared, without Lady Melbourne's approval. He could not assert that her niece had changed her views. But what was he to do if she and her aunt had exchanged positions with each other on his acceptability?

Lady Melbourne was in no hurry to make clear her position.

In the meantime he accepted Annabella's invitation to Seaham provisionally. If she was sure that she and her parents would not find his visit disagreeable, he would be glad to come.

On April 29 he wrote to her aunt again: "I don't know what to say or do about going." Sometimes he was inclined to go, sometimes the very idea seemed absurd. He was not now in love with Annabella, but he was not willing to swear that he wouldn't be. He admired her as a thoroughly superior woman, though a "little encumbered with Virtue." Were he sure of himself he would go; but he was not and not likely to be. On the next day he wrote once more, saying he did not know what to make of Annabella; her aunt had been censorious of Augusta, and he therefore enclosed a letter of hers as well as one of Annabella's for her to compare; he wanted her to concede that his sister was a highly talented woman. (No one else has ever thought so—and that alone shows how much he was in love with her.) He implied that Augusta endorsed a marriage to Annabella, an endorsement not at all pleasing to Lady Melbourne, who continued indefinite about her views.

Undecided himself, he allowed his correspondence with Annabella to lapse. In mid-May she gently chided him for owing her many letters, but her reminder bore no immediate fruit. Toward the end of the month her aunt had made up her mind, for she wrote Annabella to say she was glad they had invited Byron and that she was sure they would find him possessed of the admirable qualities of which she had always spoken.

On June 19, unable to master her impatience, Annabella begged him for a letter, and even admitted her alarm at his silence. She remarked that someone had taken exception to her writing him. This message he promptly sent to her aunt, and answered Annabella to say that it would be a pleasure to come to Seaham; but at the same time he managed to procrastinate by asking *her* to fix a date. Despite his lack of zeal to see her, he subscribed himself as very affectionately and truly hers. On June 23 she expressed her happiness on his intention of visiting them, and also her disturbance at his coldness whenever they met in London; she was anxious to acquaint him with how she really felt.

It will be remembered that during these months Lady Caroline had not ended her pursuit of Byron. On July 1 at a masquerade she was, says Hobhouse, up to "the most extraordinary tricks"; he could do nothing to prevent her "displaying her green *pantaloons* every now and then," and taking pains to make her identity underneath her mask clear to everyone. Her bitterness and mad love for Byron were evident in a letter she sent him at this time. If she had eloped with him, she said, "You would have made me make the Bed for your new favourites—you are just a Man to exact it & with all my violence you would have made me do it. I have done all but that already, have I not."

Instead of to Seaham it was to Hastings that Byron journeyed in July —with Augusta—to escape Mary Chaworth Musters in London, though he could have avoided her just as effectively at the Milbankes. Before he left town Annabella wrote to him in a style that was, for her, frank, that what she felt for him could be termed "affection." If any of her past behavior seemed mysterious to him she was ready to explain anything he wished clarified. She was, in short, now playing Ophelia to his Hamlet, with no Polonius or Claudius overhearing her pathetic attempts to awaken his seemingly dormant love. His reply from Hastings was still evasive, and the postscript was close to a complete withdrawal: he still remembered, he said, that she was attached to another man. On August 6 Annabella at last laid the ghost of the imaginary rival to her affections; she had deceived herself, she declared, in supposing she had found anyone else to whom she could give her hand; the man in question was now no more than a friend.

His answer to this hard-wrung admission was a curious mixture of sentimentality, in which his pen again ran away with his hand, and a strong bid to be excused from being considered a suitor. "I did, do, and always shall love you," he began. From what he had seen and heard he had always felt she could make any man happy; learning that she was attracted elsewhere, possibly betrothed, he was too humble and proud to gamble on winning her love. Then he heard that he had been misinformed. He was therefore completely in the dark as to why she had rejected his proposal of marriage. Whatever reasons she then had entertained must still be valid for her, but she owed him no accounting for her repugnance of him. "You would probably like me if you could." Since she obviously could not feel love for him, he was unwilling to ask for her pity.

This crucial letter was not particularly characteristic of Byron. Sometimes when in pursuit of some woman he was equal to the false sentiment which was a product of his wishing to deceive himself—but not often. Usually direct, witty and remorselessly honest with himself in his correspondence—the qualities which make his letters among the best ever written—he normally kept this sort of sentimental attitudinizing for his narrative poems. It almost seems as though having in the first section of this letter—from whatever motives, kindness toward Annabella, a deep inner sense that matrimony might save him from what his Calvinistic conscience branded as an infernal union with Augusta, or merely the impulse of the moment—portrayed himself as the victim of unrequited love, he in alarm retreated in the second half from the dread possibility of finding himself betrothed after all. Besides, he was at Hastings with his beloved, when he had heard from Annabella.

Perhaps some connection exists between his attempt to answer Annabella and an amusing episode which occurred at Hastings. As he related it to Moore: "I got into a passion with an ink-bottle." His servant had brought a jar of ink filled to the top; thinking it almost empty, Byron dipped his pen down to the bottom. When he drew it out, it was all smeared with ink. In a rage he threw the bottle out the window into the garden, where it landed on one of the leaden figures of the Muses there. "Next morning I was horrified by seeing that it had struck, and split upon, the petticoat of Euterpe's graven image . . . and grimed her as if it were on purpose. Only think of my distress,—and the epigrams that might be engendered on the Muse and her misadventure." It is not inconceivable that he had been trying to frame a reply to Annabella, and his hurling the ink-bottle out the window may have been less due to his impatience over the smudged pen than to rage at his indecision as to what he ought to be saying to her. In any case, that answer had to await his return to London.

That she was stung by his reply is not astonishing; in her pedantic, prim way she had opened her heart to him, and he was rebuffing her. She regretted, her next letter said, having extorted his sentiments from him. He did not appear to be the man she ought to choose as her mentor and support, her "example on earth, with a view still to Immortality." Nevertheless, he was the only one with whom she would be willing, under the circumstances, to continue the relationship on the basis of friendship.

The recrudescence of her religiosity annoyed him, and on August 16 he sternly wrote: "Very well—now we can talk of something else." Then, before ending, he was saying that, all things considered, perhaps it would be just as well if their correspondence were discontinued. He left that decision to her.

It is almost incredible, but nonetheless the fact, that a month after saying this he should find himself engaged to marry her.

She calmly declared on August 21 that she would renounce the pleasure of interchanging letters with him only if he found writing to her disagreeable. In the meantime, she posed him several questions upon which he might safely speak. What were his present projects? What were his activities these days? Could he recommend the books on history which she ought to be reading?

He was not of a mind to tell her what he was doing these days. For he received her letter at Newstead, and Augusta was with him. On August 25 he supplied her with a reading list, but appended that it would not be possible to come to Seaham that year.

Her family was greatly disappointed at that news, she said, and then talked more about religion; after that she added: "If we could have met, all my apparent inconsistencies would have been dispelled." Though she had no right to ask, she declared, she entreated him not to cease communicating with her.

On September 7 he was still more tart, possibly because the proximity of Augusta moved him to keep anyone else's burgeoning love at a distance. He told Annabella that he had never found her inconsistent. Indeed, he commented rudely, "your consistency has been the most formidable apparition I have encountered."

There was a further exchange of letters. Then, just when their relationship seemed at its most strained, at least on his side, he made, considering the tone in which he had been writing her, an amazing decision. Augusta had long agreed that he ought to marry, for both their sakes, and over the recent years he had halfheartedly considered this or that young woman as a candidate, speedily enough rejecting each. At Newstead, after talks with his sister, he concluded that Annabella would be the woman to be chosen.

He showed Augusta his second proposal of marriage; she pronounced it well written, but urged him to reflect seriously before sending it. Well written it is, if the criterion be the introduction in it of loopholes for escape. He waited some hours, then sealed it and sent it off on September 10. "There is something I wish to say," he wrote, "and as I may not see you for some— perhaps for a long time—I will endeavour to say it at once. . . . Are the 'objections' to which you alluded insuperable? or is there any line or change of conduct which could possibly remove them? . . . I neither wish you to promise or pledge yourself to anything; but merely to learn a *possibility* which would not leave you the less a free agent." When he had believed that she was attached to another man, he had nothing to urge—"indeed I have little now." Knowing, however, that her affections were not elsewhere engaged, he was addressing her again, though only after a struggle. "With the rest of my sentiments you are already acquainted. If I do not repeat them it is to avoid—or at least not increase—your displeasure."

It was the strangest of love letters, and throughout it breathes his dread of being accepted. He waited in a fever of anxiety for her reply, though whether in hopes or dread of an acceptance we are not told. He said to Augusta that he was sure of a second rejection; if, by chance, however, Annabella should say Yes, he would have to go immediately to Seaham.

Annabella replied at once. "I am and have long been pledged to myself to make your happiness my first object in life. . . . The fear of not realizing your expectations is the only one I now feel."

He next wrote on September 18: "Your letter has given me a new existence." He had always regarded her as the best of human beings, one whom it was almost impossible not to love. It was in her power to make him happy. In truth, she had already done so.

The same day he wrote at least two other letters conveying the news and enjoining secrecy. He asked Lady Melbourne whether she would not now give her consent too? Without it he should be unhappy. He meant to reform, to become good and true in every sense, and to make Annabella happy. Of course, his news must be considered private. He also wrote to Hanson to tell him; he was to *"keep this a secret for the present."* Two days later he sent the good word to Tom Moore, who thought Annabella "too straight-laced" for his friend. "She is said to be an heiress, but of that I really know nothing certainly, and shall not enquire. But I do know, that she has talents and excellent qualities; and you will not deny her judgment, after having refused six suitors and taken me. Now, if you have any thing to say against this, pray do; my mind's made up, positively fixed, determined, and therefore I will listen to reason, because now it can do no harm. Things may occur to break it off, but I will hope not." Moore also was to keep this "a *secret."* It reads rather as though he privately hoped that Moore could summon arguments to talk him out of his engagement.

He was certainly bent on acquiring trouble. On the same day he wrote to Annabella that he could never have had confidence in a woman who bore any doubts about the truth of religion, even though his own principles were by no means settled. He was simply bewildered by the multiplicity of faiths and not at all sceptical of the foundation of belief. From now on she should be his guide. "My whole heart is yours."

A few days later he wrote again to her aunt, suggesting it might be well to let Lady Caroline know of his betrothal. The secret could not long be kept (certainly not the way he was guarding it). He anticipated Caro's doing all possible to break up the match, but did not think Annabella an easy prey to her cousin's machinations. He was not concerned whether his bride would have any fortune; it was simply that, if she had nothing, he had better try again to sell Newstead so he could make her a good settlement. He would settle on her all he could—which is precisely what he eventually did. He was prepared to do anything to avoid losing her. He was horrified when going over in his mind his immoralities of the past two years; they might all have been avoided had Annabella accepted his first proposal. But he could hardly blame her for that, and there was still time to mend his life. (He was only twenty-six.) He ended with a quip which revealed more than he realized: A married man, he asked, never gets another woman, does he?

When Lady Caroline was informed of the engagement, she of course behaved in a way that no one had counted on. She did not threaten or attempt suicide; she did not even buy the pistol she had sworn to procure. Instead she sent her blessings and good wishes to Byron. To Murray she expressed every hope for Byron's happiness, spoke of her cousin's virtue and amiability, but could not resist that little thrust about the lower part of Annabella's face.

On October 1 Byron was still talking about going to Seaham; his delay he ascribed to shyness and a reluctance to meet strangers. On that day Augusta wrote to Annabella in order, she said, to become closer to one who would soon be her sister, and whom she professed already to love as such; she was certain her brother would find great happiness in the marriage. With no intent of sardonic *double-entendre* of the kind her brother would have meant had he composed the sentence, she assured Annabella that words failed her to indicate how dear her brother was to her.

He was pleased that Augusta had written, and to his fiancée on October 7 sang her praises as the most unselfish and the gentlest of God's creations. Lady Melbourne had continued to misjudge her, and to Annabella's aunt he protested too that Augusta was "the least selfish person in the world"; her part in their mutual sin was entirely his fault, and for that he could plead no excuse "except passion," which, he conceded is no excuse at all.

His confidante teased him with some banter on his procrastination in visiting the Milbankes, and getting to know his future father- and mother-in-law; he answered on October 12: "Well, but I *am* going, am I not? . . . I shall not be a whit nearer marriage when I get there"; besides which, she ought to understand, it was a vexing business being with one's intended and have one's intimacies limited to intentions only. To Hobhouse he declared that this sort of respectable suit, to one whose familiarity was only with the disreputable kind, was irksome; if only he could awake one morning and find himself married.

Augusta wrote again to Annabella, who thereupon invited her to come with Byron to Seaham. Augusta begged off with thanks and the excuse that her heavy responsibilities would keep her with her family. (Medora was still a babe in arms.)

Finally, on October 29 Byron set out from London, but he did not omit stopping for almost two days at Six Mile Bottom with Augusta. At Seaham he arrived at length on November 1. Since Annabella had invited him there, more than half a year had elapsed.

4.

THE MILBANKES HAD BEEN EXPECTING HIM FOR TWO DAYS, AND ANNA-bella's short-tempered mother was in a pet. Annabella herself remained calm. When she heard the wheels of his carriage she was in her room reading. She put out the candles and firmly let her parents, who were used to obeying her, know that she wished to be alone when she greeted him. He was waiting in the drawing room at the hearth as she advanced toward him; he took her hand and kissed it. She stood opposite him at the fireplace, and they were silent for a while until he remarked on the long time which had elapsed since their last meeting. Feeling overwhelmed, she made an excuse to leave the room and fetch her parents. Forty years later she recollected that she had been shocked to note that during the time they had not seen each other he had become "coarser, sullied."

When her parents joined them, the conversation was general. Before they all retired he and she shook hands.

In answer to his query he had been told they would be up and about at around ten in the morning. But she arose early, anticipating that a lover would be eager to do the same. Not so. She waited until noon, gave up, and went for a walk to ease a headache.

Later in the day she asked him if it were true, as she had been told, that he had broken off communication with Augusta for three years because of some trivial offense. He conceded they had quarreled, said, with some understatement, that he had tried to make it up to his sister since then, and added mysteriously that Annabella might very well have heard worse than *that*. He also told her that had she married him two years ago when he had first proposed, she could have saved him from the one thing for which he could never forgive himself. (The incest, of course.)

After a two days' stay at Seaham he wrote Lady Melbourne: he was delighted with her brother, his future father-in-law, as a perfect gentleman, whose only shortcoming was that the stories he told were too long; Lady Milbanke, who seemed to rule the roost, he could barely tolerate; Annabella was more emotional than anyone had suspected, but was also the most silent of women. He wished she would talk more, for talking makes women think less; if she should reflect too much, the results must surely be unfavorable to him. He had not progressed far in studying her disposition. "However, the die is cast; neither party can recede; the lawyers are here . . . I shall become Lord Annabella." He could not pronounce on their future happiness; he doubted her ability to govern him; if she could not, the marriage would prove a disaster.

But two days later he was able to say that his fiancée and he were getting along splendidly. He spoke more emphatically of her feelings—she nursed *"passions* stronger than we supposed." The next week, however, he was disturbed by the gravest doubts that any wedding would take place; Annabella was a constant victim of scruples and intermittent ill health.

This ill health was to plague her all her life. Everyone in her circle developed the habit of expecting her imminent demise. But she outlived them all—her parents and Lady Melbourne, Byron, her own daughter, Augusta, Medora, Lady Caroline, and most of her acquaintances of her generation. She ate well, Byron noted, and was, when not ill, in good spirits.

One evening they had a scene, somewhat, he said, in Lady Caroline's manner. It was too extended and over too petty a matter not to work havoc on his impressionable nature. When she was alone with him, she asked him to tell her frankly whether there was not some cause for his patently altered desire to marry her. She did not seek to know the reason, merely to know if one existed. If it did, she was prepared, as his friend, to break the engagement herself. He became livid, and staggered back upon the sofa in a faint. It was minutes before he could speak, and when he did it was in anger and reproach. He charged her with having just done him dreadful damage. She knelt at his feet for forgiveness, but he remained stony. From that hour his attitude toward her became less confiding; when he spoke of his past it was to shroud it in mystery. She determined never to raise that question again.

Without detailing the event, he summarized it for her aunt, underlining his distaste for emotional disturbance provoked by trifles. (If he felt so strongly on that score, he was manifestly unsuited to live under the same roof with any woman.) Annabella had suddenly found her tongue—alas!—for she was using it excessively; he never felt sure of her for a minute, he said. When he himself, to avoid boredom, prattled on, she was prone to draw some "significant" inference. (This drawing of significant inferences from his most flippant remark became a kind of mania with her and was the source of constant irritation.) Since talk so often ended in this unsatisfactory way, he was having more and more recourse to what he named for her remarkable aunt as the "calming process"—awaking the girl's sensuality, a skill he must by then have highly perfected, with caresses. He found that it worked very well.

This carnal awakening of the prim girl must have cost her self-torture in private; she is on record with believing "a reciprocation of Passion highly culpable and absurd." For her, the highest relationship in love was mutual esteem.

Though convinced he loved her, she had already become familiarized with the stormy interludes which inevitably became an ominous part of their marriage. It must have been on one of these days that he suddenly turned to her and said with a malevolent look, "I will be even with you yet." This threat, delivered right after some of her endearments, stuck like a bur in her memory. She was never to know whether it was due to her first rejection of him, his feelings of being trapped (which she never understood), or his despair over himself.

It was at her suggestion that, after two weeks, he left Seaham for London. She thought it better they be separated until the wedding. He, no doubt, had been accelerating his siege of her chastity—in doing that he was at least not ill at ease—and she probably had been finding it harder and harder to resist him. And finding it harder, she must have been terrified at the sensuality she had discovered within herself. It would have been at odds with her notion of herself.

On his way he stopped at Augusta's.

After leaving Seaham he exchanged letters with Annabella, though she wrote more often and with far greater warmth and love. To fill in the gaps of his silence Augusta wrote her, too. During these brief months Annabella's letters for the first time are pathetic. Seaham no longer seemed like her home once he had left, and she wished for him more and more the livelong day. She called him her dearest husband, and jokingly threatened to invade his lodgings at the Albany in London—as she never guessed a certain Eliza had in fact been doing—if he stayed away from Seaham much longer.

His letters were rather perfunctory and filled with business matters relative to the sale of Newstead; also Annabella was given a lecture via post by her aunt for sending him off until the wedding. What bothered Lady Melbourne was not at all the effect of separation upon the principals and their future, but the speculation and gossip it was engendering in London. It annoyed her to be asked by everyone, Why the delay? Why is he back in town? Moreover, he himself was grumbling at his temporary dismissal.

Before long Annabella was suggesting an immediate marriage without waiting for the financial arrangements to be ready. She was anxious that he return to Seaham. On December 23 he wrote her: "If we meet let it be to marry." Experience had shown them both, he added, the lack of wisdom of their being together under the same roof without the sanction of matrimony. (How many centuries distant seems that traditional conception of morality!)

On December 24 he left London for Six Mile Bottom—his destination actually Seaham. Augusta had been invited to the wedding, but family problems made it impossible for her to come. On December 26, Hobhouse, who had accompanied him part of the way to Augusta's, rejoined him. It was not until December 30 that they reached Seaham, Hobhouse noting that Byron grew progressively less enthusiastic about the object of their journey, and, as they neared its conclusion, positively reluctant.

The first moments at Seaham have been vividly recorded by Hobhouse. Annabella came into the library, "presently in tottered her father—Miss is rather dowdy looking . . . though she has excellent feet & ancles—the lower part of her face is bad, the upper expressive but not handsome—yet she gains by inspection. She heard B. coming out of his room—ran to meet him —threw her arms around his neck and burst into tears." Her mother was considerably upset by their delays in arriving, and John Cam was hard put to it to invent plausible excuses. Annabella was silent and modest, "but very sensible & decent and inspiring an interest which it is easy to mistake for love. . . . Of my friend she seemed doatingly fond, gazing with delight on his bold and animated bust." Lady Milbanke he found "pettish & tiresome but clever—both are doatingly fond of Miss."

The next day he revised his notion of Annabella, and thought her "most attractive." Among the guests were Sir Ralph's agent, Mr. Hoar, and the Reverend Thomas Noel, "a brisk parson." In the evening there was some merriment with the enactment of a mock marriage, Hobhouse the bride, Noel "parsonifying," and Hoar giving the "bride" away.

On the next night, preceding the day of the wedding, the dinner was "not quite so jolly," and Byron said to Hobhouse, "Well, H., this is our last night—tomorrow I shall be Annabella's (absit omen!!)."

On January 2, 1815, the wedding took place.

Hobhouse noted that Annabella "during the whole ceremony looked steadily at Byron—she repeated the words audibly and well." Byron stumbled over the first words he spoke "and when he came to 'with all my worldly goods I thee endow' looked at me with a half smile."

According to the sixth stanza of his autobiographical poem "The Dream," despite the fact that he had already become disillusioned in her and had avoided meeting her again, during the ceremony it was of Mary Chaworth he was thinking, not Annabella:

And he stood calm and quiet, and he spoke
The fitting vows, but heard not his own words,
And all things reeled around him; he could see
Not that which was, nor that which should have been—
But the old mansion, and the accustomed hall*. . .
All things pertaining to that place and hour
And her who was his destiny, came back
And thrust themselves between him and the light:
What business had they there at such a time?

There is no doubt about his confusion at the ceremony. Indeed, in Colman's *Leon to Arabella,* a companion piece which probably preceded *Don Leon,* he has the hero say to his wife:

Thou know'st, when married, from the church we came,
Heedless I called thee by thy *maiden* name.

The wedding ring, which had been his mother's, naturally proved too large for Annabella. Her mother was only too ready to find a portent of evil in that. Later she sneered that he had never had the decency to present his bride with the "common" gift of a "diamond Hoop ring."

Bound for Halnaby for their honeymoon, they got into their carriage. Annabella later remembered that at once his face changed, became somber and hostile. As was his habit when angered, he began singing wildly, and spoke hardly a word to her until they had reached Durham; there he muttered that she would have been wiser to marry someone else. As their journey continued he informed her that one of his chief purposes in marrying her had been to win out over her other suitors; he brought up again the rejection of his first proposal and spitefully promised to make her suffer for it. He went on to speak of how much he hated her mother and to recount some of Lady Melbourne's derogatory pronouncements on her brother's wife. It was surely one of the eeriest rides ever taken by a bride after the nuptials.

It was also a prelude to the peculiarities which followed when they reached Halnaby Hall, for Moore read in the memoirs before they were burned, and confided to Hobhouse, that Byron employed what he believed was the best method of pacifying women: he *"had* Lady B. on the sofa before dinner on the day of their marriage."

After dinner he said to Annabella in a mystifying tone: "Now I have you in my power, and I could make you feel it." He went on to describe how Lady Caroline was wearing away her husband's heart, and added that

* Mary's house.

Annabella would find she had got herself just such a husband as Caro was a wife—a remark that has curiously been interpreted to be merely a product of his love of fun. During the evening he asked her whether she intended to sleep with him in the same bed; she was free to do so, but he wished her to know that he detested sharing his bed with any woman.

He got up late the next morning, and greeted her with, "It's too late now—it's done—you should have thought of it sooner." It was, she felt, ice upon her heart, but she told him she had no regrets. It is possible that in all women there is a touch of masochism; if so, she, as is shown by her finding "significance" in every trivial or amusing remark, had considerably more than her allotment. As the day wore on, he fed her love of being wounded by speaking cryptically of various outrageous crimes he had committed, and summed up: "I am a villain—I could convince you of it in three words."

A letter arrived from Augusta, and he read to Annabella with exultation the salutation: "Dearest, first & best of human beings," and tormented her to interpret that. He grieved over his sister's absence and said again, as he was often to repeat, that nobody loved him as Augusta did, that no one but her knew how to make him happy.

Querulous though he was, that day he gave Lady Melbourne a quite different picture of his state: "You would think we had been married these fifty years. Bell is fast asleep on the corner of the sopha, and I am keeping myself awake with this epistle."

To please him Annabella the next day invited Augusta to join them, but she was wise enough to refuse being part of the honeymoon.

A few days after that Annabella had a sudden terrifying fear. She had made a parenthetical reference to a brother and sister who, ignorant of their relationship, had an incestuous love affair. Unexpectedly Byron flew into a rage, demanded to know where she had heard of it, and was beside himself with terror. She quietly explained that she was alluding to Dryden's *Don Sebastian,* which she had been reading. He seized a dagger from the table, left the room, and banged the door of his room shut. Her first idea was that he had been so frantic because he might have slept with some girl whom he had not known to be his father's illegitimate daughter. Captain Byron's career as a libertine made such an explanation not implausible.

One night in bed he told her he would gladly reveal what it was that preyed on his mind, if it were not that it involved another person whose secret it must remain. She asked if Augusta knew the details, and he exclaimed with horror, "For God's sake don't ask *her.*"

At Halnaby he wandered about alone a great deal and often left a room as soon as she walked into it. Sometimes he went so far as to quit her with an "I don't want you." Every night he used to rise from bed and walk up and down the long gallery of the Hall in a state of unrest, so that she dreaded his often-repeated threats of committing suicide. Perhaps some miti-gation of blame is due him for the reason that he had caught a bad cold after leaving Seaham, but the chief trouble was that he was bored. Anna-bella was heavy company, had not a grain of humor, and because of her insecurity was in a constant state of emotional upheaval. "I only want a woman to laugh," he snapped at her one day. But with her aunt he kept up appearances: "I have great hopes this match will turn out well. I have found nothing as yet that I could wish changed for the better."

Annabella wrote often to Augusta, who promptly answered her "Dear Sis." In one letter Annabella recounted her husband's recurrent declaration that he could never love anybody as well as he loved his sister. To which Augusta replied, "I wish I deserved half the kindness he feels & expresses towards me," and congratulated herself on his having a wife who was not offended by such avowals. Little did Augusta suspect the true feelings of Dear Sis, or the method behind such apparently affectionate reporting.

During their first week at Halnaby she came upon him as he was sit-ting by the fire with a collection of old letters. He singled out one she had written him in which she had hoped to reconcile him to his conscience; he furiously demanded what she had meant by the expression, and stormed at her for having rejected him for two years—until she began to fear that he would use violence upon her. To quiet him with affection, she sank to her knees before him and, throwing her arms around his neck, reminded him that they were married now. He became calmer. Then he read her parts of Lady Melbourne's letters; she was struck by a passage in which her aunt tried to turn him away from some atrocious sin he was bent on committing, a sin which could find forgiveness, neither in this world nor the next. It was plain from the passage that he was planning to run away with a certain A—— to Sicily, and that A—— had agreed to go with him. He went on to tell his bride that he had taken her aunt's advice in part, but wished he had followed it altogether. By this time his face was twisted in anguish. He also murmured that Lady Melbourne had encouraged his affair with Lady Frances Webster to save him from something worse.

This episode plunged her, after the rest of his unnerving conduct, into the most abject misery, with the consequence that she allowed herself an indiscretion quite alien to the aloofness the world saw in her. While at Halnaby she had as a servant Jane Minns, the married daughter of a farmer, a girl she had known as a child. To her she confided that she was sure that something most dreadful had passed between Byron and his sister, something which he could not obliterate from his mind and gave him no peace.

They stayed at Halnaby three weeks. Sir Ralph urged them, when they left, to return to Seaham, but Byron had no inclination to see his mother-in-law again. However, he gave in. They left on Saturday, January 21, because he thought that traveling on Friday was unlucky. Sunday, January 22, was his birthday. It is astonishing to think that he was only twenty-seven— though, to be sure, in some ways he seemed no more than seventeen.

5.

IF THE HONEYMOON HAD BEEN A FIASCO, THE STAY AT SEAHAM BROUGHT husband and wife, surprisingly enough, closer to each other. That may have been the result of his seeking her protection from her father's long-winded stories and her mother's irritating talk, as well as of her feeling less tense under the parental roof, where she was used to being pampered and adored. They walked by the sea together, climbed rocks on the shore; he seemed grateful for the little attentions she lavished on him at her home. He was always polite to her father and mother. When she asked why he was kindest to her in their presence, he explained that he loved her better when someone else was there.

She and Augusta began a frequent exchange of letters. Perhaps with her proclivity for finding in every careless phrase some deep implication —and Augusta's style was nothing if not careless—she hoped to find some clue unintended, some hint unguarded that might confirm the suspicions she had begun to form. At any rate, Augusta was at her gayest in these letters. She told, for instance, how she had laughed uncontrolledly over one of her brother's pranks. Annabella in turn recounted how Byron and she one night were having a private masquerade, he dressed as a woman, she mustachioed as a man, when he snatched the wig from Lady Milbanke's head to place on his own.

But all was far from merriment for Annabella. In the Seaham drawing room she garnered new material for increasing her doubts. She and Byron were amusing themselves writing some *bouts-rimés;* of this quatrain, for example, he composed the first and last lines, she the other two:

> My wife's a vixen spoilt by her Mamma
> Oh how I pity poor hen-pecked Papa
> The Lord defend us from a Honey Moon
> Our cares commence our comforts end so soon.

(Her contributions show two interesting things: her willingness to fall in with his whims even at the expense of her doting parents, and her bitterness over her recent experiences.) He was so much pleased with the verses they had spun off that he suggested she send them to Augusta for her delectation. Now, Annabella had already noted the crosses with which brother and sister peppered their letters to each other, and Byron had explained that these symbols referred to a frightful mystery he and Augusta shared. It may have been sheer innocence, as she later implied, though it was more likely in the vein of her Pandora-like need to open the dangerous box, that she offered to distinguish his lines of the doggerel from hers by affixing crosses to them. He at once blanched and begged her not to think of doing that, saying those signs would terrify his sister.

On the whole he was trying to behave. On February 6 he told Moore: "Since I wrote last, I have been transferred to my father-in-law's . . . and the treacle-moon is over. . . . My spouse and I agree to—and in—admiration. Swift says 'no *wise* man ever married'; but, for a fool, I think it the most ambrosial of all future states. I still think one ought to marry upon *lease;* but am very sure I should renew mine at the expiration, though next term were for ninety and nine years." He obviously was determined to make the best of his marriage, however ill equipped he was to carry through his intentions. He continued, "Upon this dreary coast, we have nothing but county meetings and shipwrecks. . . . My papa, Sir Ralpho, hath recently made a speech at a Durham tax-meeting; and not only at Durham, but here, several times since after dinner. He is now, I believe, speaking it to himself (I left him in the middle) over various decanters, which can neither interrupt him nor fall asleep."

Augusta remarked to Dear Sis that with Colonel Leigh away her cramped house had a little more room; if Annabella and Byron cared to visit they would be welcomed. She sent Dear Sis one hundred million thanks, in her usual style, for her conscientious reporting of Byron's day-by-day occupations, state of mind, and health. (Within a year she would be performing the same service for Dear Sis.) If only her brother would give up his habit of fasting until famished and then devouring more than his system could hold, his health would improve.

Why did Byron suddenly begin to speak to his wife of Thyrza? She, of course, thought Thyrza a girl and he did not disabuse her. But why, so early in his marriage, did his thoughts revert to Edleston? (At another time he enlarged for his wife on Thyrza's beauty and how eager he had been for every meeting between them, and, as he spoke of this, he paced the room in a frenzy of excitement.) At Seaham he vented his grief at being able no longer to feel what he had felt in the Thyrza days. The midnight of his pouring this out to Annabella, he composed one of his best lyrics:

There's not a joy the world can give like that it takes away,
When the glow of early thought declines in Feeling's dull decay;
'Tis not on Youth's smooth cheek the blush alone, which fades so fast,
But the tender bloom of heart is gone, ere Youth itself be past . . .

The disparity between his obsession for the Cambridge choirboy and what he could feel for his wife inspired the poem.

But he was doing his best to be sociable. Augusta was astonished that anyone could have inveigled him into playing checkers.

By early March he had had enough of Seaham. On the excuse that Augusta's quarters were so limited, his idea was that he go to see her alone, while Annabella went on to London. But she pleaded to be allowed to accompany him. Unhappily for her, she won the point. On March 8, before leaving Seaham, he wrote Moore: "I have been very comfortable here,—listening to that damned monologue, which elderly gentlemen call conversation. . . . However, they have been very kind and hospitable, and I like them and the place vastly. . . . Bell is in health, and unvaried good-humour and behaviour." The Milbankes were equally pleased with their son-in-law. Augusta was able to tell Hodgson: "Lady B. writes me word she never saw her father and mother so happy; that she believes the latter would go to the bottom of the sea herself to find fish for B.'s dinner." (The latter, the following year, would have gone to the bottom of the sea to wreck him.)

The newlyweds set out March 9 for Six Mile Bottom. As soon as they were in the carriage, he resumed his ferocity of the ride to Halnaby. What did her mother mean by confiding her to his care? Was she not fitter to take care of herself than he to take care of her? To divert him she spoke of Augusta; he retorted that Augusta was a fool, and when she tried to defend her, he reiterated the charge more fiercely. His private thought must have been that his sister had been stupid to invite them both, knowing, as he did, his wife's gift for finding in a conversation hidden meanings. Perhaps, too, knowing that Colonel Leigh was not at home, he was bitter when he foresaw that Annabella's presence would be an impediment to lovemaking with Augusta, and that Augusta should have thought of that or of the danger of exposure in having Annabella there.

Upon their arrival Augusta came downstairs, greeted her brother with affection, but, after all the effusions to Dear Sis, merely shook hands with her. Presently Byron chided her for her tepid greeting of Annabella. But her reserve could have been due to the shyness she shared with him; Annabella and she had seen each other once at a gathering, but this was the first time they actually met.

Thinking the two would want some time alone, Annabella left them for a while; when she returned he made it clear that he preferred his sister's company, and sent his wife to bed at nine o'clock—a practice he kept up all the while they were at Six Mile Bottom. Sometimes he went so far as to dismiss her with the remark that he and Augusta knew how to amuse themselves very well without her. That first night when he joined her in their room, he was in a state of frenzy, showed every sign of detesting her, and cried that he did not need her, now that he had Augusta again. He reminded her that he had warned her not to come there with him, and elaborately hinted that he had just made love to his sister—an idea so shocking that Annabella refused to credit it. Indeed, her scepticism seemed justified by the casualness with which Augusta greeted him next morning.

The stay at Augusta's was a nightmare for the young bride. When he had drunk enough brandy he would insult her until she was on the verge of tears. Recurrently he would insinuate the reason for his wishing to be alone with Augusta. Officially Medora's godfather, he once pointed to the baby and said equivocally that that was his child. One day two gold brooches which he had ordered from a jeweler arrived at Six Mile Bottom, one inscribed B and one A, with his hair and Augusta's and three crosses on each; he and Augusta wore them daily thereafter. He announced before his wife that he knew that his sister wore drawers; it was clear enough what he intended to be understood. He talked freely of the affairs he had been having during the two years of his correspondence with Annabella, and forced his sister to bring out letters in which he had discussed them, then turned sneeringly to his wife to say that all that time she had imagined he was perishing of love for her. During all these scenes Augusta was timidly obedient as if, Annabella felt, she were in her brother's power and had no choice but to do his bidding, so that she seemed even more miserable than her sister-in-law. It was his pleasure to work them both well, as he called it; lying on the sofa, for instance, he required them to take turns kissing him, and after a while he declared Augusta's kisses far more satisfying. During their visit to Six Mile Bottom he had sex with his bride only during the nights when, as Augusta informed Dear Sis, she was menstruating.

After the separation Annabella chronicled these experiences in a series of narratives. The wonder is that she did not then and there insist upon leaving Augusta's and returning to her parents. Her own explanation is that she could not believe the facts thus patently thrust upon her. Just the same, Annabella, though virginal in thought, was not a fool and was used, moreover, to having her own way, and her toleration of his humiliations at Six Mile Bottom, as she has recorded it, opens the question as to how much of all this may be embittered exaggeration after the event. One of her critics calls her a gross liar. But the evidence is against such a judgment of her. She had too high an opinion of her moral stature to allow herself barefaced lying. What she was capable of, as matters connected with the separation make eloquently plain, was telling half-truths and consoling herself with the thought that half-truths were not really lies.

In any case she relayed nothing of her sufferings to her parents. After two weeks the Byrons left Six Mile Bottom, he reluctantly—though Augusta was glad to see them go. In the carriage he eagerly asked his wife what she thought of his sister; her cryptic answer was that Augusta was far cleverer than he had delineated her.

For the next ten days he was kinder than he had ever been. And then Augusta came to stay with them. She had recently been appointed Lady-in-waiting to Queen Charlotte; it was therefore necessary for her to come to London, and her brother, with Annabella's endorsement, invited her to their new home. Later Annabella defended her agreeing by affirming that had she refused to allow Augusta to come, she must have given as her reason facts of which she was none too sure and whose open declaration would have been ruinous to Augusta and her children; she was also in dread of his vicious temper; moreover—and here the truly good woman is in evidence—she would not close the door, if the two were actually guilty, on remorse, as she phrased it, if remorse they were prepared to feel.

6.

IT WAS ON MARCH 28, 1815, THAT THEY LEFT SIX MILE BOTTOM FOR what was to be their home, Lady Devonshire's furnished house at 13 Piccadilly Terrace. After shopping around for him Lady Melbourne had chosen it as the most suitable of those available for his needs, despite its costliness and his current indebtedness and limited resources. It is rather surprising that he, with his vast superstitiousness, made no objections to the number 13; but then it was his venerated Aspasia who had selected it for him.

Their first visitor was Hobhouse, whom Byron, though professing to have the best of wives, cautioned against marrying. Two days after they had left her, Augusta was again writing to Dearest Sis; her letter makes it clear that Anabella had been urging her to stay with them in London. This was masochism with a vengeance after her recent crucifixion at Augusta's. Augusta said she needed no pressure to come to them. She came and remained for several months. The day she was expected Byron made it his business to be absent. When he returned home he greeted her with great affection, and then before her assured his wife she had been stupid to allow her sister under their roof—it was going to change everything between them, as she would soon see. Again the routine of displays of affection to his sister and savagery to his wife was renewed.

Viscount Wentworth, Annabella's uncle, whose heir she was to be, fell mortally ill toward mid-April, and Annabella hastened to be with him—she later said, with great relief at escaping the tensions of her own house, even if it meant witnessing the sufferings of a dying man—and, leaving Augusta with Byron, remained with Wentworth for three nights until his sister, Annabella's mother, came to relieve her. He died on April 17.*

She was now pregnant, and with the sickness attendant upon the early stages of that condition Annabella was unequipped to deal with the situation in her home when she came back. Her husband was annoyed rather than sympathetic with her illness, and when she retired would stay up with his sister. But she herself was too near hysteria to render her accounts of this period trustworthy. If Byron was morose she feared him; if she heard him laughing with Augusta, almost the only one who knew how to make him laugh, she became suspicious. Yet his somber moods were attributable to two causes. He had accepted membership in the management committee of Drury Lane and was undertaking his responsibilities in the theatre very seriously; for all her interest in the London theatre, Annabella seemed little aware of his efforts there. More grave, his creditors, noting the elaborate house he had rented and knowing his wife to be an heiress, had begun to hound Byron in earnest; he was deeply in debt, her father was almost in as bad straits as her husband, but she, who had never had to think about money, was totally oblivious to Byron's constant worry and depression over their financial problems.

She kept a great deal to her room and for some time was in dread of having a miscarriage. He would come to see her but briefly, she says, and then only in order to express his hatred of her. (These recollections, it should be remembered, were made during her separation from him, when she was at great pains to evolve a case against him.) One night, when he and Augusta had remained up later than usual, she became so much upset that she arose from bed and paced the floor. Hearing her, Byron sent his sister up to see what was wrong. Augusta found her in a flood of tears, and Annabella's narrative confesses that she then thought of Byron's dagger lying in the next room and wished it plunged in Augusta's heart.

In attempting to disentangle fact from overheated fancy in Annabella's later recollections, we have one document that only complicates the picture. While Annabella was at her uncle's bedside, Lady Milbanke arrived in London en route to relieving her daughter; Byron wrote to his wife at once

---

* He left no legitimate children, and so his viscounty came to an end. The barony of Wentworth eventually fell to Annabella. On Wentworth's death the entailed estate of Kirkby Mallory, together with half his considerable wealth, went to his sister, Lady Judith Milbanke, Annabella's mother. On May 20 of that year, a royal license gave Sir Ralph, Annabella's father, the right to take the name and heraldry of Noel. Lady Judith thus became in 1815 the Hon. Lady Noel. Annabella, upon her mother's death in 1822, became Lady Noel Byron until her death in 1860.

in the most tender vein: "Dearest—Now your mother is come I won't have you worried any longer—more particularly in your present situation which is rendered very precarious by what you have already gone through. Pray, come home." Besides, people who saw the newlyweds that summer thought them very happy. Harness was struck by their mutual devotion, and particularly noticed Byron's meticulous attention to her. Murray was delighted with Annabella and much impressed with her good humor and linguistic accomplishments. George Ticknor, a young American with letters to Byron, visited him in mid-June and was accorded the most gracious hospitality; he found Lady Byron pretty, ingenuous, and Byron's manner toward her most affectionate. It would be a groundless disparagement of this evidence to assert against it that Byron was putting on a show of felicity before others. Whatever his faults, he was no hypocrite, and would not have thought of stooping to that. It is perhaps more to the point to observe that by the time of Ticknor's visit Augusta had left.

Annabella could never deny later that during this visit of hers, Augusta had been most kind and considerate. In fact on one occasion, according to Annabella's account, Augusta told her brother that she refused to remain in the house and see his wife so shabbily treated. And when he launched into a tirade on a favorite subject, his aversion to his wife's parents, Augusta stoutly defended them against his abuse. Nevertheless, Annabella for once exhibited good sense: she decided that since her sister-in-law, no matter what the reason, augmented Byron's worst tendencies for sarcasm and mental cruelty, Augusta had to go. It was she who decided this and who insisted upon fixing a date for the other's departure.

Characteristically, Augusta bore Dearest Sis no ill will; she was, in any case, aware enough of her guilt not to challenge Annabella's right to terminate her visit. Within a few days, in early July, she was writing Hobhouse a glowing account of the success of the marriage. Byron never looked better, ate heartily and sensibly, drank moderately; Lady Byron was a blessing to him—the most wonderful human being she had ever known. Byron, when not at Drury Lane, was a stay-at-home; when he did go out it was always with his wife.

At the end of August Byron went again to Six Mile Bottom, this time to help Colonel Leigh, in one of his perennial financial crises. While he was there, Annabella wrote a most wifely letter to her Darling Duck—a nickname inspired by his calling Augusta "Goose"—telling him how in his absence the carpets were being torn up and the whole house was undergoing a tumultuous overhauling; she hoped he occasionally called out to his Dear Pip—his nickname for her—as he was wont to do. Such a letter is enough to disprove that her life had been so completely devoid of happiness with Byron as she later chose to remember it. The same must be said of his reply. He spoke humorously to Dearest Pip of the mousetrap Augusta had laid in his room and which nearly cost him the loss of a toe; the overtones of his letter are full of genuine warmth.

After five days he returned to London, was most loving to his wife but annoyed with his sister. But Annabella was not the woman to know how to keep him at his best. He was barely back when she began to be satirical of his obligations at Drury Lane. To her father she described witheringly her husband's duties as involving the superintendence of candle-snuffers and haranguing actors; she did not see how he was going to get out of his engagements there—he never expressed any desire to do so—and she dreaded to think of what people were going to say; she could only hope that the two of them could find some reason to leave town. Later in September she was ironically referring, in another letter to her father, to her husband as The Manager, though at the same time testifying to his calm and judicious handling of theatrical matters. There was another jab in her remarking that he had asked Lady Melbourne to accompany her to *The Merchant of Venice* since The Manager was always too busy "trotting about behind the Scenes."

She called on her cousin, Lady Caroline, in October—apparently looking for trouble—but found her not at home. Caro wrote her regrets at having missed her, and sent her the gift of a Lyonesse scarf—concerning which Annabella told Sir Ralph that she feared the Greeks bearing gifts. She did not mention her own visit.

In November she wrote a series of reflections on her husband's character, for her own delectation. In them there are no symptoms that she had any grievance against him, though their marriage was less than three months from being broken. In these notes she said that whatever impression he might create to the contrary, his religious sense was strong and indestructible; his boyhood experiences as well as later ones had merely discolored them with despair. Having never studied practical morality, he held but vague concepts of virtue, though at heart he was a good man; his imagination had operated to misdirect those ideas and in turn had been misdirected by them. His imagination was too exalted; he must do good on too vast a scale or not at all; it was, moreover, too much occupied with the past and the future to concern itself with the present. His attempts at sophistication were in violation of his own nature.

None of this suggests either desperation or hopelessness about her marriage—though there is something odd about a wife's sitting down to sketch her husband's character.

On November 8 the cause of his depression was forced upon her notice, for on that date a bailiff slept overnight at their house. Byron was almost beside himself with fury at the indignity. When he quitted his home the next day he announced that he was going to lose himself in dissipation. He violently denounced her and Augusta as well. As she wrote to her sister-in-law, he seemed to hate them both together. The following day she stood her ground and upbraided him; he at once relented, and, though still distracted, was gentle. The mental torture he suffered was unabated, however, for the bailiff was a particularly inconsiderate beast who did all he could to make the Byrons smart. It was Byron who took the situation the harder of the two. He now began to drink to excess and went about for weeks in as much of a fog as brandy could conjure.

                                    7.

IT WAS, OF COURSE, INEVITABLE THAT WHEN BYRON BECAME A MEMBER of the management of Drury Lane, some of the actresses should make an effort to attract his interest—inevitable because of his fame, his reputation as the Byronic hero in the flesh, with all the accompanying titillating overtones of wickedness, and his extraordinary personal beauty made pathetic by his clubfoot. Oddly enough for him, he seems to have resisted the advances of all but one.

Susan Boyce was an actress allotted by the company only the most trivial roles, yet nonetheless furiously jealous of her colleagues. Byron apparently began his intimacy with her during the very last months of Annabella's pregnancy. As a sensualist suddenly forced to nearly total celibacy at home, he was more susceptible at such a time. It is possibly the only case —always excepting Augusta's—of his breaking his fidelity to Annabella during the year of their marriage.

Susan's first letter to him is full of indignation at the way a Mrs. Scott had been treating her at the theatre; she referred to her sneeringly as "*much elevated*—I don't know whether it was the *smell* or *taste* of gin." The origin of the squabble had to do with Byron's attentions to Susan, which the other actresses had noted. What she herself wanted from him was his "*confidence and esteem*. If I can obtain that, most joyfully would I meet you when you please." She hoped he could be her friend "in a *quiet* way." If so, she was ready to give herself to him wholeheartedly and to devote all her "time and affection" to him and to him alone. He accepted the offer.

There were some hysterics after the night of November 14, when she lost her brooch in the carriage. She dreaded that the incident might lead to something unpleasant—just how is not clear.

She had been living at her sister's, but for his sake took a room in New Ormonde Street. He soon made her what she described as a "truly noble present," but she complained that the accompanying note contained not *"one* expression congenial" to her feelings. She felt he did not really know the sort of person she was, and prayed "night and morning" that someday he might. But she had not forgotten his observation that a woman too much in love was troublesome, and she was going to avoid troubling him.

Since he was soon quite cavalier about his visits to her, one week she stressed the fact that she would be waiting for him every evening from six to eleven, except for Thursday, her six-year-old son's birthday. Though she always spent that anniversary with the boy, she was willing to break the custom if Byron wished to come that evening.

As she became more possessive he, as ever, began to cool. She wrote a tearful letter pleading with him to be less negligent. She knew not how to account for his increasing indifference unless it was that he was a "most *uncommon* character" and herself *"a bit of an oddity."* Their mutual attraction had been perhaps the "natural consequence of two extraordinary beings meeting." He had always been candid with her, and she was going to be candid with him. She hoped they had not reached the end of their attachment, but she was in utter confusion about his present feelings. She suggested he see her for a minute in the green room, and save her from wretchedness. She had hoped her complete devotion would "make amends" for his past disappointments; was he going to throw away the happiness within his reach?

He became more and more casual. She pressed again for a meeting and an answer to her letter. She feared he was ill. (He was.) He certainly had looked unwell the last time. Was sickness the cause of his breaking his promise to come the preceding night? Her situation, she said, was not enviable; she had been alone from six o'clock to twelve.

The paper of another letter is still stained with tears. His conduct of the night before beggared understanding. He did not speak a word to her, though she had been at the theatre only because he had asked her to be. He had left without saying good night, and had forced her to run after him. If that was his method of escaping observation by others it had failed, for everyone had noticed his ignoring her and his paying so much attention to Miss Smith. This sort of thing put her at immense disadvantage with the other actresses and enabled them to "trample" on her. If by misfortune she should find herself pregnant, she might do something desperate to herself.

Poor Susan was not the one to recapture his interest. She wrote again to remind him how he had originally singled her out at a time when she was *"respected and loved by all."* She had become the subject of common gossip, and she was "the jest of the *dirt* and refuse of the theatre." She would and could love him, if he would but allow her to.

"The Green Room at Drury Lane" with "Characters in Don Giovanni," drawn and engraved by I. R. and G. Cruikshank; from P. Egan's *Life in London*. (Courtesy of the British Museum.)

LOBBY Loungers. (taken from the Saloon of Drury Lane Theatre.)

Lewis Marks / Silvester, No 98 Strand.

"Lobby Loungers taken from the saloon of Drury Lane," probably by I. R. Cruikshank. (Courtesy of the British Museum.) Byron, hair curled, is ogling the actresses, particularly Mrs. Mardyn.

FASHIONABLES of 1816 taking the air in Hyde Park!

"Fashionables of 1816 taking the air in Hyde Park," probably by I. R. Cruikshank. (Courtesy of the British Museum.) Byron is the man in the center with curly hair.

Presently he had had enough of her persistence. On April 3 she wrote him her last letter. The night past he had been so rude in answer to her query about his health that she knew her love was now only an offense. He had wounded her; since that was what he wished, she would offend him no more with her affection. It was what he wished.

This short-lived romance was ill timed for the unhappy girl. Shortly after its beginning, Annabella bore him a child; his house was overrun by bailiffs; a month later his wife left him; in the months following he was pleading for her return and contending with her, her family, and her supporters; and he himself had become gravely ill. It is not surprising that an affair which began as a physical convenience should, under those conditions, soon become more of an irritation. At first he might have been amused, as in his youth, by the girl's vulgarity and pretentious airs, but in the long run he was bound to find them irksome, certainly too burdensome to cope with in the midst of the anxieties crowding him.

8.

IN HIS DUTIES AT DRURY LANE HE HAD GOT TO KNOW VERY WELL A MAN he had long admired, one of the first writers of comedy of his day, the theatrical manager, George Colman, and found him an ideal drinking companion, "extremely pleasant and convivial." Comparing him with Sheridan, he observed that though the latter's wit was saturnine, he never laughed, "but Colman did." Byron ranked the ability to laugh very high. "I have got very drunk with them both," he noted in his journal, "but if I had to *choose*, and could not have both at a time, I should say, 'Let me begin the evening with Sheridan, and finish it with Colman.' Sheridan for dinner—Colman for supper. Sheridan for claret or port; but Colman for every thing, from the madeira and champagne at dinner—the claret with a *layer* of *port* between the glasses—up to the Punch of the Night, and down to the grog or gin and water of day-break. . . . Sheridan was a Grenadier Company of Life-Guards, but Colman a whole regiment—of *light Infantry*, to be sure, but still a *regiment*."

Such was the tenor of Byron's life during the last months of his marriage. He must have been drunk most of the time, and in his cups obviously made a confidant of Colman concerning intimate details of his life at home. (Hobhouse said, what every reader of Byron's letters must feel, that his friend's worst fault was that he talked too much to others about his private affairs.)

Annabella's pregnancy was now far advanced, and it must have been at this time that Byron performed the act which decided her upon the separation. Later, no doubt moved to anger by the burning of Byron's memoirs, an act which insured that Annabella's version of the cause of separation should be perpetuated—as it has been—Colman determined that the truth ought to be known, and therefore composed the witty ribald *Don Leon* poems.

Don Leon jumps from the passages last quoted early in this work, to the subject of the Byrons' separation. It launches an attack on "yon reptile with his squinting eyes," by whom is meant either Lushington or Romilly, Annabella's lawyers. The note tells us it was he who "plugged" the ears of our hero's wife with "vile opinions" and distortions, and was responsible for sundering the marriage. The poem, turning to Annabella, conjures up the happy days of husband and wife together:

> Methinks 'twas yesterday as both in bed
> We lay: her cheeks were pillowed on my breast,
> Fondly my arms her snowy bosom pressed.
> Love no denial found, desire no stay.
> That night it was, when tired of amorous play,
> She bade me speak of wonders I had seen.

He tells her tales that would shock chaste ears. In the East the woman is her husband's slave; he engulfs her with flowers, perfumes, rare silks, with every luxury "but that vital one of liberty." Soon tiring of her, he spurns her from his couch and will prefer a boy's kiss to hers. "To him with ithyphallic gifts he kneels," Byron is made to continue—when Belle interrupts with a question: How "can male covet male?" He enlightens her. Love of boys inspired the muse of Anacreon, Virgil, and Catullus. Belle cries that she is astonished, remembering all the praise she has heard bestowed on ancient poets.

> That time it was, as we in parlance wiled
> Away the hours, my wife was big with child.

Her once-tapered waist was swollen.

> And Love, chagrined, beheld his favourite cell
> From mounds opposing scarce accessible.

The ninth month of her pregnancy had begun, and he tells her,

> I burn to press thee, but I fear to try,
> Lest like an incubus my weight should lie.

He fears a "close encounter" would "doom" the life of their unborn child. Her charms excite him—how shall they "celebrate the marriage rite"? Medical authorities like Galen and Hippocrates have proposed that in such straits it is better "To copulate ex more pecudum." Belle ought not object to the counsel of science.

> She answered not; but silence gave consent,
> And by that threshold boldly in I went.

In this way clever statesmen

> All comers by the usual door refuse,
> And let the favoured few the back stairs use.

> Soon the languor which our limbs o'erspread
> Had ceased, I thus resumed the theme, and said
> "Thou seest how Nature's operations tend
> By various roads, to work one common end."

The "more hallowed spot" is where "sages, prelates, kings, and bards" have sought to "quench the rage of Priapeian fire." There as

> . . . misses' haunches wriggle in quadrilles
> In thought the lecher his libation spills.

There too the nobleman watches with "achromatic glass" two boys in St. James's Park on the grass busy at their gross obscenities. Neither soldier nor bishop hesitates to enjoy such pleasures, and our hero suggests that he and his wife try them now.

(In the earlier *Leon to Annabella,* the plea made by the hero for that sort of amorous congress is even stronger:

> Oh, lovely woman! by your Maker's hand,
> For man's delight and solace wisely planned!
> Thankless is she who nature's bounty mocks,
> Nor gives love entrance wheresoe'er he knocks . . .
> Matrons of Rome, held ye yourselves disgraced
> In yielding to your husbands' wayward taste?
> Ah no! By tender complaisance ye reign'd:
> No wife of wounded modesty complained.
> Though Gracchus sometimes his libations poured
> In love's unhallowed vase; yet still adored
> By sage Cornelia, 'twas her pride to be
> His paradise with no forbidden tree . . .

The Roman damsel on her wedding night, terrified of the pain facing her while losing her maidenhead,

> Would pray her lord to spare a virgin's fear,
> And take his restive courser to the rear.)

To continue with *Don Leon:* Our hero's historical justification of sodomy has plainly made an impression on his wife. He continues his plea:

> And thou, dear Anna, think'st thou I can see
> Without longing all these charms in thee? . . .
> Then turn thee round, indulge a husband's wish,
> And taste with me this truly classic dish.

Now she wavers between shame and curiosity. At last, in this "fatal hour," his entreaties persuade his wife to "enact the Ganymede" for him.

> Quick from my mouth some bland saliva spread
> The ingress smoothes to her new maidenhead . . .
> 'Tis true, that from her lips some murmurs fell—
> In joy or anger, 'tis too late to tell;
> But this I swear, that not a single sign
> Proved that her pleasure did not equal mine.

Though no one else was as forthright as Colman in identifying the chief cause of the separation, there is sufficient other evidence—to which insufficient weight has hitherto been attached—that he was telling what was basically the fact. Annabella departed with her child from Piccadilly Terrace on January 15, 1816, on a visit to her parents in the country. Writing to her husband with affection at first, with every indication they would soon be together again, she presently began an elaborate correspondence with others—which we shall follow in its complicated course—on the subject of a separation from him. After she had been but a few days under her parents' roof, her talks with them must have had something to do with her change of heart. The services of Dr. Stephen Lushington as her attorney were early procured. For some six weeks, her former governess, Mrs. Clermont; her mother; her father; her friend Selina's brother, Colonel Doyle; and Lushington were kept running around London while she remained in the country playing more or less the general, with advice from Lushington, and receiving almost daily the most circumstantial reports from Augusta, who eagerly played the spy on her brother while living in his house. On February 22 Annabella herself came to London for one express purpose; to confide in Lushington certain horrifying details which must never be made public, and of which her parents knew nothing. The effect of these details was to cause Lushington to rule out all possibility of a reconciliation. On the title page of *Leon to Annabella,* Colman quotes him:

> *Lady Byron could never cohabit with her noble husband again. He has given her cause for separation which can never be revealed; but the honor due to the female sex forbids all further intercourse for ever*
> *Opinion of Dr. Lushington on the Question of Divorce.*

In the margin of Moore's biography of Byron, where the author is attempting to account for the dissolution of the marriage, Hobhouse penned: "Something of this sort, certainly, unless as Lord Holland told me, he tried to ———— her." Lord Holland was a friend of both Lushington and Byron. Now, what has generally been overlooked as crucial, is that Lushington went to Lord Holland to procure his services in persuading Byron to agree to an amicable settlement without recourse to the courts. Since everything connected with Annabella's private interview with Lushington points to her having told him about her husband's "unnatural" act or acts with her, it is reasonable to suppose that he conveyed this damaging information to Lord Holland as a most powerful persuader to Byron's compliance with what Annabella wished, since up to that time Byron gave every token of being unprepared to agree. That Hobhouse knew that Lushington and Annabella were holding the charge of enforced sodomy over Byron's head as a threat will be obvious from Hobhouse's role in dealing with Annabella for Byron.

The "cause" in Lushington's Opinion was permitted to remain unrevealed; just the same, that the cause had to do with some kind of perversion was allowed to remain current, as Byron, to his great indignation, well knew. For example, Thomas Campbell, the poet, in his defense of Lady Byron said: "It concerns morality and the most sacred rights of the sex" that she be acquitted of any share in the blame, which was Byron's and Byron's alone. For the sake of Byron, he added, he refrained from probing into Moore's misconceptions concerning the separation. "The subject would lead me insensibly into hateful disclosures against Lord Byron." What was required, he said, was to acknowledge one great flaw in Byron, and with that exception it would be possible to feel "charity and even . . . admiration of him." Nevertheless, it would have to be admitted "that the child of genius is, in this particular, not to be defended." Campbell assured his readers that his information, came not from Lady Byron but nevertheless from an authentic source. It was this sort of thing which kept tongues wagging long after Byron's death, the more energetically just because the facts were kept clouded until the publication of the *Don Leon* poems—and they did nothing to clear the air, because when they appeared they were dismissed as irresponsible obscenities.

Why Byron should have been propelled to urge a sodomic act upon his prim Princess of Parallelograms, with her endless talk about virtue, when he must have guessed that it might prove traumatic, is not hard to explain. To begin with, his life since his earliest days of adolescence had been given over to sexual experience of various kinds, abnormal in its frequency of recurrence. Appetites increase or diminish in direct proportion to the extent to which they are satisfied. The more one eats, the more often one is hungry; the less one becomes accustomed to eat, the less one requires food—short, of course, of starvation. So it is with sex. Byron's sexual activity had almost never had a pause, and his wife's pregnancy during her last months may very well have caused him acute frustration. Together with his financial worries it was surely one of the causes for his lapsing into daily drunkenness; and his affair with Susan Boyce, apparently his sole expedition into adultery during his year of marriage—excluding, of course, that with Augusta —can be explained on no other basis.

9.

IT IS LESS EASY TO GAUGE ANNABELLA'S REACTION TO THE EXPERIENCE than Byron's impulses. It is necessary to remember that while many people today would consider congress between husband and wife "ex more pecudum" shocking, quite as many others would not be shocked; modern conceptions of the marriage relation encourage people to feel that any mode of physical intimacy between husband and wife, when both agree to it, is perfectly decent. But in Annabella's day, which, for all the dissoluteness of the London aristocracy, made a strident parade of respectability, such an act would publicly be held too horrible to admit as even possible, except among the most depraved.

The difficulty in understanding Annabella's feelings comes not from her having been shocked but from her behavior shortly after their child was born. It is fair to assume that the sodomy left her, her background considered, bewildered, and it is probably bewilderment which, despite all her suspicions of incest, caused her to implore Augusta to come and stay with them, as she did. She arrived during Annabella's ninth month and in the midst of her brother's affair with Susan Boyce, on November 15. Byron was anything but cordial to his sister when he saw her, and then proceeded to make both women the targets of his sarcasms and surliness.

From this point on we must be very careful about accepting as verbatim fact Lady Byron's later copious narratives of what took place during the last weeks she spent with her husband. The rest of her long life she made a

career of justifying herself, first at Byron's, and then at Augusta's expense—
and the act which resolved her never to return to him was never publicly
mentioned, not to spare him, for she built up an elaborate case of incest
against him, but because willingly or not she had been a partner in the act.
(An unwilling partner in that act is hard to imagine, no matter what remorse
might have followed it.) As usual, her distortions were less in the nature of
downright lies than of careful omissions and of an inflamed imagination that
exaggerated every move and word of Byron into the diabolic.

She says that she and Augusta were now left alone many nights while
he went out "to indulge his most depraved propensities," of which he would
boast before and after. It was like Byron's perversity to taunt them, since
they made so excellent an audience, with a picture of debaucheries it is clear
he had no desire to commit. Those days were chiefly given over to endless
drinking bouts with his friends at Drury Lane. Had he admitted to no more
than drinking heavily, Annabella would have branded that as the depth of
depravity; she loathed his Drury Lane companions and was, moreover, convinced that he was having all sorts of affairs with actresses with whom he
was on no closer terms than that of cordiality. He did nothing to disabuse
her. All this time bailiffs were in charge of the house; he told Hobhouse
there were "from one to four executions in his house at a time." In fact, the
bailiffs were there for weeks after the birth of the child, nearly until Christmas, and perhaps later than that. He went about more or less in an alcoholic
mist, and his behavior at home was more often than not frenetic. One night
Augusta, who seemed to suffer more from his taunts than even Annabella,
cried out to Dear Sis: "Ah—you don't know *what* a fool I have been about
him!" She looked so bitter as her trembling hand drew back her hair from
her forehead that Annabella's heart was wrung. She kissed Augusta and
left the room.

The day before the child was born, she was so much terrified that she
consulted Serjeant Heywood, an old friend of the Milbankes, as to the advisability of her leaving the house. It was doubtless because he knew of this
that Byron asked her if she intended to live with him any longer. According
to her own admission, she tried to turn the question into a jest, but he was
intransigent. He presently acknowledged that his question had been mis-
timed; but it was like her to make great capital of it against him, without
considering what might have motivated it. She put it down to a simple
desire to torture her while she was in labor.

That night he was in a state of tension common to all prospective
fathers. As he drank bottle after bottle of soda water because of all the
magnesium he had been taking, he broke off their heads, as was his impatient
habit, with a poker. That was, of course, inconsiderate at such a time, for it
made a great deal of noise. But in her hectic fancy—and she stated this as

fact—what he was doing was throwing bottles against the ceiling for the express purpose of depriving her of sleep in the room above. When Hobhouse examined the ceiling to verify the charge she had made to her physician, he found not a mark.

On Sunday afternoon of December 10, at one o'clock, Lady Byron was delivered of a girl, who was at first named Augusta Ada, and later called only Ada. Byron was delighted with his child. Mrs. Clermont, Annabella's old governess (whom Byron mistakenly came to blame as the chief cause of the separation), who had been called to Annabella's side by Augusta, told Hobhouse that she had never seen a father so proud of his offspring. "Lady Byron herself more than once said to Lord Byron that he was fonder of the infant than she was, adding also what, to be sure, might have been as well omitted, and 'fonder of it than you are of me.' "

Whatever happiness the birth of Ada brought him was dissipated by his financial worries. At the end of November he had already begun to talk of giving up the house in Piccadilly Terrace after his wife's confinement. Now he owned to Hobhouse that his "pecuniary embarrassments were such as to *drive him half-mad.* He said 'he should think lightly of them *were he not married'*—he wished 'he could go abroad.' This he said once or twice, but afterwards dropped that expression and talked of going down into the country. He said 'that no one could know what he had gone through'; that no man should marry—it doubled all his misfortunes, and diminished all his comforts. 'My wife,' he always added, 'is perfection itself—the best creature breathing.' "

His drunkenness must have made him unaware of the brutality of his conduct at home, for, discussing with John Cam his money troubles, he could remember only one occasion upon which he had been outrageous with his wife: " 'One day in the middle of my trouble I came into the room, and went up to the fire, she was standing before it, and said, "Am I in your way?" I answered, "Yes, you *are,*" with emphasis. She burst into tears, and left the room. I hopped up stairs as quickly as I could'—Poor fellow, you know how lame he was— 'and begged her pardon MOST humbly; and that was the only time I spoke really harshly to her.' " He later filled out this incident for Medwin by prefacing it with: "I do not like to be interrupted when I am writing. Lady Byron did not attend to these whims of mine." (Every writer will understand that normal wish as being far less than a whim.)

Yet she was able to remember scenes of equal or greater savagery. For instance, one night he came home from "one of his lawless parties," and, perceiving her to be in a mood of calm indignation, he was seized with remorse, called himself a monster, and, though Augusta was present, threw himself "in agony" at his wife's feet. He seemed convinced he had lost her forever. Astounded "at the return of virtue," she began to weep freely, and said, "Byron, all is forgotten: never, never shall you hear of it more!" He jumped up, folded his arms, and burst into laughter. Puzzled by his reaction, she asked what he meant. It was only a philosophical experiment, he said, to test the firmness of her resolutions. What Annabella was incapable of understanding is that Byron's penitence might have been sincere enough, and that the unctuous phrasing of her forgiveness would have sufficed to make him laugh and lapse into the sardonic. Or, as is likely, if his "lawless" party had been with people no more dangerous than Sheridan or Colman, he might very well have been annoyed at her "mood of calm indignation"—one can picture it—with which she greeted him, and decided to play a little farce in revenge.

By degrees she was trying to find consolation in the possibility that he was deranged—at least, so say her later narratives. Certainly the letter he wrote Moore on January 5, 1816, was sane enough. He boasted of his daughter's being "very flourishing and fat, and reckoned very large for her days—squalls and sucks incessantly." Her mother was in fine health.

But Annabella secretly consulted Dr. Baillie with the approval, she says, of Augusta, on Byron's possible insanity; not able to examine him, Baillie could give no opinion. He did come to their house while Byron was out, and "in Lord Byron's own parlour," as Hobhouse phrased it, "did examine these medical charges against Lord Byron by Lord Byron's own wife." This was on January 8. The best that Baillie could do was suggest that she limit her conversation to light and soothing topics.

Nor did she hesitate, in Byron's absence, to rummage through all his personal belongings for evidence of lunacy. As Hobhouse bitterly commented: "Her Ladyship thought she was only doing her duty in investigating *him* and *his* in search of those singularities and obliquities, which she considered were the proofs and features of that particular insanity under which he laboured. His *drawers* and *trunks*, and *letter-cases*, were the objects of research." Among the things she found were a small bottle of laudanum, a common enough possession in those days, and a copy of de Sade's *Justine*, which though now a best seller and very popular among the high school and college set in unabridged translations, no doubt seemed proof positive to her of his insanity.

On January 9 she pressed his attorney, Hanson, to see her. When she came to his house he was alarmed at what he felt was her intention: to have her husband taken in charge as a dangerous lunatic. He therefore warned her against such a desperate measure, which could only eventuate in catastrophe. She gave so circumstantial an account of Byron's violent language, that he asked her if she were living in any fear of her own safety. She answered, "without the least hesitation, '*O, no, not in the least; my eye can always put down his!!!*' and then added that her suspicions were that Lord Byron might make an attempt upon his own life." Hanson reminded Annabella that Byron was used to these bursts of passion and violence in his normal conversation, and that it was a mistake to interpret what he said literally. The upshot of this interview was that having already planned to go for a visit to her parents with the baby, she "begged Mr. Hanson to use his efforts *to induce Lord Byron to follow her as soon as possible to Kirkby."* [italics mine.] Hanson never told Byron he had seen his wife.

As a matter of fact, Byron, convinced that all he could do about his overwhelming debts was to give up the house in Piccadilly Terrace, had left a note for Annabella telling her how important it was to dismiss the members of their household staff, and that it was for her to decide upon the date for her visit to her parents. She could be comfortable there, as he had already observed, until further arrangements could be made. Of course, she was to consult her own convenience and wishes in fixing the date. He had already counseled her to take the safer carriage for her and baby Ada, but if she preferred the chariot she naturally was to use that.

Annabella chose to be offended with the note, as she was with everything he now said and did. They had a brief quarrel, but made up, and the matter was never mentioned again between them. The next day she informed him that she would leave London on the earliest possible day.

Knowing nothing of her moves to prove him insane—three days after her talk she sent Hanson a marked volume of the *Medical Journal* on hydrocephalus with the comment that Byron showed only too clearly the first and second stages of the progress of the disease—her husband imagined that all was well between him and his wife. He told Hobhouse that they "lived on *conjugal* terms up to the last moment—and that so far from not intending to return," she had taken his carriage and several receipts for great sums belonging to him—all of which, Hobhouse notes, "it is not likely a wife resolving to decamp for ever from her husband should venture to do."

Annabella was determined that Augusta should not remain at the house after her own departure. She calmly wrote down that she informed Augusta's aunt, Sophia Byron, that Byron had "intimated" that he had had criminal "dispositions" toward his sister, and left it to Sophia Byron to see that Augusta was not left unprotected from this danger. Byron's cousin George had recently come to stay at Piccadilly Terrace too, and that, of course, lessened the "danger."

It may be that by now Annabella was beginning to be gravely concerned about that act of sodomy to which she had lent herself, and her desire to prove insanity was her method of accounting for it. For a scarce two months later she was declaring: "In his endeavours to corrupt my mind he sought to make me smile first at Vice, and with regard to others has revealed this system of corrupting by degrees—saying, 'There is nothing to which a woman may not be reconciled by repetition, or familiarity.' There is *no* Vice with which he has not endeavoured in this manner to familiarize me— attributing the condemnation of such practices merely to the manners of different Countries, & seeking either to ridicule or reason me out of *all* principle." This declaration of Annabella makes, it seems to me, the basic authenticity of Colman's poem a matter beyond cavil. It is her euphemistic version, after the separation, of the tale told by Colman from Byron's point of view.

She left London on January 15, 1816, with Ada and her maid. Byron was not to see her or his child ever again.

When she went from Piccadilly Terrace to the house of her parents, it was apparently with the greatest affection for him. She clearly left with the intent of being absent from his side for only a brief while. He had no reason under the sun to suppose she was leaving him forever, and she herself certainly had no such intention at the time. The change came under her parents' roof. If that sexual act was the determining cause, as the evidence overwhelmingly indicates, there is only one explanation for its figuring weeks after the fact. However bewildering the experience might have been to her, in her innocence she may have had no idea of how horrifying it would have been to her contemporaries. Away from Byron and revolving it in her mind, she might by a simple assurance (in her reading or a question discreetly asked and answered) that it was immoral to the last degree, have suddenly become appalled with Byron, with herself for lending herself to his desires, and with terror at what such complaisance as she had shown might lead to in moral corruption. Her statement, already quoted, implies as much. At the moment of the act, her feverish desire to win him entirely to herself—away, perhaps, from Augusta—together with her own strong strain of masochism —would have been enough to make her grant what he asked for, despite her severe love of "virtue." Who knows? As *Don Leon* hints, she might have found the experience not altogether repugnant. If so, once she saw that she had been dragged by Byron from her rarefied plane of morality, where she was always so proud of dwelling, being Annabella she would have become all the more relentless against her putative debaucher.

10.

IN THE CRUCIAL DAYS WHICH FOLLOWED IT WAS CERTAINLY NOT BYRON whose behavior was the oddest. Annabella's is almost past belief; Augusta's is not only touched with her usual hysterics but also beyond pardon; George Gordon's, in the long run, was hardly better. Byron's wrongs against Annabella had been very grave, and had she left him at any time during the year it would have been understandable, and one would feel he had got his just desserts. But because of the disgusting machinations which were going on behind his back, it is Byron who inevitably becomes the object of one's sympathy. It is impossible not to feel that he was being betrayed by both wife and sister, and later by George Byron too.

To follow the story of that betrayal it is necessary to follow chronologically its unfolding in a flurry of letters, "statements," documents, memoranda—frequently penned with relish by persons who had no business to be meddling. Traced in this way, the facts take on the fascination of a Henry James novel.

[JANUARY 15]

ON THE AFTERNOON OF ANNABELLA'S LEAVING LONDON, AUGUSTA BE-gan a series of reports to Dear Sis. Though her presence was required at Six Mile Bottom and she was packed to go, she had been advised by Byron's lawyer Hanson to stay on a while at Piccadilly Terrace, she told Annabella. Byron was quiet, languid, and felt ill.

En route to Kirkby, Annabella wrote him:

> Dearest B—— The Child is quite well, and the best of Travellers. I hope you are *good,* and remember my medical prayers & injunctions. Don't give yourself up to the abominable trade of versifying—nor to brandy—nor to any thing or any body that is not *lawful* & *right.*
>
> Though *I* disobey in writing to you, let me hear of *your* obedience at Kirkby.
>
> Ada's love to you and mine.
>
> Pip.

The letter was obviously meant to be affectionate, but it reveals her gracelessness. What can she have been thinking to urge her husband, with a vast reputation as a poet, to give up writing poetry (presumably, it was his poetry which first made her fall in love with him), what did she mean by calling it "abominable" and a "trade," and why did she equate it with alcoholism and whoring? Was she trying to be playful? If so, could she have imagined he would be pleased by elephantine caperings? And to ask for *his* "obedience"!

She also wrote to her good friend, Selina Doyle, who had been the recipient of her confidences and grievances against Byron. She said she hesitated to take advantage of the victim of a disease, for that would be both inhuman and disgraceful; if one could not help others, however, one must preserve oneself without augmenting the sufferings of the sick. Obviously the basis of Byron's illness was physical; hereafter, she remarked, it would be understood that *she had not severed their relation* [italics mine] only because of her patience and perseverance.

She had, in short, already started work on her portrait of Lady Byron the Martyr.

[*JANUARY 16*]

FROM KIRKBY MALLORY, WHERE HER PARENTS NOW LIVED, ANNABELLA wrote Byron this loving letter:

> Dearest Duck
> We got here quite well last night, and were ushered into the kitchen instead of drawing-room, by a mistake that might have been agreeable enough to hungry people . . . *Dad . . . and Mam long to have the family party completed* [italics mine] . . . Such a *sitting*-room or *sulking*-room all to yourself. *If I were not always looking for B,* [italics mine] I should be a great deal better already for the country air. . . . "*Love to the good goose, & every body's love to you both from hence. Ever thy most loving* [italics mine]
> "Pippin . . . Pip—ip.

Whatever pretenses were advanced later, there was no reason why Byron upon receiving such a letter should have dreamed that anything could be afoot to disrupt his marriage. Yet Lady Judith, Annabella's mother, who is here represented as yearning for Byron to come, would shortly become an avenging Fury against him. According to this letter Annabella profoundly missed him, yet in a few days she was scheming to be rid of him. As for the good goose Augusta, Annabella would soon make her the villainess of the piece, and Lady Judith would develop a fixation against her as a very she-devil.

On this night the good goose continued her report to Dear Sis on Byron's health, his doctor, the pills. From Byron's conduct at the theatre the previous night Augusta was convinced that something was wrong with him. (She was already toadying to Dear Sis's preconceptions.) To Augusta's great relief, Mrs. Clermont, Annabella's old governess, had appeared that morning; it was rather touching to hear Byron talk of Le Mann, the doctor, without a suspicion of the true nature of his illness. She was, of course, implying lunacy, to please Dear Sis.

[JANUARY 17]

AUGUSTA TOLD ANNABELLA THAT BYRON WAS GOING OUT TO DINNER
but promised to drink moderately because of his bad liver, of which he was
talking to everyone. He came home early from the play but sat up late with
Augusta. She inquired about a pistol she had seen on the mantel; he replied
that there was a man whose looks he did not like lurking about the street.
He spoke of Dear Sis with great kindness; he had told Murray that Annabella was the only woman he could have lived with for even six months. He
read aloud Annabella's first letter many times, but could not understand why
she objected to his writing verse. He also remarked that the letter had in it
rather too much of what he was to do and was not to do.

Annabella wrote to George Byron and spoke of her husband as the
"Patient." *She and her parents were in agreement that the Patient ought to
join her now at Kirkby* [italics mine], where he could be kept under a
medical regimen and have fresh air and exercise to supplement it. *Her parents wished to lavish all their attention and care upon him* [italics mine].

She also wrote to Le Mann reinforcing her wish to have the Patient
[*sic*] removed to Kirkby; but she understood that the doctor must have
time to win ascendancy over him.

[JANUARY 18]

AUGUSTA'S LETTERS OF THIS PERIOD ARE MORE DISJOINTED THAN EVER,
but their disorganization is due not only to her usual fuzzy-mindedness, but
also to the fact that she wrote them at intervals during the course of the
day. Obviously, she would have been anxious that her brother know nothing
of their contents, so she could not write in his presence. Moreover, she was
beginning to enjoy the role of spy so thoroughly that every time something
happened she thought worthy of recording, she would rush to her uncom-
pleted letter and add a paragraph of trivia, to keep her correspondent informed up to the minute of posting.

She wrote to Dear Sis that despite his promise her brother had come
home with Hobhouse after midnight, both of them drunk. He had sent her
and George to bed, and called for brandy. She felt one comfort: that fiend
of a Hobhouse looked as though he were dying, and she hoped the Lord
would speedily remove him to a better world. [He fortunately lived to an
advanced age.] When he departed at three in the morning, he left the door
open—they might all have had their throats cut. His talk and Byron's last

night had been so loud that it filled the house. Augusta felt that the more ill Byron felt today the better [i.e., he would therefore drink less?]. He showed her Annabella's second letter; he was greatly pleased with it, though he felt too listless to answer it yet. But she was to tell Dear Sis he would write soon. His face was swollen and he looked very bad.

Selina Doyle also wrote to Annabella. At her friend's request she had put her brother, Colonel Doyle, in full possession of all Annabella had confided to her and asked his opinion. It was that Byron's behavior was due to jealous love exacerbated into morbid passion; that passion, worked upon by an inflamed imagination, had fathered the series of his outrages, the object of which was to make his wife love him for himself, not for his virtues, but in despite of his worst defects. [Doyle was not a bad psychologist here, and his conclusions might have been just enough if his premise, that Byron loved his wife madly and jealously, were not wholly untrue.] Selina remarked that she and Annabella had frequently spoken of Byron's wicked treatment of his wife; she felt that her brother had analyzed the cause better than either of them. She warned her friend: if Byron ever succeeded in causing her to substitute love for him for love of God, she must eventually forfeit Byron's love too.

[JANUARY 19]

AUGUSTA REPORTED TO DEAR SIS THAT BYRON WAS QUITE RECEPTIVE TO going to Kirkby as soon as he felt equal to the travel. She hoped that Hobhouse had truly disappeared; that day he had not been heard from. Dear Sis was not to torment herself; Byron was profiting during his illness by her absence. Byron has asked Le Mann whether a bad liver did not make the victim a hypochondriac—that was as near as he came to the main point, his insanity, Augusta said. [It is hard to see how Byron's beloved sister could have been more treacherous.] She wished she could be with Dear Sis in Annabella's troubled state.

Selina Doyle was also a friend of Annabella's mother, Lady Judith, who must have demanded to know what was the series of outrages of which, according to Selina's last letter, Byron was guilty, for the quick-tempered Lady Judith decided to go at once to London for legal advice. At any rate, go to London she did. This decision was the turning point in Byron's relations with his wife—though he was the last to be notified of what was being done.

Annabella drew up a statement for her mother to take with her. What is not accounted for is Annabella's change of heart. On January 16, she was "ever thy most loving" and sent him her parents' love, for they were longing to have him with them; on January 17 they all agreed he ought to be at Kirkby, where they could lavish all their attention and care upon him; yet two days later she was starting her documentation of the necessity of a separation. It would be easy to ascribe the change to the influence of her parents, but she had always been self-willed in her dealings with them, and had fairly patronized her mother with her own superiority. Indeed, it was she who dictated their opinions, not they hers, as their family letters show. It may have been the case, of course, that Lady Judith, alarmed at the extent of Byron's debts, feared that he might quickly run through the sizable fortune her daughter was due to inherit and that Annabella's mother therefore began to urge a separation. But that is merely putative. The separation will be seen as directly owing to considerations quite different.

We cannot rely upon Annabella's later attempts at self-justification wherein she did her best to insinuate the notion that separation had long been in her thoughts. The facts are provided by her loving words to Byron and her assumption, up to this day, that he would join her in the country. It was only four days since she had left him.

Annabella wrote to Mrs. Clermont that her mother was gone to London; she hoped Lady Judith would be reasonable; however, harsh measures against Byron must go as far as necessary for Annabella's own security and "justification" [!] and to permit "others" to assume as much of the blame as possible. She trusted that her advisers would support her with a minimum of injury to Byron, *since no wife will be commended by the world for making out the most extreme case against a husband* [italics mine]. She had furnished her mother with a very strong statement; at present it would suffice to know what those grounds would enable one to do. Since she could not help her husband, there was no moral reason for wishing to live with him. In any case, she would not sacrifice herself needlessly. Mrs. Clermont was invited to edit the statement; Annabella conceded that she had, perhaps left out pertinent facts.

The pertinent facts were probably the sexual ones later exposed indignantly by Colman. This letter to Mrs. Clermont reveals Annabella's amazing egotism, her deep urge to posture before herself as an exemplar of virtue, and her undying concern for standing before the world as a woman martyred because of that virtue.

[*JANUARY 20*]

HAVING BEGUN WITH HER STATEMENT, ANNABELLA NOW RENEWED HER old practice of putting down her reflections for her own purposes. Before

dramatizing for posterity her own blamelessness, she naturally had to convince herself of the justice of all she eventually might decide to do. If
Byron was really suffering from a sickness, she wrote, she as its long-time
chief victim was thereby the least qualified to remain with him. If, on the
other hand, he had acted only out of wickedness, she had no reason to
hesitate leaving him. If his conduct was due to the evil counsel of others
[Who were they?] and against which his experience of her virtue could not
prevail, what assurance had she that a future with him would not be a
repetition of the past?

[JANUARY 21]

AUGUSTA TOLD HER BYRON FELT HE WAS GETTING BETTER. HE WAS STAY-
ing at home, avoided brandy, and spoke of going to Kirkby in a few weeks.

But the Princess of Parallelograms had made up her inflexible mind.
She answered Mrs. Clermont that she wished never to see Byron again, if
that could be managed with decency. She regretted her second, affectionate
letter to him of a few days ago; she must have been insane to have written
it, for it expressed regret at not being with him. However, the letter would
only prove her tenderness[!]. She wished Mrs. Clermont's assurance that
tenderness would not seem hypocritical in view of Lady Judith's trip to
London and her own statement.

To her mother in London she wrote a long series of instructions. Augusta
and George Byron were not to know of the statement. Byron had better not
come to Kirkby; if he were received there that would annihilate her grounds
for complaining and her own "justification"[!]. Too bad that he was pleased
—out of vanity, of course—with her second letter. She simply must not have
her case weaker than his—as there was danger she might, considering that
he had never beaten her or used abusive language. But if there was any
justice, she must not fall victim to his devilish cleverness [i.e., his failure to
beat her or abuse her?] He was now playing a cunning game to win Augusta
to his side. [Byron had not the remotest idea that sides were to be taken.]
Half-measures would never work; he must be overawed by decisiveness.
Lady Judith was to convey all these opinions to Selina. Important to remember: he was always preoccupied with the figure he cut in the world [far truer
of herself than of him]. Let her mother be not taken in by any of his tender
talk; she herself had had enough of that—his kindest words had often been
followed by malice.

To Mrs. Clermont she wrote to speak ironically of Augusta's new optim-
ism. Because his liver was improving Augusta thought everything was on

the mend. She herself would follow not her feelings but, as ever, the dictates of duty.

Selina Doyle reported to Annabella that her brother had altered his analysis. He now counseled complete separation. Should the disease increase so that the world would see Byron was a lunatic, Doyle advised that Annabella claim guardianship over her husband's affairs. Lady Judith had therefore best procure expert legal opinion—that of Sir Samuel Romilly's, for example. If Byron's mental state made him unequal to the demands of negotiation, his friends ought to take out an official declaration of lunacy.

[*JANUARY 22* (*Byron's birthday*)]

MRS. CLERMONT COMPOSED A STATEMENT OF HER EXPERIENCES IN THE current situation. Around November 20 Augusta had been exceedingly shocked at Byron's conduct; she had feared for Lady Byron because of his violence. A few days later Mrs. Leigh had entreated her to come and stay at Piccadilly Terrace for Lady Byron's confinement. Convinced that he would murder his wife, Mrs. Clermont said as much to Augusta, who begged her never to leave him alone with Lady Byron until her confinement was over, and to stay at her side after that.

Mrs. Clermont also wrote a letter to Lady Byron saying that she had seen Augusta and George Byron and had found their attitude toward Annabella all that could be desired. When she told them that Sir Ralph would never allow his daughter to return to Byron [she, too, seemed unaware that Sir Ralph said only what he was told to say], they had declared that that was but just. Augusta agreed with Lady Judith on all points. Augusta had told Mrs. Clermont that only the night before Byron had abused Colonel Leigh and her own children and had dared to offer George the free use of Seaham. Everyone wondered how Annabella had been able to bear her marriage even for one year.

Byron's cousin George, who like Augusta, owed him only the completest loyalty for his kindness, was, in short, eagerly playing the traitor along with Augusta.

It was now a week since Annabella had quitted Piccadilly Terrace; she wrote her mother to caution her: Byron's must never guess that any harsh measures were being planned. As long as he had no suspicion of what these measures were, he would make all necessary admissions that his wife's conduct had been above suspicion; he would also make every provision for Ada's future. All this he would do only if he were applied to before any action was taken. For his nature was strangely generous. [Here Annabella sounds like

Claudius scheming with Laertes for Hamlet's murder.] As much as she detested publicity of any kind, she knew the world would be her warm partisan.
At present Lady Judith was to enjoin secrecy on everyone. [It is fairly miracu-
lous, with all the people Annabella had let into her "secrets" that Byron as
yet had no wind of what she was up to.] Perhaps, if Byron was not really
insane, his behavior might be due to his sorrowful awareness that he was
unworthy to have such a wife as she[!]; for she believed he loved her very
much; but the more esteem she might win from others, the more irritated
he would become against her. His ill-usage might also emanate from his
remorse for having used her so shamefully. That way indeed madness would
lie. It was therefore better for *him* never to see her again. The fact that her
reason was moving her to act in despite of her love for him could only add
to her justification (a favorite word of hers now) before the world. Lady
Judith was to pass on these ideas to Doyle. (Had typewriters and carbon
paper then existed, Annabella no doubt would have broadcast copies of her
letters to everyone she knew.)

Lady Judith wrote to her daughter that she had an appointment to
see Sir Samuel Romilly, who found the case to be one of the most distressing
ever brought to his notice. [This is almost the most disgusting breach of
ethics on record even for the legal profession. Byron had long before this
retained Romilly as *his* attorney. In all decency Romilly was required to
refuse to discuss matters with Lady Judith.] He advised against allowing
Byron to come to Kirkby and urged that Sir Ralph act for Annabella; there
must be no delay, he added, in coming to a decision. Action should begin
with a letter from Sir Ralph to Byron.

Augusta reported to Dear Sis that Byron was still drinking no brandy.
In the evening he had been in good spirits, then suddenly changed, abusing
Augusta's family for no apparent reason. How well she understood the
feelings of Dearest Sis, and how she wished she could mend them! What
was to be done? The things he said—telling George to go to Seaham and
live there as long as he liked, and announcing himself to be the greatest man
alive! George had laughingly made an exception of Napoleon, but Byron
would not except even him. [Obviously Byron was not to be allowed to have
any fun.]

[*JANUARY 23*]

AUGUSTA TOLD DEAR SIS THAT BYRON WAS HORRIFIED AT LADY JUDITH'S
appearing in London and wanted to know why she was there. Naturally,
Augusta had pretended that Annabella's mother had business of her own in

town. She had shown him such of Dear Sis's letters to her as he might safely read; he had been amused but wished to know if there were others. All evening long he harped on Lady's Judith's presence in the city and seemed to guess that she was angry with him. Augusta had asked why, and his answer was his failure to go or write to Kirkby. Augusta had lightly turned the matter aside and spoke as if unaware of what was taking place. He had asked whether his sister had remembered to send Annabella his love; she had answered that he had not told her to do so. When she next wondered why he did not write himself and taunted him with his laziness, he responded with his customary sarcasms. [Augusta, in brief, was behaving more and more like a snake.]

Lady Judith wrote to her daughter saying she would draft the text of a letter Sir Ralph was to send Byron, Romilly would correct it, and when Lady Judith was back at Kirkby, her husband could pen it. Sir Ralph must state in that letter that Byron could not be admitted to their home; his duty to his daughter and his own principles made it impossible to permit any further association between any of his family and Byron. If Byron attempted to storm their citadel by force he would be answered in kind. Lady Judith was to see Lushington to find out what measures were to be taken toward a private settlement of the separation. Annabella now could assure herself that Augusta was safely their partisan; she had so thoroughly committed herself before Lady Judith and Mrs. Clermont that she could never retract hereafter. In fact, Augusta was most anxious to have the lunacy established to free her brother of any charge of depravity. Romilly believed Lady Melbourne to be the most infamous woman alive. [Romilly must have developed the art of the weathercock to a considerable degree. Lady Judith no doubt had been venting to him her inveterate hatred for her sister-in-law, and he was apparently only too ready to second her ill opinion in order to please.] Augusta said that Byron talked so obscenely before his niece Georgiana that she was forced to keep her daughter [then aged seven] out of his range. [This is the daughter whom she so eagerly married off later to the scoundrel Trevanion, with whom Augusta was apparently infatuated.] She and George Byron felt that Annabella's life would not be safe with Byron, and they had sworn to testify as much, if there should be need. [How account for their treachery? Perhaps, after all, Augusta was anxious to inherit her large legacy from her brother, and George Byron in haste to inherit the title to which he was, thus far, heir.]

[*JANUARY 24*]

MRS. CLERMONT WAS ABLE TO TELL ANNABELLA THAT GEORGE BYRON had lectured his cousin on his abominable treatment of his wife. Byron had been astonished at the accusation, denied having treated her badly or asking her to leave his house. George then demanded how Byron could have expected his wife to be at her parents' without their learning the way he had behaved. Byron became violent and declared that if her friends wished her to have a separation she could have one. Augusta and George had assured Mrs. Clermont that whatever happened only Annabella's feelings must be considered; they could not have been more sympathetic. Selina was of great help too.

Whether George Byron's upbraiding of his cousin was fact or invention to please Annabella, the declaration was, to say the least, shabby.

Annabella wrote to her mother to give her authority for taking such measures as would ensure a separation. Byron was no longer entitled to consideration. Despite increasing evidence that he was insane, that had better not be the grounds for separation, since she could not *swear* that he was mad. However, a patent aspect of lunacy was pride like his, which defied God and mankind. Before the world the thing to stress was his manifest aversion to her and his malevolence. People might say she ought to have known his character better before marrying him, but no one could accuse her of having known he hated her. [Two days earlier she had been sure he loved her.]

Her mother wrote again. Lushington was cleverer and clearer-headed than any man she knew. He too said that Byron, if he appeared at Kirkby, was not to be allowed to stay an instant. On no account must Annabella see him alone; if she did, she would be wholly in his power; he could then appeal to the court for a resumption of his conjugal rights and force her to return to him. Nor must she answer any of his letters. Lushington was surprised to hear that Lady Judith had given exactly this advice. [Annabella came by her conceit rightfully.] All of London, she gleefully added, was saying Byron was mad and had chased his wife from the house.

Augusta sent another circumstantial report. Yesterday she had told Byron that his behavior at Drury Lane was common gossip, that his affair with Susan Boyce was a favorite topic, and that there were whispers about his intimacy with others. He laughed. He had been having severe pains in his head; he thought they were due to the mercury given him. When she told him that Mrs. Clermont had reported Annabella as unwell, he looked quite wretched. He commiserated with his poor wife for all her worries and said he must write to her soon. He was eager to know whether she wanted him to join her.

[JANUARY 25]

AUGUSTA WAS ANGRY ON TWO COUNTS: HOBHOUSE HAD REAPPEARED, she told Annabella, and Byron, with a cold in his head, had his hair cut. He came home from Drury Lane in a black humor, madder than he had been in many weeks. Hobhouse bluntly told Augusta that she seemed to hold him responsible for her brother's drinking, and Byron called her to his room and continued from where John Cam had left off. She demanded to know why Hobhouse was being defended so elaborately when no one had attacked him, and offered to tell John Cam what she thought of him whenever he cared to hear it. Byron forbade her to do any such thing and stoutly denied that his friend was in any way responsible for his treatment of Annabella.

Selina Doyle wrote Annabella that she had stated the facts as she knew them before Augusta at Mrs. Clermont's and appealed to Augusta and George Byron for their support. It was granted. They said Byron was as incapable of making his wife happy as of being made happy by her.

[JANUARY 26]

SELINA TOLD ANNABELLA THAT HER BROTHER HAD SEEN LUSHINGTON. George Byron had threatened his cousin that Annabella's parents would come to her defense, and Byron's face looked exalted as he cried that he would glory in it if they did so. He had the courage to destroy his soul but none to repent. [Everybody saw Byron as one of the heroes of his narrative poems.] He might refuse private negotiations just to force Annabella to a public exposure of his vices. He had despised her when she lived with him; now when an insuperable barrier stood between them she became a second Thyrza. Had he married Thyrza he would have treated her just as he had Annabella.

Annabella answered her mother: Augusta had been the truest of friends and Lady Judith must treat her accordingly. It would be terrible if anybody thought she was the cause of separation. [Annabella was to spend most of her life creating exactly that impression.]

Lady Judith sent on the draft of a letter, corrected by Lushington, for Sir Ralph to send Byron. All that was needed was Sir Ralph's handwriting. Lushington promised to represent them, a real condescension on his part since, if Byron intended hiring Hanson, it was not really etiquette for Lushington to meet with a mere solicitor, Lushington being the most respected member of the Spiritual Court.

[*JANUARY 27*]

HER PRESENCE IN LONDON NO LONGER REQUIRED, LADY JUDITH LEFT for Kirkby.

Annabella composed another of her numerous memoranda. The last year of her life, she wrote, had been sheer waste because of the devotion she had lavished on Byron. It was like him to cherish the past, not the present. His love for her would be awakened when he thought of her in the future; her goodness, which had only irritated him, would in retrospect endear her to him—might even lead him to better thoughts. If she should be the vehicle of bringing him to one association of virtue, she was glad to have suffered. This year had been the least blameworthy in her life; had her trials been due to happiness, she might have fallen. Sorrow is both castigator and guardian.

And she wrote at length to Augusta. She would not cease considering Byron's welfare; that had been her guiding motive in everything she had done. But Augusta must speak no more of his feelings for his wife—unless those feelings might be useful for her parents to know (!); in which case Augusta could recount them to Mrs. Clermont. (She was already letting Augusta know that she held the whip hand over her, and thus was openly converting her into a full-fledged spy, a role she was to play for many years to come.) It was important that Byron be made aware of his disease as one from which he had recurrently suffered for years. If he meditated any strange act let it be made clear to him that the oddity of his conduct had already been remarked; if he performed anything more in kind, someone might have to take *strong measures.* When he should at least learn that Annabella was no longer his, let him realize that she had discovered she could not make him happy, but that she bore no resentment for his behavior. Better, too, that he be permitted to think of her as cold and calculating; let him operate under the false idea that the separation was for her own happiness; but let him also believe that she had not surrendered hopes for his salvation. (There was no end to this woman's goodness.) He had told her twice that her prayers would help him in the Hereafter; she would continue to pray for him—and it would be well she remain in his thoughts as connected with his hopes for Heaven. But under no circumstances was Augusta to reveal to him Annabella's intentions, for he might take advantage of that knowledge. *Augusta was also to present as her own opinions* [italics mine] what Dear Sis had told her of her motives. Then, as if suddenly aware of the domineering tone of her instructions—as though she had been addressing a slave, Dear Sis concluded with a request to be pardoned for seeming to dictate—she was, after all, writing to *a friend.*

Two days earlier she had asked Augusta whether she was still to be her sister. Now Augusta replied that she would always be her own dearest Sis. Every day made her, if that were possible, only "dear*er*." Last night Byron had stayed home but had sung wildly. She had spoken again on the topic of mental derangement. He quietly took what she had to say, but at last was rather alarmed and asked her to desist.

[*JANUARY 28*]

SIR RALPH'S LETTER ARRIVED AT PICCADILLY TERRACE. SURPRISINGLY Augusta returned it undelivered and unopened to Kirkby before her brother could see it. (This was a fatal move for her relationship with Lady Judith.) Her accompanying letter said that she had for the first time in her life acted according to her own judgment, although with ten thousand fears. She asked for a few days' delay. It was of the utmost importance to Dear Sis and little Ada that Annabella pause. George Byron was leaving London the next day and hoped Annabella's parents would see him, and she wished them to hear what he had to say. Byron had seen Lady Melbourne and come home in good spirits; she had evidently scolded him for being a bad husband and son-in-law. Perhaps Lady Melbourne's interest might make a difference now. (It certainly would make a difference with Lady Melbourne's archenemy, Lady Judith.) Augusta had never been so much pleased with Annabella's aunt as she was after hearing what Lady Melbourne had said to her brother. Of course, Augusta wished all the blame to be her brother's—if even a shadow of it rested on Dear Sis it would break her heart. (Augusta was plainly, on a sudden, frightened at Annabella's intentions—probably on her own account.)

[*JANUARY 29*]

SHE WROTE ANOTHER LETTER FOR GEORGE BYRON TO TAKE WITH HIM to Kirkby. She begged Dear Sis to consider for a few days the possible effect of Lushington's letter. Most likely Byron's first reaction would be to plan vengeance. What revenge could be greater than his taking little Ada away from her mother? Who could prevent him? If he was not deranged enough to be confined, he would not be declared unfit to care for his child. And what would that do to Annabella and Ada? Augusta knew all Dear Sis was suffering; all she dreaded was her having to suffer more. Lady Melbourne had made the strongest representations of Annabella's merits and devotion;

she had said nothing against her brother, Sir Ralph, but had been less kind on the subject of Lady Judith—a subject, unfortunately, upon which Byron himself was particularly irrational. Nevertheless, Lady Melbourne had urged Byron to deal well with Annabella's parents for his wife's sake. Had Annabella any instructions for Augusta in case Lady Melbourne saw her? Augusta acknowledged being a coward with wicked people. Doctor Le Mann thought Lushington's letter might very well cause Byron to do something wild.

Despite her toadying and her reports composed to please Dear Sis, treacherous though they were to her loving brother, Augusta's interception of the letter caused a complete alteration in Dear Sis's attitude. Lady Judith had not been prepossessed in Augusta's favor, but further incensed by the complimentary references to Lady Melbourne, she was henceforth at war with Byron's sister. Dear Sis, Lady Judith, and Sir Ralph put Augusta down in their books as acting always exclusively in Byron's interest.

At once Lady Judith wrote to her. Annabella was not much longer for this world: her distress was terrifying to behold, and all of it was due to the cruelty and wickedness of Byron, who had broken her heart. Le Mann's opinions were beside the point; the doctor knew nothing of the crimes of which his patient was guilty. Augusta had had no right to intercept the letter. Did she expect wretched Annabella to suffer the acts of a lunatic or heartless savage? Byron was one or the other. Was she to live in dread of what he might do next? There was more cause to fear what he might do to his wife than to himself by way of violence. Augusta would live to repent her interference.

Apparently Annabella refused to allow her mother to send this abuse. She knew that she still had use for Augusta.

[*JANUARY 31*]

LADY JUDITH WROTE AUGUSTA A SIMILAR LETTER, WHICH AGAIN HER daughter forbade her to post. In the meantime Sir Ralph had been sent to London with the intercepted letter.

[*FEBRUARY 1*]

LADY JUDITH WROTE TO MRS. CLERMONT ON A FAVORITE SUBJECT, HER hatred of Lady Melbourne. Doyle and Lushington had better advise them what was to be done about Sir Ralph's sister—a dangerous, malevolent, and inveterate enemy to her brother's family, ready to do anything to please Byron.

This letter also contained an enclosure for henpecked Sir Ralph. It said that some two years before their marriage Byron had told Annabella that he had had unlawful copulation with both an old lady and her daughter-in-law (by whom, of course, Lady Judith meant her husband to understand his sister, Lady Melbourne, and Lady Caroline)—that the old woman had been the aggressor—and that Byron had said her age was so advanced that he had scarcely known how to manage the affair. (While this bizarre confession might have been the fact—there was nothing in Lady Melbourne's character which ruled it out—and while Byron might indeed have said this to Annabella the first year of their acquaintance, the tone of respect and anxiety to please with which his letters to Lady Melbourne were composed makes it difficult to believe this story. He could, however, have recounted it to the young country girl just for its shock value, without there being a grain of truth in it, and consoled himself that he was not mentioning names. Or the story might have been true enough of some other woman and her daughter-in-law, for 1813 was the year of his mad whirl in London society.) Sir Ralph was not to refer to this matter when he wrote to Kirkby, for Annabella insisted on reading all letters which arrived there.

Annabella wrote further instructions to Mrs. Clermont for her father. If Byron should demand more reasons for the separation, it would be just a trick to gain time; Sir Ralph was to pay no heed to it. Let Sir Ralph beware of all who called on him. When they did, he had better have them conducted into one room, and have them brought in one at a time to another room where he would receive them. In that way he could select whom he wished to see and whom he did not.

[FEBRUARY 2]

IT WAS IRONICAL THAT BYRON, HIMSELF HAVING HEARD NOTHING FROM Annabella and not guessing her plans, should on this Friday have ordered horses to take him to Kirkby on Sunday. For soon after, Lushington's letter via Sir Ralph was delivered to him by special messenger. It stated that in view of what Sir Ralph knew, there could be no excuse for Annabella's returning to her husband.

Augusta at once wrote to Dear Sis that her brother had asked her to find from Annabella whether the separation was her wish. If so, he would acquiesce. He was quiet; though admitting his past faults, he thought Sir Ralph's letter an exaggeration. He made a great point, in talking with

Augusta, of the mischief money worries had provoked him into; Le Mann also said that his long illness had made him particularly prone to irritability. But he spoke of Annabella only with kindness. Augusta pitied him, but worse, for her, was the memory of what Annabella had suffered.

To Sir Ralph, Byron replied with his usual candor. Lady Byron had never been dismissed from his house, as Sir Ralph's letter claimed. They had parted, so far as himself was concerned, with the greatest affection and harmony. He had, in truth, once suggested to her that it would be expedient that she stay temporarily with her father and mother. But his reason for this was very simple: his debts and his inability to continue maintaining the establishment at Piccadilly Terrace. Lady Byron, who never lied, would bear out the truth of this. During the past year he had had to contend with perturbations external and internal. He had tried to remove the distress in every way he could; as for the disease, he would make no reference to it had he not the authority of his physician to state that it was such as to encourage an unreasonable touchiness, which must have made him as disagreeable to others as he had been to himself. She may have seen him gloomy, even violent, at times, but she knew well enough that she had nothing to do with either mood. He might be exonerated if the causes were considered fairly. Out of justice to Lady Byron—not to satisfy Sir Ralph, for he owed him no satisfaction—it was his duty to state that there was no part of her behavior or temperament in word, deed, or thought which showed any failing or which could have been changed for the better. He had always regarded her as one of the world's most genial beings and as closer to perfection than he had thought humanly possible. As for the proposed separation, he must decline answering for a few days. Such a step, once taken, cannot be retraced. Sir Ralph was to remember that Annabella was still his wife, as well as the mother of his child; until he heard from her that she sanctioned what Sir Ralph was doing, he would take the liberty of doubting his right to meddle. Whether he spoke for his daughter or not would soon be determined. Byron's answer depended on hers.

[FEBRUARY 3]

MORE THAN TWO WEEKS OF PLOTTING FOR THE SEPARATION HAD BEEN going on—enough, it will be granted, to have occupied two months—without a word to Byron, even though members of his own family living under his roof were well aware of Annabella's purposes. It is not surprising, then, that when presented with Sir Ralph's letter he should have concluded the idea was her parents', not hers. This was a conviction of which he found it impossible to rid himself for a long time.

He wrote to his wife acknowledging receipt of her father's letter. He could not reply to the proposal for separation until he knew what *her* thoughts were, what *she* wished, and from herself. It was impossible to answer generalized and exaggerated charges made by others. If he ever decided to allow relatives to interfere, it would not be because he granted their right to do so, but only as a courtesy. Not knowing how far she had sanctioned the letter he found it difficult to address her; anything he said might be open to misinterpretation. Even the letter itself was incomprehensible. Could she explain it? He promised to abide by her decision, but begged her to weigh all the consequences. Whatever her decision would be, he had to declare in all justice that he could accuse her of no fault and that at no time had there been anything he could have imputed against her. He had no choice but to sign himself hers "ever most affectionately."

That should have fed Annabella's self-esteem. However, she was already providing the answer Byron stipulated for in a letter that same day— not to him, but to Augusta. Byron had asked his sister to find out whether Sir Ralph had acted with his daughter's concurrence. Annabella wrote that he had.

11.

OF COURSE, ANNABELLA SENT LUSHINGTON A COPY OF BYRON'S LETTER, and in seeking advice she told him that Byron was particularly vain of his ability to use words equivocally; in the enclosed letter the motive could be love, pride, or cunning. She said the same thing in a letter to Mrs. Clermont. She herself, she added, was miserable because undecided. She did not wish to be responsible for Byron's death, if there were danger of that. Augusta, she implied, was complicating matters by foolishly trying to evoke her tenderness.

Colonel Doyle was counseling an attempt to negotiate with Byron directly, rather than to go to law; although the separation would be best for her, he feared that later self-reproach might kill her. (Annabella had so successfully imposed her idealized notion of herself on her friends and *their* friends and relatives, that they all had a distorted picture of her as soft and sensitive, whereas her sensitivity was reserved almost exclusively for herself. They seemed to know nothing of that core of egocentricity she possessed, which made her durable enough. For her the most important thing was to come out of this problem with the flags of her virtue waving.)

Indeed, her comments to her father on Byron's letter show how utterly callous she was to the terrible oppression he suffered from financial problems. If they were the cause, she said with vast exaggeration, of his obvious purpose of forcing her to separate from him, why had he ever married her? But in the long run it was unnecessary to inquire whether his excuses were medical or pecuniary or both; what counted was that to live with him would be to perish from his tyranny and cruelty. If Lushington was certain that her grounds would not fail in a court of law, she would prefer going to law to putting herself to any degree in Byron's power. He would probably work for a delay, and that, at all costs, must be prevented.

Having impatiently waited for some sign from her, Byron wrote her again: "Dearest Bell—No answer from you yet— . . . do recollect—that all is at stake—the present—the future—& even the colouring of the past. The whole of my errors . . . you know—but I loved you—& will not part from you without your *own* most express and *expressed* refusal to return to or receive me. Only say the word—that you are still mine in your heart—and 'Kate!—I will buckler thee against a million'—ever yours dearest most."

Naturally, in this pass, Byron had no difficulty in persuading himself that he had always loved Annabella profoundly. That was the advantage— and disadvantage—of being a thoroughgoing romantic. But Hobhouse, coming up to London again, found him more depressed than he had ever seen him in the eleven years of their friendship. Showing John Cam the second letter from Annabella, Byron insisted that the separation could be the idea only of Lady Judith and Mrs. Clermont. Hobhouse offered to write to Annabella, Byron eagerly urged him to do so, and in great perturbation John Cam composed a letter pleading with her not to proceed with the disruption of the marriage. Would she permit him to come to Kirkby and talk with her? He was positive that five minutes' conversation would convince her that what she was doing was wrong.

Annabella's reply to him breathes her old dislike of him. He must be aware, she said, of the long history of wrongs which had forced her to seek a separation. Her decision was irrevocable. She must therefore ask him not to come to Kirkby or to attempt to discuss the matter further with her.

Lady Judith was still raging about Lady Melbourne. She wrote to Sir Ralph accusing him of never having said a word to Lushington against his sister. Was he prepared to sacrifice his daughter's happiness to a woman like that? She was sure Lady Melbourne was plotting with Byron against them. (In point of fact, Lady Melbourne had just counseled Byron either to join Annabella or have her rejoin him, in order to discredit all the rumors flying about London.) Lushington simply must be informed of her nefarious character, for he might have to deal with her too.

On February 7 Annabella at last wrote to Byron directly, her first words since her loving letter of January 16. She had already, she said, sent

Augusta what she had thought an adequate reply. His most recent letter, however, seemed to require that she put herself to the still more excruciating labor of addressing him. She had placed herself under her parents' protection, but she was a free agent and was acting on her own convictions. He knew all she had suffered to avoid the extremities to be taken, and the clear evidence she had given him of her loyalty and fondness even while experiencing at his hands the most difficult persecutions. An impartial review of her miseries had determined her to separate from him, and her father was acting on her authority. It was too bad that he had considered worthless what he had had and what he had lost as beyond price.

Not knowing this cold communication was en route, Byron wrote again to her father: her first two letters, written right after her leaving London, proved that she then had had no thought of separation; either they were duplicitous or else she had become subject to the influence of others. He would not lower himself to beg that a wife who was reluctant to come should be restored to him, but he refused to abandon his rights as husband and father. He invited his wife's return.

Mrs. Clermont wrote to Lady Judith to reprove her: Lushington and Doyle had been told all she had said about Lady Melbourne; Lushington, well acquainted with the lady, had no doubt that she had plotted the whole thing. But he thought it impractical to let her know they were aware of her wickedness. (It is not clear what Lady Melbourne, for once innocent, is supposed to have plotted.)

Having received Annabella's answer, Byron wrote that all he could now say would be useless. "Yet I still cling to the wreck of my hopes, before they sink for ever. Were you then *never* happy with me? . . . Have no marks of affection—of the warmest & most reciprocal attachment passed between us?" Was it not true that hardly a day had passed without those tokens of love? He did not deny his unfortunate state of mind, but she knew its causes. Did he not always admit his errors and had he not always repented them? "Had I not—had we not—the days before & on the day we parted, every reason to believe that we loved each other—that we were to meet again—were not your letters kind?" Let her answer her own heart. If he promised to say or do nothing to upset her, would she see him? She had said that it was his disposition to deem what he had as worthless, "did I deem *you* so?—did I ever so express myself to you—or of you to others?— You are much changed within these twenty days or you would never have thus poisoned your own better feelings—and trampled upon mine."

In the meantime Lushington had declared to Annabella that Byron's financial difficulties were no excuse for his cruelties. His pretending so was enough to confirm her wisdom in demanding a separation.

As is the way of lawyers, Lushington had not a scrap of sympathy for or interest in understanding the point of view of his client's opposite. That sort of humaneness only weakens one's case.

The Melbournes were generally furious with Annabella now. George Lamb, William's brother, called her "a damned fool." Lady Caroline, however, so Hobhouse recorded, was accusing "B of ————." The dash is to be read as homosexuality or, much more probably, sodomy. As Hobhouse well put it: "Poor fellow the plot thickens against him."

Sir Ralph's letter had put an end to Augusta's daily full reports, and Dear Sis felt she had been deserted by her. So Augusta explained her lapse in correspondence on the grounds that Annabella had better advisers than she could possibly be, though none more devoted to her. She did wish to say, however, that Byron had terrified her by the way he was taking the situation. She hoped Annabella would seriously consider seeing him. Augusta was plunged in misery for Dear Sis, as well as for her brother and Ada. All were precious to her, and she could see nothing ahead but ruin.

On February 11, in a letter to Lushington, Annabella from the heights of her self-complacency dismissed Byron's last appeal to her as containing nothing dependable. She blamed a great deal on Hobhouse. Ever since he had returned to England last summer her husband's behavior had been much worse. She also sent Augusta a ruthless command: she must insist that Augusta write to her most explicitly and omit none of the things which her last letter implied she was suppressing. In short, Augusta was failing in her self-appointed role of spy.

In addition she sent a short answer to Byron: she had made up her mind to address him only in rational terms; those matters which might ask for personal discussion could be settled through their friends.

The next day, February 12, Hobhouse called at Piccadilly Terrace and saw Augusta and George Byron. From them he learned "what I fear is the real truth that B. has been guilty of very great tyranny, menaces—furies—neglects & even real injuries such as telling his wife he was *living* with another woman & actually in *fact* turned her out of the house. [Which, of course, was not a fact.] G. B. suspected she would leave him and told him so a month before she went—but she had no intention of doing it when she went from London." Now they acquitted Byron of everything "by saying that he is mad," that "it is the consequence of a torpid liver, which has already affected his eyes, made one smaller than the other and made him squint—he had gone to the length of strutting about in his peer robes and saying he was like Bonaparte & the greatest man in the world not excepting B——— . Whilst I heard these things Mrs. L. went out and brought word that her brother was crying bitterly in his bed room—poor poor fellow. . . . The thing must not come before the public. . . . I now thought it my duty to tell Byron I had changed my opinion . . . without compromising my informants."

It is dreadful to consider that Byron never had an idea of the dual role both George Byron, to whom he had always been most affectionate, and his beloved Augusta were playing. During this trying period their behavior cannot be easily distinguished from that of his foes. Again it is forced upon one that they both were anxious to have Byron declared insane; as has been said, both would profit from a legal verdict to that effect, he with the title, she with a large inheritance. These are ugly suspicions but their treachery invites them. Moreover, how dared Augusta, of all people, tell Hobhouse that her brother had said he was living with another woman!

Later in the day, Hobhouse spoke to Byron: "I got him to own much of what I had been told in the morning—he was dreadfully agitated—said he was ruined and would blow out his brains—he is indignant but yet terrified sometimes says 'and yet she loved me once,' and at other times that he is glad to be quit of such a woman."

Presumably it was her talk in the morning with John Cam which caused Augusta to plead the bad state of her nerves in answering Dear Sis's command to be MOST EXPLICIT [capitals Annabella's]. Byron was overwhelmed with grief and was set against giving up Annabella. Did that mean that the whole sorry business would have to be exposed to the world? Would not her brother's character then be ruined forever? It would kill him, for he had vowed not to outlive the disgrace. If he died by his own hand, how would Annabella feel?

Augusta had at least a sense of what Annabella in her self-absorption ignored: that with his great reputation as a poet, not only his contemporaries but posterity as well were likely to be interested in everything having to do with Byron's life. Scandal attaching to his name was of a far graver order than that which might accumulate around the name of a man who, once dead, would not be remembered by the world. So far from being forgotten, Byron, after his death, by degrees began to be held as the greatest European poet of his century, even though there were others who were in fact his superiors. Taine, for instance, in his multivolumed and sensitive *History of English Literature,* written late in the century, gives Byron the largest chapter of any nineteenth-century poet; Shelley gets a page or two; Keats a few paragraphs, and Blake is not even mentioned.

Augusta next warned Dear Sis that Byron was determined to have Ada, and that the law would probably give her to him once she was a year old. She could not help seeing the consequences of a separation as an army of evils—the most important of which was Dear Sis's wretchedness.

Annabella tried to explain away her first two letters of the preceding month. She wrote to Byron: "It can be fully and clearly proved that I left your house under the persuasion of your having a complaint of so dangerous a nature that any agitation might bring on a fatal crisis. . . . My absence . . .

was medically recommended on that ground, as removing an object of irritation. I should have acted inconsistently with my unchanged affection for you, or indeed with the common principles of humanity, by urging my wrongs at that moment." Later she discovered that fears for his mental state were groundless. Then, quite inconsistently, she said: until she knew the facts, she had intended to induce him to join her at Kirkby where, "at every hazard, I would have devoted myself to the alleviation of *your* sufferings, and should not then have reminded you of *my own,* as believing you, from physical causes, not to be *accountable* for them. . . . I cannot attribute your 'state of mind' to any cause so much as the *total* dereliction of principle, which, since our marriage, you have professed and gloried in . . . I have *consistently* fulfilled my duty as your wife. It was too dear to be resigned till it became hopeless. Now my resolution cannot be changed.

A. I. Byron."

Beside himself, Byron alternated between fighting the separation and accepting the inevitable. A bill for £2,000 from his coachmaker inclined him to the latter view, for, as Augusta wrote Hanson, his affairs were in such a state that if Annabella came back there would be no place to receive her.

Annabella was girding herself for battle in earnest. On February 14, in sending a copy of her most recent letter to Byron, she deliberately whetted Lushington's curiosity. She could, she wrote her attorney, add other facts to her first statement.

To Augusta she said, *"Happiness* no longer enters into my views, it can never be restored, and the greater or less degree of misery I must endure will depend on the *principles* of my conduct, not on its *consequences* . . . I deem it *my duty to God* to act as I am acting, and I am resigned to the misfortunes that may flow from that source. . . . In regard to him . . . I think it a great error to regard 'worldly disgrace' as a serious evil compared to some that must ensue, with his character, from worldly prosperity. . . . It is not for *me,* but for the *accompanying circumstances,* that he feels so deeply. . . . Those who consider his welfare ought not to desire my return. . . . Don't despair absolutely, dearest . . . God bless you, from the bottom of my heart." Was Annabella's object here to disarm Augusta against any sudden public crucifixion which she might decide upon?

On February 15, exactly one month since Annabella had left Piccadilly Terrace, Byron wrote her again. Every step she had taken, he ruefully observed, had borne her further from him. Though her year with him had been full of distress and misfortune, her trial as wife and mother had not been long. Most of the distress and misfortune had fallen chiefly on him; that he had made her a partner of his desolation was embittering to him. Twice her father and his advisers had refused to state the charges to be preferred against him. He had passed two weeks of humiliation and suspense, while being exposed to the blackest kind of calumnies, without the power to contradict gossip as to what the charges were. He had been kept in ignorance of every detail. He had asked her to come back to him; she had refused. He had begged to see her; she had refused. He had asked to know the charges; that also had been refused. Whatever the outcome of all this might be, he could only say, without hope or ulterior motive, that he loved her and would always love her to the end of time. He had said nothing about Ada, but he had the right to know of his child's welfare, and through some channel he should like to be informed how his baby was doing.

Annabella had made up her mind to come to London herself now. She wrote to Lushington, significantly, on February 17, that there were things that she—and only she—could say to him personally.

On the same day, Augusta reported to her that at a large party a woman read aloud a letter from a friend staying at Kirkby (obviously Selina Doyle) containing bitter charges against Byron, and that Lady Judith's friend, Mrs. Harvey, had been guilty of the same sort of thing. Though Augusta had marked her letter as most private, Annabella sent it on to Lushington.

On February 21 Annabella left for London. She had decided not to take her maid, the wife of Fletcher, Byron's valet; Fletcher had written his wife that they ought to try to bring about a reconciliation; Annabella's caustic comment was that what he really wanted was to have his wife with him—as though that were the most unnatural thing in the world.

12.

UPON HER ARRIVAL IN LONDON ON FEBRUARY 22, 1816, SHE HAD AN interview with Lushington, during which she revealed to him matters unknown to her parents and which must remain unknown to the world. The revelation was of so startling a nature that he at once saw that she must never cohabit with Byron again. Biographers have generally agreed with the position taken by Professor Marchand that it had to do with the incest, which was not mentioned in the statement she had drawn up for Lushington. However, that statement had said that Byron's conversation "turned on images of the most indelicate nature." This could not have been a reference to incest; to sodomy it assuredly could have been. Moreover, in view of Lady Byron's subsequent consecration to building up a mass of evidence to prove the incest, it is hard to see why she should have been so sensitive of Augusta's feelings as not to have already mentioned it to her parents. She had, as we have seen, not hesitated to tell others that she suspected the incest at the beginning of her marriage. But the act of which Colman speaks was another matter. She would have managed to tell Lushington as her attorney, painting herself, as ever, a victim; the world in general, however, must never hear of it because she had, after all, been a partner in the act. Just the same, with the information in Lushington's possession, it could be used to bludgeon Byron into acquiescence. The transactions which followed fortify this theory, though unfortunately for the biographer, the essential documents were destroyed by Lushington before his death. Nevertheless, some portions of Annabella's revelations to him were written down; several individuals who later read them found them coarse in the extreme. One summer weekend many decades later Henry James at Lady Lovelace's* request, went through her archives, and came upon this material; he found it extremely significant but nauseating. An account of incest would not have affected him so.

Byron sent another letter to Annabella hoping she would make up with him. He was sick of the whole business and was sure no good could come out of it. If she would return he would make all the apologies for past conduct she could wish, and promise to be good for the rest of his days. He hoped she would understand the light tone of his letter, for he was terribly tired of the ponderous style of their recent communications.

Annabella found the letter ridiculous; he was apparently making a joke of the whole matter. She would not answer him.

For the moment Augusta was not writing Dear Sis. Hobhouse noted on February 20 that he had dined out with Byron and Scrope Davies: "B. merry . . . Mrs. Leigh has been forbid all intercourse with her [Annabella] at her lawyer's request. A story has now got around against her and B!!!" The triple exclamation indicates several things: that Hobhouse was referring to the incest; that he had never heard of it before; that his telling Byron "the worst" of what was being said, a few days earlier, had not included the incest; and that he was indignant at the imputation. For the rest of his days Hobhouse never ceased being the loyal watchdog fiercely guarding his friend's reputation.

It is fair to assume that this new bit of scandal was first broadcast by Lady Caroline Lamb. Byron had been indiscreet enough to tell her about his love affair with his sister. Annabella complacently was saying to Mrs. Clermont that Lady Caroline would be her partisan and that she was encouraged to have the approval of even the evil people of the world.

It is not to be expected that Lady Caroline could resist involving herself in the drama. From a letter she wrote Byron, professing the deepest

---

* Byron's daughter Ada became by marriage Lady Lovelace. The Lovelace archives contain all the letters, statements, memoranda, etc., which Annabella had kept to justify herself. The Lady Lovelace referred to above was of the next generation, the widow of Byron's grandson.

concern for his happiness, it is transparent that she had already written his wife blackening his character—which explains Annabella's confidence in having the support of the wicked. Now Lady Caroline wrote Byron that if a letter or report had been malevolently placed in Annabella's hands, she was ready to swear it had been written by her only to deceive Annabella. There was nothing, no matter how vile, she would not do to save him, she assured him. He was not to believe that his wife knew anything to his detriment with any certainty, no matter how confidently she might state her suspicions. He must insist on seeing his wife. A wife could and should forgive her husband anything. If she refused to see him, she must be a devil.

Byron, naturally, did not bother to reply. He had enough to keep him in ferment without her. But the consequence was that Lady Caroline suddenly assumed another role, that of a sorrowing well-wisher to both parties. She wrote him again: "When so many wiser and better" were surrounding him, she could not hope her words would "find favour" with him; nevertheless, she must "venture to intrude," even though all she might gain would be his displeasure. "All others may have some object or interest in their's; I have none, but the wish to save you. Will you generously consent to what is for the peace of both parties? . . . Even were everything now left to your choice, you never could bring yourself to live with a person who felt desirous of being separated from you." She knew him too well to believe otherwise. He would feel happier when he made such an agreement, "and all the world will approve your conduct. . . . They tell me that you have accused me of having spread injurious reports against you. Had you the heart to say this? I do not greatly believe it. . . . You have often been unkind to me, but never as unkind as this." No one could be more anxious for his happiness than she. A man superior, as he was, "in mind and talents and every grace and power that can fascinate and delight," ought to be happier. "Return to virtue and happiness, for God's sake, while it is yet time. Oh, Lord Byron, let one who has loved you with a devotion almost profane find favour so far as to incline you to hear her . . . I cannot see all that I once admired and loved so well ruining himself and others without feeling it deeply."

At the very time of writing this, she was deep in her *Glenarvon*.

Byron's finances were now so low that his library, valued at £450 had been attached by the sheriff.

He had received a letter from Moore referring to the rumors which had percolated from London and tactfully hoping that Byron would let him know the facts. Byron answered him on February 29: "I do not know that in the course of a hair-breadth existence I was ever, at home or abroad, in a situation so completely uprooting of present pleasure, or rational hope for the future, as this same. . . . You must not believe all you hear on the subject; and don't attempt to defend me. . . . All the activity of myself and some vigorous friends have not yet fixed on any tangible ground or personage, on which or with whom I can discuss matters." He spoke of Mrs. Clermont, "a kind of housekeeper and spy" of Lady Judith's, "who in her better days, was a washerwoman." He was sorriest "for Sir Ralph. He and I are equally punished. . . . Yet it is hard for both to suffer for the fault of one, and so it is—I shall be separated from my wife; he will retain his."

More than ever wrapped up in her conceit, Annabella was indignant at a certain rumor floating about town—she had no objections to rumors damaging to her husband: it condemned her as a spoiled child. She thought Byron ought not allow *that* insult to go uncontradicted. At the same time she found it expedient to start building up her case against Augusta as the destined victim along with Byron, in the event that she might have to name incest as her charge. In March she drew up another statement: her husband had *always* [underlining hers] spoken of his sister as his mistress; when he began his affair with Susan Boyce he appeared to regard it more as an injury to Augusta than to his wife.

Byron received a visit from Lord Holland as intermediary, early in March; he expressed the hope that Byron would lend his support to a friendly settlement. Byron replied that he was open to the most amicable of all arrangements—continuing his marriage with his wife; to that end he was prepared to make any sacrifice. But he would sign no separation agreement. He wrote again to Annabella: she was destroying the happiness of both of them; if he were not sure of his love for her or her love for him, he would never have endured what he had already suffered these weeks. He had rejected all proposals for a separation as he would spurn an adder, and for the same reasons. He considered the tone of her family's suggestions the greatest insult of his life. He pressed her again to see him and vowed he would never give up his fight to have them together again.

But later that same day, March 4, he wrote her once more: if indeed all hope was over and he was to encounter from her only accusations and intransigence, he could promise no more than to act according to circumstances. It was terrible to have learned it was she who had drawn up the hard, mercenary, bargaining proposals for separation. That she could so stifle and annihilate all feeling and love was far bitterer to him than any future consequences.

Annabella had already written her mother that the only recourse now was war to the finish. The best thing to do, she felt, was to present the strongest possible statement in court, then delay as long as possible in order to tire Byron out, and use his conduct during the prolonged suit against him should he commit adultery, as she apparently was sure he would.

The Hon. Mrs. George Villiers, sister of the Earl of Morley, was an old and close friend of Augusta's. During July of the previous year Annabella had begun to cultivate her acquaintance. In the years to follow, Mrs. Villiers was to be Annabella's confidante in her long, ruthless torturing of Augusta—what better choice for that role than an old friend of the enemy? Now Mrs. Villiers addressed Annabella, beginning with a civilized apology for interfering in the affairs of others. She would have refrained even now were it not that for the last few days she had been hearing the greatest calumnies against her close friend, Augusta, and she was certain that Lady Byron's affection for Mrs. Leigh had remained unaltered and that she would be anxious to see that the world did her sister-in-law justice. Mrs. Villiers had denied the reports vehemently, but the gossips had retorted that their information was proved by Lady Byron's refusal to announce a reason for her proceedings for a separation. This argument must be contradicted, and only Lady Byron was in a position to speak out against it with finality. It would be only fair that she circulate among her friends her confidence in Augusta and her affection for her—which Mrs. Villiers knew to be reciprocal.

To this well-meant plea, Annabella, anxious to maintain friendship with Mrs. Villiers—probably seeing the usefulness of having her as an eventual partisan—with as much warmth as her ingrained arrogance permitted, replied that she deplored the rumors, especially those that cast a shadow on Augusta. She could freely state that none of these reports was sanctioned by her family, and therefore she could not feel in any way that they were her responsibility. While Augusta had been living under the same roof with her, everyone had heard Annabella's gratitude for her kindness. However, present conditions made it impossible to publish the actual grounds for the separation; she had been advised to disclose nothing further.

In view of her own convictions and plans, her slights upon Augusta, the statement she had already drawn up on the incest—which she was prepared to use in evidence if necessary—her letter to Mrs. Villiers is a choice piece of hypocrisy. How could she, always posturing before herself for her unblemished virtue, have allowed herself the dishonesty? Possibly she consoled herself with the thought that if and when she came forward with the charge of incest, the world, whose good opinion was the cardinal consideration with her, was bound to admire her only the more for having refrained from a disclosure until the latest possible hour.

Lady Caroline, whose overtures to Byron had met only silence, now began working behind the scenes to inflame his wife further against him. She wrote her a series of high-pitched and voluminous letters. In the first she declared to her husband's cousin that she prayed to God to protect Annabella in her present unhappy crisis, and acknowledged that she had little right to project herself into it—let Annabella put her faith in the Lord, in her own integrity, and in her parents, whom she was fortunate enough to have to help her. Thus Lady Caroline cunningly began in a strain that had all the correct elements: appeals to Annabella's religiosity, vanity, and devotion to her parents. She went on to declare that she could say much, but would not, for her lips must remain tight shut. When she had heard that her cousin had left Byron, moved by pity because of stories that he was desperate, she had written to him as a friend, begging him to try to win his wife back. If either he or Annabella could even momentarily believe that Lady Caroline could be so basely treacherous to all sense of decency as to take Byron's part against Annabella's . . . ! No earthly consideration could move her to have any friendship or any sort of converse with anyone who had a character like his. She had been through enough suffering, which she fully merited, only because of his ruthlessness and her own unpardonably criminal behavior. She thanked God that she had thus suffered as her sufferings might perhaps atone for her susceptibility and sin. (This was calculated to please Annabella who loved nothing so much as the spectacle of a sinner brought low.) She could assure her that not until now did she know what it was to feel abhorrence for a man who deserved that one should feel nothing else for him. How different was the punishment meted out to those who deserved punishment from the undeserved barbarity visited upon a human being (Annabella, of course) not only innocent, but by Byron's own admission of exalted character. Considering that Lady Caroline must have known her cousin's undisguised disapproval of her, she must have been very sure of Annabella's rising to the bait of flattery to continue, as she did, by saying that her cousin must not speak of her with the generosity and humaneness with which she ever had spoken. For the Lord's sake let her have no further dealings with Lady Caroline now. Nevertheless, if it meant her death, she was not willing to allow another minute to go by without assuring Annabella that it was she whom she would support, not Byron, even if the entire population of the world were backing him. Here Lady Caroline offered her most tempting lure: if Byron dared to wrench Ada from her mother, Lady Caroline would tell Annabella a thing which, if it were but used as a threat by his wife would strike him with terror. And now Lady Caroline, having used the various registers of her instrument, pulled out all the stops: let Annabella conceive of what Caro went through when she understood that her husband's cousin, a pure, guileless girl, was to be offered up to Byron's selfishness and cruelty. At the time she did not interfere because he had promised to reform, but she still castigated herself for not racing to Annabella to tell her everything she knew. However, she still loved him in those days, though now she detested and loathed him from the bottom of her heart for the way he had treated his wife. Annabella was without spot or taint, while she herself was iniquitous and without worth; yet she begged to be heard. Lady Caroline was addressing her as a suppliant for the sake of Ada and Annabella's parents. Let her believe in no one. There were reptiles around Annabella who would fawn on her and "bite" her. She would be wise to be frigid with his friends and relatives, for they would prove to be his partisans, not hers. Most of all, let her discredit those who came to her with tales of his being sick and miserable. He was neither one nor the other, only cunning, and crafty in his duplicity. Mrs. Leigh seemed to be taking Annabella's side, which was certainly unnatural. Let Annabella not trust her. Most important: let Byron have the idea that his wife knew and could prove some terrible secret of his, which only extreme urgency would force her to speak. Annabella was not to think her deceitful and conniving for writing this letter, but it was a thing she had to do because of her cousin's goodness and naïveté, which rendered her defenseless. Again Lady Caroline sounded the note of piety: truth and goodness must triumph and God would look after Annabella (who was fairly sure of that herself). But to prevent her child's being seized, she was urged to follow Caro's advice; Byron had a certain secret, which he would never survive having exposed; she herself would rather die, she *thought,* than tell anyone of it. She admitted that she must seem acting shabbily toward a man she had once been equal to dying just to please. But her indignation against him for his treatment of his wife was so great that she would run any risk to save her cousin. Annabella was not to answer her, for if questioned by Lady Melbourne Caro wished to be able to say that she had not heard from Lady Byron. The postscript, in Italian, begged her to burn the letter—something Annabella would never think of doing with any paper that might thereafter serve her self-justification.

The next day Lady Caroline wrote to her again. She stressed the fact that she knew a great deal of which everyone else was ignorant, and once more suggested that Byron would probably snatch Ada from Annabella. Annabella was to trust no one. Augusta, no doubt a sincere friend, was, after all, his sister, and hence might be feigning sympathy only to help Byron. Annabella was to remember that she could ruin Caro with a single word revealing that she had been writing to her as her partisan. The world would say that the discarded mistress and the spouse were joining forces (which is exactly what Lady Caroline was trying to effect). If, however, Caro could be of service by seeing Annabella or Mrs. Clermont, they could meet somewhere in the morning or the evening. In Annabella's conversation with Lord Holland, then acting as mediator, she ought not be too trusting.

(It is hardly conceivable that Annabella would have told Lord Holland about the sodomy, but it is almost certain that Lushington had. Lord Holland might have plied her with well-considered questions to substantiate what he had been told. At any rate, it is obvious from what he later told Hobhouse that, when he left Lady Byron, he was privately convinced that sodomy was a real issue in her wish for a separation.)

Mrs. Villiers' letter may have been responsible, despite Lushington's warning against such a move, for Annabella's meeting Augusta on March 5. After it she was able to inform him that she had once more refused to see her husband, though Augusta had entreated her to do so, or to name the charges to be preferred against him. Augusta had insisted that Dear Sis must be misguided, or else that there was something more involved which Augusta knew nothing about. (There was! But also Augusta may have, in fright, been fishing to discover whether Annabella knew of the incest and intended to use it as a weapon.) She had as well delivered a letter from Byron, which Annabella sarcastically described as written as though by a saint, with much talk of forgiveness and like matters.

Annabella also saw George Byron. Hobhouse writes on March 6 that a letter had at last arrived from her after Byron had sent many messages. She had already protested to George Byron that "nothing no not her father and mother going on their knees to her should bring her back." She reminded Byron of his promise "that should she prove the whole to be her own act and will," he would "consent to a private Agreement." Augusta told Hobhouse that Lady Byron had declared: if Byron was indeed mad, "nothing should prevent her from nursing him." Byron's reaction was to write her a note quoting Goldsmith's elegy on a mad dog, with the climactic last line, *The dog it was that died,* "meaning he was not mad but she—he did not send this note."

Giving up the fight, Hobhouse nonetheless insisted that she must put an end to imputations against Byron. On March 7 he drew up a paper "as preamble to the separation in which Lady B disavows cruelty systematic and unremitted neglect gross & repeated infidelities—incest & ———," all of which he had heard currently as gossip. With Scrope Davies he brought this declaration to Piccadilly Terrace, but "B and D seemed to think those things had better not be put on record and certainly not on the same paper [with the separation agreement]."

Several years later Byron himself more or less certified that the ——— of Hobhouse's diary stood for sodomy. When he wrote to Hobhouse from Italy he said that his wife's forces had tried to stigmatize him with the crime of Jacopo Rusticucci, who was doomed by Dante to that portion of the seventh circle of Inferno allotted to the sodomites.

Robert John Wilmot, a Byron cousin, whose services were enlisted, came in and offered to take Hobhouse's statement to Lady Bryon. To make her declaration freeing her husband of the charges not read like the price of the separation, they agreed that she be asked to write a letter incorporating the points John Cam had made. The "incest & ———" were to be deleted from his document, but Wilmot was to include them *viva voce* during his interview with her.

Annabella promised very little: if the arbitration were immediately arranged and privately, she was willing to state that neither she nor members of her family had been responsible for the rumors damaging to Lord Byron's character. (She seemed to overlook the fact that she had blackened his character to Selina Doyle, Colonel Doyle, Mrs. Clermont, Romilly, Dr. Baillie, Le Mann, and anyone else who would listen to her version of the story. We have already seen how a letter of Selina's had been read out loud at a large gathering.) Hobhouse thought that this promise "was in itself not sufficient—Lady B must not only disavow the rumors having been spread but that the specific charges . . . that is incest & ——— made no part of her charges." He also wryly observed that Byron's acts could have involved "no enormity" or "she would have quitted the house at once." Of course, if the chronology of Colman's account is to be taken literally, the sodomy occurred during her ninth month of pregnancy, when she could hardly have left Piccadilly Terrace; as it is, Ada was but a month old when her mother undertook the journey to Kirkby. The reasons Colman advances for Byron's suggesting the act would make his chronology in this matter logical enough.

By this time, March 8, all of London society had turned on Byron. Miss Godfrey, weeks before, had written to Tom Moore: "The world are loud against him, and vote him a worthless profligate. . . . He is completely lost in the opinion of the world; and I fear he is the sort of character never to make an effort to recover it. So I look on him as given up to every worthless excess for the rest of his life." Despite all the clamor, on March 8 Byron wrote to Moore with his characteristic self-honesty: "I must set you right in one point . . . The fault was *not,* nor even the misfortune—in my 'choice' [of a wife] (unless in *choosing at all*) for I do not believe . . . that there ever was a better, or even a brighter, a kinder, or a more amiable and agreeable being than Lady B. . . . Where there is blame, it belongs to myself. . . . My circumstances have been and are in a state of great confusion—my health has been a good deal disordered, and my mind ill at ease for a considerable period. Such are the causes (I do not name them as excuses) which have frequently driven me into excess, and disqualified my temper for comfort. Something also may be attributed to the strange and desultory habits which, becoming my own master at an early age, and scrambling about, over and through the world, may have induced. I still, however, think that, if I had a fair chance, by being placed in even a tolerable situation, I might have gone on fairly. But that seems hopeless. . . . It is nothing to bear the *privations* of adversity, or, more properly, ill fortune; but my pride recoils from its *indignities.* However, I have no quarrel with that same pride, which will, I think, buckler me through every thing. If my heart could have been broken, it would have been years ago, and by events more afflicting than these."

Concerning the vituperations spat out against his friend, Moore said, "There were also actively on the alert that large class of persons who seem to hold violence against the vices of others to be the equivalent to virtue in themselves, together with all those natural haters of success who, having long sickened under the splendour of the *poet,* were now enabled, in the guise of champions for innocence, to wreak their spite on the *man.* In every various form of paragraph, pamphlet, and caricature, both his character and person were held up to odium;—hardly a voice was raised, or at least listened to, in his behalf; and though a few faithful friends remained unshaken by his side, the utter hopelessness of stemming the torrent was felt as well by them as by himself, and, after an effort or two to gain a fair hearing, they submitted in silence."

Various poetasters rushed into print to abuse him. *A Poetical Epistle from Delia, addressed to Lord Byron,* by one of them, contains this charming passage:

> Hopeless of peace below, and, shuddering thought!
> Far from that of Heaven, denied, if never sought,
> Thy light a beacon—a reproach thy name—
> Thy memory "damn'd to everlasting fame,"
> Shunn'd by the wise, admired by fools alone—
> The good shall mourn thee—and the Muse disown.

When it was presently learned that Byron planned going abroad, the following amiable verses appeared anonymously:

> From native England, that endured too long
> The ceaseless burden of his impious song;
> His mad career of crimes and follies run,
> And grey in vice, when life was scarce begun;
> He goes, in foreign lands prepared to find
> A life more suited to his guilty mind:
> Where other climes new pleasures may supply
> For that pall'd taste, and that unhallow'd eye;—
> Wisely he seeks some yet untrodden shore,
> For those who know him less may prize him more.

On March 9 Lady Byron told Wilmot that the "incest and ————" were not included in the charges she would feel required to list. Her magnanimity would allow her to concede no more than that. She refused to sign a statement of disavowal of the other charges. All she was willing to do was deny her family's part in the spread of the rumors. (Her family and herself having launched the rumors, they could sit back and let an anonymous world take the blame for them.) And even that she would not grant if Byron did not at once agree to a private separation.

Lady Judith was as hysterical as ever. She wrote her daughter that she was positive her suspicions of Augusta as being actually Byron's partisan were correct. Augusta would profit on Annabella's loss. She was as wicked as her brother. Annabella's maid, Mrs. Fletcher, was also a candidate for mistrust: she might admit people during the night to do some mischief to little Ada.

Augusta was near collapse. She had not seen her children at Six Mile Bottom for four months, the gossip about the incest was wearing her down, and her newest pregnancy was far advanced. (Concerning this new child, no one thus far has theorized, but it seems to me that it is at least possible, considering the history already outlined and Colonel Leigh's tendency to be where Augusta was not, that Byron was also the father of this baby. There is, of course, no way of knowing.) On March 13 Hobhouse found her in tears and "great distress." She felt she owed it to Colonel Leigh, who had "most handsomely *discredited* in every way" the rumors about her, to leave her brother's house. Particularly, one surmises, because she was pregnant again. On March 16 she left Piccadilly Terrace at last for her apartment at St. James's, where she was Lady-in-Waiting to the Queen.

It was as late as this that Byron discovered the perfidy of Romilly, whom he had retained years earlier to act as his attorney when needed. Byron innocently sent Hobhouse to Romilly to ask him to be the only and final arbitrator in the suit; it only then came to light that Romilly had from the beginning been acting for Annabella. He had, in fact, introduced Lushington to the family. Romilly naturally could not act now as final arbitrator; to cover up his nefarious behavior—his excuse being that he had forgotten that he had accepted Byron's retainer—he withdrew from the case—late enough. Byron now had two lawyers to loathe for the rest of his life. (It is interesting that his sentiments have been shared by many of the leading writers of the world from time immemorial.)

13.

THE DAY AFTER AUGUSTA'S DEPARTURE BYRON AGREED TO THE PROPOSED terms of separation. His spirits immediately began to improve, and he was soon speaking with enthusiasm of going abroad.

On March 20, he sent Lady Byron some verses he had written to her, the first and possibly the last, he told her, of which she had been the subject.

Fare thee well! and if for ever,
   Still for ever, fare *thee well:*
Even though unforgiving, never
   'Gainst thee shall my heart rebel . . .
Yet, oh yet, thyself deceive not—
   Love may sink by slow decay,
But by sudden wrench, believe not
   Hearts can thus be torn away; . . .
And when thou would'st solace gather—
   When our child's first accents flow—
Wilt thou teach her to say "Father!"
   Though his care she must forgo? . . .
All my hopes—where'er thou goest—
   Wither—yet with *thee* they go . . .
Seared in heart—and lone—and blighted—
   More than this I scarce can die.

How much of this was Byron and how much self-delusion it is impossible to guess. At any rate, Annabella found the lines quite tender and complacently remarked that he was talking in that strain of her to everyone. She, of course, was far from reciprocating.

Her observation is borne out by a letter he wrote Samuel Rogers on March 25, in which he asked whether Rogers had ever heard him speak of his wife with disrespect, even when discussing his "family disquietudes." Was it not true that he had conceded that it was his wife who always had the right of the matter in a dispute? Indeed, Byron's idea of Annabella was so far wrong that he could not entertain the notion that she could be, as she was, the chief moving force in the separation. It was sheer nonsense that he imagined her parents could have forced her to do anything against her own inclination; she had always wound them around her little finger. Quite without foundation he continued to believe, too, that the main source of his troubles was Mrs. Clermont.

On March 27 Annabella granted an interview to Lady Caroline, whose promised revelations might turn out to be useful some day. She kept "Minutes" of the meeting.

She declined to burn or return Caro's letters, but promised to seal them up with instructions that upon her death they be returned to the sender. (It did no harm to the portrait of the martyred woman to add the touch of her anticipated immediate demise. As a matter of fact, Lady Caroline predeceased her by decades.) Caro apparently did not insist. Rather, she asked a question which reminds one of the question put in *Ruddigore* by Dick to Sir Despard; having completely betrayed his foster-brother, Ruthven, and fairly ruined his life by conveying certain information to Despard, Dick says to Despard:

"Now the question I was going to ask your honour is—Ought I to tell your honour this?" Caro professed being in a similar quandary; ought she reveal the secrets she had promised Byron never to reveal? He had sworn he would never repeat those crimes, and therefore she perhaps ought to keep her lips sealed. Despard's reply to Dick is more uncertain than Annabella's—but, of course, he had already been given the information damaging to Ruthven; he says to Dick: "I don't know. It's a delicate point. I think you ought. Mind, I'm not sure, but I think so." Annabella, however, had no compunctions about the oath Caro had taken: she guaranteed her that she was released from her vow by his having broken his own—Annabella had *not* been given yet the information damaging to Byron. She said Caro might now redeem herself and all the terrible things she had done herself by providing Annabella with her information. If it would assist, she added, in saving Ada, in her opinion Lady Caroline would have nothing to repent in so unselfish an act either on earth or in Heaven. (Annabella was as knowledgeable of how things would be ordered in the hereafter as of how they ought to be on earth.) Lady Caroline therefore plunged into the subject of Byron's incest with Augusta, which he had idiotically confided to her, and stated without qualification that Medora was his child. He had told Caro all about it before the child had left her mother's womb. He had even shown her certain letters of Augusta which left no room for doubt.

From the incest Lady Caroline proceeded to speak of graver crimes. He had hinted from time to time, but eventually had admitted that from boyhood on he had indulged in unnatural sex acts, that he had corrupted his page Rushton, that he had indeed loved the boy so much that he had more or less forced Lady Caroline to name one of her pages Rushton too. He mentioned also three of his schoolmates at Harrow whom he had corrupted in the same way. In Turkey he had practiced homosexuality without restraint, though she thought he had discontinued that sort of experience since returning to England. About the homosexuality, Annabella significantly made a note that what Caro had to say on this head only confirmed her own opinions.

On her return home Caro wrote her cousin another long letter, filled again with religious overtones and flattery. Hypocrisy may triumph for a brief time, she said, but the Lord is a just God and no mask can long hide a deformity. She assured Annabella that she had the support of William Lamb (who certainly had no cause to be Byron's partisan). She rejoiced in having Annabella as a cousin, and entreated her never to forget that in Byron and Augusta she had as foes two extraordinary hypocrites, the most depraved creatures ever allowed to crawl upon the earth. Sooner or later they would be punished for their treatment of Annabella, though she knew her cousin not to be vengeful enough to wish that, for she was too benevolent and magnanimous—but *she* hoped to see vengeance visited upon both of them. Annabella was free to make whatever use she could of what Lady Caroline had told her. Even if her generosity in wishing to spare Byron kept her silent, she ought to let her innumerable and admirable friends become acquainted with the facts. She promised to follow all of Annabella's advice to her, and trusted that her cousin would heed hers.

The woman scorned at last was having her own revenge.

Utterly convinced that his chief enemy was Mrs. Clermont, on March 29 Byron composed in a spirit of vilification the lines published as "A Sketch":

> Born in the garret, in the kitchen bred,
> Promoted thence to comb her mistress' head . . .

In lines that would have done credit to Alexander Pope, he traced her elevation from "the toilet to the table," where she "dines from off the plate she lately washed." He described her as a talebearer, liar, and "general spy," all of which functions saw her raised to the position of governess to the only child:

> She taught the child to read, and taught so well,
> That she herself, by teaching, learned to spell.

Her charge by some miracle was saved from her governess's pernicious influence:

> Serenely purest of the things that live,
> But wanting one sweet weakness—to forgive;

Unfamiliar with human faults, she thinks everyone as good as herself. The little girl grown, the governess's duties over, yet the latter "rules the circle which she served before." After describing her machinations in the most violent terms, he predicted the direst consequences from her villainy, and heaped curses upon her:

> Oh may thy grave be sleepless as the bed,
> The widowed couch of fire, that thou hast spread! . . .

Exhibiting, though the poem does, Byron's satirical talents at their most powerful, it was, as Moore said of it, "generally, and, it must be owned, justly condemned, as a sort of literary assault on an obscure female, whose situation ought to have placed her as much *beneath* his satire as the undignified mode of his attack certainly raised her *above* it."

Byron's vehemence in this instance may have been attributable to an occurrence of the day before. He had procured letters from Lord Holland, Kinnaird, and Rogers stating that he had never spoken ill of his wife; these he sent to her, and on March 28, the day after her interview with Lady Caroline, she sent them back via Augusta without a word. Hobhouse, who was present, said that her silence "made B. furious." He was ready to write her a vitriolic note, but was prevented by John Cam. "A Sketch" was, in all likelihood, the method he chose for venting his indignation.

At any rate, he at once asked Murray to print fifty copies of the poem for *"private distribution"* and it was printed with changes and additions within a few days. But Murray showed the lines to various people, including Lady Caroline, who wrote him that she would rather starve or see her child dead than speak or think of Byron as other than a miserable hypocrite and wretched craven, a man utterly heartless.

14.

IT WAS PROBABLY DURING THIS SAME HECTIC MONTH OF MARCH 1816 that, while his thoughts were already on European travel, Byron had thrust upon him the attentions of a woman who was to play a fateful part in his history for the next years.

The affair began again with a letter. It is hard to believe that the writer had not heard of the separation proceedings, and was thereby moved to hope to procure the attention of so notorious a philanderer as Byron:

> An utter stranger takes the liberty of addressing you. It is earnestly requested that for one moment you pardon the intrusion, and, laying aside every circumstance of who and what you are, listen with a friendly ear. A moment of passion or an impulse of pride often destroys our own happiness and that of others. If in this case your refusal shall not affect yourself, yet you are not aware how much it may injure another. It is not charity I demand, for of that I stand in no need: I imply by that . . . that if I seem impertinent you should pardon it for a while, and that you should wait patiently till I am emboldened by you to disclose myself.
>
> I tremble with fear at the fate of this letter. . . . There are cases where virtue may stoop to assume the garb of folly; it is for the piercing eye of genius to discover her disguise. . . . Mine is a delicate case; my feet are on the edge of a precipice. . . . It may seem a strange assertion, but . . . I place my happiness in your hands. I wish to give you a suspicion without at first disclosing myself; because it would be a cruel addition to all I otherwise

endure to become the object of your contempt and the ridicule of others.
. . . If you feel tempted to read no more, . . . check your hand: my folly
may be great, but the Creator ought not to destroy his creature. . . . If a
woman, whose reputation has yet remained unstained, if without either
guardian or husband to control she should throw herself upon your mercy,
if with a beating heart she should confess the love she has borne you many
years, if she should secure to you secresy and safety, if she should return
your kindness with fond affection and unbounded devotion, could you betray
her, or would you be as silent as the grave? . . . Either you will or you will
not. Do not decide hastily, and yet I must entreat your answer without
delay. . . . Address me, as E. Trefusis, 21, Noley Place, Mary le Bonne.

The author of this elaborate letter was revising her self-portrait to
resemble one of Byron's heroines, with whom she was well acquainted; the
facts behind these melodramatic pretensions were quite different from her
representations. She could not, for instance, have loved Byron for "many
years," since she was not quite eighteen. What she had to "endure" was not
much: chiefly the frustration of watching at close quarters the romantic
escapade of her stepsister, and the annoyance of having been prosaically
named after her mother, Mary Jane—and even that grave burden she had
already shaken off, after giving due consideration to the attractions of "Con-
stantia," by adopting instead the Christian name of "Claire." Of course, she
was not E. Trefusis, but Mary Jane—or rather, as she preferred, Claire—
Clairmont.

The daughter of a defunct Swiss merchant, she had led anything but a
dull life. Her unlovable mother, whom she alone seems to have cared for,
had contracted a second marriage with a man who, in an earlier decade, had
seemed to his contemporaries the profoundest philosopher in Britain, William
Godwin. Godwin, an inveterate enemy of marriage as an irrational institu-
tion destructive of the best in the individual, had also been married before,
to Mary Wollstonecraft, the famous, tragic and much-maligned author of
the *Vindication of the Rights of Women.* Shortly after bearing their daughter Mary, this remarkable woman had died. When the widowed Mrs. Clairmont became the second Mrs. Godwin, she brought with her a son and
daughter. Mary Jane was a few months younger than her stepsister Mary,
of whom she became a close friend and confidante. Many celebrities visited
the Godwin house, and the talk was nothing if not elevated—though probably thoroughly antiromantic. Godwin's *Political Justice,* which had pro-
pounded a millennium which would see mankind living in perfection and
forever, all evils and diseases having by that time been vanquished through
the power of man's reason, held the emotions to be the chief obstacles to
man's felicity. Man would by degress learn to kill his affective processes

and live by reason alone. Never has logic been carried to such insane lengths as in that book.

However Claire may have reacted to the chilliness of those high discourses at home, there was not only Byron's *The Corsair* to read and reread, but the wonderful not-at-all chilly love affair of her stepsister Mary to observe, aid, and abet. Shelley, still a boy, though married, had begun by being Godwin's disciple, and after seeing her once had fallen madly in love with Godwin's daughter, Mary Wollstonecraft Godwin, a pale, self-contained, and brilliant girl—Claire's ideal of what a heroine should look like. (She herself was dark and not good looking.) Claire had from the first been in the confidence of this inflammable pair, had made possible their clandestine meetings, had acted as Shelley's messenger to his wife, and when he and Mary finally eloped to the continent had gone off with them. All these exciting things had happened to her between her sixteenth and eighteenth years.

It is likely that when Claire set out to bag a poet for herself—and an infinitely more famous and notorious one, celebrated as well for his great personal beauty—she disdained putting to advantage the fact that she was the stepdaughter of Godwin. Had Byron known her identity he might have been interested at once. He had, in fact, already been most generous to Godwin, who was one of the most shameless sponges in history—though he, inveterate foe of matrimony, had castigated Shelley for running off with Mary without a wedding, that did not prevent his forever whining poverty to the young poet and bleeding him of large sums for the rest of Shelley's life. Five days after Annabella had left Piccadilly Terrace, Byron, sunk in debt and personal troubles, hearing through Rogers that Godwin was in need, had sent him anonymously £600.

But E. Trefusis was an unknown quantity to him and he did not reply to her first letter. He soon received a second:

> Lord Byron is requested to state whether seven o'clock this Evening will be convenient to him to receive a lady to communicate with him on business of peculiar importance. She desires to be admitted alone and with the utmost privacy. If the hour she has mentioned is correct, at that hour she will come; if not, will his lordship have the goodness to make his own appointment, which shall be readily attended to though it is hoped the interview may not be postponed after this Evening? G.C.B.

Whether Byron was supposed to presume that this was the same Trefusis or another correspondent is a matter of conjecture. Anyhow, this note from G. C. B. did provoke an answer from him:

> Lᵈ. B. is not aware of any "importance" which can be attached by any person to an interview with him, and more particularly by one with whom it

does not appear that he has the honour of being acquainted. He will however be at home at the hour mentioned.

These were dreadful days for Byron, and if he did agree to see her, it
may have been because on an impulse he welcomed some diversion from the
crushing anxieties of March 1816. When she came, he found that she was
still very young, far from beautiful, but with great vivacity of spirit and an
extraordinarily lovely voice.

To engage his interest she pretended to be considering the careers of
playwright and actress, and brought him a story of hers to read. He gave her
letters to Drury Lane, which she never used. But she too had ill timed her
attempt to fascinate him. The world was crumbling beneath his feet, and
she, moreover, was too much of the intellectual girl, a type he detested.

Her third letter said that she had called on him twice but his servants
had told her he was out of town. She would make her letter brief since he
was "overwhelmed with affairs and cares." (Byron, as was his wont, may
have confided in her his current domestic difficulties.) She asked him to
procure from his friends in the theatre the information which might help
her start a career there. "I half suspect that you believe I am an impostor,
and that you shun me. Did my tale appear extravagant to you?" Let the
world upbraid her, she knew her actions not the "result of momentary
temptation, the impulse of passion . . . With regard to the romance of my
story it is not so improbable. How many realities and characters do I not
recollect of wonderful and strange. The German Weishaupt, the story of
Eleanor Maria Schoning in Coleridge's Friend—can you read these and not
think of mine as an every-day adventure? You think it impertinent that I
intrude on you. Remember that I have confided to you the most important
secrets." She must therefore know his sentiments toward her. Would he
answer her? This time she signed herself Clara Clairmont.

Next she sent him an extract from Shelley's *Queen Mab,* which she
said bore "marks of genius," but was "unpoetical and unpolished" in style
and therefore not admirable. *Alastor* was "a great improvement." She hoped
that if Byron did not like Shelley's work he would say so; "he may improve
by your remarks." Shelley was now twenty-three, and she was interested in
everything he was doing. Then she reverted to her own concerns. She had
written half a novel, and was wavering between writing and the theatre as
a career. Shelley thought well of her literary talents, "but his affection might
blind him." She could count on Byron's honesty—though she was afraid
that since he rather disliked her, he might be prejudiced against what she
had done. She intended to live as a recluse. Then she struck the true Byronic
vein: "I do not desire happiness, for I remember in moments of the most
exquisite delight how much they have failed from my expectations." She

transcribed for him a sonnet of Dante's, and commented: "I wonder how Dante, with such a peculiarly unpleasant countenance, could have thought of such a pleasant way of passing life. Do you remember his inscription over the gate of Hell—'Lasciate ogni speranza voi ch'entrate.' I think it the most admirable description of marriage." (This proved her an enlightened God-winian, and also sympathetic to his current difficulties.) She could never resist speaking ill of matrimony.

Byron did not hasten to reply. Another letter came from her, and another. The one after that said: "I do not expect you to love me; I am not worthy of your love. I feel you are superior, yet much to my surprize, more to my happiness, you betrayed passions I had believed no longer alive in your bosom." He might think her imprudent, vicious, depraved, but time would show that she was gentle and affectionate in her love. His future should be hers. She suggested that on Thursday evening they go out of town by the same stage or mail for some ten or twelve miles. "There we shall be free and unknown; we can return early the following morning." Could she see him for two minutes to settle where they would go? No matter what he decided she would never forget his gentleness and the "wild originality" of his face. Once he had been seen he could never be forgotten.

Leading again, by no choice of his, a celibate life, Byron was torn by conflicting impulses. He was bored and embittered by his present life; most of the London society which had lionized him had dropped him; he wanted nothing more to do with Susan Boyce; he was therefore mildly tempted by Claire's offering of herself. But not much. She was no beauty, though a girl of spirit, but her voice was enchanting; she was, however, demonstrating that she had an intellect, was bent on displaying it, and that he could never abide in a woman. Besides, rake though he was, he was always shocked by such boldly stated unconventionalities as her Godwinian disdain of marriage —that was well enough for a man to entertain, but not a woman. He there-fore disapproved of her plan for going outside the town for consummating their affair—he was even too lazy to wish to go; on the other hand, he saw no reason why Piccadilly Terrace should not do as well as any other place.

Claire replied that she would join him on Saturday at seven thirty of the evening. She was against making love in his house—there were the serv-ants, the possibility of unexpected visitors or letters at the wrong moment. Any fear of interruption would destroy her happiness. Love requires a sense of security. He had mentioned a house where they could be safe, and she would agree to any site but his home. He was about to leave for the con-tinent on Monday, he had said, and she would be—Gods knows where. He must not delay their meeting beyond Saturday; she could not endure the suspense. He had called her "a little fiend." She had asked Shelley if he thought she had a gentle disposition, and his exact words were: "My sweet

Child, there are two Claires—one of them I should call irritable if it were not for the nervous disorder, the effects of which you still retain: the nervous Claire is reserved and melancholy and more sarcastic than violent; the good Claire is gentle yet cheerful; and to me the most engaging of human creatures; one thing I will say for you that you are easily managed by the person you love as the reed by the wind; it is your weak side." Very often now she wished there were a God, that she might "teize" Him with prayers for Byron's happiness. (She apparently did not guess that atheism, though *de rigueur* at the Godwin circle, did not go down well with Byron.) She asked him to answer her without any little sarcasms. Her postscript asked him to bring her letters so she might burn them. We may be grateful that, again, he did not oblige.

Meet they did and by mid-April she was pregnant with the child who was to be called Allegra.

For a while Byron was kept in ignorance of the fact that he had sired another baby. Claire knew he was leaving England in a matter of days, and she intended to follow him. Perhaps she hoped that when he did learn he was to be a father again, it would arouse in him love for her. At any rate, she contrived that Shelley and Mary, who were also about to leave the country, should go to Switzerland, where Byron was sure to be. She thus became the instrument of effecting between the two poets a meeting that was to ripen into an important friendship between the two men. But all that, as they say, is another story.

Claire's hopes were never to be realized: at no time did Byron ever love her; eventually he would come to detest her as much as he did Lady Caroline. By September of 1816 he was already telling Augusta from Geneva: "As to all these 'mistresses,' Lord help me—I have had but one. Now don't scold; but what could I do?—a foolish girl, in spite of all I could say or do, would come after me, or rather went before—for I found her here —and I have had all the plague possible to persuade her to go back again; but at last she went. Now, dearest, I do most truly tell thee, that I could not help this, that I did all I could to prevent it, and have at last put an end to it. [So he thought!] I was not in love, nor have any love left for any; but I could not exactly play the Stoic with a woman, who had scrambled eight hundred miles to unphilosophise me."

15.

WHILE CLAIRE WAS BESIEGING BYRON IN LONDON AND HE WAS PREPAR-ing to leave England, he was forced to suffer public humiliation at a party at Lady Jersey's on April 8, when the distinguished Benjamin Constant was present. Byron had brought Augusta with him. Most of the ladies of fashion who only a few years earlier had begged for his notice, as well as most of the men, snubbed him. Lady Jersey tried to atone for her guests and made a great point of being particularly gracious and attentive to him.

Annabella presently sent a gleeful account to her mother: it was now being said that the good were being singled out from the wicked according to whether or not they turned their backs on Byron. Never before had there been an issue which exposed the morals of an individual so openly as how he behaved toward Byron. She didn't know anybody except "the Piccadilly crew of blackguards" who were against her.

Hobhouse, of course, was one of that crew. He was staying as much as he could with Byron until it should be time for his old friend to leave on April 23, just early enough in the morning to escape Lady Devonshire's bailiffs, who seized upon everything they found. John Cam wished to accompany his old friend across the Channel, but was refused a passport because his book on Napoleon had been too favorable to Buonaparte.

With him Byron was taking the twenty-one-year-old Dr. Polidori as a traveling companion—an unfortunate choice, as it turned out. (Polidori's sister later became the mother of those gifted Rossettis, Charles Dante Gabriel, Christina, and William Michael.) At Dover, as Lushington soon informed Lady Byron, the eagerness to catch a personal glimpse of Byron was contagious. Many women of rank disguised themselves as servants so they could get a close look at him while he was staying two days at the inn. Walking to embark on the boat, he had to march through a lane of onlookers. On April 25 his party sailed for Ostend. Byron was a little over twenty-eight.

Hobhouse ran to the edge of the pier to wave farewell. "The dear fellow pulled off his cap & wav'd it to me—I gazed until I could not distinguish him any longer."

One of his final acts before leaving had been to write to Annabella:

"More last words—not many—and such as you will attend to; answer I do not expect, nor does it import; but you will at least hear me.—I have just parted from Augusta, almost the last being you have left me to part with.

"Wherever I go,—and I am going far,—you and I can never meet in this world, nor in the next." He asked her, if anything should happen to him, to be kind to Augusta; if Augusta were dead, then to her children. (Her kindness to Augusta and to the fruit of his love for Augusta, Medora, was to be demonic in intensity.) "Be kind to her, for never has she acted or spoken towards you but as a friend. And recollect that, though it may be an advantage to you to lose a husband, it is sorrow to her to have the waters now, or the earth hereafter, between her and her brother. It may occur to your memory that you formerly promised this much. I repeat it—for deep resentments have but *half* recollections. Do not deem this promise cancell'd . . ."

It was not the sort of farewell letter to soften Annabella's thoughts. Particularly not, when his parting thoughts were of his beloved Augusta. Perhaps it was just as well for Byron that he was never to become enlightened that his sister had been won over to treachery against him.

As he quitted England, he left behind him a trail of wreckage and a meteoric reputation as a poet—twisted, frustrated, or vengeful lives among his former mistresses, and an army of ill-wishers. A series of popular prints, presumably by I. R. Cruikshank, indicate a general eagerness to fan public resentment against him among those who had no business to be concerned with his acts; they, moreover, totally misrepresent the facts by depicting Lady Byron as abandoned by her husband for the purpose of running off with an actress from Drury Lane, Mrs. Mardyn. In one of them, "Fashionables of 1816 Taking the Air in Hyde Park," Byron, shown with his curls, is the center of a promenade scene with a woman on each arm, one of whom is probably Mrs. Mardyn; they meet a third woman, looking pregnant, who stares angrily at Byron. Another, "Lobby Loungers," presents Byron and other men of fashion ogling actresses, who stand in a group like so many prostitutes on display; he is gazing at Mrs. Mardyn. A third, "The Separation, a Sketch from the Private Life of Lord *Iron* Who Panegyrized His Wife, But Satirized Her Confidante," is set in an anteroom of Piccadilly Terrace, where Byron is taking leave of his wife; he has his arm around Mrs. Mardyn's waist and is walking with her toward the staircase; looking over his shoulder at Lady Byron, who is holding her infant daughter, he dismisses her, while Mrs. Mardyn looks triumphant. The misinformation is made more explicit in G. Cruikshank's "Fare-thee-well" of April 1816; Byron is in a boat with three Drury Lane actresses, the pretty one standing by his side in his embrace is labeled "Beauteous Mrs. Mardyn"; he is waving farewell to Lady Byron, standing on the cliffs of Dover with her child in her arms. It is small wonder that Mrs. Mardyn felt obliged to write a letter to the *Morning Chronicle* protesting against the persecutions from which she had been suffering because she was publicly associated with the Byron scandal.

He left behind him, too, a host of parasites who had taken advantage of his great generosity as well as a few friends, and, in the single person of John Cam Hobhouse, one faithful to death and beyond.

Byron had an intuition that he would be absent long. He did not err. But he did not imagine that he would never return alive.

"The Separation, a Sketch from the private life of *Lord IRON* who panegyrized his Wife, and Satirized her Confidante!!" by G. Cruikshank. (Courtesy of the British Museum.) Byron, taking leave of his wife and child, with an arm around Mrs. Mardyn, in a room in Piccadilly Terrace.

The following abbreviations have been used in the reference notes:

Air.   Mabell, Countess of Airlie, *In Whig Society 1775–1818.*

Berg Col.   John Cam Hobhouse, MSS of Diary et al. in the Berg Collection, New York Public Library.

Col.   [George Colman, the Younger], *Don Leon.*

Dis.   Benjamin Disraeli, Earl of Beaconsfield, *Works.*

DLM   Doris Langley Moore, *The Late Lord Byron.*

Galt   John Galt, *The Life of Byron.*

Glen.   Lady Caroline Lamb, *Glenarvon.*

Gron.   Captain R. H. Gronow, *Reminiscences.*

Jenkins   Elizabeth Jenkins, *Lady Caroline Lamb.*

LBC   George Gordon, Lord Byron, *Correspondence.* Edited by J. Murray.

LBW   Malcolm Elwin, *Lord Byron's Wife.*

LJ   George Gordon, Lord Byron, *Works, Letters and Journals.* Edited by R. E. Prothero.

Lovel.   Ralph Gordon Noel, Earl of Lovelace, *Astarte.*

Ma*B.*   Ethel C. Mayne, *Byron.*

Md*B.*   Leslie Marchand, *Byron.*

Med.   Thomas Medwin, *Journal of the Conversations of Lord Byron.*

Moore   Thomas Moore, *The Life, Letters and Journals of Lord Byron.*

Or.   Iris Origo, *The Last Attachment.*

Poetry   George Gordon, Lord Byron, *Works, Poetry.* Edited by H. E. Coleridge.

Proth.   R. E. Prothero, "Childhood and School Days of Byron."

Rogers   Rev. Alexander Dyce, ed. *Recollections of the Table-Talk of Samuel Rogers.*

SP   Peter Quennell, *Byron: A Self-Portrait.*

TLB   George Paston and Peter Quennell, *To Lord Byron.*

ONE

PAGE	LINE	
13	9	*LBC* I, 261.
13	25	Lovel., 14.
14	3	Gron., 209.
14	15	Lovel., 15.
14	24	Roger Ingpen, *Shelley in England*, 474–75.
14	27	*LBW*, 141–42.
15	6	*LJ* II, 115.
15	22	Lady Sydney Morgan, *Lady Morgan's Memoirs*, II, 200–20.
15	24	MaB, 151.
15	39	*LJ* II, 451.
16	4	Berg Col. n.d.
16	11	Rogers, 234–45.
16	18	Vere Foster, *The Two Duchesses*, 362, 364.
16	24	Ibid., 375–76.
16	40	*LJ* II, 116–17.
17	22	Md*B* I, 5.
18	4	*Gentleman's Magazine*, May 1765, 227–29.
18	24	*Town and Country Magazine*, December 1773, 625.
18	27	Md*B* I, 11.
18	39	*Town and Country Magazine*, December 1773, 626–27.
19	12	John Cordy Jeaffreson, *The Real Lord Byron*, 20.
19	36	Moore, 3 n.
20	6	Md*B* I, 16–18.
20	30	Proth., 67.
21	1	*LJ* I, 19.
21	11	Ibid. 11 fn.
21	16	Md*B* I, 26.
21	29	André Maurois, *Byron*, 32–33.
21	33	Md*B* I, 30–31.
21	38	*LJ* I, ix.
21	42	Proth., 71
22	4	Moore, 6.
22	18	*LJ* I, 11 fn.
24	1	Md*B* I, 57, quoting Hobhouse MS.
24	13	*LJ* I, 10.
24	21	*LJ* V, 450.
25	6	*LJ* II, 374–78.
26	6	*LJ* V, 449–50.
27	19	Dis. I, 30–41.
27	38	*LJ* V, 455.
29	34	Moore, 24–25.
30	1	R. C. Dallas, *Recollections of The Life of Lord Byron*, 41–42.
30	13	*LJ* VI, 82.
30	24	Quoted by Md*B* III, 1257.
30	29	DLM, 210.
30	41	*Poetry* I, 5.
31	9	Ibid., 18.
32	25	Col., 11, 349–62.
33	11	Quoted by DLM, 291.
34	12	Quoted by Md*B* I, 80.
34	22	*LJ* I, 23.
35	9	Ibid., 43, 44.
35	28	*LJ* II, 389.
35	31	Quoted by Or., 55.
35	35	*LJ* V, 425.
37	17	Thomas Moore, *Poetical Works*, ed. W. M. Rossetti, 152.
38	5	Thomas Moore, *Prose and Verse*, ed. R. H. Shepherd, 431.
38	16	Moore, 28.
39	2	*Poetry* IV, 34–35.
39	18	Med., 46.
39	25	Moore, 272.
39	35	Md*B* I, 74.
40	20	*LJ* I, 22.
40	31	*LJ* I, 30–31.
40	36	Ibid., 46.
40	41	Moore, 13.
41	4	Ibid., 34.
41	42	on November 30, 1807. See Moore, 46–47.
42	4	*LJ* V, 427.
42	14	Moore, 28–29.
42	32	*LJ* V, 445–46.
42	37	Ibid., 169.
43	38	Col., II, 197–98; 386 et seq.
44	4	*LJ* I, 132.
44	37	Ibid., 133–35.
45	9	*Poetry* I, 66–67.
45	15	Ibid., 232–33.
45	22	Ibid., 240.
45	31	Md*B* I, 313.
46	8	*Poetry* III, 435–36.
46	18	*SP* I, 277.
46	20	Ibid., 285.
46	21	*LJ* V, 154.
46	26	Ibid., 199.
46	31	Marguerite, Countess of Blessington, *Idler in Italy*, April 16, 1823.
47	1	Hobhouse MS quoted by Md*B* I, 245.
47	18	Md*B* I, 128.

PAGE	LINE	
47	21	*LJ* II, 52.
47	23	Ibid., 101–02.
47	36	*Poetry* III, 33–34.
48	13	R. Glynn Grylls, *Claire Clairmont*, 67–68.
48	18	Mary Shelley, *Letters*, ed. by F. L. Jones, II, 61.
48	22	Moore, 54 fn.
48	25	*Poetry*, III, 36.
48	28	Ibid., 36.
48	30	Ibid., 36–38.
48	35	Ibid., 41–44.
49	2	Ibid., 46–48.
49	14	*LJ* I, 85.
51	5	*Poetry* I, 36–38.
51	6	Quoted by Md*B* I, 114.
51	8	Sir Harold Nicolson, *The Last Journey*, 300.
51	24	*Poetry* I, 63–66.
51	26	Ibid., 248.
51	40	*LJ* I, 126.
52	3	*SP* I, 36.
52	4	*LJ* I, 127.
52	24	Rogers, 231–32.
52	33	*LJ* I, 152.
52	42	Ibid., 170–73.
53	6	Quoted by Md*B* I, 147.
53	14	*SP* I, 40.
53	34	*LJ* I, 171.
54	26	Ibid., 344–49.
54	27	Ibid., 183.
54	30	Md*B* I, 148.
54	37	Ibid., 150.
55	3	*LJ* V, 269–70.
55	35	*Poetry* I, 316.
55	38	Ibid., 314.
56	2	*Ibid.*, 316–17.
56	8	Ibid., 309.
56	14	Ibid., 319.
56	22	Ibid., 377.
56	25	Ibid., 381.
57	3	Moore, 70.
57	7	Thomas Moore, *Prose and Verse*, 418–19.
57	12	*SP* I, 40–41.
57	14	*LJ* I, 302.
57	20	MS letter quoted by Md*B* I, 401.
57	32	*LJ* I, 193–94.
58	2	*Poetry* I, 277–79.
58	13	Washington Irving, *Works* III, 78.
58	15	MS letter quoted by Md*B* I, 165.
58	33	*LJ* I, 153, 156, 157, 159–60.
59	12	Ibid., 154–55.
59	33	*LJ* I, 156.
59	fn	Med., 87.
60	4	*LJ* I, 157–58.
60	19	Ibid., 153–54.
60	24	*Childe Harold*, Canto I, stanza 7.
60	42	MS letter quoted by Md*B* I, 178.
61	18	*LJ* I, 230.
61	30	*Ibid.*, 233.
62	7	Ibid., 239–40.
62	21	Moore, 93.
62	31	*LJ* I, 242–43.
62	38	Galt, 50.
63	18	Ibid., 60–63.
63	36	Ibid., 65.
63	40	Quoted from Hobhouse's Journal by DLM, 355.
64	15	*TLB*, 11.
64	28	*LBC* I, 78.
64	36	*LJ* I, 249.
65	9	Ibid., 249–50.
65	14	Ibid., 252.
65	21	Ibid., 254–57.
66	30	Colonel Leicester F. Stanhope, *Greece in 1823 and 1824*, 526.
67	17	*LJ* I, 253–55.
67	38	*Ibid.*, 269.
69	14	John Cam Hobhouse, *Travels in Albania*, 390.
69	22	*Poetry* III, 15–17.
69	25	Letter quoted by Md*B* I, 240.
69	35	*LJ* I, 266.
70	10	Galt, 130–32.
70	31	*Poetry* III, 13.
70	38	Ibid., 13–14.
71	5	*LJ* I, 272.
71	18	*Poetry* III, 418.
72	21	"Recollections of Turkey," in *New Monthly Magazine*, Oct. 1826, 311–14.
72	26	Ibid., Feb. 1827, 147–48.
72	36	Stanley Edward Lane-Poole, *The Life of the Right Honourable Stratford Canning* I, 84–86.
72	38	"Recollections of Turkey," Feb. 1827, 147.
73	5	*LJ* I, 286.
73	17	*LJ* II, 399.
73	22	Quoted by Md*B* I, 256.
73	30	Moore, 110.
74	7	*SP* I, 74–77.
74	fn	J. B. Priestley, *The Prince of Pleasure and his Regency*, 183–84.
76	4	*SP* I, 77–82.
76	33	Col., 11. 598 et seq.
77	9	Ibid., 682 et seq.
77	28	G. Wilson Knight, *Lord Byron's Marriage*, 169.
78	42	Col., 11. 733 et seq.
79	15	Ibid., 785 et seq.
80	16	Ibid., 850 et seq.
81	8	Col., 11. 895 et seq.
81	fn	["Holloway"], *The Phoenix of Sodom or the Vere Street Coterie*, 10–14.
82	6	Col., 11. 927 et seq.

T W O

PAGE	LINE	
117	42	Lord Granville Leveson-Gower, *Private Correspondence, 1781–1821* ed. Castalia, Countess Granville, II, 447–48.
119	3	Air., 128–31.
120	2	*LJ* II, 135–39.
120	5	Md*B* I, 361.
120	13	Ma*B* I, 234–37.
120	15	Frances Winwar, *The Romantic Rebels*, 114.
121	14	See *TLB*, 44.
121	22	*TLB*, 45.
122	12	*LBC* I, 71–84.
122	18	Ibid., 104.
122	20	Ibid., 95.
123	3	Air., 149–51.
123	7	*LBC* I, 104.
123	9	*TLB*, 45.
123	22	Air., 151–52.
123	fn	*Glen.* III, 80.
124	1	*LBC* I, 104–5.
124	10	Ibid., 117.
124	12	*TLB*, 45.
124	13	Rogers, 235; Md*B* I, 378.
124	32	*LJ* II, 447.
124	36	*LBC* I, 124.
125	22	*LJ* II, 325.
125	28	*LBC* I, 122.
125	33	Lady Charlotte Bury, *The Diary of a Lady-in-Waiting*, ed. A. T. Steuart, II, 287.
125	39	*LJ* II, 197–99.
126	3	*LBC* I, 148.
126	7	Ibid., 127.
126	9	Ibid., 132.
126	22	Ibid., 137.
126	38	Ibid., 143–47.
127	9	Ibid., 152–53.
127	15	*LJ* II, 452.
127	28	*TLB*, 46.
127	35	*LBC* I, 155.
127	38	Ibid., 158.
128	11	*LJ* II, 226–27.
128	20	*LBC*, I, 160–61.
128	33	Ibid., 163–64.
129	15	*LJ* II, 453.
130	3	Jenkins, 182.
130	9	Air., 154.
130	18	*LBC* I, 198–99.
130	27	*TLB*, 52.
130	29	*LBC* I, 214–15.
131	3	Md*B* I, 457.
131	10	*See* Md*B* I, 457.
131	15	*LJ* II, 333, 336, 339.
131	19	*TLB*, 57.
131	34	Ibid., 60–62.
133	12	Med. II, 68–69.
133	31	*TLB*, 67.
133	37	Jenkins, 166.
134	7	*TLB*, 68–69.
134	14	Jenkins, 171.
134	23	*TLB*, 67 and fn.
135	5	Lady Sydney Morgan, *Passages from My Autobiography*, 352.
135	11	*TLB*, 222.
135	14	Lady Jerningham, *The Jerningham Papers, 1780–1843*, ed. Egerton Castle, III, 111.
135	19	*Glen.* I, 24–25.
135	25	Ibid., 71.
135	29	Ibid., 130.
135	31	Ibid., 201.
135	37	Ibid., 284–86.
136	1	Glen. II, 27–30.
136	5	Ibid., 86.
136	13	Ibid., 80–89.
136	27	Ibid., 94–108.
136	30	Ibid., 109.
136	35	Ibid., 125.
136	40	Ibid., 126–28.
137	7	Ibid., 137–38.
137	10	Ibid., 142–43.
137	12	Ibid., 148.
137	13	Ibid., 150.
137	23	Ibid., 152–54.
137	25	Ibid., 160.
137	34	Ibid., 183–88.
137	38	Ibid., 197–200.
138	4	Ibid., 213–30.
138	11	Ibid., 233–36.
138	19	Ibid., 252–53.
138	33	Ibid., 282–84.
138	36	Ibid., 300.
138	37	Ibid., 318.
139	3	Ibid., 358.
139	9	*Glen.* III, 8.
139	17	Ibid., 45.
139	26	Ibid., 49–51.
139	30	Ibid., 61.
139	35	Ibid., 80.
139	38	Ibid., 84–87.
140	7	Ibid., 93–95.
140	16	Ibid., 120–56.
140	21	Ibid., 158–92.
140	22	Ibid., 302.
140	30	Ibid., 312.
140	36	Ibid., 315–22.
141	2	Cecil, *Melbourne*, 137.
141	12	Jenkins, 184.
141	19	Cecil, *Melbourne*, 138.
141	24	Ma*B*, 165.
141	40	Air., 185–86.
141	42	Ma*B*, 166.
142	18	*The British Critic*, June 1816, 627–31.
142	28	*TLB*, 78.
142	35	Jenkins, 173.
143	9	Ibid., 246.
143	22	*TLB*, 76.
144	2	Ibid., 83–85.
144	14	Lady Caroline Lamb, *A New Canto*, 7.
144	17	Ibid., 16.
144	22	Ibid., 16.

PAGE LINE

144 25 *TLB*, 87.
144 31 Ibid., 88.
144 34 Ma*B*, 167.
145 8 *TLB*, 77–78.
145 15 Michael Sadleir, *Bulwer: A Panorama, Edward and Rosina*, 29.
145 18 E. *Bulwer-Lytton by his Son*, I, 328.
145 27 Sadleir, *Bulwer*, 52.
146 1 Edward Bulwer-Lytton, *Life and Literary Remains*, I, 266; 328.
146 18 Ibid., 272.
146 21 Ibid., 268.
146 28 Ibid., 334.
146 35 Sadleir, *Bulwer*, 79.
146 39 Ibid., 57.
147 16 Lady Caroline Lamb, *Ada Reis*, xvi.
147 26 Ibid., I, 7–8.
147 37 Ibid., 25–28.
148 4 Ibid., 169.
148 14 Ibid., 191–92.
148 21 *Ada Reis* II, 65–71.

PAGE LINE

148 28 Ibid., 75–80.
148 31 *Ada Reis* III, 27.
148 37 Ibid., 38.
148 41 Ibid., 95–96.
149 4 Ibid., 127–28.
149 9 Ibid., 128–41.
149 15 Thomas Henry Lister, *Granby*, I, 56.
149 18 Ibid., 61.
149 21 Ibid., 62.
149 26 Ibid., 71.
149 30 *Granby* II, 127.
150 7 *Dis.* I, 284–309.
150 11 Ibid., 395–96.
150 31 Ibid., 408–13.
151 2 Jenkins, 264.
151 8 Ma*B*, 169.
151 10 Jenkins, 275.
151 15 *Gentleman's Magazine*, March 1828, 269.
151 19 *London Gazette*, February 1828, 277–78, quoted by Jenkins.
151 24 Jenkins, 276.

THREE

153 10 *LJ* II, 229–30.
154 37 *Poetry* III, 162.
155 6 Ibid., 169.
155 12 Ibid., 170–71.
155 21 Ibid., 171.
155 26 Ibid., 172.
156 8 Ibid., 174.
156 10 Ibid., 176.
156 26 Ibid., 232.
156 30 Ibid., 234.
157 11 Ibid., 331.
157 29 Ibid., 413–15.
158 5 Ibid., 508–9.
158 8 Ibid., 511 n.
158 19 Ibid., 545.
158 25 *Manfred*, III, iii.
158 32 *Manfred*, II, i.
159 1 Ibid., i.
159 2 Ibid., iv.
159 35 *Cain*, I, i.
158 38 *Cain*, III, i.
160 12 *LJ* II, 276, 340, 408, 410.
160 23 *LJ* II, 277.
160 26 Quoted by Md*B*, I, 451.
162 3 *LBC* I, 175.
162 16 Lovel., 263.
163 28 *LJ* II, 4.
164 12 Ibid., 4–5.
164 14 Ibid., 16.
164 19 *LBC* I, 56.
164 22 *LJ* II, 301.
164 26 Unpublished portion of a letter quoted by Md*B* I, 307.

164 37 *LJ* II, 254.
164 38 *TLB*, 92.
165 10 *LBC* I, 180–81.
165 22 *LJ* II, 267.
165 34 Ibid., 270.
167 19 *LBC* I, 188–95.
167 24 Thomas Moore, *Memoirs, Journal, and Correspondence*, ed. J. Russell, III, 292.
167 42 *LBC* I, 197–200.
168 9 *LJ* II, 276.
168 37 *LBC* I, 201–5.
169 17 *LBC* I, 212.
169 22 *TLB*, 98.
169 38 *LBC* I, 217–18.
169 41 Ibid., 227.
170 9 Ibid., 231–32.
170 32 *The Important Trial in the Common Pleas for Libel* etc., 3–5.
171 2 Ibid., 7.
171 16 *LJ* III, 262.
171 24 John Gore, " 'When We Two Parted,' A Byron Mystery Resolved," in *Cornhill Magazine*, January 1928, 39–53.
172 12 John Wedderburn Webster, *Waterloo*, 32–34.
172 21 Ibid., 82.
172 23 *LJ* IV, 60–61.
172 26 Ibid., 79.
172 31 *SP* II, 436.
172 33 *LJ* V, 371.

PAGE LINE
173 18 Gore, "When We Two Parted," 44.
173 21 SP II, 109–10.
173 27 LBC II, 237.
173 31 Edward J. Trelawny, Recollections of the Last Days of Shelley and Byron, 47.
173 38 Gore, "When We Two Parted," 49.
176 2 TLB, 165–69.
176 22 LBC I, 226–28.
176 36 Ibid., 240.
177 4 TLB, 171.
177 12 Ibid., 174.
177 39 LJ III, 210.
179 13 TLB, 124–25.
179 38 Ibid., 128.
180 40 Ibid., 137.
181 34 MdB II, 486.

PAGE LINE
184 12 Quoted by MdB II, 500.
184 24 Countess Teresa Guiccioli, My Recollections of Lord Byron, Pt. II, 56.
185 4 LBC I, 251.
185 8 DLM, 302.
185 12 LBC I, 251.
185 25 Lovel., 37.
187 21 Quoted by DLM, 452 and fn.
188 13 Lovel., 159–61.
194 4 Charles Mackay, Medora Leigh, a History and an Autobiography, 25.
194 19 Ibid., 26.
196 16 Ibid., 37–38.
196 39 This letter and Medora's autobiography are MSS in the Pierpont Morgan Library, New York.

FOUR

197 12 Percy B. Shelley, Letters, ed. F. L. Jones, II, 662.
197 18 LJ II, 344.
197 21 Ibid., 345.
197 23 Ibid., 347.
197 26 Ibid., 369.
197 27 Ibid., 402.
198 3 Ibid., 402.
198 5 Ibid., 283.
198 10 Berg. Col., March 28, 1814.
198 24 LJ II, 313.
199 4 Isaac Nathan, Fugitive Pieces and Reminiscences of Lord Byron, 101–2.
199 7 Berg Col., March 28, 1814.
199 11 LJ II, 319.
199 19 Amelia Opie, Memorials of the Life of Amelia Opie, ed. C. L. Brightwell, 141.
199 24 Quoted by Benjamin Haydon, Autobiography, ed. E. Blunden, 68–69.
199 27 LJ II, 331–32 n.
199 33 Ibid., 353.
199 35 Ibid., 354.
199 37 Ibid., 366.
200 1 Ibid., 384.
200 5 Ibid., 373.
200 8 Ibid., 389.
200 11 Ibid., 398.
200 12 Ibid., 402.
200 14 Ibid., 405.
200 17 Ibid., 410.
200 23 Ibid., 387.
200 30 Med., 72.
200 35 LJ I, 302–3.
201 3 LJ II, 10.

201 5 LBC I, 79.
201 9 LJ II, 231.
201 11 Ibid., 253.
201 13 Ibid., 324.
201 15 LJ III, 118.
201 16 LJ II, 318.
201 19 Ibid., 360.
201 24 LBC I, 237.
201 38 LJ II, 380.
202 7 SP II, 530.
202 25 LBW, 74.
202 32 Ibid., 79.
204 5 Ibid., 85.
204 9 LJ II, 385.
204 15 LBW, 86.
204 19 Vere Foster, The Two Duchesses, 362.
204 20 Ibid., 370.
204 27 Ibid., 365.
205 15 LJ II, 111-12.
205 20 Ibid., 117.
205 29 Ibid., 165–66.
205 37 Col., note 88, quoting from Galingnani's Messenger of June 11.
206 36 LBW, 105–8.
206 40 Ibid., 109.
207 6 Ibid., 111.
207 12 LJ III, 157.
207 24 Ibid., 119–21.
207 41 LBW, 115.
208 6 LBC I, 75.
208 9 Ibid., 79.
208 12 Ibid., 86.
208 14 Ibid., 88.
208 38 LBW, 119.
209 9 LBC I, 94–95.

PAGE LINE

209 16 Ibid., 108.
209 20 *LBW*, 157.
209 24 *LBC* I, 134.
209 37 *LBW*, 167.
210 22 *LJ* III, 397–99.
210 26 Ethel C. Mayne, *The Life and Letters of Lady Byron*, 60–62.
210 29 *LBW*, 169.
210 35 *LJ* III, 399–401.
211 2 *LBW*, 171.
211 7 *LJ* III, 401–3.
211 16 *LBW*, 173.
211 27 Ibid., 175–77.
211 35 *LJ* III, 406–8.
212 15 *LBW*, 178–80.
212 26 Ibid., 187.
212 33 *LJ* III, 408.
212 35 *LBW*, 190.
212 37 *LJ* III, 401.
213 5 *LBW*, 191–92.
213 16 *LBC* I, 250.
213 17 Mayne, *Lady Byron*, 94–95.
213 29 *LBC* I, 253–55.
213 42 *LBW*, 196–97.
214 1 *LBC* I, 260.
214 8 *LBW*, 197.
214 12 John Cam Hobhouse, *Recollections of a Long Life*, ed. Lady Dorchester, I, 157.
214 32 *LBW*, 198–202.
215 2 Mayne, *Lady Byron*, 103.
215 28 *LJ* III, 124.
215 35 *LBW*, 203.
215 41 Mayne, *Lady Byron*, 104.
216 11 *LBW*, 204.
216 24 Mayne, *Lady Byron*, 108.
217 15 Ibid., 111–12.
217 19 *LBC* I, 267–68.
217 23 *LJ* III, 137–38.
217 32 Ibid., 138–39.
217 40 *LBW*, 210.
218 5 *LBC* I, 269.
218 19 *TLB*, 66–67.
218 27 *LBW*, 221.
218 33 *LBC* I, 276.
218 38 Ibid., 280.
219 2 Ibid., 282.
219 5 *LBW*, 222–23.
219 36 Ibid., 227–29.
220 17 *LBC* I, 287–91.
220 29 *LBW*, 231.
221 3 *LBC* I, 290.
221 9 Air., 139; 153.
221 13 *LBW*, 232.
221 34 Mayne, *Lady Byron*, 133–34.
221 41 *LBW*, 239.
222 2 Mayne, *Lady Byron*, 151.
222 36 Berg Col., December 30, 1814.
222 38 Med., 46.
223 9 *Poetry*, IV, 37.
223 21 *LBW*, 250.
223 35 Berg Col., May 15, 1824.

223 37 *LBW*, 251.
224 16 Ibid., 255.
224 22 *LBC* I, 292.
225 6 *LBW*, 256.
225 8 *LBC* I, 293.
225 32 *LBW*, 267–69.
226 31 Ibid., 276 n.
227 22 *LJ* III, 175–76.
227 37 *LBW*, 282–83.
227 42 *Poetry* III, 423.
228 13 *LJ* III, 185–86.
228 16 Ibid., 185.
228 25 *LBW*, 292–93.
230 32 Ibid., 296–301.
231 16 Ibid., 302–3.
231 fn Ibid., 301; 473.
232 4 Mayne, *Lady Byron*, 183.
232 15 George Ticknor, *Life, Letters and Journals*, ed. A. Ticknor, I, 50 et seq.
233 12 *LBW*, 315–16.
233 18 Ibid., 319.
234 3 Ibid., 321–25.
235 42 *TLB*, 179–85.
239 30 *LJ* V, 461.
240 18 Col., 11. 1057 et seq.
241 7 Ibid., 1180 et seq.
241 19 Col., 1. 1208.
241 36 *Leon to Annabella*, 11. 293 et seq.
242 18 Col., 11. 1258 et seq.
243 11 Quoted by Md*B*, 587 fn.
243 14 *LBW*, 418.
243 35 *New Monthly Magazine*, April 1830, 377–82.
245 11 *LBW*, 333.
245 26 Mayne, *Lady Byron*, 196–97.
245 31 Sir John Fox, *The Byron Mystery*, 97.
246 13 Hobhouse, *Recollections* II, 279–80.
246 19 Ibid., 201–2.
246 34 Murray MS quoted by Md*B* I, 556.
246 36 Med., 52–53.
247 4 Lord Lindsay's letter to the *Times* quoted by Harriet Beecher Stowe, *Lady Byron Vindicated*, 306.
247 16 LJ III, 252–54.
248 6 Hobhouse, *Recollections* II, 250–54.
248 16 Lovel., 39.
248 18 Hobhouse, *Recollections* II, 215.
248 27 Ibid., 255.
249 1 *LBW*, 349.
250 25 Fox, *Byron Mystery*, 98.
251 5 *LBW*, 351–52.
251 20 Fox, *Byron Mystery*, 98–99.
253 5 *LBW*, 353, 354, 355.
253 19 Ibid., 359–60.
255 9 Ibid., 357–61.

PAGE LINE
255 12 Ibid., 368.
256 9 Ibid., 361–62, 364, 366.
256 18 Ibid., 334.
258 10 Ibid., 365–69.
259 29 Ibid., 373–77.
260 27 Ibid., 370–72.
264 27 Ibid., 377–89.
264 34 Ibid., 382, 385.
265 31 Hobhouse, *Recollections* II, 211-13.
266 15 Mayne, *Lady Byron*, 209–10.
266 23 *LBW*, 393–94.
266 37 DLM, 138.
267 16 Mayne, *Lady Byron*, 210.
267 30 *LBW*, 396.
267 40 Ibid., 401.
268 17 Hobhouse, *Recollections* II, 235–38.
268 22 *LBW*, 402.
268 38 Hobhouse, *Recollections* II, 239–41.
269 9 *LBW*, 405–6.
269 15 Ibid., 398.
269 20 Ibid., 340–41.
269 22 Ibid., 407.
269 26 Hobhouse, *Recollections* II, 242.
270 9 Berg Col., Feb. 12, 1816.
270 38 *LBW*, 407–8.
271 33 *LJ* III, 309–11.
272 9 Hobhouse, *Recollections* II, 257–58.
272 19 *LBW*, 412–15.
272 21 *LJ* III, 315.
272 31 Fox, *Byron Mystery*, 59.
273 12 Quoted by Md*B*, II, 582 fn.
273 20 *LBW*, 418.
273 24 Berg Col., Feb. 29, 1816.
273 35 *LBW*, 420.
274 10 Murray MS quoted by Md*B* II, 585–86.
274 33 *LJ* II, 449–50.
275 7 *LJ* III, 266–68.

PAGE LINE
275 10 *LBW*, 420.
275 17 Ibid., 341.
275 29 Ibid., 422–23.
275 36 Hobhouse, *Recollections*, 288–89.
275 41 *LBW*, 426.
276 16 *Quarterly Review*, Jan. 1870, quoted in *LBW*, 425–26.
278 36 DLM, 231–35.
279 11 *LBW*, 427.
279 22 Berg Col., March 6, 1816.
279 29 Ibid., March 7, 1816.
279 35 *LBC* II, 110.
279 42 Berg Col., March 8, 1816.
280 42 *LJ* III, 272–75.
281 33 Moore, 297.
281 38 Berg Col., March 9, 1816.
282 16 Ibid., March 13, 1816.
282 18 Ibid., March 14, 1816.
283 16 *Poetry* III, 537–40.
283 19 *LBW*, 448.
283 25 *LJ* III, 275–76.
285 6 DLM, 240–45.
285 19 *Poetry* III, 540–44.
285 35 Moore, 302.
286 6 Berg Col., March 18, 1816.
286 14 Murray MS quoted by Md*B* II, 596.
287 11 *LJ* III, 429.
288 26 Ibid., 255–56.
291 12 Ibid., 430–37.
291 14 Grylls, *Claire Clairmont*, 58.
291 35 *LJ* III, 347–48.
292 11 *LBW*, 463.
292 26 Lovel., 53.
292 30 April 25, 1816, quoted on Md*B* II, 608.
295 3 *LJ* III, 280–81.
295 31 M. D. George, *Catalogue of Personal and Political Satires*, IX, 714.

Airlie, Mabell, Countess of. *In Whig Society, 1775–1818.* London, 1921.
Bigland, Eileen. *Passion for Excitement: The Life and Personality of the Incredible Lord Byron.* New York, 1956.
Blessington, Marguerite, Countess of. *The Idler in Italy.* London, 1834–40.
————. *Journal of Correspondence and Conversations between Lord Byron and the Countess of Blessington.* Cincinnati, 1851.
Borst, William A. *Lord Byron's First Pilgrimage.* New Haven, 1948.
British Critic, The.
Bulwer-Lytton, Edward. *Life and Literary Remains.* London, 1883.
Bury, Lady Charlotte. *The Diary of a Lady-in-Waiting.* Edited by A. T. Steuart. London, 1908.
Byron, George Gordon, Lord. Correspondence. Edited by J. Murray. New York, 1922.
————. Manuscripts in the Berg Collection, New York Public Library.
————. Manuscripts in the Pierpont Morgan Library, New York.
————. *Works, Letters and Journals.* Edited by R. E. Prothero. London, 1898–1901.
————. *Works, Poetry.* Edited by H. E. Coleridge. London, 1898–1904.
Cecil, David. *The Young Melbourne.* Indianapolis, 1939.
————. *Melbourne.* Indianapolis, 1954.
Chew, Samuel C. "The Pamphlets of the Byron Separation," in *Modern Language Notes,* March 1919, 155–62.
Clayden, P. W. *Rogers and His Contemporaries.* London, 1889.
Clinton, George L. *Memoirs of the Life and Writings of Lord Byron.* London, 1827.
Collins, V. H. *Lord Byron in His Letters.* London, 1927.
[Colman, George, the Younger.] *Don Leon.* London, 1866.
————. *Leon to Annabella.* London, 1835.
Dallas, R. C. *Recollections of the Life of Lord Byron, from the Year 1808 to the End of 1814.* London, 1824.
Dictionary of National Biography.
Disraeli, Benjamin (Earl of Beaconsfield). *Works.* New York, 1904.
Drinkwater, John. *The Pilgrim of Eternity.* London, 1924.
Du Bos, Charles. *Byron and the Need of Fatality.* London, 1932.
Dyce, Rev. Alexander (ed.). *Recollections of the Table-Talk of Samuel Rogers.* New Southgate, 1887.
E. Bulwer-Lytton by his Son. New York, 1883.
Edinburgh Review.
Egan, Paul. *Life in London.* London, 1821.
Elwin, Malcolm. *Lord Byron's Wife.* New York, 1963; London, 1963.
Elze, Karl. *Lord Byron: A Biography.* London, 1872.
Erdman, David V. "Lord Byron as Rinaldo," in *Publications of the Modern Language Association,* March 1942, 189–231.
Foster, Vere. *The Two Duchesses.* London, 1898.
Fox, Sir John S. C. *The Byron Mystery.* London, 1924; New York, 1924.
Galt, John. *The Life of Lord Byron.* Philadelphia, 1830.
Gentleman's Magazine.

George, M. D. *Catalogue of Personal and Political Satires.* London, n.d.

Gore, John. " 'When We Two Parted,' A Byron Mystery Re-Solved," in *Cornhill Magazine,* January 1928, 39–53.

Gower, Lord Granville Leveson. *Private Correspondence, 1781–1821.* Edited by Castalia, Countess Granville. London, 1916.

Grebanier, Bernard and Thompson, Stith. *English Literature and Its Backgrounds.* New York, 1950.

Greville, Charles Cavendish Fulke. *Memoirs.* Edited by H. Stoddard. New York, 1875.

Gronow, Capt. R. H. *The Reminiscences and Recollections of Captain Gronow.* London, 1950.

Grylls, R. Glynn. *Claire Clairmont, Mother of Byron's Allegra.* London, 1939.

Guiccioli, Countess Teresa. *Lord Byron jugé par les temoins de sa vie.* Paris, 1868.

————. *My Recollections of Lord Byron.* Philadelphia, 1869.

Gunn, Peter. *My Dearest Augusta.* New York, 1969.

Haydon, Benjamin R. *Autobiography.* Edited by E. Blunden. London, 1927.

Hobhouse, John Cam (Lord Broughton). *Contemporary Account of the Separation of Lord and Lady Byron.* London, 1870.

————. Manuscripts in the Berg Collection, New York Public Library.

————. *Recollections of a Long Life.* Edited by Lady Dorchester. London, 1909–11.

————. *Travels in Albania.* London, 1855.

Holland, Henry Richard V., Lord. *Further Memoirs of the Whig Party, 1807–1821.* New York, 1905.

["Holloway."] *The Phoenix of Sodom or the Vere Street Coterie.* London, 1813.

Important Trial in the Common Pleas for Libel Concerning Adultery etc., The. London, 1816.

Ingpen, Roger. *Shelley in England.* London, 1917.

Irving, Washington. *Works.* London, 1855.

Jeaffreson, John Cordy. *The Real Lord Byron.* London, 1883.

Jenkins, Elizabeth. *Lady Caroline Lamb.* London, 1932.

Jerningham, Lady. *The Jerningham Papers, 1780–1843.* Edited by Egerton Castle. London, 1896.

Joyce, Michael. *My Friend H., John Cam Hobhouse.* London, 1948.

Knight, G. Wilson. *Lord Byron: Christian Virtues.* London, 1952.

————. *Lord Byron's Marriage.* London, 1957.

————. "Who Wrote Don Leon?" in *The Twentieth Century,* July 1954, 67–79.

Lamb, Lady Caroline. *Ada Reis.* London, 1823.

————. *Glenarvon.* London, 1816.

————. Manuscripts in the Berg Collection, New York Public Library.

————. *A New Canto.* London, 1819.

Lane-Poole, Stanley Edward. *The Life of the Right Honourable Stratford Canning.* London, 1888.

Leigh, Elizabeth Medora. *Autobiography.* Manuscript in the Pierpont Morgan Library. New York.

————. Manuscript Letters in the Pierpont Morgan Library.

Lister, Thomas Henry. *Granby.* New York, 1826.

Literary Gazette.

London Gazette.

Lovelace, Ralph Gordon Noel, Earl of. *Astarte.* New York, 1921; London, 1921.

Lovell, Ernest J., Jr. *His Very Self and Voice.* New York, 1954.

Mackay, Charles. *Medora Leigh, a History and an Autobiography.* New York, 1870.
Malmesbury, James Howard, Earl of. *Memoirs of an ex-Minister.* London, 1885.
Marchand, Leslie. *Byron.* New York, 1957.
Maurois, André. *Byron.* New York, 1930.
Mayne, Ethel C. *Byron.* London, 1912; New York, 1912.
———. *The Life and Letters of Lady Byron.* London, 1929.
Medwin, Thomas. *Journal of the Conversations of Lord Byron.* London, 1824.
Monypenny W. F. and Byckle, G. E. *The Life of Benjamin Disraeli.* New York, 1929.
Moore, Doris Langley. *The Late Lord Byron.* London, 1961; New York, 1961.
Moore, Thomas. *The Life, Letters and Journals of Lord Byron.* London, 1866.
———. *Memoirs, Journal, and Correspondence.* Edited by J. Russell. New York, 1858.
———. *Poetical Works.* Edited by W. M. Rossetti. London, 1911.
———. *Prose and Verse.* Edited by R. H. Shepherd. London, 1878.
Morgan, Sydney, Lady. *Lady Morgan's Memoirs.* London, 1862.
———. *Passages from My Autobiography.* New York, 1859.
Nathan, Isaac. *Fugitive Pieces and Reminiscences of Lord Byron.* London, 1829.
New Monthly Magazine.
Nichol, John. *Byron.* London, 1883.
Nicolson, Sir Harold. *The Last Journey.* London, 1940.
Notes and Queries.
Opie, Amelia. *Memorials of the Life of Amelia Opie.* Edited by C. L. Brightwell. Norwich, 1854.
Origo, Iris. *The Last Attachment.* London, 1962.
Paston, George and Quennell, Peter. *To Lord Byron.* London, 1939.
Priestley, J. B. *The Prince of Pleasure and His Regency.* New York, 1969.
Prothero, R. E. "Childhood and School Days of Byron," in *The Nineteenth Century,* January, 1898, 61–81.
Quarterly Review.
Quennell, Peter. *Byron: A Self-Portrait.* London, 1950.
———. *Byron: The Years of Fame.* London, 1950.
"Recollections of Turkey," in *New Monthly Magazine,* October 1826, 311–14; February 1827, 127–49.
Sadleir, Michael. *Bulwer: A Panorama, Edward and Rosina.* Boston, 1931.
Shelley, Mary. *Letters.* Edited by F. L. Jones. Norman, Oklahoma, 1944.
Shelley, Percy B., *Letters.* Edited by F. L. Jones. Oxford, 1964.
Stanhope, Leicester F., Colonel. *Greece in 1823 and 1824.* London, 1825.
Stowe, Harriet Beecher. *Lady Byron Vindicated.* London, 1870.
Ticknor, George. *Life, Letters and Journals.* Edited by A. Ticknor. Boston, 1877.
Trelawny, Edward J. *Recollections of the Last Days of Shelley and Byron.* London, 1858.
———. *Records of Shelley, Byron and the Author.* London, n.d.
Vulliamy, Colwyn Edward. *Byron.* London, 1948.
Webster, John Wedderburn. *Waterloo.* Paris, 1816.
Whipple, A. B. C. *The Fatal Gift of Beauty.* New York, 1964.
White, Newman Ivey. *Shelley.* London, 1947.
Winwar, Frances. *The Romantic Rebels: Byron, Shelley and Keats.* Boston, 1935.

DON LEON

Probably by George Colman the Younger and attributed by him to Byron

The original line numbering has been kept although inaccurate, and some two dozen of the less interesting notes have been omitted, and eccentricities of spelling and punctuation in the poem have not been altered.

Reprinted by permission of the Pierpont Morgan Library, New York

THOU ermined judge, pull off that sable cap!
What! Cans't thou lie, and take thy morning nap?
Peep thro' the casement; see the gallows there:
Thy work hangs on it; could not mercy spare?
What had he done? Ask crippled Talleyrand,
Ask Beckford, Courtenay, all the motley band
Of priest and laymen, who have shared his guilt
(If guilt it be) then slumber if thou wilt;
What bonds had he of social safety broke?   10
Found'st thou the dagger hid beneath his cloak?
He stopped no lonely traveller on the road;
He burst no lock, he plundered no abode;
He never wrong'd the orphan of his own;
He stifled not the ravish'd maiden's groan.
His secret haunts were hid from every soul,
Till thou did'st send thy myrmidons to prowl,
And watch the prickings of his morbid lust,
To wring his neck and call thy doings just.
And shall the Muse, whilst pen and paper lie   20
Upon the table, hear the victim's cry.
Nor boldly lay her cauterising hand
Upon a wound that cankers half the land?
No! were the bays that flourish round my head
Destined to wither, when these lines are read:
Could all the scourges canting priests invent
To prop their legendary lies, torment
My soul in death or rack my body here,
My voice I'd raise insensible to fear.
When greedy placemen drain a sinking state,   30
When virtue starves and villains dine off plate;
When lords and senators untouched by shame,

For schemes of basest fraud can lend their name;
When elders, charged to guard the pauper's trust,
Feast on the funds, and leave the poor a crust;
When knaves like these escape the hangman's noose,
Who e'en to Clogher a pardon would refuse?
Who would not up and lend a hand to save
A venial culprit from a felon's grave?
Sheer indignation quickens into rhyme,
And silence now were tantamount to crime.   40
I know not in what friendly breast to pour
My swelling rage save, into thine, dear Moore.
For thou, methinks, some sympathy will own,
Since, love, no matter in what guise 'tis shown,
Must ever find an echo from that lyre,
Which erst hath glowed with old Anacreon's fire.
Death levels all; and, deaf to mortal cries,
At his decree the prince or beggar dies.
So, when I'm gone, as gone I soon may be,
Be thou, dear Tom, an honest, firm trustee;   50
And, nor for filthy lucre, nor to dine
At Holland House, erase one single line.
To titled critics pay no servile court;
But print my thoughts through good or ill report.
And if these musings serve but to dispense
One little dose of useful common sense,
I fain would hope they greater good had done
Than all the pious tracts of Rivington.
Can it be justice in a land like ours,
Where every vice in full luxuriance flowers—   60
Where schoolboys' eyes can recognise afar
Soho's green blinds and Lisle-street doors ajar—

Where bold-faced harlots impudently spurn
The modest virgin's blush at every turn,
Where every pavement hears their ribald laugh,
Spite of the Bow-street gang and watchman's staff,
That one propensity (which always hides
Its sport obscene, and into darkness glides,
Which none so brazened e'er presume to own,
Which, left unheeded, would remain unknown,
Should be the game their worships will pursue
With keenest ardour all the country through.
No parson of the quorum feels a blush
To claim the honours of the stinking brush):
Whilst at the scent unkennelled curs give tongue,
Until the poor misogynist is hung.
Yet naught can satisfy the foul-mouthed crew;
Laid in his grave their victim they pursue;
And base Smellfunguses insult his ghost
With sainted columns in the *Morning Post*.
    I grant that casuists the Bible quote,
And tell us how God's tardy vengeance smote
Lot's native town with brimstone from the sky,
To punish this impure delinquency,
Unmindful that the drunkard's kiss defiled
(Whilst yet the embers smoked), his virgin child.
But reason doubts the Jewish prophet's tale.
Does history then no other place bewail?
Descend the Nile, and steer your bark along
The shores recorded in Homeric song.
Where's centi-portalled Thebes? The crumbling stone
Marks well its site, but sandy mounds have grown
O'er granite fanes that line the public way,
And seem to bid defiance to decay.
Why seek we Priam's palaces in vain?
Why howls the blast o'er Lacedæmon's plain?
Where's Memphis? Wherefore in Persepolis

Do jackals scream, and venomed serpents hiss?
What! were thy ramparts, Babylon, so thick;
And hast thou left us not a single brick?
But where's thy house, Zenobia? Thou wast Queen
Of Tadmor once; and now the Bedoween
Erects his tent, and scares the fleet gazelle,
That comes to drink at thy sulphureous well.
Where's Cæsarea now, or Antioch? Where?
And yet their domes deserved God's special care,
There Paul was honoured; there our faith proclaimed
There true believers first were Christians named.
        Who has not seen how Mother Church can press;
Each vain tradition to her purposes,
And from the cradle to the grave supply
Proofs sacred of infallibility?
Would you be damned? a text conveys her curse;
Or rise again? you have it in a verse.
Her rites as means of revenue are prized:
For mammon's sake our infants are baptized.
With golden offerings marriages are made;
Woe to the union where no fee is paid.
Who weds or fornicates, no matter which,
Children begets, and makes the altar rich;
But, where no offerings to the surplice fall,
The taste forthwith is anti-physical.
Hell-fire can hardly expiate the guilt
Of that damned sin—the church's rubric bilked.
The tree we plant will, when its boughs are grown,
Produce no other blossoms than its own;
And thus in man some inborn passions reign
Which, spite of careful pruning, sprout again.
Then, say, was I or nature in the wrong,
If, yet a boy, one inclination, strong
In wayward fancies, domineered my soul,
And bade complete defiance to control?

What, though my youthful instincts, forced to brood
Within my bosom seemed awhile subdued?
What, though, by early education taught,
The charms of women first my homage caught?
What, though my verse in Mary's praises flowed?
And flowers poetic round her footsteps strewed,
Yet, when her ears would list not to my strain,
And every sigh was answered with disdain,
Pride turned, not stopped, the course of my desires,   140
Extinguished these, and lighted other fires.
And as the pimple which cosmetic art
Repels from one, invades another part,
My bubbling passions found another vent,
The object changed, but not the sentiment.
And, e'er my years could task my reason why,
Sex caused no qualms where beauty lured the eye.
Such were my notions ere my teens began,
And such their progress till I grew a man.   150
With thee, dear Margaret, whose tender looks
Made me forget my task, my play, my books.
Young though we were, our union soared above
The frigid systems of Platonic love.
Untutored how to kiss, how oft I hung
Upon thy neck, whilst from my burning tongue
Between thy lips the kindling glow was sent,
And nature fanned the new-born sentiment!
How oft, beneath the arbour's mystic shade,   160
My boyish vows of constancy were made!
There on the grass as we recumbent lay,
Not coy wast thou, nor I averse to play;
And in that hour thy virtue's sole defence
Was not thy coldness, but my innocence.
   Among the yeomen's sons on my estate
A gentle boy would at my mansion wait:
And now, that time has almost blanched my hair,

And with the past the present I compare,
Full well I know, though decency forbad
The same caresses to a rustic lad;
Love, love it was, that made my eyes delight   170
To have his person ever in my sight.
Yes, Rushton, though to unobserving eyes,
My favours but as lordly gifts were prized;
Yet something then would inwardly presage
The predilections of my riper age.
Why did I give thee gauds to deck thy form?
Why for a menial did my entrails warm?
Why? but from secret longings to pursue
Those inspirations, which, if books speak true,   180
Have led e'en priests and sages to embrace
Those charms, which female blandishments efface.
Thus passed my boyhood: and though proofs were none
What path my future course of life would run
Like sympathetic ink, if then unclear,
The test applied soon made the trace appear.
I bade adieu to school and tyro's sports,
And Cam received me in his gothic courts.
Freed from the pedagogue's tyrannic sway,   190
In mirth and revels I consumed the day.
No more my truant muse her vigils kept;
No more she soothed my slumbers as I slept;
But, idling now, she oft recalled the time
When to her reed I tuned my feeble rhyme.
She knew how those 'midst song and mirth grow dull
Whose tender bosoms soft emotions lull.
As manhood came, my feelings, more intense,
Sighed for some kindred mind, where confidence,   200
Tuned in just unison, might meet return,
And whilst it warmed my breast, in his might burn,
   Oft, when the evening bell to vespers rung,
When the full choir the solemn anthem sung,

And lips, o'er which no youthful down had grown,
Hymned their soft praises to Jehovah's throne,
The pathos of the strain would soothe my soul,
And call me willing from the drunkard's bowl.
Who, that has heard the chapel's evening song,
When peals divine the lengthened note prolong,
But must have felt religious thoughts arise,
And speed their way melodious to the skies.
    Among the choir a youth my notice won,
Of pleasing lineaments named Eddleston.
With gifts well suited to a stripling's mood,
His friendship and his tenderness I wooed.
Oh! how I loved to press his cheek to mine;
How fondly would my arms his waist entwine!
Another feeling borrowed friendship's name,
And took its mantle to conceal my shame.
Another feeling! oh! 'tis hard to trace
The line where love usurps tame friendship's place.
Friendship's the chrysalis, which seems to die,
But throws its coil to give love wings to fly.
Both are the same, but in another state;
This formed to soar, and that to vegetate.
    Of humble birth was he—patrician I,
And yet this youth was my idolatry
Strong was my passion, past all inward cure
And could it be so violent, yet pure?
'Twas like a philter poured into my veins—
And as the chemist, when some vase contains
An unknown mixture, each component tries
With proper tests, the draught to analyze;
So questioned I myself: What lights this fire?
Maids and not boys are wont to move desire;
Else 'twere illicit love. Oh! sad mishap!
But what prompts nature than to set the trap?
Why night and day does his sweet image float

Before my eyes? or wherefore do I doat
On that dear face with ardour so intense?
Why truckles reason to concupiscence?
Though law cries "hold!" yet passion onward draws:
But nature gave us passions, man gave laws,
Whence spring these inclinations, rank and strong?
And harming no one, wherefore call them wrong?
What's virtue's touchstone? Unto others do,
As you would wish that others did to you.
Then tell me not of sex, if to one key
The chords, when struck, vibrate in harmony.
No virgin I deflower, nor, lurking, creep,
With steps adult'rous, on a husband's sleep.
I plough no field in other men's domain;
And where I delve no seed shall spring again.
Thus with myself I reasoned; then I read,
And counsel asked from volumes of the dead.
Oh! flowery path, thus hand in hand to walk
With Plato and enjoy his honeyed talk.
Beneath umbrageous planes to sit at ease,
And drink from wisdom's cup with Socrates.
Now stray with Bion through the shady grove;
Midst deeds of glory, now with Plutarch rove.
And oft I turned me to the Mantuan's page,
To hold discourse with shepherds of his age;
Or mixed with Horace in the gay delights
Of courtly revels, theatres, and sights;
And thou, whose soft seductive lines comprise
The code of love, thou hadst my sympathies;
But still, where'er I turned, in verse or prose,
Whate'er I read, some fresh dilemma rose,
And reason, that should pilot me along,
Belied her name, or else she led me wrong.
I love a youth; but Horace did the same;
If he's absolv'd, say, why am I to blame?

210

220

230

240

250

260

270

When young Alexis claimed a Virgil's sigh,
He told the world his choice; and may not I?
Shall every schoolman's pen his verse extol,
And, sin in me, in him a weakness call?
Then why was Socrates surnamed the sage,
Not only in his own, but every age,
If lips, whose accents strewed the path of truth,
Could print their kisses on some favoured youth?
Or why should Plato, in his Commonwealth
Score tenets up which I must note by stealth? 280
Say, why, when great Epaminondas died,
Was Cephidorus buried by his side?
Or why should Plutarch with eulogiums cite
That chieftain's love for his young catamite,
And we be forced his doctrine to decry,
Or drink the bitter cup of infamy?
    But these, thought I, are samples musty grown;
Turn we from early ages to our own.
No heathen's lust is matter of surprise;
He only aped his Pagan deities; 290
But when a Saviour had redeemed the world,
And all false idols from Olympus hurled,
A purer code the Christian law revealed,
And what was venial once as guilt was sealed.
With zeal unwearied I resumed again
My search, and read where'er the layman's pen
In annals grave or chronicles had writ;
But can I own with any benefit? 300
'Tis true, mankind had cast the pagan skin,
But all the carnal part remained within
Unchang'd, and nature, breaking through the fence,
Still vindicated her omnipotence.
    Look, how infected with this rank disease
Were those, who held St. Peter's holy keys,
And pious men to whom the people bowed,

And kings, who churches to the saints endowed;
All these were Christians of the highest stamp—
How many scholars, wasting o'er their lamp, 310
How many jurists, versed in legal rules,
How many poets, honoured in the schools,
How many captains, famed for deeds of arms,
Have found their solace in a minion's arms!
Nay, e'en our bard, Dame Nature's darling child,
Felt the strange impulse, and his hours beguiled
In penning sonnets to a stripling's praise,
Such as would damn a poet now-a-days.
    To this conclusion we must come at last: 320
Wise men have lived in generations past,
Whose deeds and sayings history records,
To whom the palm of virtue she awards,
Who, tempted, ate of that forbidden tree,
Which prejudice denies to you and me.
Then be consistent; and, at once confess,
If man's pursuit through life is happiness,
The great, the wise, the pious, and the good,
Have what they sought not rightly understood;
Or deem not else that aberration crime, 330
Which reigns in every caste and every clime.
    Harrassed by doubts, I threw my books aside,
Oh! false-named beacons of mankind, I cried,
Perdition's in your light! The gleam you show
Guides to a haven where no bark should go.
'Tis you that foster an illicit trade,
And warp us where a strict embargo's laid.
'Twere just as well to let the vessel glide
Resistless down the current, as confide 340
In charts, that lead the mariner astray,
And never mark the breakers in his way.
    But tell us casuists, were statutes meant
To scourge the wicked or the innocent?

What! if the husbandman, among the seeds
Of wholesome grain, detects unwholesome weeds;
What! if amidst the standing corn appear
Destructive tares, and choke the goodly ear;
Is evil, not prepense, a crime defined?
Are caitiffs those, whose sin was undesigned?
   In vice unhackneyed, in Justine unread,
See schoolboys, by some inclination led:
Some void, that's hardly to themselves confest,
Flying for solace to a comrade's breast.
In lonely walks their vows of friendship pass,
Warm as the shepherd's to his rustic lass.
Their friendship ripens into closer ties:
They love.   Then mutual vague desires arise.
Perhaps by night they share each other's bed,
'Till step by step, to closer union led,
Like wantons, whom some unknown feeling charms,
Each thinks he clasps a mistress in his arms.
Imperious nature's sensual prickings goad,
They own her dictates, but mistake the road.
Fond parents, speak! if truth can find her way
Through fogs of prejudice to open day.
Is there a father, when, instead of this,
His offspring sickens with a syphilis,
Who can unmoved his tender banting see
Devoured with chancres, writhing with chordee,
His blooming looks grown prematurely old,
His manhood wasted ere its hours are told,
His means with harlots and in brothels spent,
His breath infected and his body bent,
And will not own that any means were good
To save from taint so foul, if save he could?
Reflect, and chide not errors that arise
Less from design than man's infirmities.
Shut, shut your eyes, ye pedagogues, nor keep

350

360

370

Too close a watch upon your pupils' sleep:
For though, in boyish ignorance they may
Stumble perchance on some illicit play,
Which looks like lechery the most refined,
In them 'tis not depravity of mind.
Ingenuous souls, oft innocent of wrong,
For some enjoyment yet untasted long:
'Twas ye who roused the latent sense of shame,
And called their gambols by an odious name.
Harrow, thy hill unblemished had remained
Through years to come; but senseless fools arraigned,
With noisy zeal the rumours faintly spread,
And fixed a stigma on thy honoured head.
Thus feverish fancies floated in my brain.
Longing, yet forced my purpose to restrain,
Upon the brink of infamy I staid,
Now half resolved to plunge, now half afraid.
But fate, that turns the eddy of our lives,
And, at its will, like straws our fortune drives,
Saved me, ere yet the desperate chance was run;
For death deprived me of my Eddleston.
   I pass the useless hours in college spent—
The morning's lounge, the evening's merriment,
The tutor's lecture flippantly disdained,
The bottle emptied and the punch-bowl drained,
The restless slumber and the spewy bed,
And all the horrors of an aching head;
Some of our proud aristocratic joys;
Youth's vision that reality destroys;
The course pursued to people, church, and state,
And rear up senators for grave debate.
These classic pastimes had no charms for me;
They filled my breast with languor and ennui.
The daily round of dull scholastic rules
Amused me not.—"I'll quit these wordy fools,"

380

390

400

410

Cried I, "who pass unprofitable days
"To square a circle or collate a phrase.
"Be mine a wider field to till the mind,
"I'll ramble, and investigate mankind."

    Launched on the main to distant climes I sailed,
And mental freedom's pure Aurora hailed
With all the glow that ardent youth inspires,
Borne on the tempest of its own desires,
What splendid cities and what navied ports,
What feasts, what revels, and what princely courts
I saw, were matter foreign to my theme: 420
Love, love, clandestine love, was still my dream.
Methought there must be yet some people found,
Where Cupid's wings were free, his hands unbound
Where law had no erotic statutes framed,
Nor gibbets stood to fright the unreclaimed.
I'll seek the Turk—there undisputed reigns
The little god, and still his rights maintains.
There none can trespass on forbidden ground:
There venial youths in every stew are found,   430
And with their blandishments inveigle man,
As does in Christian lands the courtezan.

    Lo! to the winds the sail its bosom heaves,
Bland zephyrs waft us and the port receives,
Where sable Euxine past is seen to glide,
To join his waters with a fairer bride.
'Tis there Byzantium's minarets arise
Tipt with their golden crescents to the skies:
And trees and palaces from height to height
With vivid hues enrich the novel sight.

    Here much I saw—and much I mused to see
The loosened garb of Eastern luxury.
I sought the brothel, where, in maiden guise,
The black-eyed boy his trade unblushing plies;
Where in lewd dance he acts the scenic show—

His supple haunches wriggling to and fro:
With looks voluptuous the thought excites,
Whilst gazing sit the hoary sybarites:
Whilst gentle lute and drowsy tambourine
Add to the langour of the monstrous scene.
Yes, call it monstrous! but not monstrous, where   450
Close latticed harems hide the timid fair:
With mien gallant where pæderasty smirks,
And whoredom, felon like, in covert lurks.

    All this I saw—but saw it not alone—
A friend was with me; and I dared not own
How much the sight had touched some inward sense,
Too much for e'en the closest confidence.   460
Deep in the dark recesses of my mind
I hid my thoughts, nor told what they designed.
Quit we (I cried) these prostituted walls—
A second Sodom here my heart appals.
Spare us good Lord! like patriarchal Lot!
If fire and brimstone falls, oh, burn us not!

    This mask of horror served my purpose well—
Resolved to do what yet I feared to tell.
I found no kindred leaning in the breast   470
Of those around me, and I felt opprest.
We bent again our topsails to the breeze,
And reached unharmed those smooth cerulean seas,
Whose surface, studded with a hundred isles,
Heaves like the nurse that hugs her babes, and smiles.
"Shipmates, farewell! and thou John Cam, adieu!"
The nimble sailors up the mainsail clew:
"Starboard the helm,"—the topsails fall aback,   480
And the ship's course seems suddenly to slack.
Down from the davits swiftly glides the boat—
The boatswain whistles, and away we float.
"Now pull together, lads!"   We reach the land,
And Zea's rock receives me on the strand.

Hail, freedom, hail!   For though the soil I trod,
Still groaning lay beneath the Moslem's rod,
Here first to me her benisons were known,
For mental freedom is to think alone.
    Ah! little wots the friend I quitted here,
What strange adventures marked the coming year.
He sought his native shores; and, ever brave
In danger's hour the freeman's rights to save,
Stood in the senate by a people's choice,
And, not unheeded, raised his patriot voice.
I, wicked Childe, pursued a different course:
A demon urged, and with Satanic force
Still goaded on. Retrieve the moment lost,
He whispered) —Haste, and pleasure's cup exhaust.
Go, lay thee down beneath the shady plain,
Where Phædrus heard grave Plato's voice complain.
Another Phædrus may perchance go by,
And thy fond dreams become reality.
    Thou knows't the land where cool Ilyssus flows,
Where myrtles blossom and the olive grows,
Where ruined temples overhang the plain,
And lawless Klephts in devastation reign:
Though reckless times has scarce preserved a trace
Of what it was, I hied me to that place.
    Ye virtuous dead, whose names shall never die,
Long as the sun illumes earth's canopy;
Long as divine philosophy shall dwell
In mortal breasts; long as the sacred well
Of Helicon shall pour the stream of song,
And noble deeds to poesy belong.
Ye falling monuments and mouldering fanes,
Where still the magic of past greatness reigns;
Thou tall Hymettus, on whose honied top
Fresh odours rise, and dews in fragrance drop;
Piræus, with thy never angry wave,

Where oft my languid limbs I used to lave.
Scenes, where my soul in stillness and retreat,
Indulged in thought and lucubration sweet:
Ne'er till this body in corruption rot,
Shall those loved moments ever be forgot.
    In Athens stands an antiquated tower,
Built to the winds, whose good or evil power
Can one while fan with soft and balmy breath,
Then blow the rushing mighty blast of death.
This tower, composed by nicest rules of art,
And richly chiselled round in every part,
Which still the wonder of the traveller wins,
Served as a cell for hooded capuchins,
Whose walls monastic, girding it around,
Had changed the Pagan spot to holy ground.
'Twas here the pilgrim, doubtful where to lay
His weary head, a welcome guest would stay;
And, for his humble mite, could hope to share
The frugal monastery's daily fare.
Historians still some old traditions quote,
That here Demosthenes his speeches wrote;
And hence the temple with the vulgar famed,
The lantern of Demosthenes was named.
There dwelt I long, the tenant of that cell:
And not a mountain's side or hidden dell,
And not a classic spot, or fragment rude,
Or lettered plinth, but what in turn I viewed.
    Chance led me once, when idling through the street,
Beneath a porch my listless limbs to seat,
Where rudely heaped, some sculptured marbles lay,
Of pediments now crumbled to decay.
There the fallen building as I musing eyed,
Which meditation to the mind supplied,
And called me back to epochs now remote,
When Zeuxis painted and when Plato wrote,

490

500

510

520

530

540

550

Aloof my faithful Tartar waiting stood,
(Derwish Tahiri); for he understood
His master's fancies, and with naked blade,
The near approach of boorish men had staid.
Close to the spot a Grecian dwelling reared
Its modest roof. A courteous man appeared;
And, bowing low, with invitation pressed
To enter in, and on his sofa rest.
I crossed the threshold of the courteous man,
And smoked and chatted. Close by the divan   560
His son, as Eastern usages demand,
In modest attitude was seen to stand.
And smiling watched the signals of my will,
To pour sherbet, or the long *chibook* fill.
Grace marked his actions, symmetry his form;
His eyes had made an anchorite grow warm,
His long attire, his silken *anteri*,
Gave pleasing doubts of what his sex might be;
And who that saw him would perplexed have been,
For beauty marked his gender epicene.   570
    Day after day my visits I renewed,
His love with presents like a mistress wooed;
Until his sire with dreams of greatness won,
To be my page made offer of his son.
I took him in my train, with culture stored
His mind, and in it choice instruction poured;
Till like the maiden, who some budding rose
Waters with care and watches till it blows,
Then plucks and places it upon her breast,
I too this blossom to my bosom pressed.   580
    All ye who know what pleasure 'tis to heave
A lover's sigh, the warm caress receive
Of some fond mistress, and with anxious care
Watch each caprice, and every ailment share.
Ye only know hard it is to cure

The burning fever of love's calenture.
Come, crabbed philosophers, and tell us why
Should men to harsh ungrateful studies fly
In search of bliss, when e'en a single day
Of dalliance can an age of love outweigh!   590
How many hours I've sat in pensive guise,
To watch the mild expression of his eyes!
Or when asleep at noon, and from his mouth
His breath came sweet like odours from the south,
How long I've hung in rapture as he lay,
And silent chased the insect tribe away.
How oft at morn, when troubled by the heat,
The covering fell disordered at his feet,
I've gazed unsated at his naked charms,
And clasped him waking to my longing arms.   600
How oft in winter, when the sky o'ercast
Capped the bleak mountains, and the ruthless blast
Moaned through the trees, or lashed the surfy strand,
I've drawn myself the glove upon his hand,
Thrown o'er his tender limbs the rough capote,
Or tied the kerchief round his snowy throat.
How oft, when summer saw me fearless brave
With manly breast the blue transparent wave,
Another Doedalus I taught him how
With spreading arms the liquid waste to plough,   610
Then brought him gently to the sunny beach,
And wiped the briny moisture from his breech.
    Oh! how the happy moments seemed to fly,
Spent half in love and half in poetry!
The muse each morn I wooed, each eve the boy,
And tasted sweets that never seemed to cloy.
Let those, like Œdipus, whose skill divine
Can solve enigmas strange, unriddle mine.
How can two rivers from one fountain flow,
This salt, that fresh, and in two channels go?   620

Why one while would a living well-spring gush
Forth from my brain, and with pure waters rush
In copious streams to fertilize the rhyme,
Which haply yet shall life to later time?
And why, anon, like some Artesian fount
Would oozings foul e'en from my entrails mount,
Salacious, and in murky current wet
The urn beneath with interrupted jet?
    In Athens lived a widow poor and old,   630
Who once could boast of coffers filled with gold;
But when her husband died, misfortune came,
And left her nothing but her honest name,
With three young bantlings. 'Twas her lot to see
Their years and charms increase to puberty.
    Theresa, Catherine, and Marianne,
(For so their Christian appellations ran),
Had eyes like antelopes, with polished skins,   640
And that ingenuous modesty that wins
Men's admiration by no schooling taught,
And wields a sceptre which was never sought.
Much talk their beauty had in Athens made;
Like others I my court and homage paid;
For rich men find an access where they will.
Methought 'twere good my vacant hours to fill
In adoration at their beauty's shrine,
And if they yielding proved, to make them mine.
They proved but statues: rarely would their speech
Beyond a simple affirmation reach.
They never heard of Almack's, never knew
Whose play was damned, who made the last *debut*.
On Broadwood's keys, arranged in ivory row,
Their taper fingers never learned to go.
Bound in morocco, there no album lay
To register each poetaster's lay.
They read no page beyond the morning mass,

Spelt with the aid of some revered papas:
But, half reclined upon a low settee,
With naked feet, and waist from corset free,
Their joy was mocha's beverage to sip   660
From small finjans of Chinese workmanship,
Or count their rosaries in listless ease,
Whilst dying swains were sighing at their knees.
Felt I their charms?   I felt them not; for me,
They just sufficed to tune my poetry.
And though some leaf, which to the winds I cast   670
Might say Theresa all her sex surpassed,
I did as doctors do, who potions make,
Which they prescribe much oftener than they take;
Or as the preacher lauds the angels, more
To make his hearers than himself adore.
Women as women, me had never charmed,
And shafts that others felt left me unharmed.
    But thou, Giraud, whose beauty would unlock   680
The gates of prejudice, and bid me mock
The sober fears that timid minds endure,
Whose ardent passions women only cure,
Receive this faithful tribute to thy charms,
Not vowed alone, but paid too in thy arms.
For here the wish, long cherished, long denied,
Within that monkish cell was gratified.
And as the sage, who dwelt on Leman's lake,   690
Nobly his inmost meditations spake,
Then dared the man, who would like him confess
His secret thoughts, to say his own were less;
So boldly I set calumny at naught,
And fearless utter what I fearless wrought.
For who that's shrived can say he never slipped?
Had conscience tongues what back would go unwhipt?
    Is there an idiosyncracy prevails
In those whose predilection is for males?

And like the satirists, who gravely said,
"When wives are tiresome take a boy to bed."
Are female charms too feeble to resist
The rooted bent of the misogynist?
I know not; but from boyhood to the hour
Which saw my wish accomplished in that tower,
One thought undying ever would intrude
In pleasure's moments or in solitude.
So twigs, kept down by force, remount again,
So casks infected still their smell retain.   700
So needy spendthrifts, who are forced to pawn
Their goods and chattels, when their credit's gone,
From rooted instinct, where the brokers use
A double entrance, will the back one choose.
    Sometimes I sauntered from my lone abode
Down to the palace of the town waiwode.
Methinks I see him on his rich divan,
In crimson clad, a proud and lordly man.
An amber-headed pipe of costly wood
Adorned his hand: around kawasses stood.   710
A sable beard his gravity bespoke,
His measured words the silence rarely broke.
Beside him sat a boy of gentle mien,
In rich attire, in age about fifteen.
His red tarbúsh o'ertopped his jet black hair,
His cheeks were comely and his skin was fair.
His faultless form, in Grecian garments cloaked,
Thoughts more than mere benevolence provoked.
Not Ganymede, whose all bewitching shape,
Could in Olympus sanctify a rape.   720
Nor Ali, long the Moslem prophet's joy,
Bloomed with such graces as this Grecian boy.
Waiwode, this stripling was thy catamite,
And if by grave examples men do right
To mould their lives, say, Was my conduct weak?   730

Was it a crime to imitate him?   Speak.
Full well I know the answer; thou woulds't cry
Shun, shun the monster, from his presence fly.
Alas my friend, and whither should I go?
The self same usage reigns with high and low.
There's not an envoy our good king has sent   740
His royal majesty to represent;
To lay a snuff-box at the sultan's feet;
To coax, to lie, to threaten, or to treat;
But must have known that, from the Grand Signor
Down to the Tartar squatted at his door,
All drink alike from that forbidden spring,
And with reluctance wear Hans Carvel's ring.
Upon that altar friendship's vows are pledged;
There young ambition's soaring wings are fledged;
There the fond wife, whene'er the marriage rite   750
Palls on her husband's sated appetite,
The wily Parthian's stratagem has learned,
Most sure to vanquish when her back is turned.
For this the Mufti has no need to brave
The scoffer's jest or dread the judge's glaive;
And fearless of the Alcoran's rebuke,
O'er female tenderness would almost puke.
On Albion's chaster sod we never dare
Consort with such delinquents; nor so there.
    Come Malthus, and, in Ciceronian prose,   760
Tell how a rutting population grows,
Until the produce of the soil is spent,
And brats expire for want of aliment.
Then call on God his mercies to dispense,
And prune the mass by war and pestilence.
Arm with your sophistry oppression's hand,
And interdict coition through the land.
Poor fool! the ruddy milkmaid's blooming cheek
Can language stronger than your volumes speak.   770

E'en in the cot, where pinching want assails,
Love still finds time to tell his tender tales;
Or else, when ousted from his lawful bed,
Resorts to grosser substitutes instead.
    Economists, who seek the world to thin,
'Tis you that teach this so named deadly sin;
And the poor wretch, denied a wife's embrace,
Appeases nature in another place.
In sterile furrows why not sow his seed?
Why follow not the strict Malthusian creed?
The Scripture says, "increase and multiply."
Malthus cries "No," till doubt brings jeopardy.
    God, like the potter, when his clay is damp,
Gives every man, in birth, a different stamp.
Divergent tastes his appetites disclose;
These reason justifes, example those.
Adair delights his manhood to display
From window casements, and across the way
Woos some sultana's fascinated eyes,
Convinced the surest argument is size.
The reverend doctor, with a hernial taste,
Goes fastening trusses round a ruptured waist.
The Wadham fellow on a barber leers;
The bishop drills the foot guard grenadiers;
Bred in the poisoned atmosphere of courts,
Ernest, in youth, with maids of honour sports
Expert on levee days their rumps to pinch;
Then grown a whiskered roué every inch,
Tumbles the pillow of a sister's bed,
And trusts his secret only with the dead.
Too proud to tilt upon plebeian ground,
Of Norman blood a minion Beckford found;
But caught perchance, in some unseemly play,
Years have not served to wipe the stain away.
H—— D—— paws, and red-haired Charlton sips,

Tiptongued, the nectar from vaginal lips.
Some take a flogging, till the smart supplies
Incentives to their dormant energies.
Some hoary captains oft their yards have braced
Where Jean Secundus only basia placed;
For Mother Wood has maidens complaisant,
With mouth piece ready for each old gallant;
And Mother Windsor plies her dirty work,
To suit the taste of Hebrew, Greek, or Turk.
Professors there peep through the wainscot hole,
And watch the needle dipping at the pole.
Or nicely solve by observations found,
The problem of the oval and the round.
Some in the flask can give their prowess leaven;
Whilst some in corners make themselves a heaven.
The strumpet, Myrrha, steals by night, and stirs
Her sire to incest—Cenci poignards her's.
Dixie, to vengeance and to lust less prone,
Nor saves her father's honour nor her own.
A pair of breeches S—— and W——k shock,
They ask no joys beyond each other's smock.
Penelope, the model of a wife,
Grasps in her hand all night the staff of life,
And e'en in sleep to lose that bauble fears,
For which she sighed, a widow twenty years.
Lucretia drives a dagger to her heart,
Unwilling with her chastity to part.
The stern Virginius views his daughter dead
Unmoved, to save that film—a maidenhead;
Which modern virtue is so used to slight,
It hardly serves to make rich gudgeons bite.
For things when new, not always will command
A price as great as when they're second hand.
So good Cremona fiddles sell for more,
Which amateurs have played upon before.

So able navigators sail secure,
Where previous soundings make the passage sure.
Had Foote been prudish, nobody would meet
Her carriage rolling down St. James's Street.
Had Blessington resolved her charms to bring
Into the market for a wedding ring,
She now might toil an honest farmer's bride,
And one fair flower unseen had bloomed and died.
    Oh! England, with thy hypocritic cant,
To hear the bench declaim, the pulpit rant,   850
Who would not say that chastity's pure gems
Had shed their lustre o'er the muddy Thames?
That self condemned, decried, ineffable,
Innominate, this blackest sin of hell,
Had fled dismayed to some Transalpine shore,
To sully Albion's pudic cliffs no more?
    Marked you the thousand inkhorns that indite,
With ruthless glee the name of some poor wight,
By Bow Street bloodhounds to their Jeffreys brought,
With flap unbuttoned, in some tap-room caught?
Heard you the thousand post-horns that diffuse
The foul details, and pimp to lust for news?
Saw you the wealthy, who profusely dine
On viands rich; and o'er their evening wine,
With well-feigned horror prophecy his end,
Nor at his fate one saving accent lend?
Barbarians! know you whence his failings sprung?
Know you what Mentor tutored him when young?
Perhaps he scorned the maiden's troth to win,
And thought seduction was the greater sin;   870
Or feared the scald of that infectious taint,
Which makes a man or sodomite or saint.
Perhaps he was ill favoured, humpbacked, shy;
Or shunned the harlot's laugh and ribaldry.
He kept no miss to dandle on his knee,

Or could not pay a bed room at the Key.
This was his fault, to weigh with scales too nice
Between a heartless crime and harmless vice.
    Yes, London! all thy chastity is show;
Bear witness Vere Street and the Barley Mow.   880
Lives there a man, whate'er his rank may be,
Who now can say, my caste from stain is free?
Are you a soldier?   Pace the barrack room,
Just as the morning dawn dispels the gloom.
See where the huddled groins in hot-beds lie,
Each fit to be a garden deity.
Though all the Messalinas of the shire,
Devote their days and nights to quench the fire,
And misses club in every country town,
To keep the martial priapism down.   890
The fermentation still much scum supplies,
Which to the bunghole will o'erflowing rise.
Drummers may flog, judge advocates impeach,
The soldier's post is ever at the breach.
    Are you a sailor?   Look between the decks:
What sinews thewed are there! what sturdy necks!
Pent in their hammocks for a six months' cruise,
They dream of Portsmouth Point and Wapping stews.
No deep-sea lead, suspended from a weight,
Could keep their manhood in quiescent state:
Or if the urinary organs prest
By grog o'ernight, should interupt their rest,
Not all the founts that Marly's height supplies,
In surer perpendicular would rise.
The prurient mettle hot desire begets;
Their mouths delight in foulest epithets;
And that gross word, which crowns a seaman's phrase,   910
The latent thought if not the deed betrays.
At college bred, and destined for the church,
You turn a Busby, and you wield the birch.

320

Think you there's no incentive in the sight
Of sixth-form bottoms, naked, round, and white?
Ask Drury, Butler, sleek-gilled Goodenough,
How looks a kallipygic disk in buff?
Ask him of Eton, who if fame speaks true,
Made open boast he all his scholars knew
By their posteriors better than their face,
As most familiar with the nether place.
Flog, lechers, flog, the measured strokes adjust:
'Tis well your cassocks hide your rising lust.   920
Are you a senator? But come with me,
And seat yourself beneath the gallery.
Faugh! how the steams of fetid stomachs rise,
In belchings fresh brought down from Bellamy's.
Now look: those crowded benches contemplate,
Where legislators sit in grave debate.
They make our laws, and twist the hempen cord,
That hangs the pennyless and spares the lord.   930
Behold that shining forehead, scant of hair:
Our learned schools are represented there.
He moves his seat. His limping steps denote,
The gout has found a passage down his throat.
Yet judge not rashly; for his mind's a hoard,
With Bodley's tomes and Boyle's acumen stored.
Alas! the time shall come, when he, like me,
Shall fall a victim to foul calumny.
Then all his love of learning, all his worth,
The seat he holds by talent and by birth,
Shall count as dross; whilst basest rumours, spread
Folks care not how, shall light upon his head.
Then friends shall shun him, and a venal press
Shall seal in blackest types his wretchedness.
Whilst some false lawyer, whom he called his friend,
To damn his name his arguments shall lend.
Shall take a brief to make his shame more clear,

And drop his venom in a jury's ear.
But had that tongue with earnest friendship glowed,
His words had lighted, not increased the load;
Had poured a balmy unguent on his sore,   950
And chased mendacious slander from his door.
To uncorked hartshorn, when its odour flies
Forth from the phial, almost blinds the eyes;
But, if the stopper is replaced with care,
The scent diffused evaporates in air.
    Look at that row where elder Bankes is placed,
There sits a youth with courtly manners graced.
He fought his country's wars, and fixed his tent
Where Etna burns with fuel never spent.   960
'Twas there, where summer suns eternal beam,
And life's the doze of one delicious dream,
Where pleasure loves to twine her silken chains,
And builds her altars in a thousand fanes,
There, nursed by heated sap, new blossoms shot,
And the rich soil exotic fruit begot.
For there, e'en rivers in their course are found
To run not on the bosom of the ground.
But when from Alpheus Arethusa fled,   970
And, frighted, sought a subterranean bed,
Not face to face his stream with her's combined,
But mixed his nasty waters from behind.
Ah! youth beware! forget Trinacria's isle;
A deadly blight lies hid beneath her smile:
And when the day shall come (for come it will),
The honoured station, which in life you fill,
Will only add momentum to your fall,
And stain the scutcheon in your father's hall.
    Now turn your eyes athwart the speaker's chair: 980
A pious orator is seated there.
In vain the negro's cause he nightly pleads;
Tells how the gangrened back with lashes bleeds;

Delights with philanthropic zeal to rail,
And paint the horrors of the felon's jail,
Let but some knave vituperate his name,
Adieu to all his former well-earned fame!
An exile to a foreign land he'll fly,
Neglected live, and broken-hearted die.
    Britons! and will no penalty suffice,
Except the gibbet for a lecher's vice?
To lose his country, to behold the chain
That linked his best affections snapt in twain,
To find no refuge for his stricken head,
Wher'er he goes to know his shame is spread,
And is not this enough, without he's cast
By judge and jury? fiends would cry "Avast!"
Blot out the crimson leaf! the glaive forbear!
Count o'er the wretched victims of despair.
The panic flight, the suicidal beam,
The knife, the bullet, do they trifles seem?
Thirst ye for blood? and will no punishment,
But what Old Bailey metes, your hearts content.
Oh! Peel, for this nefarious deed alone,
Do what thou wilt, thou never canst atone.
Why blow the bubble of thy own repute
For laws amended. and on this be mute?
Mute! no, not mute; for heretofore there lay
A stumbling block in every jury's way;
But, Draco like, thou (gainsay who that can)
Didst add a clause to drown the sinking man.
Why were the listening Commons silent then?
Martin has mercy—yes, for beasts, not men;
And Brogden's modesty his voice impedes,
Who, when the sections of a bill he reads,
With furs of coneys, to a gentle hush
Subdues his tone, and feigns a maiden's blush.
But answer, Mackintosh; wert thou asleep?

Or was the tide of feeling at its neap?
Why gull the nation, with thy plans to mend
The penal code, in speeches without end,
And, like a jelly bag, with open chops,
Dwindle and dwindle into drizzling drops?
Who dreamt of witchcraft? antiquated theme,
And fall'n from long disuse in Lethe's stream,
Whilst every circuit death was riding post
With warrants, signed by Sidmouth o'er his toast
Was it to do thy native soil a turn,
Where hags are found yet weird enough to burn?
Or hadst thou learnt the Scotchman's wily tricks,
To make thy fortune by thy politics,
And meddled only with those points of law,
Which raise a talk, and matter not a straw?
    Statesmen, in your exalted station know
Sins of ommission for commission go;
Since ships as often founder on the main
From leaks unstopped as from the hurricane.
Shore up your house; it totters to the base;
A mouldering rot corrodes it; and the trace
Of every crime you punish I descry:
The least of all perhaps is sodomy.
    Close to the chair, where Sutton half the year
Counts Ayes and Noes to make himself a peer,
Behold yon reptile with his squinting eyes:
Him shall my curses follow till he dies.
'Twas he that plugged my Anabella's ears
With vile opinions, fallacies, and fears;
The richest treasure of my youth purloined,
And put asunder those whom God had joined.
Forgive these railings, much lamented bride!
Who said I wronged my Ada's mother lied.
Thee, whom remembrance, wheresoe'er I go,
Maketh a source of happiness and wo:

990
1000
1010
1020
1030
1050

Since, when dejected to the past I turn,
I fancy griefs like mine thine thy bosom burn.
For if the vows we plighted once were true,
So needs must be our mutual sorrows too.
    And are those happy days for ever fled!
Methinks 'twas yesterday, as both in bed
We lay: her cheeks were pillowed on my breast;
Fondly my arms her snowy bosom pressed.
Love no denial found, desire no stay.
That night it was, when tired of amorous play,   1060
She bade me speak of wonders I had seen
In cities where my wandering steps had been.
"Tell me," she said, "of strange and jealous men
"In secret harems who their consorts pen,
"Of bluebeard Turks on Ottomans reclined,
"And young sultanas to their will resigned."
And then she added, "Leon have a care;
"Say not we English ladies are so fair.
"Some Eastern maid has heard thy plighted vows."
"She was thy love, I'm nothing but thy spouse."
    The veil of night, that hid her blushing cheek,
Had made her bold to ask and me to speak:
And though her words but half her thoughts betrayed
I knew their drift, and thus my answer made:
"My tales, sweet Bell, will shock chaste ears like thine,
"The Moslem's wife is but a concubine.
"The nuptial night no altar sanctifies.
"No priest nor knot indissoluble ties,
"A marriage bond of half a dozen lines,   1080
"Short as a billet doux, the cadi signs,
"And from that hour, whate'er her lord may say,
"Or do, 'tis hers to honour and obey.
"For her 'tis true, the carpet spreads its flowers;
"For her the arbour twines its roseate bowers;
"For her the vase exhales its choice perfume;

"For her rich sofas cushion every room;
"Bazaars supply their muslin and brocade,
"And pearls of many a carats' worth are weighed.
"The jet black girl, from Darfur's burning sands,   1090
"Bear fragrant Moka to her lily hands;
"And slaves unnumbered all her wants supply,
"All, but that vital one of liberty.
"Ah! hopeless wish to see those doors unbarred,
"(Which lynx-eyed eunuchs, never dozing, guard)
"Save to a mother's or a sister's call,
"Or female guest on days of festival;
"Save when close muffled in her feridjee,
"She walks abroad her relatives to see,
"Or to the bath her weekly visit pays,   1100
"And pleased her jewels and her silks displays;
"Save when the araba, by oxen drawn
"Jolts her afield, where some secluded lawn
"Spreads its green sward, and no intruder checks,
"The harmless gambols suited to her sex.
    "Thus through the morn (for that at least is her's)
"She sits immured, or else well-guarded stirs.
"But, when the hour is on the noontide tick,
"Her Aga slowly quits the selamlik;
"The harem opens to his loud testoor;   1110
"Humbly she greets his entrance at the door,
"Serves him his pipe, and, crossing both her hands
"Before her waist, expects his stern commands.
"His dinner set, she like a menial waits,
"Watches his looks, his wants anticipates,
"Nor honoured sits beside him at his meat,
"Honour enough to see her husband eat!
    "Perhaps, if still her cheeks their bloom possess,
"He lets her sit—vouchsafes a cold caress,
"Or when the day is sultry, bids her chase   1120
"The gnats away, that buzz about his face.

"But ah! the worst remains behind to tell—
"How must her breast with indignation swell,
"To see that tenderness by marriage owed
"To her, upon a minion's form bestowed!
"Spurned from his couch, or with neglect dismist
"Another lip than her's, a boy's, is kissed;
"To him with ithyphallic gifts he kneels;
"And that bright spark, which from Sol's chariot wheels   1130
"Prometheus stole to animate our clay,
"He husbands not, but throws the boon away.
    "Dear Leon," interrupting here my tale,
My wife exclaimed, "can male then covet male?
"Can man with man hold intercourse of love,
"And mar the ends designed by God above?
    "Nay, Anna, hush! no falsehood I advance,
"Yet wonder little at thy ignorance.
"On maidens' shelves, with chastest volumes lined,
"Systems like these, perchance 'tis rare to find.
"But we, whose thirst of love no draughts appease,
"Exhaust the cask, and swallow e'en the lees;
"Watch proud philosophy in dishabille,
"Catch Parr with Meursius or with Fanny Hill;
"Stir up the ordure of the cynic's tub,
"And prove the sage a butterfly or grub.
"Know then that boys strung old Anacreon's lyre,
"That boys the sober Virgil's lines inspire.
"Catullus pours his elegiac strains,
"Soothed by the portrait of a stripling's reins;
"And" — "hold," she cried, "How little had I thought
"Catullus such abominations taught,
"That Virgil's swains beneath the shady beech
"In songs of lewdness dared the muse beseech.
"I oft have heard my venerable sire
"The ancients praise, their doctrines too admire;
"But, sure I am, such things he never read

"To dear mamma, unless it was in bed."
    That time it was, as we in parlance wiled
Away the hours, my wife was big with child.
Her waist, which looked so taper when a maid
Like some swol'n butt its bellying orb displayed,
And Love, chagrined, beheld his favourite cell
From mounds opposing scarce accessible.
"Look, Bell," I cried; "yon moon, which just now rose   1160
"Will be the ninth; and your parturient throes
"May soon Lucina's dainty hand require
"To make a nurse of thee, of me a sire.
"I burn to press thee, but I fear to try,
"Lest like an incubus my weight should lie;
"Lest, from the close encounter we should doom
"Thy quickened foetus to an early tomb.
"Thy size repels me, whilst thy charms invite;
"Then, say, how celebrate the marriage rite?
"Learn'd Galen, Celsus, and Hippocrates,
"Have held it good, in knotty points like these,
"Lest mischief from too rude assaults should come,
"To copulate ex more pecudum.
"What sayst thou, dearest?   Do not cry me nay;
"We cannot err where science shows the way."
    She answered not; but silence gave consent,   1180
And by that threshold boldly in I went.
So clever statesmen, who concoct by stealth
Some weighty measures for the commonwealth,
All comers by the usual door refuse,
And let the favoured few the back stairs use.
    Soon as the languor which our limbs o'erspread
Had ceased, I thus resumed the theme, and said
"Thou seest how Nature's operations tend,
"By various roads, to work one common end,   1190
"Just as a vessel, from opposing rhumbs,
"Though winds may vary, to her haven comes.

"But ah! thou little dream'st how wide her hand
"Has spread her gifts o'er Cytheria's land,
"Another path untrodden yet remains,
"Where pleasure in her close recesses reigns.
"The neophyte to that more hallowed spot
"But rarely ventures; 'tis the favourite grot
"Where sages, prelates, kings, and bards retire
"To quench the rage of Priapeian fire.
"How many view this grotto from afar,
"Whilst fear and prejudice the entrance bar!
"There fain the pedagogue's lewd glance would reach
"Through the convulsions of a schoolboy's breech.
"There as the youth with tightened pantaloons,
"Whirls through the dance in waltz or rigadoons,
"Or misses haunches wriggle in quadrilles,
"In thought the lecher his libation spills.
"There, as my lord, with achromatic glass,
"O'erlooks St. James's Park, and on the grass,
"Beneath his mansion's half-closed window spies
"Two crouching urchins' gross obscenities,
"He turns his eager gaze, adjusts the screw,
"And brings their unwashed nudities in view.
"That spot, concealed by two o'er hanging hills,
"Foul sweat and foetid excrement distils,
"Yet frowsy, there the pipe-clayed soldier sports,
"And bishops hold episcopalian courts.
"'Tis there the Bath empiric's finger guides,
"The oiled bougie; and as the dildo slides
"Besmeared, to meet last night's descending meal,
"Oft makes the strictures he pretends to heal.
"'Tis there Sir Astley, as his rounds he goes
"In Guy's sick wards, to gaping pupils shows
"How art can grope to find a schirrous gland,
"And in his cambric kerchief wipes his hand.
"But when ablution purifies its gates,

1200

1200

"And from within no odour emanates;
"Or when the bath its thermal waters lends
"The oppilated passages to cleanse,
"Its shade can e'en ambrosial gods delight,
"And make great Jove become a proselyte,
"Thus to the Cnidian Venus men inclined
"The knee, in homage to her parts behind;
"Despised her face, and greater pleasure found
"In buttocks smooth, protuberant, and round."
        "And thou, dear Anna, think'st thou I can see
"Without a longing, all these charms in thee?
"Thou'lt say the seed that useless there is spilt,
"Thwarts nature's purposes, and argues guilt.
"Thou'lt tell me how we God's commands defy,
"Who bade mankind increase and multiply.
"Vain fear! to fancy he bestows a thought
"What germ is fruitful, or what ends in naught.
"Else show me why, for nine long months thy womb
"Is closed; since there that germ would find a tomb.
"And were no foetus in it, still we know
"Those lenten days when women's courses flow.
"How oft in dreams, that ape the hour of bliss,
"Our passions wander, 'till we wake, and miss
"The lovely phantom clasp't in our embrace,
"And find a lost emission in its place.
"Then turn thee round, indulge a husband's wish,
"And taste with me this truly classic dish.
        "Who that has seen a woman wavering lie
"Betwixt her shame and curiosity,
"Knowing her sex's failing, will not deem,
"That in the balance shame would kick the beam?
"Ah, fatal hour, that saw my prayer succeed,
"And my fond bride enact the Ganymede.
"Quick from my mouth some bland saliva spread
"The ingress smoothed to her new maidenhead,

1220

1230

1250

The Thespian God his rosy pinions beat,
And laughed to see his victory complete.
'Tis true, that from her lips some murmurs fell—
In joy or anger, 'tis too late to tell;
But this I swear, that not a single sign   1260
Proved that her pleasure did not equal mine.
Ah, fatal hour! for thence my sorrows date:
Thence sprung the source of her undying hate.
Fiends from her breast the sacred secret wrung,
Then called me monster; and, with evil tongue,
Mysterious tales of false Satanic art
Devised, and forced us evermore to part.
    Pardon, dear Tom, these thoughts on days gone by: 1270
Me men revile, and thou must justify.
Yet in my bosom apprehensions rise,
(For brother poets have their jealousies),
Lest, under false pretences, thou should'st turn
A faithless friend, and these confessions burn.
Scott, you and I, rule o'er Parnassus now:
Who next may wear the laurels on their brow
I care not. To my country I bequeath
My works; posterity our crowns shall wreath,
Then why should malice vex us during life?   1280
Between us bards unseemly is the strife.
Why fight for fame? Thou hast not now to learn
On what small pivots empty honours turn.
We, paper kites, in vain essay to rise,
Unless some wind propels us to the skies.
Scott would have been plain, simple Walter still,
Had not a monarch smarted from my quill.
And, sick with spite, to give my rival fame,
Planted a Sir before his Christian name.
GEORGE little cared for Walter's doggrels; he,   1290
Exalting him, had hoped to lessen me.
Light paste makes puffs, but solid dough makes bread,

On that we cloy, on this are daily fed.
The fearless man, in conscious virtue clad,
Endures the persecution of the bad,
Pursues his road by envy's shafts assailed,
Nor reaps renown until his coffin's nailed.
    Then should you, tempted by some Lintol, print   1300
My strange career, allow one friendly hint.
Be true to nature; paint me as I am;
Abate no sin I had, no virtue sham;
Be simple in your style; for truth looks best,
Not spangled o'er with tropes, but plainly drest,
Shun meretricious ornaments; for why?
You've whored enough, men think, in poetry.
With judgment sound, unmoved by passion, write,
And leave to Rogers all an author's spite.
Yet not unsung be his and Southey's praise: 1310
Mine be the task their monuments to raise.
My verse shall live, more durable than brass,
And make their names to future ages pass.
    But, whilst St. Stephen's candles still give light,
Let us resume our seats. A luckless wight
Sits on the left, one rich in classic lore,
Who roamed, like me, strange countries to explore.
In Moslem lands, like me, long time he dwelt,
The subtil venom of their customs felt.
And could I, as the Pythoness of old,   1320
His morrow in these distichs rude unfold,
Nor warn in riddles understood too late,
Haply might I avert his future fate.
"Hearken, oh gifted youth!" (my voice should be)
"The Abbey walls reserve a niche for thee;
"And where to fame the great and good consign
"Their ashes, living thou shalt blazon thine."
    Portentous hour for him, who's doomed to feel
The iron grasp of some rude alguazil;

When through the streets the sanguinary crowd
Shall mouth their curses horrible and loud,
When e'en a father shall avert his face,
And fear to own his progeny's disgrace,
Then Peel, if conscience be not wholly dumb,   1330
Within thy bosom shall compunction come.
How shalt thou sorrow for the moment, when
A single scratch of thy reforming pen,
Had from our code erased a peccant lust,
And left its punishment to men's disgust.
Nor wilt thou pass that house without a pang,
Which erst with social joy and revels rang,
When rendered desolate by his disgrace,
Whose hand had helped to prop thy tottering place.
For think not, man, the speeches thou hast made,
And all thy frothy sophistry, has weighed
One single vote!   Their breaths 'twas filled thy sail,
Who threw their rotten boroughs in the scale.
Backed by Corfe Castles orators have sense,
And there find sinews for their eloquence!
    So stands a unit on a schoolboy's slate,   1350
A figure of no consequence or weight.
It cannot multiply, it can't divide;
But place some hollow zeros by its side,
And what alone for things of nothing tell,
By union into vast importance swell.
'Tis thus the bolstered minister requires
A row of booby lords and country squires,
To cry out "Aye" to every wicked law,
For every sop to sit with open maw.   1360
    Let my example one great truth unfold!
And in the mirror of my life behold
How foulest obloquy attends the good,

Whose words and deeds are never understood.
Oh! strange anomaly, that those should wage
War on my actions, who approve my page.
Whate'er I write, the town extols my song;   1370
Whate'er I do, the vulgar finds me wrong.
Their feelings are not mine; in vain they scoff:
I hate the vulgar, and I keep them off.
They've done their worst, and now I heed them not;
On me long since their farthest bolts were shot.
Admired and shunned, now courted, now contemned.
By many eulogized, by more condemned.
I stand a monument, whereby to learn
That reason's light can never strongly burn
Where blear-eyed prejudice erects her throne,
And has no scale for virtue but her own.
    That little spot, which constitutes our isle,   1380
Is not the world!   Its censure or its smile
Can never reason's fabric overthrow,
And make a crime what is not really so.
The willing maid who plights her marriage vows,
Owes blind obedience to her lawful spouse.
Flesh of his flesh, and knitted bone to bone,
As in a crucible two metals thrown,
The ores commixt, but one amalgam form,
And fuse more sure the more their natures warm.
At Hymen's altar mystery presides,
Spreads her dense veil, and in oblivion hides,
The sacred orgies of the nuptial bed,
Where timid nymphs to sacrifice are led.   1390
    God of the universe, whose laws shall last,
When Lords and Commons to their graves have past,
Are good and evil, just as man opines,
And kens he thy inscrutable designs?
Love, like the worship which to thee is paid,
Has various creeds by various nations made:

One holds as dogmas what the other mocks;
That schism here which there is othodox.
Some mode of faith finds favour in your eyes,
But must you, therefore, damn my heresies?
Behold two nooks obscure, where, side by side,   1040
His feathered pinions Cupid loves to hide.
What! if the little urchin I pursue,
As fancy guides, in either of the two,
'Tis hard to say why erring mortals think
This fount is pure, and that unfit to drink;
And still the more the problem I revolve,
The more I find it difficult to solve.
When laws are made, which common sense decries,
Inert, they prove no bugbear to the wise.
Philosophy the wiles of priestcraft scans,   1410
And shows what code is God's, and what is man's.
Does not the gunner, who his mark would reach,
First load the muzzle, and then prime the breach?
Boys, tickled by the tail in wisdom grow,
And by their tails bashaws their honours show.
Health through the tail by doctors is infused,
And to a bum debts seldom are refused.
Amidst the firmament when comets sail,
Where are our eyes directed?—on its tail.   1420
The ship goes better with the wind astern;
The horse well figged appears the ground to spurn;
The learned student, poring o'er his books,
Like one absorbed in gravest study looks;
Yet, mark him well! and sometimes I'll engage,
His finger's on the bottom of a page.

Women and watches have one common power;
We look on both their faces by the hour;
Hung round our necks, their hands in secret move
In parts, where most we warm emotions prove:
Both are wound up at night—the watch behind;   1430
But where you place the key to womankind,
Divulge it not, lest Lushington should know,
And fill your cup with calumny and woe.
   Look through the world! whatever mortals do,
They still must keep their latter end in view—
Not death; for that let bloated parsons quail:
Our latter end—what is it, but our tail?
Where honour, sensitive, a shelter seeks,
Whose mouth in oracles to physic speaks;
Whose voice can soothe a rumbling belly's moan,   1440
And, conscience like, is loudest when alone;
Whose motions imperceptibly controul
The energies of body and of soul.
Health, ease, and honour centre in that spot,
But, at the risk of life, approach it not.
Oh, glorious privilege of kings! in this,
That they alone can give the part to kiss.
   Once these were epigrams to raise a laugh:
The world is grown too scrupulous by half.
Deprived through life of fundamental joys,   1450
Things can no longer find their equipoise.
Closed is the Cnidian temple, and we see
Writ on its walls "*Hic nefas mingere.*"

THE END

NOTES TO DON LEON,*
AN EPISTLE TO THOS. MOORE,
BY THE RIGHT HON. LORD BYRON.
Author of Childe Harold, Don Juan, *&c. &c.*

Note 1, Line 1.
"Thou ermined judge, pull off that sable cap!"

In reading the opening of this poem, it would almost seem that the author of it had in his eye Mr. Justice Park, were it not that the supposed date of the poem would imply an anachronism. In the Courier, of August 1833, and the Chronicle of the same month and year, we read "Captain Henry Nicolas Nicholls, who was one of the unnatural gang to which the late Captain Beauclerk belonged, (and which latter gentleman put an end to his existence), was convicted on the clearest evidence at Croydon, on Saturday last, of the capital offence of Sodomy; the prisoner was perfectly calm and unmoved throughout the trial, and even when sentence of death was passed upon him. In performing the duty of passing sentence of death upon the prisoner, Mr. Justice Park told him that it would be inconsistent with that duty if he held out the slightest hope that the law would not be allowed to take its severest course. At 9 o'clock in the morning the sentence was carried into effect. The culprit, who was fifty years of age, was a fine looking man, and had served in the Peninsular war. He was connected with a highly respectable family; but, since his apprehension not a single member of it visited him."

Mr. Justice Park might not have remained long enough at Croydon to see the poor man hanged, but, if he did, his peep out of the window at the gallows would have been any thing but agreeable.

Note 2, Line 16.
"Till thou didst send thy myrmidons to prowl."

Two persons, James Bryan and Frederick Symonds, who were recently apprehended in Hyde Park, for indecent practices, were yesterday tried at the Westminster Sessions. It was proved that the police disguised themselves on the occasion, &c. &c. *Sun, April 29th,* 1830.

In the case of an information, in the beginning of the year 1825, before a magistrate who presided on the S. side of the river, a scheme was devised under his immediate direction, whereby a lad, who alleged that he had been tampered with in the streets, for the gratification of what is called abominable lusts, was taught how he should deliberately lead his seducer into the snare, which was to be set for him, and how, just when his seducer's breeches were unbuttoned, he was to make a signal, by which a police officer, planted for the unworthy purpose, was to take him in a state of unequivocal delinquency. The plot succeeded, and the magistrate had the pleasure of beholding in the gentleman who was brought before him, one whom he knew, and who, in the common acceptation of the word, was a friend. The reward of his over done vigilance was to have blasted the reputation of that individual for life, and to have plunged an innocent wife and family into the deepest distress.

A plot somewhat similar was also concocted against Mr. Muirhead to whom a mere hint thaat his proceedings were watched would have been sufficient for the purpose of moral decorum, and have saved that publicity by which thousands of girls and boys were informed of the existence of obscene manœuvres of which they were totally ignorant.

Note 3, Line 36.
"Who e'en to Clogher a pardon would refuse?"

In the *Times*, of January 2, 1844, appeared the following paragraph, extracted from the *Scotchman* of the preceding Saturday, relative to the individual named above.

* The discrepancies between the text and the Notes for *Don Leon* are faithful to the original volume from which these were reproduced. Likewise, typographical errors that appeared in the original have been retained.

"A person died here a short time since, who obtained an unenviable celebrity more than twenty years ago. This was the bishop of Clogher, who was indicted for an unnatural crime committed in St. James's, London, (at the St. Alban's Tavern, Charles Street, Haymarket, in the year 1822,) forfeited bail, and fled, was degraded from his ecclesiastical dignity, and has never been heard of until now. He kept house, under the assumed name of Thomas Wilson, at No. 4, Salisbury Place, Edinburgh, to which he removed four years ago, having previously resided at Glasgow. His mode of living was extremely private, scarcely any visitors being known to enter his dwelling; but it was remarked that the post occasionally brought him letters, sealed with coronets. His *incognito* was wonderfully preserved; it was only known to one or two individuals in the neighbourhood, who kept the secret until after his death.

Note 4, Line 58.
"Than all the pious tracts of Rivington."

In the preceding lines two things occur to make the reader ascribe this epistle, or the outline of it, to some correspondent of Mr. Thomas Moore's. If we could suppose for a moment that the poetry is worthy of Lord Byron, then we might conjecture that a letter written from Ravenna, September 3, 1831, makes some allusion to this very epistle. Lord B. says (Moore's Life, vol. IV., page 175.) "I yesterday expedited to your address, under cover, one or two paper books, containing the *Giaour-nal* and a thing or two." The journal, no doubt, was the M.S. which Mr. M. thought proper to burn; or was it this epistle?

[Or, if the gift was made at an earlier period, it may be that which Moore alludes to in a letter to Samuel Rogers, Paris, December 23, 1819. (See vol. VIII, Memoirs of Thomas Moore, by Lord John Russell.)

Lord John has, I suppose, told you of the precious gifts Lord Byron made me, at Venice—his own Memoirs, written up to the time of his arrival in Italy.]

Note 5, Line 124.
"Of that damned sin, the church's rubrick bilked."

Hume makes an observation to the same effect, (Note B. ch., ii., History of England.) "If Edwy says he, speaking of the marriage of Edwy and Elgiva, had only kept a mistress, it is well known that there are methods of accommodation with the church, which would have prevented the clergy from proceeding to such extremities against him; but his marriage, contrary to the canons, was an insult to their authority, and called for the highest resentment."

Note 6, Line 146.
"The object changed, but not the sentiment;"

It does not follow as a natural consequence that pœderasts are mysogynists, or that a culpable indulgence in inclinations for the one sex argues an insensibility to the charms of the other. Theodore Beza, himself, in his youth and before he bcame a father of the church and one of the pillars of the protestant faith, addressed some lines to his beloved *Candia,* in which we find the following phrase—
"Amplector hunc et illam."
In a dialogue to be found in Plutarch (Morals, vol. 8, edit. 1718), one of the disputants is made to say "Where beauty tempted him the sex was a matter of indifference to him, for there was no reason why a sensible man should be tied down to the parts only which distinguish the sex."

Here is a little *post mortem* scandal by way of revenge:—

"As we were crossing the Apennines he told me that he had left an order in his will that Allegra, the child who soon after died, his daughter by Miss C., should never be taught the English language. You know that Allegra was buried at Harrow; but probably you have not heard that the body was sent over to England in two packages, that no one might suspect what it was."

Note 7, Line 137.
"What though my verse in Mary's praises flowed."
Afterwards Mrs. Musters, Byron's first love.

———

Note 8, Line 151.
"With thee, dear Margaret, whose tender looks."
Margaret Parker is the young lady here meant. Lord Byron, in one part of his correspondence, (vol. 1. page 46., Moore's Life,) says "I have reason to know she loved me."

———

Note 9, Line 173.
"Yes, R...sh...n, though to unobserving eyes,'
Robert Rushton, see Moore's Diary, vol. V. page 247, Jan. 21, 1828, "Had some conversation after breakfast with Rushton (the Robin of Childe Harold), who now is master of a free school some miles off."
There is also mention made by Moore of another cottage boy, near Newstead, for whom Lord B. had an early predilection. See Moore's Life of Byron.

———

Note 10, Line 226.
"And could it be so violent, yet pure?
Speaking of his infatuation for this chorister, Lord Byron calls it "A violent, though pure love and passion." Moore's Life, vol. 1, page 312.

———

Note 11, Line 266.
"The code of love, thou hadst my sympathies;"
Ovid appears to have been generally orthodox in his amours, not because he imagined for a moment that there was any sin in cohabiting with boys, but because the enjoyment with women seemed to him to be less selfish since it was mutual.
"Odi concubitus qui non utrumque resolvunt;
Inde fit ut pueri tangar amore minus."

———

Note 12, Line 271.
"I love a youth;—but Horace did the same;"
Horace's inclinations may be gathered from his odes,
"Nunc gloriantis quamlibet mulierculam
Vin ere mollitie,
Amor Lycisci me tenet."
Lyciscus was a boy.
And again,—
"Amore, qui me proter omnes, expetit
Mollibus in pueris
. . . . . urere."
He paints the lubricity of his country, and his own, in these two lines,
"Presto puer, impetus in quem
Continuo fiat."

———

Note 13, Line 280.
"Could print their kisses on some favoured youth?
Castiglione, in his Corteggiano, in confirmation of some assertion that he makes, says "I am more certain of that, than you, or any one else, can be, that Alcibiades rose from the bed of Socrates as sons rise from the beds of their fathers, for night was a strange time, and bed a strange place, for contemplating that pure intellectual beauty, which it is said, Socrates loved independent of any improper desires. And it is strange too, that loving especially the beauty of the mind more than the body, he should have sought for it in boys, and not in old men who are certainly the most wise of the two."

———

Note 14, Lines 305, 306.
"Look how infected with this rank disease,
Were those who held St. Peter's holy keys."
Dante, when he visits hell, finds a great portion of it set apart for pœderasts. He spies out among them his own preceptor, and accosts him with *Siete voi qui, Ser Brunetto?* He then asks him who his companions principally were. The preceptor answers—
Il tempo saria corto à tanto suono,
In somma sappi, che tutti fur cherci,
E letterati grandi e di gran fama.
                DELL INFERNO, Cant xv. juxta finem.

In confirmation of the truth of what Dante here asserts, the reader is referred to the Decameron of Boccaccio (2 Nov. First day) to the Histoire des Papes (4to á la'Haye 1733), vol. 11, p. 48, p. 371, p. 435, and p. 599.

"In the year 1120, when William, son of Henry I. was drowned, on his return home from France, some authors represent his untimely end as a judgment on him and his followers for being contaminated, among other vices, with an unnatural one, which had been first introduced by the crusaders."

William son of Henry drowned off Boulogne, see History of England. Also for Charles II., see Pepys's Diary, 27th July, 1667, where he says "He tells me that the King and Court were never in the world so bad as they are now, for gaming, swearing, women and drinking, and the *most abominable vices,* that ever were in the world."

Note 15, Line 313.
"How many captains famed for deeds of arms."
Ld. Col. Maitland.   Sir Eyre Coote.   Julius Cesar. &c., &c.

Note 16, Line 331.
"Harassed by doubts, I threw my book aside."
"It has been too much the custom with such modern writers as have expressly discoursed on antiphysical propensities, or have incidentally mentioned them, to couple them only with the vices of a Tiberius, a Nero, a Caligula, or a Heliogabalus, endeavouring to disguise or conceal from their readers this important truth, that the virtuous, the brave, the generous and the temperate, have equally sympathised in the same predilection and that, if such examples can stamp any disordinate inclination as praiseworthy, it will be in the reader's recollection that many such men have been avowedly and notoriously slaves to it." This remark is taken from *A Free Examination into the Penal Statutes,* xxv. Hen. VIII., c. 6, and v. Eliz. c. 17, a book which we recommend all persons to peruse, if they can get it, for it is become very scarce. From this work is appears that among the Romans, ridiculous as it may appear, there was a law in force, which forbad arsenerasty. It was called *Lex Scantinia* or *Scatinia.* There are two accounts of this law, some say it was Scatinius Aricinus, a tribune of the people, who first caused it to be passed, whilst others suppose it to be called Lex Scantinia, and not Scatinia, from one Scatinius, against whom it was first put into execution. It was particularly levelled at the keepers of catamites and at such as prostituted themselves for the service. (*Quintilian,* 1. v. c. 2, and lib. vii. c. 4.) The penalty enjoined by the framer of it was only pecuniary; but Augustus Cœsar made it capital. (JUST. Inst. l iv.) This serves to add another trait to the hypocrisy of that emperor. It is hardly possible to imagine how he could meddle with this law, except to repeal it, when those Romans, in whose society he delighted to pass his hours, could have made no secret of their predilection for the male sex in their amours, since one of them, Horace was daily addressing his erotic productions to the beautiful boys whom he, in common with the rest, courted and idolised. (Id. p. 15)

This *Lex Scantinia* was also called *Lex Julia,* and is the same to which Sir Walter Scott, in his novel, entitled Kenilworth, alludes, c. viii. v. 2, when Michael Lambourne calls Demetrius Doboobie 'The infractor of the Lex Julia." Sir Walter more than once gives intimation of his having read and reflected a good deal on the subject of pœderasty. Thus in chaper viii. of the same volume he makes Michael use the word *ingle* to imply that this abomination had existed between him and Foster, the puritan.

That this law was subsequently repealed or became obsolete, we learn from the Theodosian Code (9. viii. 6.) which mentions as things tolerated *Lupanaria puerorum patientiumque exoletorum*—brothels for handsome boys and ingles.

Note 17, Line 357.
"Perhaps by night they share each other's bed."
The ancients had resort to contrivances for preserving chastity even in boys. Celsus describes them,—One was the *fibula*, a mode of "ringing" the prepuce, and thus preventing not only coition, but even masturbation. Med. vii. 25.

Infibulation or *ringing* of females is a usage of the highest antiquity. The ring was passed through the labia.

The same end is partially obtained by another method, still used in France. A waistcoat with sleeves closed at the ends, after the manner of those made for lunatics, is put on boys and girls on going to bed, and the cuffs of the sleeves are tied together, and to the neck with tapes, which admit only of extension of the arms, just enough to scratch the nose or to reach half way down the body.

Note 18, Lines 377, 378.
"Shut, shut your eyes, ye pedagogues, nor keep
Too close a watch upon your pupils' sleep."
From the Times, 1850.
ROYAL MILITARY ACADEMY.

WOOLWICH, OCT. 10.
Major-General J. Boteler Parker, C.B. Lieutenant-Governor of the Royal Military Academy, Woolwich, has issued an order, of which the following is a copy:—
"ORDERED BY THE LIEUTENANT-GOVERNOR.
"Royal Military Academy, Woolwich, Oct. 7.
"The unprecedented occurrences of 10 cadets being, by the minute of the Master-General of the 20th ult., removed from the Royal Military Academy, appears to the Lieutenant-Governor to call for a slight remark or two, principally to quiet the feelings of all interested in the reputation of the establishment.
"It having come to the knowledge of his Lordship the Master-General that certain obscene habits and practices had most unfortunately been introduced into the Ordnance School at Carshalton, his Lordship instituted a committee to proceed there and examine evidence, the result of which is most calamitous, and has ended in the removal of many of the pupils as well as the 10 cadets lately admitted from that school.
"It cannot fail to satisfy any one capable of forming an opinion that the Master-General, in coming to this determination, has evinced the utmost jealousy for the reputation of this academy by cutting off all sorts of contamination,
"This severe but just measure will, it is believed, give confidence to the parents and friends of boys remaining in the school, and be the most effectual method of restoring the reputation and moral character of the establishment."

Note 19, Line 385.
"Harrow, thy hill unblemished had remained."
Some twenty years ago (it being now 1842) an allusion was made in the public papers to certain rumours which had spread about concerning the unnatural propensities of the boys in Harrow school. November 15th, of this year, a paragraph appeared in the *Times* newspaper, headed Miscreants, wherein it was distinctly stated that the youths of the Harrow and Sandhurst schools had been tampered with, not unsuccessfully, for the indulgence of criminal passions by Mr. Patrick Leith Strachan, residing at 65, Quadrant. For more of this see Galignani's Messenger, of November 18, of the same year.

And that which is said of Harrow, no doubt has occurred in other schools. Thus in the SUN of October 3, 1842, we read "Edward George Caston, school master of Wivenhoe, was apprehended on Tuesday last at Ipswich, on several charges of abominable character. The offences were alleged to have been perpetrated on pupils under his care.

On Wednesday the prisoner underwent an examination. Only one case was gone into, the details of which are too gross for publication, and the prisoner was committed for trial."

Note 20, Line 397.
"And death deprived me of my Eddleston,"
This was the youth's name and I have put it at full length, although in the printed work the letters E.....n are only used. He died in 1811. Stanza ix. of Canto 11. Childe Harold is addressed to his memory.

Note 21, Line 432.
"As does in Christian lands the courtezan."
Prostitution is the act of a person towards him or herself, or rather it is the disposal of his or her own body, which no one has a right to contest. Therefore, so long as the use of this liberty injures the rights of no one else, and causes not great and public scandal, prostitution comes not within the pale of the law."

Encycl. Method. v. x., p. 678.

Note 22, Line 449.
"While gazing sits the hoary sybarite."
Such houses are constantly open at Constantinople, as any one knows who has been there; and it was customary, twenty years ago, (i.e. in the beginning of the nineteenth century,) for all English travellers, who visited that city, to be conducted to them as to one of the curious sights of that metropolis. It is not wonderful that therefore that Lord Byron went, and it is probable that Mr. John Cam Hobhouse went with him; for in conversation with Moore, (see *Memoirs of Thomas Moore,* vol. viii., p. 347) Hobhouse said, "I know more of Byron than any one else, and much more than I should wish any body else to know.' Hobhouse's nervousness on one occasion when the subject of Byron's Life to be written by Moore, was under discussion, seems also to have reference to some such feeling. See Moore's Diary.

Among the ancient Romans there were *lupanaria, ganeœ* and *fornices,* all places of the same sort and filled with young persons of both sexes, but kept in separate rooms, the girls appearing in boys clothes, and the boys assuming the habiliments of women. Nothing was more common than for the Roman citizens to frequent these brothels.

As a note to the word *monstrous,* a few lines lower down, I would add, that in Constantinople, female prostitutes, when their doings are too flagrant, are put into a sack and thrown into the Bosphorus; but the pœderasts and catamite have the sanction of the police. How differently do magistrates in Galata and in Bow Street act in such cases!

"The modern Greeks, as living under the Government of the Turks, naturally follow their usages. If therefore they indulge in antiphysical pleasures, it might be said that they owe it to the example of their masters; however in a Greek grammar, printed at Vienna some years ago, there are some *Golden Rules for Youth, by Phocylides,* in hexameter verse, in which there is a line shewing that the thing at least was spoken of familiarly to and before young persons, and seems to have been forbidden in the same strain as we are accustomed to hear fornication forbidden, and probably with about the same effect."

Free Examination into the Penal Statutes, (p. 671.) *by A. Pilgrim.*

Note 23, line 604.
"And clasped him waking to my longing arms."
Dr. Frazer, in his *Travels in Khorasan,* speaking of the *Soofies,* a fraternity of Mahometan enthusiasts, says (p. 567), "Meerza Selim told me that he once conceived so strong an attachment for a boy, that he would sit for hours gazing on him, playing with his hands, or kissing his feet. At night he would put him on his own bed, and watch by the side of him, sometimes sighing or bursting into tears, and occasionally stealing a kiss."

Martial, in a strain equally animated, says—"The kisses of my boy are sweeter than any perfumes, more fragrant than flowers, more precious than pearls, and more delicate than the caresses of any girl. In a word, nothing singly can describe them; mix together the things most delicious in nature, and these combined will be like the morning kisses of him I love."

Note 24, line 614.
"Another Dedalus, I taught him how
With spreading arms the liquid wave to plough."
"His (Lord Byron's) early youth in Greece, and his sensibility to the scenes around him, when resting on a rock in the swimming excursions he took from the Piræus, were strikingly described" (*i.e.* in the burnt biography).—DIARY OF THO. MOORE, p. 192, vol. iv.

Note 25, line 665.
"From small Fingans of Chinese workmanship."
Fingans are small coffee cups.

Note 26, line 676.
"Women as women, me had never charmed."
The stories which were current up the Archipelago about Lord Byron's amours, seem to have originated in reports spread by his Greek servants, who, finding how eagerly every tale respecting his lordship was listened to by travellers and naval officers, may possibly have added this to the number. Two of these servants were named *Demetrius* and *Basilius,* and the latter afterwards set up as a watchmaker at Cyprus. One of Basilius's stories was that Lord B. consulted an English doctor who was passing through Athens at the time of his lordship's sojourn there, touching a relaxation in the *sphincter ani* with which the boy Giraud was troubled. The disease of a ragged fundament, arising from the frequent distension of the *podex* in antiphysical concubinage, was frequent among the ancient Greek and Roman *cinœdi,* and the city of Clazomenæ, in Ionia, notorious for this species of debauchery, became a synonymous expression with it. To have the clazomenæ was to have what the Italians now-a-days call *fichi.*

Note 27, line 678.
"But thou, Giraud, whose beauty would unlock."
G . . . . d means Nikolaki, or Nicholas Giraud, the son of the "courteous man" mentioned a few lines back. Moore speaks of him in Byron's Life, v. 1, p. 312.

Note 28, line 684.
"For here the wish, long cherished, long denied,
Within that monkish cell was gratified."

"There is a moment we may plunge our years,
In fatal penitence."
CHILDE HAROLD, c. iii., st. 70.

Note 29, line 733.
"Waywode! this stripling was thy catamite."
The late Lord Plymouth, who was at Athens when Lord B. was there, used to speak of these visits to the governor of Athens, and to mention the presence of this minion as a matter that seemed to be of ordinary occurrence, and that excited no remark, except among the English and French who were sojourning in that city at the time.

Note 30, line 774.
"Or else when ousted from his lawful bed,
Resorts to grosser substitutes instead."
"The Rev. Mr. Malthus is not the first political economist who had thought that a too numerous population might prove injurious to a commonwealth. We read in Aristotle (Pol. 1. ii., c. 8) that Minos made a law which compelled married persons in Crete

to discontinue cohabiting with each other after a certain time, lest too many children should over populate the islands; but the same law permitted arsenerasty as an equivalent for the privations which it imposed."

PENAL STATUTES, 25 Hen. 3, by A. PILGRIM.

Note 31, line 788.
"Adair delights his manhood to display."

The following anecdote is derived from a foreign ambassador's lady, who resided with her husband a long time near Portman-square. Sir Robert Adair, whilst he was ambassador at Constantinople, is known to have carried on an amorous parley across the street with a Greek lady by dumb signs; a significant one was the display of his pœnis in a plate on the sill of the window. It was supposed, as the Greek women have latticed windows as well as the Turkish, and dare not be seen openly looking out, that some one had taken, unobserved, the lady's place, and afterwards divulged the ambassador's innocent practices; for the circumstance was very generally spoken of in the diplomatic circles at the Porte.

Note 32, line 797.
"Bred in the poisoned atmosphere of courts,
Ernest in youth with maids of honour sports."

The story of the Duke of Cumberland's having got his sister, the Princess Sophia, with child is perfectly true. What first led to a discovery was the giving a thousand pounds to the people (a tailor, I believe, at Weymouth, or somewhere near) where they placed the child at nurse; this awakened inquiry, and blew everything. The queen gave them some reason for their conduct, for she was dreadfully severe to the princesses, and shut them up in a sort of prison.

The royal duke and his sister, whose unfortunate attachment made such a noise about three or four years ago, might have found many parallel cases in history. " 'Scay-je bein toute-fois, qu'elle ajouta tost après à ses sales conquestes ses jeunes freres." This is said of Marguerite, Queen of Navarre. (See Journal de Hen. III., by de l'Estoille, vol. 1, p. 174.) Sauval, speaking of the same princess, affirms "Non selement elle anima tous ses freres, mais, &c." (Mem. Hist. et secr. concernant les amours des Rois de France, p. 101). The confession of Monseigneur d'Espignac, archbishop of Lyons, is curious, as given in the Memoires de Daubigné.

> "Je suis né à l'inceste, et, dès mon première age,
> J'ai de ma belle sœur abusé longuement:
> Puis avec ma sœur je couche maintenant,
> Ayant à cet effet rompu son marriage."

Note 33, line 801.
"And trusts his secrets only to the dead."

The story of Sellis, said to have committed suicide in St. James's Palace, is here alluded to.

Note 34, line 803.
"Of Norman blood a minion Beckford found."

Mr. Beckford, when he reached manhood, was pronounced to be one of the most promising young men in England. Lord Courtenay, then about seven years old, was on a visit with his sisters at Mr. Beckford's house, and having been missed one evening from his bedroom, search was made after him, and, some suspicion being excited, persons in the house went into Mr. Beckford's bed-room, and found Lord Courtenay in bed with him. The king wanted to hang them both; but the relations of the parties, who had great parliamentary interest, threatened to oppose the king's measures if he did; and so Mr. B. was desired never to go beyond the walls of Fonthill, and never to speak to any nobleman; and that is the reason why, for a number of years, no nobleman ever saw the inside of Fonthill Abbey.

Note 35, line 810.
"Some hoary captains oft their yards have braced,
Where Jean Secundus only Basia placed."

It may be gathered from a perusal of the ancient classic authors that antiphysical lusts were named with a precision unknown to our language. Where, indeed, is the equivalent in English for the word *irrumatio,* which designate's Nestor's and Priam's failing, if we may believe Juvenal (Sat. 6).

"Quibus incendi, jam, frigidus œvo,
Laomedontiades, et Nestoris hernia possit."

and is the last resort for debauchery. Suetonius relates of Tiberius, that "Pronior erat ad id genus libidinis" (irrumationem scilicet) "et naturâ et ætate." (Tib. 44). Calda Vetustillæ nectibi bucca placet. (Mart. ii., 28). Such women were called at Rome *Fellatrices* and *Labdæ.* When men lent themselves to such abominations towards their own sex (which they did) they were *fellatores,* towards women *liguratores* or *cunnilingi.*

"Quid cum fæminio tibi, Bœtice Gallo, barathro?
Hœc debet medios lambere lingua viros."

[Mart. iii, 81.]

"Labda, the same as fellatrix, is derived from *labia dare.* Cui ipse linguam quam dedit suam, labda est."

ANSON, Epig. cxix., 8.

"Lesbiantes enim id est, tenta virorum vorantes, alba sib labra reddebant; ut rubra, Phænicissantes.

Parrhasuis, the celebrated painter, represented Atalanta in this attitude with Meleager, and Tiberius hung the picture up in his bed-room. [See Suetonius Vitâ Tiberii.]

It is recorded of the great Captain Gonsalva, that he kept a young mistress for the sole purpose of such an unsoldierlike gratification.

Note 36, line 821.
"While some in corners make themselves a heaven."

These persons were called *masturbatores,* but if they complaisantly did the same office for another (which was a trade in Rome) they were named *deglubatores.*

Note 37, line 822.
"The strumpet Myrrah steals by night, and stirs
Her sire to incest."

Incest was common enough at Rome. Suetonius, speaking of Nero, says, "Olim etiam, quoties lecticâ veheretur cum matre, libinatum incesté ac maculis vestem proditum affirmant."

"Prædicabat (Caligula) matrem suam ex incesto, quod Augustus cum Julia filiâ commisisset, procreatam."

SUET.

In Henderson's "Biblical Tour in Russia," in his account of the Polish Jews we find these words, "It is not rare among these Jews for a father to choose for a wife for his son some young girl who is personally to his (own) taste, and with whom he lives in criminal intimacy during the minority of the young husband." Pericles cohabited with his son's wife.

Brantôme has some anecdotes on this subject; here is one: "J'ai ouy parler aussy d'un grand seigneur estranger, lequel, ayant une fille des plus belles du monde, et estant recherchée en marriage d'un autre grand seigneur qui la meritoit bien, luifut accordée par le père; mais avant qu'elle sortit jamais de la maison il en voulut taster; disant qu'il ne voulait laisser si aisément une si belle monture, qu'il avoit si curieusement` eslevée, que premierement il n'eut monté dessus, et sçeu ce qu'elle auroit sçeu faire à l'advenir."

Keating, in his "Narrative of an Expedition to the source of St. Peter's River," 1825 (p, 112, v. 1) relates that, among the tribe of the Potawatami Indians, one Wagakenagon married his mother-in-law, previous to which he had cohabited with two of his daughters. Both the women openly confessed their guilt, but with very little appearance of shame.

The disposition to similar licentiousness does not seem to be wanting in England, were it not repressed by punishment and the disgrace attached to it. In spite, however, of both, the newspapers abound from sessions to sessions with examples as gross as any that ancient history or savage life can furnish us with.

EXTRAORDINARY OCCURRENCE.
(From the *Bradford Observer*.)

The quiet village of Horbury, near Wakefield, has been thrown into a state of great excitement by a painful occurrence that has come to light within the last week. An independent gentleman of the name of Craven lived in the village in respectable style. He was a bachelor, and a young lady lived with him as housekeeper, who was known as Miss Craven, and was reputed to be his natural daughter. In the middle of last week a report prevailed that this young person had given birth to a child, which had been made away with, and that the body had been found buried in the plantation belonging to the house. The report was, of course, not long in coming to the ears of the constables, who instituted proper inquiries, traced the report to a man who had seen the body of the child, and then informed the coroner, who thereupon directed that an inquest should be held forthwith. Accordingly, on Saturday last, the body of the child having been produced, an inquest was held over it at the Fleece Inn, when the following extraordinary facts were elicited in evidence:—

Thomas Nettleton said—I live at Horbury, and am a butcher. I was told by Ellen Sykes (Mr. Craven's servant) that she saw Mr. Craven burying something in the plantation, and in consequence I went to the place. I took some earth up with my hands, and found a bundle wrapped in brown paper. I took it up and opened it, and found a newborn child. I made another hole and buried it again. I showed it to Ellen Sykes before I buried it; it was a boy. This was on Tuesday morning. I was called upon by Mr. Roger Hirst, Mr. Joseph Berry, and Mr. John Gee, on Friday morning. They are constables for Horbury. They asked me to meet them at the Fleece Inn, in Horbury, and to bring the bundle I had found. I went and dug up the bundle and brought it to the Fleece. I laid it on the table in the room, in the presence of the constables and other persons. I left it with them. Ellen Sykes told me not to say anything; so I did not mention the finding of the child to the constables nor to any one. Ellen Sykes told me she saw Mr. Craven digging something. She told me she suspected something was up. I never denied I knew anything about the child, or had had it in my possession. I groom and occasionally work for Mr. Craven.

Ellen Sykes, upon her oath, said—I am a single woman. I was servant to Mr. Edward Craven, but was discharged last Thursday by Miss Craven. Mr. Craven is a bachelor. Miss Craven is about 24 years old, and lives in his house as his daughter. I had been there three years the 1st of last June. I never told Nettleton I saw Mr. Craven digging or burying in the plantation, but I did tell him I saw Mr. Craven graving in the garden; by "graving" I mean working in the garden. He was in the habit of doing so. He (Nettleton) said he suspected something was up, and said he supposed I suspected. I laughed and put it off, and a little girl came in, and we said no more at that time. This conversation took place on Tuesday evening. I never told Nettleton not to mention the finding of the child to any one. It was last Monday morning, between 9 and 10, when I saw Mr. Craven working in the garden. Nettleton told me I was not to name it to any one that he found the child. At the time Miss Craven was confined to her bed I had reason to suppose she was delivered of a child. My reason for supposing so was the difference in her appearance before she was confined to her bed and after she came down stairs. She came down stairs about 4 o'clock last Monday afternoon. I saw the bed linen was changed and taken away. There were finer sheets on the bed than were put on before. I did not attend her on Saturday and Sunday. Mr. Craven himself attended to her on those two days, but I went into her bedroom occasionally. No medical man was sent for to Miss Craven. Mr. Craven on Saturday shut the inner door leading from the kitchen to the room after him, as he often does. It was betwixt 12 and 1 o'clock. I also heard him shut the stairs door. I heard Miss Craven crying out, as if in much pain, all Saturday morning, and she was very poorly. On Wednesday night, I think it was, I went into

Miss Craven's bedroom. She was undressing. I saw her apply something to her breasts, but did not notice what it was. I shut the door and went away without going in to her. It was bedtime and I had my shoes off. I had not spoken to Nettleton on Wednesday morning before he brought the child. I have looked at the piece of cloth the child is now wrapped in. It is a piece of linen cloth; the child was wrapped in calico that Nettleton produced to me on Wednesday morning.

Medical testimony concluded the evidence, and the coroner went over the evidence very minutely, and directed the jury as to the law of the case. The jury returned a verdict of "still-born."

Mr. J. Stringer, solicitor, of Horbury, was present on behalf of the authorities, and three other solicitors were also present to watch the inquiry.

On Monday, Mr. Stringer applied to the magistrate for warrants of apprehension against the parties concerned in the above offence; but the magistrates required some evidence to be produced before taking this step, and issued summonses to the witnesses already named to appear before them. This no doubt has been done, and the warrants have doubtless been granted, although we have no information to that effect. Mr. and Miss Craven have left Horbury, no one knowing whither they are gone.—*Times,* Aug. 21, 1849.

Nisi Prius Court.—(*Before Mr. Justice* Williams.)

Emma Craven and Edward Craven were indicted, the female prisoner with having endeavoured to conceal the birth of an illegitimate child on the 6th of August last, at Wakefield, and the male prisoner with aiding and abetting in the concealment.

Mr. Blanchard and Mr. Shaw prosecuted; and Mr. Overend and Mr. Pickering defended the prisoners.

It appeared that the prisoners lived near Dewsbury, and that a woman servant, named Ellen Sykes, lived with them, and a man servant, named Thomas Nettleton, out of the house. In August last the appearance of Miss Craven excited suspicions in the mind of the maid-servant, and on the 4th of that month she was taken ill, and Mr. Craven attended her in bed. Cries were heard coming from her room in the course of the day, Mr. Craven remaining there, and the maid-servant observed the chamber-utensil had been emptied by some one, and marks of blood were upon it. The next day she observed that the sheets had been changed on Miss Craven's bed. Mr. Craven continued to wait upon her, carrying her up her breakfast. On Monday, two days after, she saw Mr. Craven go into the garden, and watched him, in consequence of her suspicions being aroused, and there she saw him dig a hole near a cucumber frame, and she was sent out. She returned in about an hour, and then saw Miss Craven downstairs, looking much thinner. After tea she went into the garden, and then saw that the hole Mr. Craven had been digging was filled up. She was soon afterwards directed to make a linseed poultice by Miss Craven, for a pain in her head, and she saw Miss Craven applying this poultice to her breast. She told the man-servant, Nettleton, of what she had seen, and he dug up and searched the hole in the garden, and in it he found a paper parcel containing a male child, wrapped in white calico sheets. This was given to the police, and the sheets, in the opinion of medical men, had been used by some person delivered of a child. On this discovery taking place, Mr. and Miss Craven suddenly disappeared from the neighbourhood. Mr. Craven eventually surrendered himself, and Miss Craven was taken into custody in October last. About two months before this discovery, a sweetheart of Miss Craven had gone to Australia, and when she first complained of being poorly, her father, the male prisoner, wanted to send for a doctor. Some baby linen had been seen in a box of Miss Craven's, and it appeared that when Mr. Craven was digging he saw the servant watching him and was evidently digging a little grave, and that Miss Craven's door was not locked.

His Lordship here interposed, and said this was no concealment of the birth, but of the body of the child, and directed the jury to find a verdict of *Not Guilty.*

Mary Skinner was indicted for having, on the 13th of September last, wilfully murdered her male child at Dunnington.

Mr. Matthows prosecuted, and Mr. Dearsley defended the prisoner.

In this case it appeared that the prisoner resided with her father in a cottage at

Dunnington, in which also lived a woman named Hannah Granger. The cottage was divided by a badly made partition, through the crevices of which it could be discerned what took place on the other side. It had been observed that the prisoner was pregnant; and about 2 o'clock on the morning of the 13th of September cries were heard in the prisoner's room. Hannah Granger looked through the partition, and saw the prisoner seated on a chair. The prisoner was then observed to look cautiously out of the door, and go into the garden with a spade, and dig a hole, into which she placed a bundle. Hannah Granger gave information of what she had seen, and in the hole which the prisoner had made the body of a new-born male child was found. Mr. Hay, surgeon, of York, stated that the child had been born alive, and that there were marks of bruises upon it, which had caused its death. His opinion, however, was not infallible.

His Lordship asked the jury if, on this evidence, they could convict of murder.

The jury found the prisoner *Not Guilty*.

The prisoner was then charged with concealing the birth of the child, and to this she pleaded "Guilty."

His Lordship, in passing sentence, said, considering the long time she had been in prison, he should only sentence her to six weeks' further imprisonment.—*Times,* Dec. 20, 1849.

Joseph Preston, a man of respectable appearance, aged 48, was tried at the Stafford assizes in March, 1828, for a rape on two of his daughters, one eleven and the other sixteen years old, and was convicted. At the Rochdale sessions, on the 14th of March, of the same year, a woman, aged 22, was brought up to affiliate a child. She refused, at first, to take the oath, but, on being committed for contumacy, she swore that her own father was the father of the child, She had had another child six years before by him. [Galignani's Mess., March 27, 1828.]

The Windsor Express (as quoted in Galign. Mess. April 11, 1828) says, "It appears by the confession of a young woman at Datchet, nineteen years of age, that her own father, a master blacksmith of that village, named Allen, has been in the habit of violating her person. Another daughter, about a year older, is in the family way, it is supposed, by the father also.

Note 38, line 824.
"Dixie to vengeance and lust less prone,
Nor saves her father's honour or her own."

The incest alluded to here will be found in the daily newspapers of May, 1827. "Miss Dixie, a girl hardly in her teens, acquainted her relatives that her father had made repeated and successful attempts to possess himself of her person; and in consequence of an information lodged against him, Sir Willoughby Dixie, Bart, was committed to Leicester gaol on the 20th May, 1827.

"On the 30th ult., at Gumley, by the Rev. Mr. Mathews, Capt. Henry T. Boultbee, Royal Artillery, only son of J. M. Boultbee, Esq., of Springfield Park, County of Warwick, to Julia, widow of the late Chas. Goring, of Wiston Park, Sussex, and daughter of the late Sir Willoughby Dixie, Bart., of Bosworth Park.—TIMES, Sept. 2, 1856.

Note 39, line 826
"A pair of breeches S......n and W.....k shock.
They ask no joys beyond each other's smock."

These two names (Lady Strachan and Lady Warwick) seem to have been selected by the author, because they had obtained some notoriety for a species of lasciviousness, probably common enough nowadays, but of frequent practice among the Roman ladies. There was a caricature of these two ladies in the window of Fores' shop in Piccadilly some years ago. Females addicted to these modes of mutual gratification were called *tribades* and *frictrices.*

The beautiful ode of Sappo, beginning
"Ille mi par esse deo videtur."

is addressed to a woman. Beranger, the French ballad writer, admits that tribades are not rare among his own people:

> "Qui ne juge, aux harangues
> Des Saphos de nos jours,
> Que ces mauvaises *langues*
> Font la guerre aux amours?"
>
> SERMON D'UN CARME.

So common was this abominable complaisance among the Roman ladies, that even matrons were not exempt from the imputation.

In one of Lucian's "Dialogues between Courtezans," Clonarium, speaking of Megilla, a rich lady of Lesba, says to her friend Leona, "I fancy that she was a tribade, of whom it is reported there are many here, who dislike men, and have to do with their own sex."

We have Brantôme's testimony that the French ladies of fashion of his time had not suffered these lesbian practices to fall into disuse. In his "Discours de Cocus," (p. 169, v. 8) we read:—"J'ai oui couter à Mons. de Clermont Tallard la jeune, qui mourut à la Rochelle, qu'etant petit garçon, et ayant, l'honneur d'accompagner M. d'Anjou, depuis notre roi, Henri III. en ses études, et étudier avec lui ordinairement, duquel M. de Gournay etait precepteur, un jour etant a Tolouse, étudiant avec son dit maitre dans son cabinet, etant assis dans un coin apart, il vit par une petite feute dans un autre cabinet deux fort grandes dames, toutes retroussés et leur caleçons bas, se coucher l'un sur l'autre, s'entre baiser en forme de colombe, se frotter, s'entrefrotter, s'entrefrigeur,—bref, se remiser fort, paillardeur, et imiter les hommes, et dura leur abattement pres d'une bonne heure, s'etant si fort échauffées et lassées, quelles en demeurerent si rouges et si en eau, bien qu'il fit grand froid, quelles non purent plus et furent contraintes de se reposer autant, et disoit qu'il vit jouer ce jeu quelques autres jours, tant que la court fu là de même façon."

A French author of a later date, le Marquis de Sade, has given a most obscene description of this unnatural coitus:—"Oh, my friend, what a woman was that Charlotte!" and the reader is informed in a note that the Charlotte here spoken of was the Queen of Naples, sister to Marie Antoinette, Queen of France.

Note 40, line 761.
"Come, Malthus, and in Ciceronian prose,
Tell how a rutting population grows."

It is perhaps invidious to designate by any particular examples that system of limited procreation adopted from motives of prudence and economy by married couples in some countries of Europe, but the ladies of the moral city of Geneva will pardon me if I mention here what is very generally asserted of them by the ill-natured English who have resided a long time among them, namely, that it is quite a rare thing to see any of them mothers of more than two, or at most three or four children, and that their husbands make no secret of the precautions they use, with the consent of their wives, to prevent begetting a numerous family, when their means of providing for it are unsufficient. The Genevan wife's recipe is what Beranger, in his songs, called "eating the eel without the sauce." It is to be observed, however, that people there, and in several parts of the continent, take a very different view of such matters from what the English do. In France, for example, a magistrate will openly recommend some such practice as necessary in poor families; witness the following extract from the circular letter of M. Denoyer, prefect of the department of la Somme, to his under prefects; his words are:—"Il n'y a pas pour les familles pauvres deux manières de se tirer de l'affaire, ces familles ne peuvent s'élèver qu'à force d'activitè, de raison, d'economies, de prudence—prudence surtout dans l'union conjugale, et en évitant avec un soin extrême de rendre leur marriage plus fécond qui leur industrie." (Exam. of the Pen. Stat. xxv Hen. viii. and v. Eliz. by A. Pilgrim.)

Note 41, line 836.
"Which modern virtue is so used to slight."

In ancient Greece and Rome chastity does not seem to have been necessary to a woman's elevation in life, any more than in our own times. For one Cæsar's wife we find a dozen Cleopapatras.   Among the Romans, Flora, Pompey's mistress, was the admiration of the age for her charms and the sweetness of her disposition   Cytheris, a dancer, the mistress of Marc Antony, is celebrated by many authors for the graces of her person, to which she added exalted sentiments and moral duties, which have set her above many a married woman.   She never quitted Marc Antony in all the reverses of his fortune: she shared his sufferings and afforded him consolation, thus rendering herself as estimable by her conduct as she was admirable for her beauty.   Among the Greeks we are told that Aspasia was idolised by Pericles.   Phryne's statute was enshrined in the same temple and honoured with the same solemnities as Cupid's, and the reader must recollect that Cupid, in the Heathen Mythology, was a real deity.   Of Thais we read "Ad cujus jacint Grecia tota pedes."   Aristophanes Byzantius relates that at the time of which he writes, Athens contained one hundred and thirty-five courtezans, who were distinguished by the statesmen and geniuses of the day for their beauty and accomplishments.   (Plutarch's Morals of Love.)   Theoganes, a philosopher, killed himself, because the courtezan of Migara, whom he was in love with, would not yield to his solicitations.   (Lucian's Tyrant.)   Aristotle kept Herpyllis as his mistress till his death.   Plato—the divine Plato—loved Archeanissa, a prostitute.

Sophocles, the tragedian, when advanced in years, became enamoured of Theoris, a woman of the same class.   Towards the close of his life he fixed his affections on another, named Archippes, whom he made his heiress, if we are to believe Hegisander and Hierony-mus, the Rhodian.   Hermippus informs us that Isocrates, the rhetorician, when old, kept Lagisca, and had a daughter by her.   (Gron. Theo. Antiq. Grec. in Muson.   Philos. de lux Græc. Tract., vol. 8, p. 2522.)   Pitho became the wife of Hieronymus, the king of Syracuse, although he had her from a brothel.   Timotheus, who reigned over the Athen-ians, was the son of Conon, by Thoessa, a prostitute.   Phillip of Macedon kept Philinna, a dancer, by whom he had a son, named Aridæus, who reigned after Alexander.   Demetrius raised Myrina, a Samian courtezan, to share his throne.   Ptolemy, son of Philadelphos, lived openly with Irene, a harlot.   (Grov. Thes. vol. viii., p. 2518.   The Syrian Semiramis was a poor wench, kept by one of Nenus's slaves, partly as his servant, partly as his con-cubine, till Ninus, seeing her by accident, and taking a fancy to her, at length doated on her to that degree that she governed him as she pleased, and finally came to reign over Asia.

In our own days we have Lady Holland, Lady Darlington, Mrs. Whitbread, Mrs. Fox, Lady Blessington, Lady Canterbury, the Countess of Harrington, Lady Berwick, Lady Heathcote, the Duchess of St. Albans, two or three Lady Abercorns, and many more besides.

Note 42, line 856.
"Had fled dismayed from some transalpine shore
To sully Albion's pudic cliffs no more."

Italy of late years, and indeed in all times, has enjoyed the distinction of being con-sidered the hotbed of pœderasty.   Sterne seems to make some rather obscure allusion to the risk men's morals run by going beyond the Alps, in the following passage:—"My shirts!   See what a deadly schism has happened amongst 'em, for the laps are in Lom-bardy, and the rest of 'em here.   I never had but six, and a cunning gipsy of a laundress at Milan cut me off the fore-laps of five.   To do her justice, she did it with some con-sideration, for I was returning out of Italy.   (Tristrim Shandy, ch. 303.)

There is another passage in Tristrim Shandy which denotes that Sterne had observed the frequency of this propensity in the Italians:—"I am not ignorant (says he) that the Italians pretend to a mathematical exactness in their designations of one particular sort of character among them, from the forte or piano of a certain wind instrument they use, which they say is infallible.   I dare not mention the name of the instrument in this place; 'tis sufficient to have it among us, but never think of making a drawing of it.   This is enigmatical, and intended to be so—at least *ad populum*.   (p. 65, Ed. Paris.)

Beranger's words, in the song entitled "l'Accouchement," are:—

"Ce n'est pas mon Italien—
Il a prouvé son gout trop bien:
Il n'aura jamais de famille."

Had the author's sole object been to attest the very general prevalence of arsenerasty throughout the world, he would have had no difficulty in collecting his evidence, but as he confines himself to his own country, let us endeavour to help him out; and it will not be difficult, within the compass of a single year, to select from police reports cases enough to force from the strongest stickler at the morality of this church-going generation an avowal that no class of English society has been exempt from the stain, and moreover, that neither disgrace nor punishment can cool these Priapeian fires. The gravest men, and those whose situations and characters would have justified us in supposing that their education, honourable pursuits, rank, or religion, would keep them aloof from these grovelling weaknesses, have nevertheless yielded to these as an infirmity of nature; and, without going back to a warden of Wadham College, a Lord Aston, or a Beckford, we may content ourselves with a list made up during the year 1833, which does not include numerous committals in provincial towns, and among the lower ranks of people.

1. The Rev. C. E. Holden, aged 70, vicar of Great Cornard, Suffolk, and the Rev. Rob. Fiske, his curate, accused by Thos. Prigg, their parish clerk, of sodomy, acquitted. Galignani's Messenger (from the *Globe*) Aug. 8, 1833.

2. The Rev. E. P. Benezet, of Bungay, accused by the constable of that town of sodomy, with one Barton. Benefit of clergy. Galignani's Messenger (from *Norwich Mercury*) May 13, 1833.

3. An inhuman murder has been committed on a boy named Paviour, whose body was discovered in the Regent's Canal, bearing marks of the most unnatural treatment; he was about 13 years of age. Mr. Laing was occupied at Hatton Garden office in the investigation, and a clue was obtained to a gang of miscreants, who have for some time carried on their infamous practices. Nicholls, the associate of Beauclerc, and concerned with him in inveigling boys from their houses, has escaped to the Continent. A colonel of the West End and a rich merchant of the City, are supposed to have been associates of Nicholls.

4. A rev. gentleman, upwards of 70 years of age, was yesterday held to bail at the Marylebone Office for an indecent assault on a lad of 17, servant to Mr. Denison, M.P. for Nottingham. Galignani's Messenger (from the *Guardian*) June 28, 1833.

5. It is with equal regret and disgust that we hear that a person in the upper class of society, a member of the senate, was yesterday held to bail for an indecent assault on a policeman. The person here alluded to was Mr. Baring Wall, M.P.

6. A miscreant, attired in the first style of fashion, was brought before the magistrate at Lambeth-street Office on Thursday, charged with having been guilty of disgusting practices towards a young man named Meadows. Mr. Hoskins asked the prisoner his name, when he, after some hesitation, faintly said, Herbert Benet, &c. April 12, 1833.

Note 43, line 877.
"Or could not pay a bed room at the Key."
A celebrated brothel in Chandos Street, since pulled down.

Note 44, line 881.
"Bear witness Vere Street and the Barley Mow."
Two gangs of miscreants (as they were called when this poem was written) were discovered at these two places.

Note 45, line 894.
"Drummers may flog, judge-advocates impeach;
The soldier's post is ever at the breech."
Not only common soldiers, but generals have been enslaved to these morbid feelings. Sir Eyre Coote had his escutcheon taken down from among those of the Knights of the Bath, owing to such an accusation.

Note 46, line 919.
"As most familiar with the nether place."
This anecdote must have some truth in it, for it was related by Mr. Freemantle in an after-dinner party over his wine. Mr. Jephson, of Trinity College, Cambridge, probably could have made the same recognition of his pupils.

Note 47, line 954.
"But if the stopper is replaced with care,
The scent diffused evaporates in air."
Mr. Richard Heber, M.P. for Oxford, the great book collector, is the gentleman here meant. Mr. Heber's shame was brought to light in consequence of an action for libel, instituted by Mr. Hartshorn against the editor of a newspaper, wherein pointed allusions were made to a supposed intimacy between Mr. Heber and Mr. Hartshorn's son. In this action Mr. Scarlett, afterwards Lord Abinger, was counsel for the plaintff.

Note 48, line 993.
"Where'er he goes to know his shame is spread."
"Such delinquents are sufficiently punished by the shame and infamy of a discovery."
(Bentham, Theorie des peines et recomp. v. i. p. 55, 3d. ed. French.)
Sterne was of the same opinion, for he seems to consider that, where the matter had no natural results, it was folly to create legal ones, and that, where nature was blind, man too might honestly pretend to shut his eyes. This is his argument (See Tristram Shandy, c. 259): "It is a great pity, but 'tis certain, from everybody's observation of man, that he may be set on fire, like a candle, at either end, provided there is a sufficient wick standing out; if there is not, there's an end of the affair, and if there is—by lighting it at the *bottom*, as the flame in that case has the misfortune, generally, to put out itself—there is an end of the affair again."
In another part of the same work the author's allusions bears evidently on the same subject.
"I beseech you, Dr. Slop," quoth my uncle Toby, "to tell me which is the *blind* gut?" "The blind gut," answered Dr. Slop, "lies between the *Ilion* and the *Colon*." "In a man?" said my father. " 'Tis precisely the same," cried Dr. Slop, "in man or woman." "That's more than I know," quoth my father.

Note 49, line 976.
"Will only add momentum to your fall,
And stain the scutcheon in your father's hall."
The youth here alluded to is probably the Honourable James Stanhope, brother of the present Lord Stanhope, who served in Sicily, was the intimate friend of Mr. Heber, and, soon after the disclosures made respecting the latter gentleman hung himself in an outhouse at Caen Wood, the residence of his father-in-law, Lord Mansfield.

Note 50, line 986.
"An exile to a foreign land he'll fly;
Neglected live, and broken-hearted die."
Mr. Grey Bennett, who was maligned in the Age newspaper, in some verses which had reference to the name of a Brussels valet-de-place, one Valle, with gross insinuations of an improper intimacy between them. His death is recorded in Galignani's Messenger as having taken place at Florence some few days before, June 16, 1836.

Note 51, line 998.
"The panic flight, the suicidal beam,
The knife, the bullet, do they trifles seem?"
In the *Ledger* Newspaper, (as quoted in *Galignani's Messenger* of May 28, 1836) we read the following account of a gentleman who cuts his throat, driven to desperation by the most dastardly and ignoble treatment of a brutal mob at Brighton:—"An inquest

was held at Brighton on Tuesday on the body of Mr. Stanley Stokes, a proctor, of Doctor's Commons, who cut his throat in East Street in that town on Saturday night. Saunders, the landlord of the New Ship Hotel, on Saturday night had laid a plan to intercept him, and, accompanied by a crowd of fellows, after charging him with an indecent assault on a boy's person, they simultaneously mobbed him, smeared his face with tar, gave him severe blows on the head with fists, sticks, etc., until he fell down. Whilst undergoing this persecution, the unhappy man, in the open street, drew a penknife from his pocket, and inflicted a severe wound in his throat. He was immediately conveyed to the hospital, and for a day or two the wound went on favourably, but the nervous excitement under which he laboured, and the blows which he had received, producing fever, he gradually sunk and expired."

Note 52, line 1000.
"Thirst ye for blood? and will no punishment
"But what Old Bailey metes, your hearts content?"
The whole purport of what has been said, may be summed up in a paragraph extracted from a French newspaper of July 18, 1833, of which this is the translation;—"A noble marquis was recently fined for an indecent attempt upon a gen d'arme; the laugh went amazingly against the Marquis; many persons would not believe the story: yet incredible as it is, the same thing has recurred this day. A M. Briene was accused before the Sixth Chamber of an indecent assault upon a city serjeant. From the precise evidence given by the serjeant no doubt could be left in the judges' minds; Briene was condemned to fifteen days' imprisonment." Here we have the fine and the laugh for the Marquis, and the fortnight's prison for the humbler individual. Will Mr. Peel please to say this is not better than death warrants and gibbets; not to mention the distress of innocent families rendered miserable for ever. (Free Exam. Pen. Stat. by A. Pilgrim, p 74.)
It is pleasing to be able to quote the celebrated author of *Scienza della Legislatione*, Filangeri, in favour of milder laws against anti-physical propensities, having a passage from Œschines (in Timarchum) which shows that any Athenian who had become a notorious catamite, was ineligible as archon, priest or magistrate, or herald, was excluded from the temples, and, in fine, lost his civil rights; he then adds:—"I cannot omit comparing this law with the horrid punishment of burning, inflicted on pœderasts by tha emperors Constantius, Constans, and Valentinian. (Vid. Cod. Theod. tit. ad Leg. Jul.) "I shudder," he then continues, "to see laws so ferocious so universally adopted. I shudder when I find that the only alteration made in England in the ancient statute is confined to changing the stake for the gallows. I shudder more than any man can do in thinking that Justinian, when he promulgated a law against this delinquency, was satisfied with the deposition of a single witness, even if that witness were a child." (Lib. iii, c. 48, tit. 6.)

Note 53, line 1008.
"But, Draco like, thou (gainsay who that can)
Did'st add a clause to sink a drowning man."
These strictures are not altogether just. It was in May, 1828 that Mr. Peel, in revising the criminal code, introduced some changes respecting the punishment of sodomy. Before this time the punishment was death, but then it was necessary that the witness should swear to having seen the actual perpetration; now the punishment is not capital, but the conviction is rendered considerably easier. The reader must decide upon the amendment.

Note 54, line 1042.
"Behold yon reptile with its squinting eyes:
Him shall my curses follow till he dies."
"Do you suppose I have forgotten or forgiven it? It has comparatively swallowed up in me every other feeling, and I am only a spectator upon earth till a tenfold opportunity offers; it may come yet! There are others more to be blamed than * * * *, and it is on them my eyes are fixed unceasingly."—(Moore's Life of Byron, vol. 3, p. 249.)

Lord Byron's animosity against Dr. Lushington, for the advice he gave Lady Byron, seems to have known no bounds;—or is it Sir Samuel Romilly who is meant?

Note 55, line 1098.
"Save when close muffled in her feridjee."
Feridjee, cloak or mantle of cloth, generally of a gay colour, worn by Turkish women out of doors.

Note 56, line 1102.
"Save when the araba, by oxen drawn."
Araba, a light wagon, drawn by oxen, in which Turkish women are carried out of town, in thir daily excursions. There is a tilt over it; and is covered in by curtains all round.

Note 57, line 1108.
"Her Aga slowly quits the selamlik."
Aga, the master of the house.
Selamlik, or salutation room, a small room just within the entrance door, where the master receive his male visitors.

Note 58, line 1110.
"The harem opens to his loud testoor."
Testoor, or by your leave.

Note 59, line 1143.
"Catch Parr with Meursius or with Fanny Hill."
At the sale of Dr. Parr's library, Mersuius (Eleg. Lat. Serm.) was among the books.

Note 60, line 1154.
"I oft have heard my venerable sire
The ancients praise; their doctrines, too, admire."
Catullus sings of his Juvencus's caresses with a feeling of voluptuousness so touching that a female must necessarily be envious of it.

Horace and Martial are two out of a hundred learned and eminent men among the ancients who wrote freely on erotic subjects; cotemporary with Martial was Sabellus, an amatory writer, Calvus, the rival of Cicero, Hortensius, a more formidable rival still, were authors of lascivious works; Samius another.

Many female authors on such subjects are mentioned by ancient writers; thus Philænis wrote a treatise *Die variis Modis Cocundi,* Elephantis another on the same subject, Cyrene another, yet they are all said to have been "Claræ literis et philosophia." Calistrata, also, a Lesbian Poetess, and Nico, a Samian maid, may be included in this list.

Note 61 line 1176.
"Lest mischief from too rude assaults should come
To copulate *ex more pecudum.*"
I have read somewhere the following couplets, alluding to this mode of copulation:—
————"Which some have named
The Trojan horse, whereby is meant, instead
Of copulating by the usual mode,
You enter from behind the dark abode."

Note 62, line 1208.
" 'Tis there the Bath empiric's finger guides
The oiled bougie, and as the dildo slides.
Whoever has visited Bath must have heard of a surgeon, by the name of Hicks, who pretends to cure strictures in the rectum by the insertion of bougies of enormous dimen-

sions up the anus in male and female patients. The morning meetings of ten or a dozen persons of both sexes, all waiting to undergo the same mode of cure (for he never fails to discover stricture or tendency to stricture, in all those persons who consult him), must be ludicrous and somewhat obscene. Why does he not follow the plan of Enothea, a harlot spoken of by Petronius? "Profert Enothea scorteum fascinum, quod, ut oleo et minuto pipere atque urticæ trito circumdedit semine, paubatim cœpit insere ano meo." It may not be amiss to observe that the *fascinum* (Gallice *godmiche*, Anglice *dildo*) was a substitute for the human penis, known to the ancients as well as to the moderns.

Note 63, line 1216.
"But when ablution purifies its gates,
And from within no odour emanates."

"As man is gifted with the power of perfecting whatever nature has granted him, so he has perfected love. Cleanliness, and attention to the person, by rendering the skin more delicate, increase the pleasure of the touch, and add sensibility to the organs of voluptuousness.—Mirabeau.

BOW-STREET.—Inspector Reason and Sergeant Hunt, officers appointed to enforce the regulations of the Common lodging-house Act, attended before Mr. JARDINE to prefer complaints against several of the occupiers of rooms in Wyld-court, Drury-lane,—one of the worst localities within the jurisdiction of the court.

Sergeant Hunt proved that between 12 and 3 o'clock in the morning of the 12th inst. he visited a room occupied by James Donovan, at 8, Wyld-court, having previously given him the usual notices to register, and repeatedly informed him of the necessary regulations, by which he was prohibited from taking lodgers while his own family (already exceeding the number allowed) were living with him. Witness found two beds in the room, the first containing the defendant and his three daughters, aged 17, 16, and 15, and a boy aged 8. The second bed contained a man and his wife, who were paying 8d. per week for the lodging. Witness visited the room again yesterday morning, and found the defendant and his daughters sleeping together as before, but the second bed was empty.

Mr. Jardine inflicted a penalty of 20s., upon which Donovan declared that he had not a penny in the world, nor any goods worth seizing. He was consequently committed for 21 days; but, having been subsequently detected in passing a stocking containing about 40s. to one of his daughters, his worship had him replaced in the dock and compelled him to pay the fine.

Daniel Carthy and Michael Sullivan (an old offender) were next charged.

The usual caution had been given to the defendants, but when Hunt visited Carthy's room, in which four persons only were allowed by the regulations, he found two dirty beds on the floor, the first of which contained the defendant, his wife, a girl of 16, and two boys aged 15 and 10; and the second a man and his wife, a girl of 13, and two boys (15 and 13.) The room was very filthy, and yesterday morning, on repeating his visit, witness found the same persons there, and the room in the same condition. In Sullivan's room there were five beds, all on the floor. The first bed contained the defendant, his wife, a boy of 16, and a girl of 14, with another boy of 10, and an infant. In the second bed there were a woman, a girl, and a child; in the third bed a man, his wife, a girl of 16, and two boys (12 and 7); in the fourth bed a woman and two boys; and in the fifth a man. There were no partitions of any kind to separate the sexes. The total number of persons in the room was 20, but seven only were allowed.

It appeared that Sullivan had been before convicted, once or twice, while occupying a room in Lincoln-court, which he had given up to his wife. Hunt stated that Carthy had shown a disposition to comply with the regulations since the summons had been taken out, but the same people were in the rooms on the occasion of witness's second visit.

Mr. Jardine, after commenting with indignation upon the swinish manner in which these people were huddled together, without a sense of decency or morality, fined Sullivan £5, and committed him for two months in default.

The summons against Carthy was suspended.

Jeremiah Donovan, of 2, Wyld-court was proved to be the occupier of a room on the ground floor, in which there were two beds, one of them containing the defendant, his wife, his two daughters aged 18 and 10, and a servant girl out of place aged 14.

The sergeant stated that only one person would be allowed in the room. The beds were made up of loose dirty straw on the ground, and emitted a horrible stench—there being no means whatever of ventilating the room.

Mr. Jardine fined him £3 and costs, committing him for a month in default of payment.

Another man named John Lynch, occupying a room in the same court, was fined £4, or a month's imprisonment in default.

Note 64, line 1233.
"Thou'lt say the seed that there is spilt
Thwarts Nature's purposes and argues guilt."

It is quite clear that the author of this epistle had read *Justine, ou Les Malheurs de la Vertu,* by the Marquis de Sade, as the arguments used in the sixteen following lines are assuredly taken from that extraordinary work. The public journals have lately been filled with execrations against the memory of that nobleman, who had recently died in an advanced age; but why is he worse than Pliny the Younger, who wrote lascivious poetry, and takes no great shame to himself for having done so? (Vid. *Epist.* xviii. *Epist.* iv, 14, 15), and Ausonius (*Cent. Nupt.*) alludes to these writings of Pliny as something very obscene.

Note 65, line 1255.
"Quick from my mouth some bland saliva spread,
The ingress smoothed to her new maidenhead.",

Juvenal tells us (Juv. xi. 171.) that the Romans used to lubricate the same orifice in the same way.

Note 66, line 1263.
"Ah, fatal hour, from thence my sorrows date.
Thence sprung the source of her undying hate."

In vol. iv, p. 555, of Byron's Life, Lady B. is made to say, when speaking of her separation from her husband, "Although I had reason for reserving a part of the case from the knowledge of even my father and another, &c." Was this the part of the case that Lady B. meant.

Note 67, line 1273.
"Lest, under false pretences thou shoulds't turn
A faithless friend, and these confessions burn."

"It was a pity that nothing, save the total destruction of Byron's memoirs would satisfy his executors, but there was a reason."—LIFE OF BYRON.

Note 68, line 1323.
"And where to fame the great and good consign
Their ashes, living thou shalt blazon thine."

In *Galignani's Messenger* of June 11 (quoted from the *Globe*), we find who it was that the writer meant in the preceding lines. Here is the paragraph. "We yesterday stated that a case was under inquiry during the day at Queen Square Office, with closed doors. From delicacy we withheld the name of the individual charged; but the publicity given to it by the morning papers renders further concealment unnecessary; it is Mr. William John Bankes, M.P. for Dorsetshire. On its being known outside the office that the public were excluded, the greatest murmuring took place, and frequent were the cries of "It is because he is a rich man." One of the witnesses, who was highly indignant at the exclusion of the reporters, promised to take copious notes of the evidence adduced; and the public are indebted to him for the account of what transpired at this second examination of the wealthy individual. Mr. Bankes was accused of having been seen standing behind the screen of a place for making water against Westminster Abbey walls, in company with a soldier named Flower, and of having been surprised with his breeches and braces unbuttoned at ten at night, his companion's dress being in similar disorder. Other circumstances transpired, inducing a belief that a criminal connexion had taken place between them. When the evidence was finished, Mr. White, the magistrate, required bail in two sureties for £3000 each. Mr. Bankes, senior, the prisoner's father, soon after arrived with another gentleman. Their bail was accepted. Mr. Bankes, senior, never once looked on his son. The prisoner was then escorted by a strong body of the police into the Birdcage Walk, followed by an immense crowd, hooting and reviling. As soon as the prisoner got into the park, the constables blocked up the gateway, whilst he (Mr. Bankes, jun.) got into his father's carriage, which immediately drove off.

At Mr. Bankes's trial, the Duke of Wellington,—Montgomery, Esq., Samuel Rogers, the poet, Mr. Bankes, the father, Lord F. Somerset, Dr. Butler, Master of Harrow, Dr. Chambers, Lord Burghersh, Mr. Galley Knight, the Earl of Ripon, Lord Caledon, The Rev. Mr. Jones, Sir E. Kerrison, Mr. Rose, Mr. Seaton, a barrister, Mr. Harcourt, M.P. for Derby, Dr. Batten, the Earl of Brownlow, Captain York, M.P., for Cambridge, Mr. Clive, M.P., Mr. Bond, Mr. R. Gordon, M.P., Mr. Harris, one of the judges of the Insolvent Court, Honourable Mr. Duudas, Lord Gage, Sir C. Beckwith, Mr. Peach, Honourable Mr. Best, Mr. Arbuthnot, Lord Cowley, Lord Brecknock, Sir C. Grant, Mr. William Smyth, professor at Cambridge, Mr. Alexander, Mr. Beachey, Lord Stuart de Rothsay, Mr. D. Bailey, the Rev G. Picker, and Mr. D. Brown. Some of these noblemen and gentlemen had known Mr. Bankes, the prisoner, for thirty years, the majority of them from twenty up to thirty years. They were all on terms of the greatest intimacy with him, and they all declared that, although Mr. Bankes was a most open, candid, agreeable, and lively person, he was never yet known to be guilty of any expression bordering on licentiousness or profaneness. The Lord Chief Justice then summed up the evidence, and the jury, after consulting together about twelve minutes, returned a verdict of Not Guilty. The foreman, Colonel Astell, added, "I am farther directed by the jury to declare their unanimous opinion that the defendants leave this court without the least stain upon their characters from this trial."

THE GLOBE.

In September, 1841, this same Mr. Bankes was again brought before a magistrate for indecently exposing himself in the Green Park, and was set at liberty on bail. Mr. B. this time forfeited his recognizances, disappeared from society, and has not been heard of since.

Note 69, line 1381.
"The willing maid who plights her marriage vows,
Owes blind obedience to her lawful spouse."

The women of Rome were so convinced of the necessity of this blind obedience to their husband's caprices, that they had sometimes no resource left them but to endeavour to assimilate themselves to boys. Accordingly, we find Martial's wife inviting him to use her person in the manner most agreeable to his perverted taste; though, for reasons not very obvious to uninitiated persons, he declines her offer.

Note 70, line 1419.
"Amidst the firmament, when comets sail,
Where are our eyes directed? On its tail."

"Blessed Jupiter! and blessed every other heathen god and goddess! for now you all come into play again, and with Priapus at your tails. What jovial times!"

TRISTRAM SHANDY, ch. c.

Note 71, line 1454.
"Closed is the Cnidian temple, and we see,
Writ on its walls—Hic nefas mingere."

Mingere, besides its usual acceptation, has another meaning, familiar to the later satirists, who use it for *semen emittere*.
